LATIN AMERICAN HISTORICAL DICTIONARIES SERIES
Edited by A. Curtis Wilgus

Historical Dictionary
of
Chile

by

Salvatore Bizzarro

Latin American Historical Dictionaries, No. 7

The Scarecrow Press, Inc.
Metuchen, N. J.   1972

Library of Congress Cataloging in Publication Data

Bizzarro, Salvatore.
    Historical dictionary of Chile.

    (Latin American historical dictionaries, no. 7)
    1. Chile--Dictionaries and encyclopedias.
I. Title.
F3054.B5   983'.003   72-3161
ISBN 0-8108-0497-2

To Albina and Ann

Editor's Foreword

Chile has been described as a "geographical extravaganza" by one of its leading writers. Its northern section
contains one of the most absolute deserts in the world, while
its southern extremity is one of the wettest, windiest and
coldest areas in the Western Hemisphere. The central heart-
land, the "Valley of Chile," has often been called the "California of South America." Its mountainous backbone, snow
covered and earthquake prone, shares with Argentina several
"Switzerlands." Its banana shape, if placed on a map of
North America, would extend from Canada to Cuba, while if
placed horizontally on a map of the United States it would
reach from New York City to Los Angeles.

Historically, Chile may be as well described as a "political extravaganza." It has had some 60 political parties
and scores of political factions and splinter groups ranging
through every political persuasion: Conservative, Liberal,
Social, Christian Democrat, Communist, Marxist, and mul-
tiple combinations of these and others. Innumerable cabinet
changes, which give the impression of political fickleness,
have allowed politicians to express their individualism and to
let off political steam from the body politic. With all its
numerous large and small political disturbances, Chile has
had only nine constitutions, and relative political stability has
been the rule. One factor contributing to this characteristic
has been the largely European immigrants who have helped to
establish a modicum of political maturity and have provided a
social leaven and a cultural stimulus during more than a century. As the most militant country in South America, Chile
has made use of Germans to train the army and of British
to develop the navy. And to finance many national projects
and to improve life in general the government has encouraged
Americans from the United States to develop its industry and
promote its prosperity. At present, however, national political, economic and social objectives are changing, as may
be clearly seen from this presentation.

Dr. Bizzarro, like other compilers of volumes in this
series, was given the assignment of selecting topics for

inclusion which to him seemed logical, comprehensive and justifiable so that a well-balanced guide to historical facts would result. Here as a result is a concise and detailed historical dictionary showing a clear comprehension of the Chilean people and their problems.

The author's understanding of Latin people results in part from the fact that he was born of Italian parents and lived in Italy for 16 years, after which he went to the United States and became a citizen. His B.A. degree, taken at Fordham University in Spanish, was followed by an M.A. and a Ph.D. (1965; 1969) at Stanford University where his dissertation on a Chilean topic was entitled "Social and Political Themes in the Poetry of Pablo Neruda from 1936 to 1950." He acquired early teaching experience at Stanford and he is now Assistant Professor of Spanish and Latin American Studies at Colorado College, Colorado Springs.

In the course of his investigations and academic activities, Dr. Bizzarro has studied and carried on research at the Universidad Católica (1962-63) in Santiago, Chile, in Cuernavaca, Mexico, and in Brazil, and he has several times visited all South American countries except Paraguay. He has been assisted in his research by grants from Stanford, Colorado College, the Ford Foundation, the United States Department of State, and the Foundation on the Arts and Humanities. His writings have appeared in scholarly publications and in the Encyclopaedia Britannica. In his present position Dr. Bizzarro has helped to create a Latin American program and he is offering a course on "Brazil and Hispanic America since Independence." This volume, which is the culmination of his special interest in Chile, makes an important contribution to a better understanding of that country.

A. Curtis Wilgus
Emeritus Director
School of Inter-American Studies
University of Florida

Introduction

The following pages aim to present a global view of the history and politics of Chile, emphasizing the contemporary period. As a subject of study, the <u>Historical Dictionary of Chile</u> possesses all the liabilities which a balanced sense of intellectual concern would persuade any writer to avoid. It is not always easy to deal at the same time with controversial historical figures, living persons, contending political forces, and, in recent years, a massive polarization and urbanization of the people. At that level, one tends to examine historical data in a sketchy way. And how much more vulnerable classifications in a dictionary become when they are meant to give a factual identification of important people and events in the stormy contemporary scene.

All this is by way of admitting openly that much of what will be included here is subject to any number of qualifications and additions. And yet Chile, a country known for its political stability in the mercurial world of Latin American politics, has received much commentary in the United States but surprisingly little objective study. Hence it seemed useful to publish a brief up-to-date dictionary which would analyze not only the past, but also contemporary events.

Just as in other volumes in this series the arrangements here are alphabetical. There are inevitably a number of cross-references about people, geographical places and names of institutions. There are also some abbreviations, including political parties, organizations and companies which are referred to by their initials. Spanish words peculiar to the regions of Chile are listed. An asterisk is used throughout the text to indicate that an entry has been made under the preceding name, place, historical site, etc. "See" followed by an ENTRY NAME indicates that, unlike the entries asterisked, the cross-reference is directly related to the subject being discussed. Names of persons in Latin America are given in the following fashion: first name, family name, mother's name. To look up a name which has been asterisked, such as Eduardo Frei Montalva* or Salvador Allende Gossens* do not look up Montalva or Gossens; rather look up the family names Frei and Allende.

Any user of this work is invited to consult the various sub-entries under CHILE first, which together provide an overview of the country itself as well as of this book.

Acknowledgments

Most of the research for this dictionary was done in Santiago de Chile, during the summers of 1968 and 1969, and during my four-year graduate studies at Stanford University, where I had the opportunity to collaborate with Lionel Cross on the preparation of the section on Chile for the Hispanic American Report (1964-65). In doing this book, I have been indebted to many people. I should like to thank first all the writers who have preceded me in the study of Chile, especially Lía Cortés, Jordi Fuentes, Jaime Eyzaguirre, K. H. Silvert, Luis Galdames, Sergio Guilisasti Tagle, Eduardo Labarca Goddard, Ernst Halperin, and Andre Gunder Frank.

I am grateful to Lionel Cross for working with me on an unpublished monograph on Chile, under the direction of Ronald Hilton. I owe to Lionel Cross the entries dealing with the Chilean economy, the armed forces, and the geography. I am also grateful to Lía Cortés, Jordi Fuentes, and the Editorial Orbe for giving me permission to quote from their Diccionario Político de Chile, and for having "stolen" countless details from their excellent study.

I am also indebted to Ronald Hilton for convincing me to undertake the writing of the book, to A. Curtis Wilgus for his editorial advice, to Nora Laughlin for her maps, and to Colorado College for a grant to go to Chile in the summer of 1969.

Finally, I am deeply grateful to Ann Christine Rennie for her helpful editing, to my student Katherine Boyd for assisting me with some research and translation, and to my secretary Elaine Johnston, who provided the expertise in typing this manuscript that she brings to all her work.

I apologize for having included so few Chilean women of note in my dictionary; however, the sources I consulted had very little information on the subject.

MAPS

ABC TREATY. In April 1915, three South American nations, Argentina, Brazil, and Chile, signed a treaty to act as a block in inter-American relations. This alliance lasted until the era (1945-55) of dictator Juan Domingo Perón, when both Brazil and Chile rejected the domineering attitude of Argentina in guiding their international interests. Argentina, which by the end of the 19th century was one of the most prosperous countries in Latin America, had created the block in order to offset the United States' concept of being the only country in the Western Hemisphere with a "manifest destiny" policy. The most important function of the ABC countries was that of mediation in international disputes. As early as 1915, President Woodrow Wilson accepted the mediation of the ABC countries in the dispute between Mexico and the United States. The ABC powers were also responsible for drafting the peace plans between Bolivia and Paraguay during the costly War of the Chaco (1928-35). The peace conference was held in Buenos Aires on July 1, 1935. A settlement of the war was finally achieved three years later in the Argentine capital, with the ABC countries mediating the peace terms with the aid of Peru and the United States.

ACADEMIA DE LA LENGUA. The purpose of this scholarly academy is to be the guardian of the Spanish language. There is an Academia de la Lengua in virtually every Spanish-speaking country. In Chile, Rodolfo Oroz Scheibe is the director of the Academia, which now has 21 honorary members.

ACCION CHILENA ANTICOMUNISTA (ACHA). A reactionary military institution formed in 1946 to protest the admission of three Communist Party members to form the first cabinet of the then President (1946-52) Gabriel González Videla*. It was presided over by Artero Olavarría Bravo, Minister of Agriculture in the government (1938-41) of Pedro Aguirre Cerda*. The aim of this group was to prevent a Communist take-over in

Chile. As part of the armed forces of Chile, ACHA
had seven regiments and was responsible for many public demonstrations until it achieved its goal in 1948,
when the Communist Party was outlawed by González
Videla.

ACCION NACIONAL. 1) Political party of the right formed
in 1935 and dissolved in 1937, when it fused with the
Unión Republicana*. The Executive President of the
Acción Nacional was Eulogio Sánchez Errázuriz, who
had also been the founder of the Milicia Republicana*.
The ideology of the party was: 1) to oppose all extremist ideas; 2) to oppose dictatorships; and 3) to
create a new political force to give Chile a strong and
effective government. The objectives of the party included the establishment of liberty and justice for all
men, the protection of private property, and the formation of a corporate state.

2) A resurgence of the old Acción Nacional. Re-
established in November 1963, it lasted until March
1965. In the presidential elections of 1964, the Acción
Nacional backed the candidacy of Jorge Prat Echaurren*.
In the parliamentary elections of 1965, the Party announced the senatorial candidacies of Prat Echaurren
and Sergio Onafre Jarpa Reyes, but neither one won
representation. As a result, the party ceased to exist
legally after the elections. Its members joined the newly formed Partido Nacional*, a coalition of three parties from the right and the Independents in June, 1966.

ACCION REPUBLICANA. Political party organized in 1937 by
the merging of the Acción Nacional* with the Unión Republicana*. The fusion of both parties was possible because of their similar doctrines, which were reflected
in their common aims: 1) to awaken a sense of re-
sponsibilities in the electors; 2) to respect the political
Constitution of 1925*; 3) to preserve law and order and
oppose dictatorships; 4) to incorporate power in the
political life of Chile; 5) to have universal suffrage;
6) to repudiate the class struggle. and 7) to have equal
employment opportunities for all Chileans. In March
1937, the new party elected two deputies, one of whom,
Benjamín Claro Velasco*, became president of the
Acción Republicana. The party organ was the newspaper La Aurora*. The party did not win representation in the parliamentary elections of 1939 and was
dissolved.

ACCION REVOLUCIONARIA SOCIALISTA. A precursor of the
    Socialist Party of Chile (see PARTIDO SOCIALISTA*),
    founded in 1931 by Oscar Schnake Vergara, Eugenio
    González Rojas, Augusto Pinto, Julio E. Valiente,
    Gregorio Guerra and Mario Inostrosa, most of whom
    dropped out of politics or left the country. The party's
    aim was to unify the Socialist groups in Chile and, on
    April 19, 1933, the Socialist Party was founded.

ACCION SINDICAL CHILENA (ASICH). A private institution
    founded in 1950 to educate and advise Catholic trade
    unionists.

ACHA see ACCION CHILENA ANTICOMUNISTA.

ACHARAN ARCE, CARLOS. Elected representative of the
    Liberal Party (Partido Liberal*). From 1926 to 1930
    he was a deputy from Valdivia, La Unión, Villarica
    and Río Bueno. From 1933 to 1953 he represented
    Valdivia, La Unión and Osorno in the Congress. From
    1953 to 1961 he was a senator from the 9th district.
    In the senate, Acharan Arce was the promoter of a
    university reform bill which created the Universidad
    Austral in Valdivia. He was also responsible for bring-
    ing government funds to the flooded zone of Valdivia,
    badly damaged by the earthquake of 1960 and by inces-
    sant rains.

ACOMODADO. A person who is well-off financially; wealthy,
    or fond of comfort.

ACONCAGUA. A province of Chile located just north of
    Santiago; population (1971 estimate): 159,752; area:
    9,873 sq. km.

ADELANTADOS. Royal appointees authorized to stake their
    own fortunes in the colonization of new lands. The
    term comes from the Spanish verb adelantar ("to advance")
    and describes in Spanish America all the discoverers,
    colonizers, and conquerors who came to the new world.
    The adelantados had a wide range of powers. They were
    not only the military leaders of the expedition, but also
    the governors and legislators of the territory discovered.
    They had the right to apportion lands and Indians, and
    to oversee the development of the new lands. After the
    conquest there was a period of consolidation and settle-
    ment, and the office of adelantado began to disappear.

ADUANA DE IQUIQUE. (Literally, "the customs of Iquique.")
Iquique* is a city in northern Chile, but when Chileans
refer to Aduana de Iquique they are reminded of a
bloody battle between the troops of President (1886-91)
José Manuel Balmaceda Fernández*, who tried to occupy the city, and the defenders of the city, who sided
with the revolutionary army of Congress. This battle
is recorded in the Civil War of 1891 (Guerra Civil de
1891*), during which two antagonistic ideologies prevailed; that of the President of the Republic, who
wanted to abide by the Constitution of 1833, and that of
Congress, which accused Balmaceda of attempting to
set up a dictatorship in Chile. The battle was won by
the revolutionaries, and the event precipitated the establishment of Parliamentarism in the country, and the
eventual defeat of the Balmaceda régime.

AFUERINO. A migrant farm worker.

AGRICULTURA, INDUSTRIA Y COLONIZACION, MINISTERIO
DE. The Ministry of Agriculture, Industry and Land
Colonization was created by statute No. 43, on October
14, 1924 (when the Ministry of Industry and Develop-
ment--Ministerio de Industria, Obras Públicas y Ferrocarriles*--was divided into two ministries, the other
being the Ministry of Public Works--Ministerio de
Obras y Vías Públicas*). It coordinated the development of the agricultural, mining and industrial sectors
of the economy, as well as forestry and fishing, until
1927, when the ministry was dissolved and the Ministerio de Fomento* was created in its place.

AGRICULTURA, MINISTERIO DE. The Ministry of Agriculture was created by statute No. 3524 on August 5, 1930,
when the Department of Agriculture separated from the
Ministry of Development (Ministerio de Fomento*). The
functions of the Ministry of Agriculture have been to
coordinate the development of agricultural products,
cattle, and forestry, and to implement the agrarian reforms of 1962, 1965, and 1971. Other branches of
this ministry are the Corporación de la Reforma Agraria (CORA*), and the Instituto de Desarrollo Agropecuario (INDAP*). Before 1930, the Ministerio de Agricultura was known as the Ministerio de Agricultura,
Industria y Colonización*.

AGRICULTURE see THE ECONOMY: Internal: B. Agriculture; C. Forestry; etc.

AGUIRRE CERDA, PEDRO, 1879-1941. Lawyer, large landowner, leader of the Radical Party (Partido Radical*),
Aguirre Cerda became President of Chile from 1938 to
1941, the year he died. He won the Presidential elections with the help of the Frente Popular*, a Socialist-
Communist-dominated coalition, defeating Gustavo Ross,
the candidate of the Right, by some 9,000 votes. A
major earthquake in January 1939 slowed down the economic progress made under his and the previous administration. Assuming the Presidency, Aguirre Cerda
had pledged "to end conditions in which the Chilean
masses lack food, culture, clothes, and dwellings."
But the earthquake brought much ruin from Santiago to
Valdivia. More than 50,000 were killed, 60,000 were
injured and 750,000 made homeless. The government,
as a result, had to bend every effort for the relief of
the sufferers. Nevertheless, a year later the Aguirre
Cerda Government announced a vast industrialization
program involving the expenditure of $24 million dollars
($12 million of which came from a loan extended by the
U.S. Export-Import Bank). Great strides were made
in electrification and in the explorations of oil fields.
The boundaries of the Chilean territory of Antartica
were fixed, a minimum wage was established and the
government embarked upon a massive program of social
welfare.

When the Republicans were defeated in the Spanish
Civil War (1936-1939), Aguirre Cerda opened the door
to emigrants from Spain. His wife, Juana Aguirre
Luco de Aguirre, undertook many charitable works for
the poor, especially for children. Of all the Chilean
governments to date, only that of Aguirre Cerda had
a popular base. The President had insisted on identi-
fying himself with the people, gaining the support of
the masses and of the Frente Popular. Before becoming President, Aguirre Cerda held many important
posts in government. He was a Radical deputy from
the province of San Felipe (1915-18), and from Santiago (1918-21). In 1921 he was named Minister of Justice and Public Education and made education compulsory for children through grade school and reduced the
number of illiterates in the country. From 1921 to
1924 he was senator from Concepción*, and in the
latter year he was the leader in the cabinet of President (1920-24) Arturo Alessandri Palma*.

ALALC. Asociacíon Latino Americana de Libre Comercio
see LATIN AMERICAN FREE TRADE ASSOCIATION
(LAFTA).

ALAMEDA VIEJA DE LA CONCEPCION. Site of a battle
fought in the city of Concepción* on November 27, 1820,
between the Spanish forces led by Vicente Benavides*
and the Chilean forces led by Ramón Freire Serrano*.
It was an episode of the so-called Guerra a Muerte*
("War to the Death"), during which these two opposing
forces committed cruelties and war crimes. The
troops of Benavides, fighting to restore Spanish power
in Chile, surrendered.

ALCALDE BASCUÑAN, JUAN AGUSTIN, 1798-1860. He
fought in the Wars of Independence (1810) and held numerous public offices in the newly formed Chilean
state. He was fourth Count of the Quinta Alegre. He
was regidor* of the Cabildo Abierto* of 1810. His parliamentary activities are listed as follows: deputy from
Santiago at the first National Congress of Chile (July 4,
1811); senator in 1818; President of the Conservative
Senate from 1820 to 1822; Vice-President of the Provisional Assembly of Santiago (1827); and representative
in Parliament (1827-31). In 1831, he created the Commission on Agriculture and Mining; in 1834, the Commission on War and the Navy. He was senator again
from 1840 to 1860, the year he died in office.

ALCALDES MAYORES. Royal appointees chosen in the colonies at the recommendation of the viceroys for a three-
year period. They presided over municipalities and
other administrative units of varying sizes and importance.

ALCALDES ORDINARIOS. Magistrates and municipal clerks
in colonial times. They performed unimportant functions within the municipality.

ALDUNATE CARRERA, LUIS, 1842-1908. Candidate of the
Right for the Presidential elections of 1866, Aldunate
Carrera held many important diplomatic posts during
his lifetime. As a lawyer, he was sent to Peru in
1865 to sign the treaty of Chincha Alta between Chile
and Peru (later, Ecuador and Bolivia also signed). A
year later, in 1866, he was sent to the United States
as Secretary of the Chilean Delegation in Washington,

D. C.   In the same year he returned to Santiago to run
for the Presidency.   Backed by the Radicals, the Liberals, and the Nationals (Partido Radical*, Partido Liberal* and Acción Nacional*), he lost the elections to José
Francisco Vergara Echevers*.   Among his many official
appointments, he was subrogate judge in the Chilean
highest court, and served in the Ministries of the Interior, of Foreign Affairs and of the Treasury.   In 1865
he was designated Plenipotentiary minister to Chile by
the Government of Guatemala, an honorary post which
he declined.   The Queen (1833-68) of Spain, Isabel II,
conferred upon him the Cross of the Order of Isabel
the Catholic.   From 1895 to 1896, he was Minister of
the Anglo-Chilean Tribunal.   Before he died, he wrote
numerous treatises on the economic and commercial
status of Chile.

ALDUNATE ERRAZURIZ, FERNANDO, 1895- .   As a lawyer, Aldunate Errázuriz excercised his skills in various
commercial, mining, and industrial enterprises.   After
obtaining his degree, he became Professor of Law at
the Universidad de Chile, and also taught at the Universidad Católica.   From 1930 to 1932 he was a member
of the Commission which drew up the Mining Labor
Code.   As a conservative, he was elected deputy and
later senator to Congress from 1934 to 1953.   Among
his civic posts, he was President of the Banco Central
de Chile, of the Compañía Acera del Pacífico*, of the
Banco de Crédito e Inversiones, and of various other
companies.   From 1956 to 1957 he was named Chilean
Ambassador to Argentina, and from 1959 to 1963 he
was Chilean Ambassador to the Vatican.   Until recently, he was one of the directive members of the Conservative Party (Partido Conservador*).

ALDUNATE PHILLIPS, ARTURO, 1900- .   Chilean author
and critic who wrote the first book of criticism on the
now famous Veinte poemas de amor y una canción desesperada, a collection of poems by Pablo Neruda*.
From 1940 to 1960 he was president of Endesa*, the
Chilean equivalent of Con-Edison in electricity.   During the last few years he has been writing books on
scientific research and space travel, having become an
expert on unidentified flying objects (UFO's).   His last
book is A horcajadas en la luz, and deals with life in
the universe.   Aldunate Phillips has taken many trips
abroad and has visited Russian and U.S. space centers,

where he has collected materials for his books.   He
was recently named a member of the Academia de la
Lengua*.

ALDUNATE TORO, JOSE SANTIAGO, 1796-1864.   A career
   military officer who participated in the Chilean struggle
   for independence from 1810 to 1818.   He was captain
   in the army of Bernardo O'Higgins and took part in the
   battle of Rancagua*.   In 1820, he was sent to Peru by
   the Argentine liberator José de San Martín* and fought
   for the independence of that country.   He was wounded
   in Peru, and for his military services received the
   gold medal.   In 1839, he retired from the military.
   Three years later, he was named Minister of the Interior in the conservative cabinet of President (1841-51)
   Manuel Bulnes Prieto*.   In 1847, Aldunate Toro became
   director of the Escuela Militar, a post he abandoned to
   run unsuccessfully for the Presidency of Chile in 1851.

ALESSANDRI PALMA, ARTURO, 1868-1950.   Twice President (1920-24; 1932-38) of Chile.   He was born in the
   central province of Linares* (south of Santiago), and
   died in the capital.   In 1893 he received a law degree
   and became an active member of the Liberal Party
   (Partido Liberal*).   Between 1897 and 1920, he was
   elected to Congress as a representative and held many
   governmental offices, including that of Minister of Industry and Public Works (1898), and Minister of the
   Interior (1918).   Backed by the Alianza Liberal* and
   the Partido Democrático*, he ran for President of
   Chile in 1920 and won, being inaugurated on December
   23 of that year.   The Alessandri government incurred
   a period of economic depression, due to a drastic decrease in nitrate exports, and was afflicted by unrest
   within the military.   In the Senate, conservatives con-
   sistently refused to cooperate with the program presented by Alessandri, which would draw funds from a
   wealthy minority (land and income taxes) to aid the
   poor and improve working conditions, health, education
   and welfare.
        The general unrest between 1920 and 1924 was in-
   creased by the fact that the pay of public servants and
   of the military had fallen in arrears; unemployment
   was on the rise; the masses were ragged and hungry.
   Allessandri reworked his cabinet 16 times and finally
   brought to Congress a majority favorable to his programs.   Although the army's pay was increased, the

military tried to force the President to devaluate the
Chilean peso in order to alleviate the economic conditions of the population.   Unable to cope with the demands, and harrassed by Congress, Alessandri took
the initiative in September 1924 and resigned.   Ironically, Congress would not accept his resignation and
granted him a six-month leave of absence.   Alessandri
went to Europe, and a military junta, headed by General Luis Altamirano, assumed the government of Chile.
The junta, in turn, was forced to resign by army officers who accused Altamirano of not bringing about social reforms.

Alessandri was invited by Carlos Ibáñez del Campo*,
head of the new military junta, to return to Chile, and
did so by March 1925.   A constituent assembly was
called immediately to amend the constitution.   Church
and state became separate and in August the new constitution became, and still is, the law of the land (see
CONSTITUTION OF 1925).   Because of a quarrel with
Ibáñez, who had been appointed Minister of War, Alessandri resigned again on October 1, 1925, appointing
Luis Barrios Borgoño* to succeed him.   New elections
were held in the same year, and Emiliano Figueroa
Larraín* became President, resigning in 1927.   In May
1927 Carlos Ibáñez emerged again as President of Chile.
His government was greatly upset by the world depression, and in 1931 he resigned.

In 1932 Alessandri began his second term as President of Chile.   The Constitution of 1925 gave him six
years in office and strong powers, which the President
was determined to use.   One of the first measures he
took was to reorganize the nitrate industry, abolishing
COSACH*.   As the decade advanced, Chile enjoyed a
considerable economic advance.   Measures were taken
to improve education, agriculture, and industry.   In
1935 the exports of nitrate were double that of the preceding year.   In April 1937, the Nazi movement began
to spread in Chile.   On September 5, the Nazis attempted to carry out a revolution in order to return
Carlos Ibáñez del Campo to power.   Ibáñez was arrested and Alessandri was given additional extraordinary powers.   Order was kept until Alessandri stepped
down from office, and Pedro Aguirre Cerda* was elected as the new president.

ALESSANDRI RODRIGUEZ, JORGE, 1896- . Son of Arturo
Alessandri Palma*, he was President of Chile from

1958 to 1964, and an unsuccessful candidate to the
same office in the elections of September 4, 1970. He
received an engineering degree in 1919, and taught engineering at the University of Chile*. He served in the
Chilean Congress as a deputy (1926-30), and as a senator (1956-58). In 1947, he was Minister of the Treasury in the cabinet of President (1946-52) Gabriel González Videla*. Urged on by his Presidential aspirations, Alessandri ran in the elections of 1958 backed
by the Conservative Party (Partido Conservador*), the
Liberal Party (Partido Liberal*), a faction of the Radical Party (Partido Radical*), and other minor parties
of the center who refused to support their nominee
Eduardo Frei Montalva*. The elections of 1958 were
very close, and were resolved by Congress. Alessandri defeated his major opponent, Socialist Salvador
Allende Gossens*, by only 33,000 votes. Although
Alessandri had not won a mandate, Congress confirmed
him President in October 1958 and he was inaugurated
for a six-year term on November 4, 1958.

Backed by the moderates and conservatives, Alessandri was able to bring about some reforms in industry and agriculture. The first law of Agrarian Reform
was passed in 1962. It permitted the expropriation for
cash of some unproductive or inefficient private holdings and provided for the consolidation of the "minifundia*." A year before, Chile had joined the Latin
American Free Trade Association* (LAFTA). In 1963,
Chile signed the American Continent Treaty as a de-
nuclearized zone, accepted the ruling of Queen Eliza-
beth II of England to settle a border dispute at Palena*,
between Chile and Argentina, and signed a treaty for
disarmament in South America. In 1960, Chile was
plagued by another major earthquake. More than
10,000 died, and the homes of some two million Chileans were destroyed. The losses were estimated at
more than $500 million. As a result, Chile faced one
of the most severe inflations in the history of the
country. The Chilean peso* was devalued, and a new
monetary unit was introduced in Chile, the escudo*.
In 1960, the exchange rate was one escudo to the dollar (one escudo = 1,000 pesos), but by 1962 the Chilean currency had been devalued again to 1,500 pesos
to the dollar.

In January 1961 a ten-year development program was
announced by the government, with assistance from the
U.S. World Bank and the Export-Import Bank of Wash-

ington, D. C.   As a result, the copper, tin, nitrate,
and steel industries were able to finance their operations.   In 1962, the Chilean Government did not sanc-
tion the Cuban blockade officially, even if it approved
it tacitly.   But two years later, in 1964, in accordance
with the decision of the Organization of American States
(OAS), Chile broke relations with Cuba.   In the same
year, President Alessandri visited the United States and
toured other Latin American countries.   He was succeeded on the third of November, 1964, by Christian
Democratic President (1964-70) Eduardo Frei Montalva*.
In 1970, Alessandri ran again in the Presidential elections, but was defeated by a narrow margin by Salvador
Allende Gossens*.

ALGARROBO.   This largest and newest of the Chilean iron
mines is located in the province of Atacama*, some 27
miles inland from Huasco.   Purchased by the Compañía
de Acero del Pacífico (CAP*) in 1959, Algarrobo is
looked upon as the future supplier for Chile's integrated
iron and steel industry.   The deposit has known reserves of 50 million tons with additional probable reserves of 75 million tons, and is expected to supply
ore for two blast furnaces for at least 50 years (as
opposed to El Romeral's 20-year supply for only one
blast furnace).   Moreover, recent geological surveying
and projecting to determine the ore reserves of the
Algarrobo mine (and adjacent sector) have led experts
to believe the mineral content of the mine to be substantially greater than originally estimated.   The Peno-
so hill facing the mine has also been surveyed and iron
ores have been found there.
    Partial operation of the Algarrobo mine started in
1960, but it was not until 1962 that full-scale operation
was begun.   At the time, the mineral extracted from
the open-pit mine amounted to 2. 3 million long tons
(1 long ton = 2, 240 lbs.).   A year later, production
increased to 2. 7 million long tons.   Although the increased production of iron ore in the world today makes
competition more severe in Chile's traditional ore markets, the quality of Algarrobo ore places CAP in a
favorable competitive position (the mineral at Algarrobo
has high iron and low phosphorous content).   Algarrobo
ore is not only well known and widely accepted in Japan
and the United States, but is beginning to find new
European markets.

ALIANZA DE PARTIDOS Y FUERZAS POPULARES. A coalition of political parties formed in 1958 to back the candidacy of Jorge Alessandri Rodríguez*. The components of this organization were: the Partido Radical Doctrinario*, the Partido Social Cristiano*, the Partido Agrario Laborista Recuperacionista*, the Movimiento Nacional del Pueblo*, and the Movimiento Republicano*. After Alessandri emerged as victor, becoming President of Chile (1958-64), the Alianza de Partidos y Fuerzas Populares was dissolved to the dismay of many of its members, who were shocked that the President showed so little interest in the organization.

ALIANZA DEMOCRATICA DE CHILE. A political coalition of Communists, Socialists, and Radicals, formed in 1942 to back the Presidential candidacy of Juan Antonio Ríos. Ríos won the elections, and the Alianza Democrática remained active until dissolved upon the President's death in 1946.

ALIANZA LIBERAL. A political combination of liberals and radicals formed in 1875 and dissolved in the same year. After the Civil War of 1891 (Guerra Civil de 1891*), the Alianza Liberal was organized once again and lasted until 1925. During this period, Chile functioned as a parliamentary republic, which made it necessary for parties to form coalitions in order to attain a majority in both chambers of Parliament. The Alianza Liberal achieved its greatest importance during the Presidencies of Germán Riesco Errázuriz* (1901-06), Pedro Montt Montt* (1906-10), and Arturo Alessandri Palma* (1920-25).

ALIANZA POPULAR. A coalition of five parties formed in 1952 after the triumph of Carlos Ibáñez del Campo* in the Presidential elections of that year. The member parties were the Partido Agrario Laborista*, the Partido Socialista Popular*, the Partido Democrático del Pueblo*, the Partido Radical Doctrinario*, and the Partido Femenino de Chile*. Their objective was to unite the political groups who had backed Ibáñez del Campo. The Alianza Popular was dissolved shortly after its inception.

ALIANZA POPULAR LIBERTADORA. A political alliance which supported the presidential candidacy of Carlos

Ibáñez del Campo* in 1938, formed by the pro-Nazi
Movimiento Nacional Socialista de Chile*, the Unión
Socialista*, and a group of military politicos. The
electoral campaign in 1938 was marred by incidents
sparked by the activities of the pro-Nazis, and Ibáñez
del Campo was forced to withdraw his nomination in
order not to be mixed up with his extremist sympathizers. On September 4, 1938, other demonstrations
occurred in favor of Ibáñez. The Seguro Obrero*
building was occupied by students, and the clash with
the police resulted in various deaths. When Ibáñez del
Campo was arrested, the Alianza Popular Libertadora
gave its support to Pedro Aguerre Cerda*.

ALLENDE GOSSENS, SALVADOR, 1908- . Doctor by profession, Socialist candidate for the Presidency in the
last four elections (1952, 1958, 1964, 1970), and President of Chile for the term 1970-1976. In 1932, Allende
Gossens received a degree in medicine, alternating his
practice with his political career. As a student activist, he helped to organize the Socialist Party (Partido
Socialista*). He was arrested twice for political disturbances and regarded by many potential employers as
a troublemaker. In 1937, he was elected deputy from
Valparaíso*, a post he held until 1939 when he became
Minister of Health and Welfare in the government (1938-
41) of Pedro Aguirre Cerda*. In 1939, Allende married Hortensia Bussi, a geography student at the University of Chile*. In 1943, he became secretary general of the Socialist Party and in 1952 he was the leftist
candidate for the Presidency but was defeated at the
polls by Carlos Ibáñez del Campo*, Allende receiving
a mere 6% of the popular vote.

In 1955, he became president of the Frente Nacional
del Pueblo*, a leftist coalition of parties. In 1958, he
was once again the leftist candidate to the Presidency,
losing that election to Jorge Alessandri Rodríguez* by
only 33, 000 votes, Allende receiving 28. 9% to Alessandri's 31. 6%. From 1961 to 1965 Allende was an elected senator from Aconcagua* and Valparaíso*. In 1964
he ran once more for President, but lost to Christian
Democrat Eduardo Frei Montalva*, with 38. 6% of the
vote--the highest Allende has ever received--to Frei's
55. 6%. After his third defeat, Allende joked about being
the perennial candidate of the left. He said that if he
lost the 1970 elections, he would demand that the following inscription be placed on his tombstone: "Here

lies Salvador Allende Gossens, future President of
Chile. "

Even though Allende received a mere 36% of the vote
in the 1970 Presidential election, it was enough to edge
former President (1958-64) Jorge Alessandri Rodríguez,
who received 35% of the vote, and the Christian Democratic candidate, Radomiro Tomic*, who received 28%
of the vote.   At final count, Allende got 1, 075, 616
votes to 1, 036, 278 for conservative Alessandri, and
824, 849 for Tomic.   Since no candidate had received a
majority of votes, the Congress was required by the
Constitution to choose the new President from the top
two vote-getters.   Allende, who was supported by the
Communist-Socialist-dominated Unidad Popular*, counted
on 83 votes in Congress and needed only 13 more to be
confirmed.   The Christian Democratic Party agreed to
support Allende unanimously in return for constitutional
guarantees that he would preserve the democratic process in Chile.   Allende signed the agreement and on
October 24, 1970, the Chilean Congress confirmed him
President giving him 160 votes of confidence as opposed
to 35 for Alessandri.

A political assassination that occured two days before confirmation is worth mentioning because such an
event had not happened in Chile for the last 132
years.   The army chief of staff, General René Schneider, had announced that the army would support which-
ever candidate Congress chose.   On October 22, General Schneider was mortally wounded in an attack by
gunmen.   The day before, General Schneider had spoken publically against right-wing plots to keep Allende
from taking office.   Soon after being confirmed President, Allende pledged that his government would continue the investigation into the death of General Schneider.   On November 3, 1970, Allende was sworn in.
Shortly after, the President named three Communists
to his 15-man cabinet, but kept four posts, including
the key interior and foreign ministries, in the hands of
his own Socialists.

The line-up in Allende's cabinet is: Ministry of the
Interior, José Toha, 43 (Socialist); Foreign Ministry,
Clodomiro Almeyda, 47 (Socialist); Economics Ministry,
Pedro Vuskovic, 46 (Independent Marxist); Ministry of
Agriculture, Jacques Chonchol, 44 (MAPU*, an off-
shoot of the Christian Democratic Party); Ministry of
Mines, Orlando Cantuarias, 40 (Radical Party); Labor
Ministry, José Oyarce, 44 (Communist); Finance Min-

istry, Américo Zorrilla, 58 (Communist); Housing Ministry, Carlos Cortés, 48 (Socialist); Ministry of Lands,
Humberto Martones, 43 (Social Democrat); Defense
Ministry, Alejandro Ríos, 68 (Radical); Education Ministry, Mario Astorga, 39 (Radical); Health Ministry,
Dr. Oscar Jiménez, 55 (Social Democrat); Ministry of
Public Works, Pascual Barraza, 60 (Communist); Justice Ministry, Lisandro Cruz, 59 (API, a minor non-
Marxist leftist group); and Government Secretary General, Jaime Suárez, 46 (Socialist).   Chile has no vice-
president.   In the event of the President's death or
disability, the Minister of the Interior succeeds him.
The last time Communists held cabinet posts in Chile
was 25 years ago, when President (1946-1952) Gabriel
González Videla* appointed three in an effort to get
Communist backing.   But he had them thrown into a
concentration camp several months later because he
feared they were getting too powerful.

As a Socialist, Allende has pledged to initiate the
socialization of Chile.   But he said that his administration would be "neither Marxist nor a Socialist government Castro-style."   One of the first measures taken
by the Allende government has been that of recognizing
Castro's Cuba.   Allende has said he aims to achieve
four major objectives by 1976:   1) to recuperate basic
resources, meaning nationalization of copper and other
minerals such as nitrate, coal and iron; 2) to radically
speed up agrarian reform by expropriating most of rural Chile for conversion into rural farm cooperatives;
3) to nationalize banks and credit; and 4) to control exports and imports (the Popular Unity program calls for
nationalization of domestic and external commerce).
Allende also stated that if his Marxist successor does
not win the 1976 Presidential elections "I will go into
the history books as a failure."

ALMAGRO, DIEGO DE, 1475-1538.   A celebrated Spanish
Conquistador and discoverer of the Reino de Chile who was
born in the city of his own name, the illegitimate son
of Spanish peasants.   In 1524, fleeing a murder charge,
he came to Panama, where he became a close friend
of Francisco Pizarro.   He marched with Pizarro and
Fernando de Luque in Peru, acquiring for Spain territories rich in gold and silver.   As a result, Pizarro
was given the governorship of Peru, whereas Almargo
was designated governor of Túmbez at only half the
salary of Pizarro.   Thus ended their friendship and

began a long and bitter rivalry between the two men.
Nevertheless, they continued together, and Almagro
took part in operations which resulted in the death of
the Inca Atahualpa and the conquest of the Peruvian
territories.   In 1535, Almagro was granted the title of
adelantado* to the regions south of Pizarro's territory,
which comprised northern Chile and Argentina.   He set
out to inspect these territories with an expedition of
approximately 500 Spaniards and thousands of Indians,
but their march was marked by hardships and priva-
tions.   More than 10, 000 Indian carriers, nearly all
of the animals, and many Spaniards died.   Finding no
gold, the resentful Almagro returned determined that
the ancient Inca capital of Cuzco should be his.

In Cuzco, he found the Spaniards, led by Francisco
Pizarro, under the siege of an Indian revolt.   The
Chilean forces, however, soon forced an Indian retreat,
and Almagro claimed the city.   Almagro was victorious
in the conflict that ensued with the Pizarro brothers
and captured Hernando, whom he set free at the en-
treaties of his brother Francisco.   In 1538, however,
there was another battle between the aging rivals, in
which Hernando Pizarro took Almagro as prisoner.
The latter was executed on July 8, 1538, leaving Pizarro the undisputed master of the Inca empire.

ALMEYDA MEDINA, CLODOMIRO, 1923- . A lawyer and
university professor, he has been a militant in the Socialist Party (Partido Socialista*).   In 1952 he was
named Minister of Labor, a post he resigned a year
later to become Minister of Mines.   He was the secretary general of the Partido Socialista Popular*, and a
member of the Central Committee of the Socialist
Party.   In 1970, he was named Minister of Foreign
Affairs in the cabinet of President (1970-76) Salvador
Allende Gossens*.

ALTAMIRANO TALAVERA, LUIS.   A career military officer
who entered the Civil War of 1891 (Guerra Civil de
1891*) as a captain in the army.   Afterward, he passed
through the usual military grades and had commissions
in Europe and South America.   He was a lieutenant
general in the Chilean army, and Minister of the Interior (September 5, 1924), at the beginning of the
revolutionary movement in 1924.   He presided over
the Military Junta which replaced President (1920-24)
Arturo Alessandri Palma* on September 11, 1924, and

headed that body until the following January, when a
second military coup asked for the return of Alessandri.

ALTO DEL HOSPICIO.   Situated in the northern province of
Tarapacá, Alto del Hospicio was the site of a battle
during the Civil War of 1891 (Guerra Civil de 1891*)
between the loyalist troops favoring the government of
President (1886-91) José Manuel Balmaceda Fernández*
and revolutionary troops backing the Congress.   The
loyalists won and occupied the northern city of Pisagua
(January 27, 1891).

ALVAREZ SUAREZ, HUMBERTO, 1895- .   Lawyer by profession, businessman, and member of the Radical Party
(Partido Radical*).   In 1936, he was Minister of Justice and in 1940, Minister of the Interior.   Between
1941 and 1965 he served in both chambers of Congress.
He was Chilean delegate to the United Nations in 1947,
and President of the Senate in 1949.   He has also been
very active in the international business world.

AMPUERO DIAZ, RAUL, 1917- .   A lawyer by profession,
he became very active in the Chilean Socialist Party
(Partido Socialista*).   In 1934 he was one of the
founders of the Socialist Youth Movement in Chile, and
in 1938 he went to New York for the World Congress
of Socialist Youth.   In 1946 he was elected Secretary
General for the party, and has held that post many
times.   From 1953 to the present he has been serving
as senator from Tarapacá and Antofagasta*.   In the
Presidential elections of 1970, he backed Salvador
Allende Gossens*, as he had done in 1952, 1958, and
1964.

AMUNATEGUI ALDUNATE, MIGUEL LUIS, 1828-1888.   Author of many books on the history and politics of Chile,
and various biographies, Amunátegui Aldunate was very
active in politics and ran for the Presidency of Chile
in 1876.   In 1867 he was elected Vice-President of the
Chamber of Deputies, and, in the same year, President.
In 1868 he was named Minister of the Interior and of
Foreign Affairs.   In 1871 he was once again elected
President of the Chamber of Deputies.   In 1874 he
presented a proposal for the separation of church and
state, which was finally put into law in the Constitution
of 1925 (see CONSTITUTION OF 1925).   In 1875 he was
nominated by the Liberal Party (Partido Liberal*) to be

a candidate for the Presidency of the Republic, but declined.   A year later, he was convinced to run but
lost the elections to Aníbal Pinto Garmendia*, backed
by the Partido Nacional*.

From 1876 to 1888, Amunátegui Aldunate held many
important elective offices and was named President of
the Chamber of Deputies for the third time.   His literary contributions have great historical importance.
Among his best known works are: Títulos de la República de Chile a la soberanía y dominio de la extre-
midad austral del continente americano; La reconquista
española; Apuntes para la historia de Chile; La cuestión
de límites entre Chile y Bolivia; and, La crónica de
1810.   In 1863 he founded a newspaper, El Independiente, which reflected the ideology of the Partido Doctrinario, of which he was a member.   In 1888 he died
while holding the office of deputy to Congress from
Valparaíso.

AMUNATEGUI JORDAN, GREGORIO, 1901- .   Engineer by
profession and member of the Liberal Party (Partido
Liberal*).   He served in the Chilean Congress as a
deputy from 1933 to 1941, and became President of the
Chamber of Deputies in 1937.   He also served as a
senator from 1941 to 1965.   In the 1950's, he was
elected president of the Liberal Party.   In the Presidential campaign of 1964, however, he refused the
nomination of his party and backed Socialist Salvador
Allende Gossens*.

ANACONDA COPPER MINING COMPANY.   Copper is the
biggest dollar earner in Chile, providing about 68% of
foreign exchange receipts, and Anaconda has been the
giant of the Chilean copper industry, providing twice
as much copper as Kennecott*.   The largest and best
known of the Chilean copper mines is Chuquicamata*,
located between the Atacama* desert and the western
Cordillera*, at an altitude of 10, 000 feet.   The leading
copper-producing property in South America, and the
largest copper deposit in the world, Chuquicamata was
acquired and developed by the Guggenheim brothers,
who later sold it to Anaconda.   The third of Chile's
great copper deposits was located at Potrerillos* (province of Atacama) up to 1959.   In that year production
from the mine was exhausted and Chileans were lucky
to find a new mine located 12. 5 air miles from Potrerillos.   Symbolically, the new mine was called El

Salvador* ("the Saviour").

Potrerillos was purchased in 1913 by William Braden, and was later sold to Anaconda. For over 50
years it yielded only low grade ore until it finally
stopped production. From 1927 to 1959, the Potrerillos mine averaged only 55, 000 short tons of copper
per year. El Salvador, on the other hand, in the
short period of 11 years has raised its production to
about 100, 000 short tons of copper annually. The
rated annual capacity of El Salvador is estimated at
8, 500, 000 short tons of ore. El Salvador and Chuquicamata have been producing copper at capacity rate.
During the 1960s, the tax rate on Anaconda has been
of about 60% (10 to 25% lower than that of Kennecott*),
the reason being that Anaconda has behaved more to
the national interests of the Chileans by expanding production. In 1969 the firm drew about 70% of its total
profits (after taxes) from its two Chilean subsidiaries,
increasing capacity both at the mines and at the refinery.

In 1965, the Anaconda company insisted on retaining
sole ownership of its Chilean subsidiaries during the
negotiations with the Chilean government to "chileanize"
the copper industry, which would have given the government a greater participation in regulating copper prices,
production, and marketing. In 1969, for fear that a
leftist government would nationalize the copper industry,
Anaconda was prepared to make greater concessions to
the administration of President (1964-70) Eduardo Frei
Montalva*. The new agreement, called "nacionalización pactada, " or contracted nationalization, had the
following stipulations: a) as of 1970, the Chilean government would have acquired 51% of the stock of the
Anaconda mining operations; b) the Chilean government
would pay Anaconda US $197 million, with a 6% annual
interest; c) the sum Chile would pay due to interest
would amount to US $75 million, meaning that 51% of
the stock would be worth approximately US $272 mil-
lion; and d) the government and Anaconda also agreed
to the future sale of the remaining 49 per cent. Under stipulated conditions, the government could buy the
entire Anaconda stock after 1973.

In spite of these concessions, the new Chilean government (1970-76) of Socialist Salvador Allende Gossens* has promised to nationalize immediately not only
Anaconda, but other large American companies (from
the iron and nitrate industries) which in the past 60

years have taken out of Chile US $10.8 billion in
profits. The figure is of tremendous significance for
Chile if one compares it with the fact that the G.N.P.
achieved throughout the entire existence of the country
(about 400 years) amounts to US $10.5 billion. Ac-
cording to Chilean government sources, the conclusion
is clear: in a little over half a century these large
American companies took out from Chile an amount
greater than that created by Chileans in terms of industries, highways, schools, ports, hospitals, trade,
etc., during the country's entire history.

ANARQUIA POLITICA. If one excludes the period which
followed the death of the Conquistador Pedro de Valdivia*, Chile has experienced two periods of political
anarchy: from 1823 to 1830, and from 1924 to 1932.
The first period was a result of the Chileans' struggle
for independence from Spain. From 1823, when Ber-
nard O'Higgins* was ousted as Supreme Director of
Chile, until 1830, when the Republic was established,
Chile lived in a state of constant disturbance. Different congresses and Supreme Directors succeeded each
other amidst revolts and military coups. The most
important events during this period were the abolition
of slavery (1823), the Constitution of 1823*, the Constitution of 1828*, and the Civil War of 1829-30 (Guerra
Civil de 1829-30*). The second period of political anarchy (1924 to 1932) followed the first administration of Arturo Alessandri Palma*. This period was heightened
by the departure of Alessandri Palma before he could
end his term of office, and the activities of the military in the political arena, especially those of Carlos
Ibáñez del Campo*. The most important event during
these years of strife was the Constitution of 1925*,
which was implemented in 1932.

ANCUD. Capital city of the central-southern province of
Chiloé; population: 21,700 (1971 est.).

ANTOFAGASTA. 1) City in northern Chile in the province
that has the same name. Situated 720 kilometers south
of Arica*, and 1,373 kilometers north of Santiago*.
The city overlooks the Pacific Ocean and faces the
desert to the east. In 1971, the population was
124,500.
2) Province of norther Chile; population: 271,197
(1971 est.); area: 125,306.3 sq. km.

API. Acción Popular Independiente. A political party which is left-of-center but not Marxist, founded in 1969 to aid the Presidential candidacy of Social Democrat Rafael Tarud Siwady*. In December of the same year, API joined a coalition of leftist parties which backed the candidacy of Socialist Salvador Allende Gossens* (see UNIDAD POPULAR).

ARAUCANA, LA. An epic poem about the Spanish conquest of Chile, and the valiant efforts and sacrifices of the natives, the Araucanian Indians*, who fought against them in a war to the death. Written by Alonso de Ercilla y Zúñiga* (1533-94), La Araucana portrays a series of events that give a historical account of the wars against the Indians. Ercilla y Zúñiga admired the bravery of the Indians, and recorded, in truly Homeric proportions, the fortitude of men like Caupolicán*, Lautaro*, and Colocolo*. La Araucana is considered today to be the best Spanish epic of the 16th century.

ARAUCANOS. A nomadic tribe of Indians who occupied most of central Chile south of the Río Bío-Bío. Before the arrival of the Spanish Conquerors in 1539, the Araucanians had been able to supplant every other tribe and dominate the land known as Arauco (present-day south-central Chile). Among the Indians of South America, the Araucanians have the distinction of never having been conquered by force of arms. For more than three centuries, the Spaniards tried to subdue them, but failed. After the Declaration of Independence, the Chileans fought the Araucanians, but they were not able to incorporate them into Chilean life until the end of the 19th century. It was then that the last punitive expeditions against the aborigines were waged. It was mere contact with white man's civilization, however, and not rifles, that finally conquered the Araucanians.

Today there are 170,000 of them in the valley of the Toltec River, south of Temuco*, and in south-central Chile. Their number is increasing, though slightly, and their skills are limited to basket-weaving and pottery. Their artifacts are then sold to tourists. After 400 years of conditioning, these Indians, who were known for their warlike attitude and their hunting skills, have finally been given a place in Chilean society. The government of Eduardo Frei Montalva* (1964-70) made land grants to them and their communal holdings have been redistributed in the form of private property. It is questionable whether the concept of private property has been fully advantageous to them, since the Araucanians have been accustomed to a communal life style.

ARAUCO. Province of south-central Chile; population: 105,267 (1971 est.); area: 5,240.1 sq. km.

ARAUCO DOMADO. An epic poem of some 16,000 verses written by Pedro de Oña* to celebrate the deeds of Diego Hurtado de Mendoza* in the conquest of Chile. The book describes the arrival of the Spanish Conquistador in the south of Chile, and the battle with the Araucanian Indians (see ARAUCANOS). Oña's work is inferior to another epic poem, La Araucana*, written by Alonso de Ercilla y Zúñega*.

ARICA. Northernmost Chilean city and a free port. Peruvian Arica became a Chilean possession after the War of the Pacific* (1879-83). Arica is located on Chile's northwestern border with Peru.

ARMED FORCES. The struggle for independence convinced Chile's leaders of the need for effective armed forces. Despite Chile's limited resources, Bernardo O'Higgins* had by 1820 established an army of 5,000 men. First through purchase, and later through combat, O'Higgins acquired a navy of four ships of war, manned by 2,000 men. Chile's infant navy, enlarged by the Scottish seamen Lord Cochrane*, carried San Martín's army to Peru. Chilean arms were victorious against Bolivia and Peru in the War of the Pacific*; in this conflict Chile added to its national domain the arid, mineral-rich northern region.

At the present time, every able-bodied male citizen must serve a compulsory 18-month term in the armed forces. Following active service is a mandatory 12-year term in the active reserve, and a final period of inactive reserve duty through age 45. The army includes 1,500 officers and 20,000 enlisted men (enlisted men are not allowed to vote; they share this disenfranchisement with illiterates and convicted criminals). There are three army combat groups: one infantry division, one more-or-less mechanized cavalry division, and a mobile railway regiment. The navy numbers 1,000 officers and 16,000 men. An air force was established and trained in 1918 by British officers. During and since World War II, all three branches

have received equipment from the United States. Three
national service academies, all in the Santiago area,
train officers for their respective branches of Chile's
military establishment.

ASICH see ACCION SINDICAL CHILENA.

ATACAMA. A province of northern Chile; population:
161, 948 (1971 est.); area: 78, 267.5 sq. km.

ATACAMEÑOS. Indians who settled in the semi-desert provinces of Atacama* and Coquimbo* before the arrival
of the Spanish conquerors. They were pastoral Indians
and were soon absorbed by the more numerous Diaguitas* hordes, who had come from western Argentina.
Both tribes have long since been extinct.

AUDIENCIA. A Royal law court established in colonial Spanish America, with a ranking official--viceroy, governor,
captain-general--presiding over the body. It served as
the highest court of appeals and excercised practically
all the function of government within its territorial
jurisdiction. Its members were judges or oidores
("those who hear"), and their number varied according
to the importance of the audiencia (Mexico had ten
oidores while Guatemala only three, for example). The
first Audiencia was established in Santo Domingo in
1511. Soon, the most important trading centers had
their own audiencia. Mexico had one in 1527 and Peru
one in 1542. The first audiencia in Chile was that of
Santiago, in 1609.

AURORA, LA. A newspaper published in Santiago in 1937
to disseminate the ideology of the political party known
as the Acción Republicana*.

AURORA DE CHILE. A political weekly published from
February, 1812 to April, 1813, when it was replaced
by the Monitor Araucano. Its main objective was to
popularize the cause of independence from Spain.

AUTORIDAD EJECUTIVA. The executive branch of the newly established (July 4, 1811) Chilean Congress. It
came into existence on August 11, 1811.

AVELLANO. Site of a battle fought on December 10, 1819
between Conservatives, who wanted to retain the Span-

ish crown to control the affairs of Chile, and the Independents, who wanted total separation from Spain.

AYLWIN AZOCAR, PATRICIO, 1918- . Lawyer by profession, and one of the founders of the Christian Democratic Party (Partido Demócrata Cristiano*). In 1951, he was president of the Falange Nacional*, a political party which was the precursor of the Christian Democratic Party. From 1958 to 1960, and again in 1965, he was president of the Christian Democratic Party. In 1965, he was elected senator to Congress for a term of eight years.

AYSEN. Province of southern Chile; population: 50,100 (1971 est.); area: 103,583.9 sq. km.

-B-

BALANCE OF PAYMENTS see THE ECONOMY: External: B. Balance of Payments; etc.

BALMACEDA FERNANDEZ, JOSE MANUEL, 1840-1891. Member of the Partido Nacional*, and one of the most admired orators of the time, Balmaceda was elected President (1886-91) of Chile with the backing of Liberals and Radicals. During the first years of his regime, he was able to increase publich revenues and to embark upon an ambitious public works program which included a 600-mile expansion of the railways, the building of highways, the improvement of harbors, the assurance of safe aqueducts, the lengthening of telegraph lines and postal routes, and the provision of better sanitation and health services. There were also improvements in education, in agriculture, and in manufacturing. Despite general prosperity, the Balmaceda's administration alienated a slow Congress, which was not ready for such radical changes, and relations between the President and his cabinet began to deteriorate.

A controversy ensued over congressional criticism of governmental spending, and Balmaceda's programs met violent opposition. The President was accused of being extravagant, and of attempting to free himself from Congress so that he could rule dictatorially. By 1890 Balmaceda counted on only a few political supporters. Congress challenged his cabinet choices and re-

fused to approve his budget. Balmaceda played into
the hands of his enemies when, in January 1891, without convening Congress, he appropriated funds for the
new fiscal year. A week later, Congress met in a
National Assembly, deposed the president, and created
a revolutionary junta, appointing Jorge Montt*, a naval
officer and son of the late President (1851-61) Manuel
Montt*, to head the provisional government. Balmaceda, exercising dictatorial powers, refused to yield. A
civil war ensued (Guerra Civil de 1891*).

Although the army remained loyal to the president,
the revolutionary junta, with the support of the Navy
which controlled the ports, defeated the government
forces in two encounters: the battle of Concón*, near
Valparaíso*, and that of La Placilla*, near Santiago*.
Both battles, which left more than 10, 000 dead, occurred in August 1891. The defeated Balmaceda found
asylum in the Argentine Embassy, refusing to resign
until the expiration of his term, on the 18th of September, 1891. A day later, he wrote an eloquent state-
ment defending his actions and pleading for mercy for
his supporters, and then committed suicide. The death
of Balmaceda marked the end of 30 years of liberal
rule.

BALMACEDISTA. A partisan or sympathizer of President
(1886-91) José Manuel Balmaceda Fernández*.

BALTRA CORTES, ALBERTO 1912- . Lawyer by profession and member of the Radical Party (Partido Radical*). He taught at the Universidad de Chile, and was
director of the School of Political Economy at the university. From 1942 to 1945 he was General Director
of the Ministry of Economy and Commerce. He was
later named Minister of Economy and Commerce by
President (1946-52) Gabriel González Videla*. In 1950
he was president of the Chilean delegation at the Third
Congress of CEPAL* (Comisión Económica para América Latina), held in Montevideo, Uruguay. In 1958 he
was president of the Radical Party. Since then, he
has been active in Chilean economic circles, and has
written various books on political economy.

BANKING see THE ECONOMY: Internal: L. Banking.

BAÑADOS ESPINOSA, JULIO, 1858-1899. Newspaper cor-
respondent; writer of various books on Chilean history;

professor of law at the Universidad de Chile; holder of
various ministerial posts in the government (1886-91)
of José Manuel Balmaceda Fernández*. In 1885 he was
elected deputy to Congress and in 1888 he was appointed
Minister of Justice. From 1890 to 1891 he was editor
of the newspaper La Nación. In 1891 he was Minister
of the Interior when the Civil War (Guerra Civil de
1891*) began. As a result, he became Minister of War
(August 3, 1891) and participated in the battles of Concón* and La Placilla* (August 27th and 28th, respec-
tively). The government troops having been defeated,
he left Chile and went to Peru, where he asked for
political asylum. In 1894 he returned to Chile after a
short stay in Paris. He was elected deputy to Congress and was named director of the Liberal Democratic Party (Partido Liberal Democrático*). In 1897
he was named Minister of Industry and Public Works.
As a newspaper man he won many honors for his objective reporting. He left many works which were published posthumously. In 1889 he was honored with the
Cross of the Order of Rosa by the Emperor Pedro II
of Brazil.

BAQUEDANO GONZALEZ, MANUEL, 1826-1897. A preco-
cious military genius who ran away from home when
he was only 12 years old, in 1838, to fight against the
Peruvian-Bolivian Confederation. At the age of 13 he
was promoted to lieutenant, and, by the end of the War
of the Pacific (Guerra del Pacífico*), he had reached
the rank of general. He was also active in politics
as a member of the Liberal Party (Partido Liberal*)
and in 1881 was nominated for the Presidency of Chile,
an honor he refused. From 1882 to 1888 he was a
member of Congress, having been elected senator from
Santiago*. He did not participate in the Civil War of
1891 (Guerra Civil de 1891*) and as a result, was
named by President (1886-91) José Manuel Balmaceda
Fernández* to succeed him as the head of an interim
government on August 28, 1891.

BARBOSA BAEZA, ENRIQUE, 1882- . Lawyer by profession and active member of the Liberal Democratic Party (Partido Liberal Democrático*). When a faction of
the party split to become the Partido Liberal Democrático Aliancista*, he became its president (1926).
In 1925, he supported Emiliano Figueroa Larraín*,
who became President (1925-57) of Chile. In 1932, he

again joined the Liberal Democratic Party and backed
the candidacy of Arturo Alessandri Palma*, who became President (1932-38) of Chile for the second time.
In 1956, Barbosa Baeza joined the newly formed Movimiento Republicano*, becoming the vice-president of
this political party.   From January to May, 1956, he
served as Minister of Foreign Affairs in the cabinet of
President (1952-58) Carlos Ibáñez del Campo*.

BARBOSA PUGA, ORZIMBO, 1838-1891.   A career military
officer who fought in Valparaíso* in 1866 against the
Spaniards.   He also fought against the Araucanians* in
1868.   He became colonel in 1876, and in 1880 and
1881 was highly commended for his bravery in the War
of the Pacific (Guerra del Pacífico*).   In 1891, he was
elected senator to Congress and remained true to President (1886-91) José Manuel Balmaceda Fernández* during the civil war (Guerra Civil de 1891*).   He was
commander-in-chief of the loyalist troops in the final
battle of La Placilla*, where he was defeated in a
skirmish, taken prisoner by a superior force of the
enemy's cavalry, and barbarously assassinated.   His
body was paraded nude through the streets of near-by
Valparaíso.

BARRA LASTARRIA, EDUARDO DE LA, 1839-1900.   Nine-
teenth-century Chilean author and member of the Radical Party (Partido Radical*).   In 1864, he became
popular through his book of poems, Poesías líricas.
He also wrote various treatises on linguistics and on
the rhetoric of the Spanish language.   His best work
in linguistics concentrates on the Spanish epic Poema
de mio Cid.   He kept himself immersed in political
disputes and in 1891 participated in the civil war
(Guerra Civil de 1891*), condemning the actions of the
revolutionary congress.   Because of his loyalty to
President (1886-91) José Manuel Balmaceda Fernández*,
Barra Lastarria was forced into exile and went to
Montevideo, Uruguay.   He also spent about three years
in Buenos Aires, Argentina.   His reputation as educator and poet led the Argentine Government to bestow
numerous commission upon him, but in 1895 he decided to return to Chile.   Upon his arrival, he was
received and acclaimed by many young Chilean intellectuals.

BARRENECHEA PINTO, JULIO. Member of the Socialist
Party (Partido Socialista*), who in 1931 led a student
movement against the government (1927-31) of Carlos
Ibáñez del Campo*. In 1932, he was elected president
of the student government at the University of Chile.
From 1937 to 1945 he was a deputy in the Chilean Congress, and, in 1944, he was named second vice-president of the Chamber of Deputies. From 1945 to 1952
he was Chilean ambassador to Bolivia. In 1956 he became president of PADENA (Partido Democrático Nacional*), leaving the Socialist Party. Since his youth,
he has written many books of poetry, and in 1960 he
received the Premio Nacional de Literatura*. In 1966,
he was named by President (1964-70) Eduardo Frei
Montalva* as ambassador to India.

BARRIOS HUDTWALCKER, EDUARDO, 1884-1963. Chilean
writer and author of many literary works. He was Director of the National Library of Chile, and held many
important ministerial offices. He was Minister of Public Instruction in 1927; Minister of the Interior in 1928;
and Minister of Public Instruction again in 1928. In
1946, he won a very coveted literary prize, the Premio
Nacional de Literatura*. In 1953, he was named Minister of Education, and from 1953 to 1960 he was General Director of Libraries and Museums. Barrios' best-
known novels are: El niño que enloqueció de amor
(1915); Un perdido (1917); and El hermano asno (1922).

BARRIOS TIRADO, GUILLERMO, 1893- . He studied in
the Military Academy of Santiago, and was a career
military officer. In 1946, he became General of the
armed forces. From 1947 until 1952 he was Minister
of the National Defense. From 1958 until 1960 he was
governor of Arica*, the northern-most city in Chile.
He has written many books and articles on military
science.

BARROS ARANA, DIEGO, 1830-1906?. Chilean historian and
man of letters. He wrote many important biographies,
among them the well-known Galería de hombres céle-
bres de Chile, and his 10-volume Historia general de
la independencia de Chile. The latter, begun in 1854
and finished in 1858, is one of the best accounts of the
wars of independence. Among his other well-known
works are Historia de Chile (1860), Los cronistas de
India (1861), Historiadores chilenos (1862), Vida y

viajes de Hernando de Magallanes (1864), and Proceso
de Pedro de Valdivia (1873).
   In 1858, Barros Arana was imprisoned because he
was accused of conspiring against President (1851-61)
Manuel Montt Torres*, and was later exiled. He
traveled widely to Europe and to other South American
countries. In 1862 he returned to Chile, where he
continued his literary work, publishing many books on
history and diplomacy. He became a member of the
Partido Liberal Doctrinario*. In 1881 he represented
Chile in a treaty to fix the boundaries between Chile
and Argentina, and was accused of losing 7/8 of Patagonia to Argentina. When he died in 1906, Chileans
recognized that he was a great historian, but thought
of him as a poor diplomat because of the loss of territory to Argentina.

BARROS BORGOÑO, LUIS, 1858-1943. He received his law
    degree in 1880 and while still a student taught history
    at the Chilean National Institute of Higher Education.
    In 1883, while holding the office of chief of staff in the
    Ministry of Foreign Affairs, he participated in the fi-
    nal negotiations that ended the War of the Pacific (Guerra
    del Pacífico*). Later he assisted in bringing about
    peace with Bolivia, and filled various ministerial posts
    from 1889 to 1918. In 1920, backed by the Unión Na-
    cional*, he opposed Arturo Alessandri Palma* in the
    Presidential elections, but lost. At the end of Ales-
    sandri's term of office, Barros was named Minister of
    the Interior (1925). As such, Barros succeeded Ales-
    sandri when the latter resigned in October of that year,
    remaining in power for two months. On December 23,
    1925, Barros was replaced by the elected President,
    Emiliano Figueroa Larraín*.

BARROS GREZ, DANIEL, 1834-1904. A student of engineer-
    ing and mathematics, he was best known as a novelist
    and writer of fables. He also was interested in the
    theater, especially in the dramatic art. He did most
    of his writings in the city of Talca (central Chile), and
    his Pipiolos y pelucones (Pipiolo*; Pelucone*), is ac-
    cepted as a very fine interpretation of Chilean life af-
    ter independence was won.

BARROS LUCO, RAMON, 1835-1919. Was born and edu-
    cated in Santiago, where he received a law degree
    from the National University. He was President (1910-

15) of Chile.   After a distinguished political career
which saw him elected deputy, senator, and named
subrogate Minister of War, Barros Luco participated
in the revolutionary junta of 1891 which deposed President (1886-91) José Manuel Balmaceda Fernández*.   In
1896, Barros Luco was named President of the Senate,
and in 1903, during the illness of Germán Riesco
Errázuriz*, served as acting President of Chile.   In
the crisis of 1910, all parties turned to him to run for
President.   Since his two opponents, Agustín Eduardo
MacClure and Juan Luis Sanfuentes Andonáegui, did not
receive the necessary votes to be nominated, Barros
Luco was elected President by Congress and inaugurated
on December 23, 1910.

The government of Barros Luco has been severely
criticized by Chilean historians for not being able to
put a stop to political quarreling within his administration.   His first cabinet, named on December 26, 1910,
lasted only 18 days.   Subsequent cabinets lasted only a
little longer.   It became apparent to many that the interests of politicians were to themselves above those
of the country.   In spite of these setbacks, Barros
Luco was able to bring some progress to Chile.   The
School of Engineering was established; the port of San
Antonio was opened; the National Library was built in
Santiago; and the Historical Museum was inaugurated.
Many public works were undertaken, including the establishment of sanitary waterways, and the building of
roads and bridges.   In 1913 a school for pilots was
set up, one of the first in South America.   In 1915,
Chile signed a commercial and political treaty with Argentina and Brazil known as the "A B C Treaty*."   In
the same year, Barros Luco was responsible for the
electoral law known as "La Ley de las Elecciones"; a
very important measure to stop the scandalous frauds
of the ballot box.

BELLAVISTA.   Site of a battle fought on January 14, 1826,
between the Independientes* and the Realistas*.   The
Independientes, who wanted to liberate the island of
Chiloê* and incorporate its territory within the Chilean
national boundaries, were victorious.

BELLO CODECIDO, EMILIO, 1869-1941.   Grandson of Andrés Bello* and brother-in-law of President (1886-91)
José Manuel Balmaceda Fernández*, he was a lawyer
who entered upon an administrative and congressional

career at an early age.   He was a member of the
Liberal Democratic Party (Partido Democrático Liberal*), served as deputy to Congress, and held very
important ministerial offices from 1894 to 1938.   In
1925, he was President of the junta government that
succeeded Arturo Alessandri Palma*.   Since the political overturn of 1925, he spent some time in exile but
in 1936 was called to assume the War portfolio in the
second administration (1932-38) of Alessandri.

BELLO LOPEZ, ANDRES, 1781-1865.   Man of letters, and
     founder of the Universidad de Chile*.   He was born in
     Caracas and died in Santiago, where he spent more
     than 30 years of his life.   In 1802, he was named
     Secretary in the colonial government of Venezuela.   In
     1808 he was an adherent to the Independence movement
     in Venezuela, and was sent to England with Simón
     Bolívar to woo the English for aid in the revolutionary
     cause.   In 1810 he returned to England, where he re-
     sided for almost two decades.   During that time, he
     cultivated the friendship of philosophers, men of letters,
     and scientists.   In 1829 he was invited to Chile to fill
     a high post in the Ministry of Foreign Affairs, and to
     lead the intellectual life of the young republic.   After
     founding the Universidad de Chile, he became its first
     president in 1842.   By that time he had obtained Chil-
     ean citizenship, and was already active in politics.   He
     was elected to the Senate in 1837, 1846, and from 1855
     through 1864.   His literary contributions were many.
     Besides writing poetry, he was the author of one of the
     best grammars of Spanish, Gramática de la lengua es-
     pañola (1847).
          He was also the intellectual leader of the Neo-class-
     ical period in Chile, which began around 1830 and lasted
     for about 15 years.   As a contributor to the literary
     supplement of the newspaper El Mercurio* in Santiago, An-
     drés Bello was at odds with the Argentinean Domingo Faus-
     tine Sarmiento*, who had been exiled by the Argentine dic-
     tator (1829-52) Juan Manuel Rosas, and had come to
     Chile.   Sarmiento became a contributor to El Mercurio
     in Valparaíso, and soon attacked Bello for writing un-
     imaginative poetry in the style of the neo-classics:
     cold, simple, without guts.   Sarmiento espoused the
     romantic ideals in writing, and soon there was a po-
     lemic between the two writers which lasted until Sar-
     miento returned to Argentina, later to become Presi-
     dent (1868-74) after the fall of Rosas.   Bello left be-

hind many outstanding works in addition to his well-
known grammar and poetry. His Tratado de derecho
internacional (1834), and his Código Civil (1855) are
among the great contributions to the political history
of Chile. Among Bello's many disciples are José
Victorino Lastarria Santander* and Miguel Luis Amunátegui Aldunate*.

BENAVENTE BUSTAMANTE, DIEGO JOSE, 1790-1867.
Chilean patriot who took part in the struggle for independence. In 1811, he formed part of the junta government that the patriots proclaimed in Concepción*. Two
years later he was wounded at the Battle of the Roble*,
but recovered to take part in the battle of Rancagua*
in 1814. He emigrated to Argentina with José Miguel
Carrera Verdugo* after the patriots' defeat at Rancagua,
and remained in that country until 1823. On his return
to Chile, he married the widow of José Miguel Carrera
Verdugo, doña Mercedes Flotecilla Valdivieso, and held
various ministerial posts. He reorganized the Ministry
of the Treasury, and served as counselor and Minister
of State. In 1826, he became a member of the Federalist Party (Partido Federalista*), and was President of
the Chamber of Deputies. He opposed conservative
statesman Diego Portales Palazuelos* with energy, but
was absolved from participation in his death. In 1857,
he was Vice-President of the Senate; later he became
President of the same body. He was one of the founders of the National Party (Partido Nacional*). Before
he died, he wrote various essays on the campaign for
Chilean independence, the most notable of which is the
Memorias de las primeras campañas de independencia.

BENAVIDES, VICENTE, 1777-1822. One of the central figures in the Chilean struggle for independence. In 1811,
Benavides espoused the cause of independence against
Spain, fighting in the army of Juan José Carrera Verdugo*. Two years later, however, he changed sides
and became a realista*, fighting at the battle of Rancagua* in 1814 on the side of Spain. During the battles
for the so-called "Spanish Reconquest," Benavides distinguished himself. He was imprisoned, however, in
1818, and was going to be shot. The intercession of
some independientes* who had fought with him in 1811
saved his life at the last moment, and he was sent into
exile in Argentina. In 1820, he came back to Chile
and became the commander of the Spanish troops fight-

ing to recuperate lost territory from the Chilean patriots. Thus began the "War to the Death" (Guerra a
Muerte*). After Benavides was defeated by the patriots
on numerous occasions, he resolved to leave Chile and
go to Peru, to fight on the side of Spain against Peruvian independence. He was captured at the border by
Chilean authorities, brought to Santiago where he received a summary trial, and was executed on the morning of February 23, 1822.

BIBLIOTECA NACIONAL   see NATIONAL LIBRARY.

BIENESTAR SOCIAL, MINISTERIO DE. The Ministry of Social Welfare was created by statute No. 7, 912 on November 30, 1927. This ministry was created to replace the Ministry of Hygiene, Social Security and Assistance, and Labor (Ministerio de Higiene, Asistencia
y Previsión Social y Trabajo*). The functions of the
Ministry of Social Welfare were to secure the well-
being of all Chileans by providing a minimum wage,
social security, and sanitation. In 1932, this ministry
was divided into two new ministries: the Ministry of
Public Health (Salubridad Pública*), and the Ministry of
Labor (Ministerio del Trabajo*).

BILBAO BARQUIN, FRANCISCO, 1823-1865. Chilean writer
who spent many years of his life in exile for his anti-
clerical views and his opposition to the conservative
government (1851-61) of Manuel Montt Torres*. At the
age of 11 he accompanied his father into exile in Peru.
In 1839, he returned to Chile and entered the National
Institute, where he studied with Andrés Bello* and José
Victorino Lastarria*. In the late 1830's he published
a book, La sociabilidad chilena, in which he criticized,
among other things, the priestly vocation in Chile.
Soon a polemic began when La Revista Católica, a
Church publication, launched a campaign against Bilbao
Barquín. He was brought to trial, and his book was
found to be blasphemous, immoral, and seditious. The
author was fined and in lieu of payment was sent to
prison. His admirers paid the fine and threatened to
mob the judges.
    Life in Santiago, however, proved insupportable for
Bilbao Barquín, and he went into voluntary exile to
France, where his book was well received. In 1850,
he returned to Chile and founded with Eusebio Lillo*
the "Sociedad de la Igualdad*, " a society created to

defend the plight of the poor and to organize them into
a political body. Religious polemics continued, and
Bilbao Barquín accused the Church of misusing its vast
land holdings. Within the Church, the young priests
sided with the controversial author on the grounds that
Christ himself had accursed and thrown out the penny-
pinching merchants from the temple.

The more conservative within the Church, and the
government of Montt Torres, launched a bitter campaign against the Sociedad de la Igualdad. There was
violence, and Bilbao Barquín's life was threatened. He
was exiled and had to leave Chile disguised as a priest
to cross the Peruvian border. Meeting with further
persecution in Peru, he went to Europe in 1854, and
to Argentina in 1856. In Buenos Aires, where he died,
he devoted himself to the task of unifying Argentina.
His second major book was Los boletines del espíritu
(1850). His writings inspired the formation of the
Radical Party (Partido Radical*).

BIO-BIO. 1) A province of central Chile; population:
196, 005 (1971 est.); area: 11, 134.7 sq. km.
2) A navigable Chilean river that crosses three provinces, Concepción*, Bío-Bío*, and Malleco*.

BLANCO CUARTIN, MANUEL, 1822-1890. News reporter,
poet, and editor of El Mercurio* from 1866 to 1886.
He is credited with writing various articles and poems
that attracted wide attention in Chile and outside the
country and made El Mercurio one of the most widely-
read papers in South America. Son of the Argentine
poet Ventura Blanco Encalada, Blanco Cuartín received
his education in Santiago, at the National Institute. He
had planned a career in medicine but because of deaf-
ness turned to journalism. In 1876, while still on the
editorial staff of El Mercurio, he joined the faculty of
Philosophy and Humanities at the University of Chile*.
He was a member of the Conservative Party (Partido
Conservador*).

BLANCO ENCALADA, MANUEL, 1790-1876. Born in Buenos
Aires, he was sent to Spain to complete his education
and returned to America at the outbreak of the wars of
independence. In 1813, he joined the Chilean patriots
in the fight against Spain, was taken prisoner after the
battle of Rancagua* in 1814, and condemned to death.
His sentence, however, was commuted to exile on the

Juan Fernández* island. In 1817, after the patriot's victory at Chacabuco*, he was freed and returned to Chile. He participated in the battles against the Spaniards at Cancha Rayada* and Maipú (both in 1818), and after independence was won began the organization of the Chilean navy under Lord Thomas Cochrane*. When the latter retired in 1823, Blanco Encalada became Admiral of the Navy. In 1837, he participated in the war against the Peru-Bolivia Confederation. Between 1849 and 1858 he served as senator to Congress. He also went to France in 1852 on a diplomatic mission as Chilean plenipotentiary minister. At the age of 75, he went to Peru to repatriate the body of Bernardo O'Higgins*. In the same year, 1865, he directed naval operations against the Spanish fleet.

BLEST GANA, ALBERTO, 1830-1920. Chilean novelist who considered himself a realist, and who described the transformation of Chilean society from "an energetic world of pioneers to a lax, degenerate society." He wanted to become the Balzac of Chile, and had a wide knowledge of French literature. Among his best works are Martín Rivas, considered a classic in depicting Chilean mores of the 1850's; Durante la reconquista (1897), which portrays the city of Santiago during the wars of independence against Spain from 1814 to 1818; and Los transplantados (1904), a critique of Chilean emmigrants who leave their country and their traditions to go to Paris to be absorbed in luxury and ostentation.

BLOQUE DE IZQUIERDA. (Literally, "Leftist Block.") A political coalition of leftist parties, organized in 1934 and dissolved in 1936. The Communist Party (Partido Comunista*) refused to join the coalition, formed mainly by Socialists (Partido Socialista*), Radical Socialists (Partido Radical Socialista*), and Democrats (Partido Democrático*). This block represented the major opposition to the second government (1932-38) of Arturo Alessandri Palma*. When the Alessandri administration proposed to use the profits from copper and nitrate to liquidate the national debt, the Bloque de Izquierda opposed the idea vehemently. But both chambers of Congress approved it in 1936. As a result, the coalition dissolved, and, in the same year, the Frente Popular* was organized, made up once again of leftist parties, this time including the Communists.

BLOQUE DE SANEAMIENTO DEMOCRATICO. A coalition of
Christian Democrats, Radicals, Socialists, Communists,
and National Democrats (Partido Democrata Cristiano*,
Radical*, Socialista*, Comunista*, and Nacional Democrático*) formed in 1958 to oppose the Presidential
candidacy of Jorge Alessandri Rodríguez*. When Alessandri was elected for the term 1958-64, the block was
dissolved.

BOLETIN OFICIAL DE LA JUNTA DE GOBIERNO. When the
forces backing the rebellious Congress of 1891 established a provisional government in the city of Iquique*, the Boletín Oficial was published. It was the organ of the revolutionary junta which gave an account of
the Civil War (Guerra Civil de 1891*), and accused
President (1886-91) José Manuel Balmaceda Fernández*
of causing the conflict which claimed some 10,000 lives.

BORGOÑO NUÑEZ, JOSE MANUEL, 1789-1848. Chilean patriot who fought in the wars of independence. In 1821
he went to Peru to liberate that country from Spanish
rule. On his return to Chile, he was elected deputy
in 1823, and in 1827 he was named Minister of War in
the cabinet of President (1827) Francisco Antonio Díaz*.
In 1838 he was sent to Madrid to accelerate a peace
treaty between Chile and Spain. There he was deco-
rated by the Spanish King Carlos III, but refused to accept the honorary title conferred upon him. He was
Minister of Justice in the government (1841-51) of
Manuel Bulnes Prieto*.

BOSSAY LEYVA, LUIS, 1912- . Active member of the
Radical Party (Partido Radical*), he was a Presidential
candidate in the elections of 1958. He was defeated by
Jorge Alessandri Rodríguez*. In 1939, Bossay Leyva
was president of the Radical convention held in Valparaíso*. He assumed various important ministerial
posts in the government (1946-52) of Gabriel González
Videla*. In 1946 he was named Minister of War; in
1947, Minister of Economy and Commerce; and, also
in 1947, he was subrogate Minister of Foreign Affairs.
From 1953 to 1965 he was senator from Aconcagua*
and Valparaíso*. In 1963, he was appointed by Alessandri Rodríguez to be president of the Chilean delegation to the United Nations.

BRADEN COPPER COMPANY see KENNECOTT COPPER
CORPORATION

BULNES PRIETO, MANUEL, 1799-1866. Twice President
of Chile, from 1841 to 1846 and from 1846 to 1851.
He continued the conservative rule in the country which
had begun in 1831 and was to last until 1861. His
strong regime suppressed the Radical press and exiled
radical leaders, while at the same time continuing the
general prosperity that Chile was experiencing through
economic and educational reforms. As a young career
military officer, Bulnes participated in the struggle for
Chilean independence. He joined the Chilean patriot
army when he was only 12 years old, and took part in
every major battle, distinguishing himself at Maipú*.
In 1838, he fought against the Peru-Bolivia Confederation over commercial rivalries. Elected President in
1841, Bulnes embarked upon a program of governmental reforms. He founded the Office of Statistics, and
called for the second census in the history of the young
Republic (1843). He also elevated to the status of
provinces Valparaíso* and Atacama*. In a law of
1844, he signed a treaty with Spain for the recognition
of Chile as an independent republic.
      The second Bulnes Government was much more tu-
multuous than the first one. Although the first few
years were peaceful and many programs of public
works were implemented, the President ruled with an
iron hand to stifle opposition and to secure the continuation of conservative rule in Chile. As the election
of 1851 approached, a military coup d'état was organized to overthrow the President and prevent Manuel
Montt Torres* from succeeding him. The revolt was
headed by Colonel Pedro Alcántara Urriola Balbontín*
(Mutiny of Urriola*), but troops backing the President
were prepared for such an emergency, and defeated
the opposition. After the election of Montt Torres, a
civil war broke out (Guerra Civil de 1851*). Bulnes,
who was at the head of the army, was able to restore
peace. During Bulnes' second administration, the
School of Agriculture, the Academy of Painting, and
the Music Conservatory were erected. Roads and
bridges were built, and two important railroad lines,
the Copiapó-Caldera and the Santiago-Valparaíso, were
added.

BULNES SANFUENTES, FRANCISCO, 1917- . Lawyer by
profession and member of the Conservative Party (Partido Conservador*). He became involved in politics
since his university days (he received the law degree

in 1939), and was elected President of the Conservative
Youth Movement (Juventud Conservadora*).   From 1945
to the present, he has served as deputy to Congress,
and in 1962 he was the President of the Conservative
Party.   In the Presidential elections of September 4,
1970, he supported the candidacy of Jorge Alessandri
Rodríguez*.

BUSTOS LAGOS, MARIANO, 1900- .   Member of the Demo-
    cratic Party (Partido Democrático*) who has held var-
    ious important government posts in the last 30 years.
    In 1942, and again in 1946, he was Minister of Labor.
    In 1944, he was vice-president of the International
    Labor Conference held in Philadelphia.   From 1946 to
    1950, he was Chilean consul general to Canada, and in
    1953 he was named Chilean plenipotentiary minister to
    Belgium and Luxembourg.   On his return to Chile in
    1958, he was named administrative director in the
    Ministry of Foreign Affairs, a post he held until 1965.

-C-

C. R. A. C.   see CONFEDERACION REPUBLICANA DE
    ACCION CIVICA.

CABILDO.   A municipal council.   It was the basic town or-
    ganization of the Spanish American colonies.   The body
    comprised several judges, a commissioned officer, a
    police chief, and a board of aldermen.   In the early
    days of the colony these officials were elected by the
    townsmen, but in the 1700's that practice was changed
    and they were appointed.   The cabildo supervised pub-
    lic works and sanitation, and regulated prices and
    wages.   The enforcement of the law, as well as the
    collection of taxes, were also relegated to this body.
    Besides the municipal council, there was also a cabil-
    do abierto, an open meeting attended by all townsmen
    who had an opportunity to vote and express themselves
    when matters of grave importance were before the
    community.   This type of open gathering became very
    important during the period of independence from Spain.

CABILDO ABIERTO   see CABILDO.

CALDERA.   A naval battle that took place in the Bay of
    Caldera, situated in the province of Copiapó, north of

Santiago, in 1891. In the battle, the Almirante Condell
and the Almirante Lynch, two ships supporting the government (1886-91) of José Manuel Balmaceda Fernández*,
were engaged with the warship Blanco Encalada, which
was supporting the rebellious Congress during the civil
war (Guerra Civil de 1891*). The government ships
were able to sink the Blanco Encalada, which went under in only five minutes with an estimated 140 people
aboard. Among the few who escaped death were Ramón
Barros Luco*, President of the Chamber of Deputies,
and some 180 sailors.

CALLAMPAS. (Literally, "mushrooms.") Shantytown; city
slums.

CALVO DE ENCALADA RECABARREN, MARTIN, 1756-1828.
A military officer and a conservative politician, Calvo
de Encalada was one of the most ardent promoters of
the wars for independence. In 1811 he was appointed
Vice-President of the First National Congress (July 4),
and he formed part of the ruling junta on August 11 of
that year. In 1814 he was exiled by the Spaniards for
his participation in the battle of Rancagua*. When
Chile won its independence in 1818, he returned to
Santiago and was elected senator to Congress. In
1823 he was a member of the Council of State (Consejo
del Estado).

CAMELOT see PROJECT CAMELOT.

CAMPINO SALAMANCA, ENRIQUE, 1794-1874. Chilean patriot who participated in the wars for independence.
In 1810 he joined the revolutionary army and distinguished himself in every major battle against the
Spaniards. In 1814, he took part in the battle of Rancagua, but was defeated and had to flee to Mendoza,
Argentina. He came back to Chile with the legendary
army of the Andes (Ejército de los Andes*), under the
command of the Argentine liberator José de San Martín*. Campino Salamanca fought in the battles of
Chacabuco* (1817) and Maipú* (1818). In 1820 he was
sent to Peru to liberate that country from Spain, and
was promoted to colonel. Back in Chile, he participated in the "Campaña de Chiloé"* (1825-26). In 1827
he participated in a military coup d'état with his brother Joaquín (see SUBLEVACION DE CAMPINO). In
1832 he was promoted to general. From 1826 until

1861 he was deputy to Congress as a member of the Partido Federalista*, and from 1861 to 1870 he was senator from the province of Santiago.

CAMPINO SALAMANCA, JOAQUIN, 1788-1860.   Brother of Enrique, and lawyer by profession.   Active member of the Federalist Party (Partido Federalista*) and President of the Chilean Congress, he was named Minister of Foreign Affairs and held that post in 1825 and 1826. In 1827, he helped his brother organize a military coup d'état (see SUBLEVACION DE CAMPINO).   In the same year, he was named Chilean plenipotentiary minister to the United States, and in 1830 held the same office in Mexico.   He returned to Chile and was elected deputy to Congress, holding office from 1840 to 1849.

CANCHA RAYADA.   Plains near the city of Talca*, and site of two important battles during the war of independence, both won by the Spaniards.   The first battle occurred in 1814, when 450 Spaniards dispersed more than 1,400 Chileans in a surprise attack.   The second battle occurred in 1818, and had much more importance at least in a psychological sense.   The Spaniards were losing the grip they had on their South American colonies. When things were getting much worse in Chile for the Spaniards, the troops loyal to the King of Spain pulled another surprise attack on the Chilean camp.   The Chileans panicked, thinking that a massive Spanish army concentration was surrounding their camp.   They fled north towards Santiago but their retreat was cut off by the Spaniards.   The Chilean camp was under the command of Bernardo O'Higgins* and José de San Martín*.   O'Higgins was (wrongly) reported killed and San Martín organized the retreat.   It was a humiliating defeat which lowered the morale of the Chilean troops.

CAP.   An acronym for the Compañía de Acero del Pacífico or Pacific Steel Company.   A publicly-owned company founded in 1950, CAP has established the basis for national heavy industrial development in its integrated steel plant at Huachipato*.   CAP is a subsidiary of CORFO*.

CAPITULACION DE PURAPEL.   The last battle of the Civil War of 1851 (Guerra Civil de 1851*).   With the conclusion of the conflict, President (1851-61) Manuel Montt Torres* declared a general amnesty for those who participated in the war.

CARABINERO. A member of the Chilean national police
force. See also CUERPO DE CARABINEROS.

CARMONA PERALTA, JUAN DE DIOS, 1916- . Lawyer by
profession and Minister of National Defense in the government (1964-70) of Eduardo Frei Montalva*. He was
a member of the Falange Party (Falange Nacional*) and
student leader of the Falange Universitaria. From
1949 to 1961 he was deputy to Congress. He is an active member of the Christian Democratic Party (Partido Democrata Cristiano*).

CARO, JOSE MARIA, 1866-1958. Bishop of Santiago who in
1945 became the first Chilean to be named a cardinal.
In 1958, after his death, Pope John XXIII named Raúl
Silva Henríquez to be his successor.

CARRASCO CARRASCO, ARNOLDO, 1893- . A career ar-
my officer who is now retired. He graduated from the
Escuela Militar* and was one of the founders of the
present-day Chilean Police (Cuerpo de Carabineros*),
formed in 1926. In 1944, he was promoted to general
in the army. From 1944 to 1946, he was Minister of
National Defense in the cabinet of President (1942-46)
Juan Antonio Río Morales*. In 1947, he was named
Chilean ambassador to Canada, and in 1953 he was
Chilean ambassador to Brazil.

CARRERA CUEVAS, IGNACIO DE LA, 1755-1819. Father
of José Miguel*, Luis*, and Juan José*; three Chilean
patriots who fought in the struggle for independence
from Spain. In 1777, Carrera Cuevas was serving the
King of Spain as lieutenant colonel in the "Milicias del
Príncipe," the Royal militia. Two years later he was
promoted to colonel. He retired in 1803 but, because
of his sons' activities for the cause of independence,
he returned to the army and became a colonel in the
independent troops. In 1810, he took part in the first
junta government (Junta de Gobierno de 1810*), and a
year later he was a member of the Supreme Tribunal
of independent Chile. He closely observed the vicissi-
tudes and adverse fortune that befell two of his sons,
Luis and Juan José, and had to pay the costs for their
execution in Mendoza, Argentina. He died heartbroken,
shortly after.

CARRERA FONTENCILLA, JOSE MIGUEL, 1820-1860. Became a political activist in Santiago against the Conservative Government (1851-61) of Manuel Montt Torres*.
In 1851, Carrera Fontencilla participated in the mutiny
of Urriola*, a thwarted military coup d'état against the
government. The attempt having failed, he escaped to
La Serena*, and with Benjamín Vicuña Mackenna* and
others, organized an army which was also defeated by
the government troops in Petorca. As a result, he
went into exile, but returned to Chile and participated
in the Civil War of 1859 (Guerra Civil de 1859*). Once
again he was defeated, this time at Cerro Grande*. He
was condemned to death in 1859, but managed to escape
to Lima, Peru, where he died a year later of a liver
ailment.

CARRERA VERDUGO, JOSE MIGUEL, 1785-1821. Chilean
patriot who was executed in 1821, in Mendoza, Argentina, where three years earlier the same fate had be-
fallen his brothers Juan José and Luis. Son of Ignacio
de la Carrera Cuevas, José Miguel was sent by his
father to study at the military academy in Cádiz, Spain
(1806-11). It was there that, in 1808, he met the Argentine liberator José de San Martín*. In 1809, Carrera Verdugo was promoted to captain of the cavalry.
Two years later, learning that Chile had proclaimed a
junta government (Junta de Gobierno de 1810*), he
tried to return to his fatherland, but was arrested on
suspicions that he wanted to go back to Chile to work
for the collapse of the Spanish hegemony in South America. Freed shortly after, Carrera Verdugo arrived in
Valparaíso* on July 25, 1811.
      On September 4, 1811, he participated in the first
revolutionary action against Spain, and on November 15
of that year he replaced the revolutionary junta for a
new one, in which he and Bernardo O'Higgins*, who
was later to become his great enemy, participated.
O'Higgins resigned his position, and so did other delegates to the junta, leaving Carrera Verdugo as the only
person in charge. From 1812 to 1813 the latter ruled
Chile on a broad basis of political reforms. The first
provisional constitution of the land was proclaimed, a
step toward complete independence from Spain. A
Chilean flag was designed, and diplomatic relations
were established with the United States. Carrera Verdugo refused to recognize edicts from Spain, set up a
printing press, opened primary and secondary schools,

established a public library, and controlled the newspapers in the province of Santiago.

As a result, his popularity grew, and his followers,
many of whom were conservatives who still professed
allegiance to Ferdinand VII of Spain, became known as
carreristas*.   But troubles were in the making for the
Chilean statesman, at home and abroad.   Fernando de
Ascabal y Souza, then Viceroy of Peru, decided to
send an expedition against the rebellious Chileans.   Two
thousand Spaniards left Peru to fight the revolutionaries
in Santiago.   In 1813, because of imminent danger,
Carrera Verdugo had to abandon the governing junta
and was designated commander of the Chilean army.
In August of that year, the opposing armies met in
Chillán*.   The royalists routed Carrera Verdugo in a
bloody battle, where the Chileans suffered great losses.

Discouraged by the defeat, the junta government appointed Bernardo O'Higgins as commander of the Chilean army.   Soon a rivalry between the two men began,
as Carrera Verdugo refused to give up his command.
An armed confrontation between the two was in the
making, as O'Higgins was approaching the city of Santiago from the south.   News of another royalist attack
reached both camps before orders of fire were issued.
Due to the gravity of the situation, Carrera Verdugo
and O'Higgins decided to set differences aside and to
fight together the common enemy.   O'Higgins stepped
down and Carrera Verdugo was selected commander of
the Army.   It is not clear whether the fate of the
Chileans would have changed had O'Higgins commanded
the troops, but the battle of Rancagua* (October 1,
1814), marked a decisive royalist victory.   Both Carrera Verdugo and O'Higgins found refuge in Mendoza,
accompanied by their followers.

The quarrels of Chile were carried over into Argentina.   San Martín, who was also in Mendoza, received
Carrera Verdugo coldly while accepting O'Higgins' aid
to retake Chile.   Carrera Verdugo, as a result, accused both O'Higgins and San Martín of excluding him
from the reconquest of his fatherland.   Disgusted, he
went to Buenos Aires, where he stayed briefly to collect money for the cause, and then to the United States,
where he purchased two men-of-war, the Clifton and
the Salvaje.   He returned to Buenos Aires, where his
services were once again refused by San Martín and
O'Higgins.   Carrera Verdugo swore to revenge himself from the ingratitude of his opponents.   From 1816

to 1821 he perpetrated acts of war in Argentina against
the rival armies of San Martín, O'Higgins and Juan
Martín de Purreydón, who had been elected Argentinean
Supreme Director at the National Congress of Tucumán
(1816), and who had avowed help to the Chilean and
Peruvian struggle for independence.

Carrera Verdugo published a newspaper, El Hurón,
in which he attacked the three, and demanded justice
for the innocent deaths of his two brothers in Mendoza
(1818).   On September 1, 1821, Carrera Verdugo was
captured near the city of San Juan (Northwestern Argentina).   He was accused of seeding discord in the revolutionary camp and two days later was taken to Mendoza and shot as a traitor.   Thus was eliminated one
of the most controversial patriots of Chilean Independence.   Even today, the conservatives in Chile praise
José Miguel Carrera Verdugo and want him remembered
as a misunderstood hero who, in reality, was not sel-
fish because he had proved his love for his country.

CARRERA VERDUGO, JUAN JOSE, 1782-1818.   Chilean patriot who was executed in Mendoza, Argentina.   He
participated in the Chilean struggle for independence,
and was a career military officer.   When his brother
José Miguel* came from Spain to aid the cause of independence, Juan José was a major in the patriot army.   In 1813, he was president of the junta government in Santiago, and a year later he fought in Rancagua*, with his brothers Luis* and José Miguel*.   After
the Chilean defeat at Rancagua, the three brothers
went into exile to Mendoza, Argentina.   Juan José was
involved in the political contention for power between
his brother José Miguel and Bernardo O'Higgins*.
Juan José plotted with his brothers to bring about the
downfall of O'Higgins.   In 1818, he was accused of organizing an uprising against the local authorities in
Mendoza and was captured and executed with his brother Luis.   Three years later the same fate was to be-
fall his brother José Miguel.

CARRERA VERDUGO, LUIS, 1791-1818.   Chilean patriot who
was executed in Mendoza, Argentina.   Youngest of the
Carrera Verdugo brothers, he was involved in the
armed conflict to liberate Chile from Spain and also
in the struggle between his brother José Miguel* and
Bernardo O'Higgins*, both of whom sought to gain political control of Chile.   From 1810 to 1814, Luis

Carrera Verdugo participated in the campaign against
Spain fought mainly in southern Chile and around the
capital, Santiago.   After the defeat of the Chilean army at Rancagua* in 1814, he emigrated to Argentina
with a score of patriots.   In the same year, he killed
General Juan Mackenna*, a O'Higgins' supporter, in a
duel.   In 1818, Luis Carrera Verdugo was executed
with his brother Juan José* for bringing discord in the
Chilean camp in exile, where Chilean and Argentine patriots were organizing an armed revolt against the
Spanish hegemony in South America.   He was also accused of organizing the overthrow of the local authorities in Mendoza.   Three years after, the same fate befell José Miguel Carrera Verdugo.

CARRERINO   see PARTIDO CARRERINO.

CARRERISTA.   A follower or sympathizer of José Miguel
Carrera Verdugo* during the Chilean struggle for independence from Spain.

CARTAGENA AGREEMENT   see PACTO ANDINO.

CASA DE CONTRACTACION.   This institution was developed
by the crown in 1503 for the purpose of regulating
commerce, navigation and emigration.   It was responsible for its operation to the Consejo de las Indias*.
The west coast trading center was in Lima, Peru.
The Casa was abolished in 1790.

CASTILLO VELASCO, JAIME.   President of the Falange
Nacional*, and of the Christian Democratic Party in
Chile (Partido Demócrata Cristiano*).   In 1965, he
was appointed Minister of Lands and Colonization (Ministro de tierras y colonización).   He is considered the
theoretician in the PDC.

CASTRO PALMA, BALTASAR, 1919- .   He has been the
leader of the Frente Nacional del Pueblo*, a coalition
of leftist parties which later became known as the
Frente de Acción Popular* (FRAP).   From 1949 to
1953 he served as a deputy in Congress, backed by
the Socialists.   In 1953, he became President of the
Chamber of Deputies.   In 1956, and in 1961, he was
elected senator.   He backed Salvador Allende Gossens*
in the Presidential elections of 1952, 1958, 1964, and
1970.

CATHEDRAL, THE (LA CATEDRAL). Located in the Plaza
de Armas, Santiago. Originally a colonial building, it
was transformed during the 19th century. Its treasures
are a silver altar standing on the left aisle, and a silver custody, covered with precious stones, made during the colonial period in Calera de Tango, Chile.

CAUDILLO. A leader, political boss, or chief, generally
with a military background.

CAUPOLICAN. Famous Indian chief who led the Araucanians*
to victory until he was captured and executed by the
Spaniards in 1558. He was born in the beginning of the
16th century, and in 1533 was named "Toqui" (chief)
by Colocolo*. During the Spanish occupation and conquest of Chile, Caupolicán surprised the Spaniards in
the Valley of Tucapel*, destroying their camp and killing most of them (December 2 and 3, 1553). Pedro
de Valdivia*, who fought in the battle, was executed by
the Indians on December 25, 1553. In April 1554, with
the help of Lautaro*, another Indian Chieftain, Caupolicán defeated Francisco de Villagrá*, who had succeeded
Valdivia. García Hurtado de Mendoza*, who succeeded
Villagrá, finally defeated Caupolicán at the battle of
Monte Pinto (Concepción). Aided by an Indian traitor,
Hurtado de Mendoza took the Araucanians by surprise,
capturing them and sentencing them all to death. It is
reported that some 6,000 Indians were executed. Caupolicán promised the Spaniards that he would give back
the sword, helmet, and a gold chain which had belonged
to Valdivia in exchange for his life. An Indian emis-
sary was sent to get these objects, but when he failed
to return after various days had gone by, the Spaniards
executed Caupolicán. The Indian chief died a horrible
death as he was forced by the Spaniards to sit on a
sharp, pointed wooden pole.

CAUQUENES. Capital city of the central province of Maule*;
population: 45,000 (1971 est.).

CAUTIN. A province of central Chile, located south of Santiago; population: 444,177 (1971 est.); area: 18,376.7
sq. km.

CELAM see CONSEJO EPISCOPAL LATINOAMERICANO.

CENTRAL UNICA DE TRABAJADORES (CUT). One of the
most influential unions of Chilean workers, the Central
Unica de Trabajadores was established on February 12,
1953, to bring together the various factions of the
Chilean labor movement. In spite of the fact that the
CUT represents 30% of the Chilean working force, it
does not have legal status. According to the Labor
Code of 1925, the merger of various labor unions was
forbidden, and a union could not represent workers engaged in different labor activities, as the CUT does today. As a result of that law, the CUT cannot enter
into legal negotiations on behalf of its members, nor
can it engage in collective bargaining. Since its inception, however, the CUT has influenced many labor
laws, and continues to be one of the most active forces
within the labor movement. Its historical antecedent
dates back to 1909, when Luis Emilio Recabarren*
founded the Federación Obrera de Chile* (FOCH). The
CUT has preserved the revolutionary principles upon
which the FOCH was organized.
    The social and political goals of the CUT have been
to establish socialism in Chile, and to pressure the
state to give it legal recognition by amending the Constitution of 1925* and the Labor Code contained in it.
Today the CUT is one of the staunchest supporters of
the Marxist government (1970-76) of Socialist Salvador
Allende Gossens*. After he was sworn in, President
Allende sent legislation to Congress to give legal status
to the CUT, but his proposal was defeated by the opposition of Conservatives and Christian Democrats. The
internal organization of the CUT consists of a national
council, made up of 35 members elected through secret
ballot. The members, in turn, choose a president,
two vice-presidents, a secretary general, and a treasurer. The national council remains in power for three
years, at which time a general congress is summoned
to elect a new council. Besides the national council,
there are local organizations representing the provinces,
the cities, and the small rural towns. In 1968, Communist Deputy Luis Figueroa was elected president of
the CUT for a three-year term, and Socialist Hernán
del Canto, secretary general. See also LABOR.

CEPAL. Comisión Económica para América Latina, or Economic Commission for Latin America (ECLA). Its center is in Santiago* de Chile.

CERRO GRANDE. Site of a battle between the revolutionary
  forces of Pedro León Gallo* and the loyalist troops of
  President (1851-61) Manuel Montt Torres* during the
  Civil War of 1859 (Guerra Civil de 1859*). Although
  Gallo had an army of over 2,000 men, with a cavalry
  and 12 pieces of artillery, the battle was won by the
  government troops, who were much inferior in number
  and equipment.

CHACABUCO. Site of a decisive battle won by the Chilean
  patriots during the war of liberation, fought on February 12, 1817. The army of the frontier (See EJERCITO
  DE LOS ANDES), led by the liberators José de San
  Martín* and Bernardo O'Higgins*, swept across the
  Andes and attacked the Spaniards at Chacabuco*, in-
  flicting upon them heavy losses. The royalist troops
  of Governor Francisco Casimiro Marcó del Pont had
  to retreat and San Martín and O'Higgins victoriously
  marched to the capital city of Santiago. San Martín
  was hailed as a deliverer and unanimously elected
  governor of Chile, an honor he refused so that it could
  be conferred on the Chilean O'Higgins.

CHICHA. A popular fermented beverage made from grapes,
  or various other products such as maize or pineapple.

CHILE. The name comes from the Quéchua chilli or tchili
  ("cold," "snow," or "the deepest point of the earth")
  and it was used by the Indians to designate the river
  and the valley of Aconcagua*. It was they who called
  the region Tchilimapu ("land of Chile"). Their language was the Tchili-dugu ("language of Chile"). Upon
  the arrival of the conquistadors, the name was changed
  to Chile. There is another hypothesis about the name
  Chile, and it is that it comes from the Chilean birds
  "triles," which during their flights emit the sound "chi-
  lí, chi-lí."
      Location, Size, Extent, and Time: Chile is distinc-
  tively long and narrow, extending 2,650 miles from
  Peru to Cape Horn. Of its total area of 286,396
  square miles, 7.6% is arable, and 2% is actually cultivated. At its widest point, Chile spans 221 miles;
  its average width is 109 miles. Chile is bordered on
  the north by Peru; on the east by Bolivia and Argentina (with the latter it shares a 2,000 mile, oft-disputed
  boundary); on the south by the Drake passage, including
  a small Atlantic seaboard; and on the west by the Pa-

cific. Chile is compressed between the Andes and the
Pacific and lies between 17° 25' and 55° 59' south
latitude. Chile lies entirely within one time zone;
8:00 A.M. Chile time is 12 noon Greenwich Mean Time.

Dependencies: Chilean sovereignty extends to the
Juan Fernández Islands*, Easter Island*, and to a number of arid, volcanic, and uninhabited Pacific islands
(the Diego Ramírez Islands*, the Sala y Gómez Island*,
and the San Félix and San Ambrosio Islands*). Some
boundary disputes with Argentina remain unresolved.
Chile, Argentina, and the United Kingdom have con-
flicting claims to the Palmer Peninsula in Antarctica.
These claims have not seriously disturbed relations
among the three nations.

Topography: Chile is a long ribbon of land composed
of three narrow parallel divisions: to the east is the
Cordillera*; to the west is a lower coastal plateau;
and, in the middle is the Central Valley. The Central
Valley is poorly defined in the north and in the south,
and more precisely defined in the central area. The
Andex descend more or less abruptly on the Chilean
side, while they fall more gradually into Argentina. In
altitude, there is a gradual decline from north to south;
while northern peaks exceed 15,000 feet, those of the
Tierra del Fuego* attain less than 2,000 feet. The
Andes are geologically recent, as is evidenced by their
numerous peaks and their frequent earthquakes. The
Central Valley is delimited to the west by the older
coastal range, with its low, rounded hills. It consists
of an extensive northern plateau some 3,000 feet in altitude.

The Central Valley is 600 miles long and up to 45
miles wide. It is drowned by the ocean and interrupted
by transverse canyons and fjords to the far south. The
northern desert is one of the world's driest regions.
Its three provinces include the territory won from Bolivia in the War of the Pacific (Guerra del Pacífico*).
The coastal plateau in this desert region falls some
3,000 ft. to the sea, providing an unbroken coastline with
no natural harbors. Vegetation and animal life are
almost nonexistent. Here are found immense layers
of raw nitrate or caliche, long a source of wealth for
Chile. Central Mediterranean Chile extends from 30°
south latitude to 37° south latitude. In the Santiago-
Valparaíso area, climate and vegetation are very mediterranean. The coastal hills are lower than those of
desert Chile, but the coastline continues largely un-

CHILE
NATURAL REGIONS

BOUNDARIES:
---- PROVINCIAL
—— REGIONAL

DESERT
CHILE

MEDITERRANEAN
CHILE

FOREST
CHILE

ATLANTIC
CHILE

PROVINCES

1 TARAPACÁ
2 ANTOFAGASTA
3 ATACAMA
4 COQUIMBO
5 ACONCAGUA
6 VALPARAISO
7 SANTIAGO
8 O'HIGGINS
9 COLCHAGUA
10 CURICÓ
11 TALCA
12 MAULE
13 LINARES
14 ÑUBLE
15 CONCEPCIÓN
16 BÍO-BÍO
17 ARAUCO
18 MALLECO
19 CAUTÍN
20 VALDIVIA
21 OSORNO
22 LLANQUIHUE
23 CHILOÉ
24 AYSÉN
25 MAGALLANES

broken by natural harbors, with the exception of Valparaíso and Talcahuano. Extensive and fertile transverse alluvial fans have been built by the Mapocho, Maipo, and Maule rivers. Natural precipitation and water from the Andes mountains provide an abundant water supply.

For centuries, during both colonial and republican periods, Mediterranean Chile was considered to be Chile. Only during the last 75 years has natural growth brought increased population to the north and the south. Southward from the Bío-Bío River, marine climate and vegetation predominate. Still further south, from the island of Chiloé to Cape Horn, is an almost uninhabited archipelago, a wilderness of rocky terrain, scrub vegetation and tundra, glaciers, and ice-sheets. Atlantic Chile includes territory on both sides of the Strait of Magellan, east of the southern Andes. It also includes the plains of Tierra del Fuego. The only province in Atlantic Chile that has achieved economic progress up to date is Aysén*, in which the wet grasslands support a colony of sheep herders. There is also hope that more petroleum will be found in this region.

Climate: northern Chile, or desert Chile, is predominantly arid. Most of its uninhabited expanse receives no rainfall at all. Except for the high Andes, its highest annual precipitation is at La Serena* and in the Valley of Elquí*, a mere four and a half inches. The coast, influenced by the Humboldt or Peru Current, is cooler and more even in temperature throughout the year than the inland desert. Coastal skies are sometimes cloudy. Inland, skies are uniformly clear, the day-time temperatures constantly high, and the relative humidity very low, with marked extremes in temperature between day and night. In short, the climate follows a pattern which is typical of inland deserts elsewhere.

In Mediterranean Chile, mean annual rainfall ranges from 19 inches in Viña del Mar, on the coast, to 38 inches at Angol, farther inland. Seasonal temperature variation is from 15° Fahrenheit in Viña del Mar to 22° F in Angol. While total rainfall is adequate for agriculture, frequent summer droughts have made irrigation projects necessary in the Central Valley.
Forest Chile experiences rainfall throughout the year. Mean annual rainfall varies from 53 to 113 inches, and reaches as high as 200 inches in some isolated regions.

The mean annual temperature is about 50° F. In the southern archipelago, the climate is even colder; rain falls two days out of three. Atlantic Chile is uniformly cold and wet, with an annual variation in temperature of less than 6° F. Normal rainfall exceeds 100 inches annually.

Flora and Fauna: Botanical and zoological life varies with the topographic and climatic zones described above. Desert Chile is virtually barren of plant and animal life. On the inhospitable slopes of the northern Andes, scattered desert brush and grasses subsist. The Central Valley supports more abundant life in its mediterranean environment, including such native botanical species as the Chilean pine, several varieties of cactus, and the national flower, a red, bell-shaped species known as the copihue*. South of the Bío-Bío, the marine climate has induced dense forestation, with the beech predominating over other native trees such as laurels, magnolias, and diverse conifers.

Further south, cold temperatures and high winds stunt tree growth, and inhibit heavy forestation. The grassland of Atlantic Chile has made possible extensive grazing of sheep. The dominant Andean barrier has caused a separate botanical and zoological evolution in Chile and Argentina. Chilean faunal life includes the puma, the guanaco, and vicuña, the guemal [huemul]--species of deer--and the Andean wolf. The chinchilla has been harvested almost to extinction. Native to forest Chile are several varieties of marsupials, pouch-equipped mammals related to the Australian kangaroo. The bird population of Chile is without many of the varieties common to the rest of Latin America. The waters of the Humboldt Current abound with fish, and support a growing fishmeal industry.

History: Pre-colonial Chile had no great cradle of civilization like those of the Middle East and Asia. There were prehistoric inhabitants of a stone age culture, about whose origin, appearance and customs we remain largely ignorant. Archaeological evidence suggests that their achievements were similar to those of Cro-Magnon man in Central Europe. But historic times in Chile, in the usual sense of a literate civilization, does not antedate the first Spanish explorations under Diego de Almagro* or Pedro de Valdivia*. These Conquistadors had a very hard time in trying to

subdue the Araucanian Indians (Araucanos*).   Like the
Seminoles, the Araucanians were never conquered by
Spain.   Under Lautaro*, Caupolicán*, and other leaders,
the Araucanians maintained their hegemony over the territory south of the Bío-Bío River.   Legend reports the
irony of these Indians rewarding the greedy Spaniards
whom they captured by pouring molten gold down their
throats.   Before the outbreak of the independence movements in 1810, Chile was among the most neglected of
Spain's colonies.   An agricultural economy supported
about half a million persons, including some 100, 000
southern Indians; 150, 000 Creoles; 20, 000 Peninsulares;
250, 000 Mestizos; 4, 000 Negroes; and a handful of European immigrant families of non-Spanish origin.   The
economic and social pattern was feudal; European culture, land, and education were the property of the oligarchy.   The Church, after the expulsion of the Jesuits
in 1767, was weak.

Chile's history from the end of the colonial rule may
be divided into five main periods.   The years from
1810 to 1831 saw independence established, and were
characterized by a conflict between the partisans of
centralized government and those who wanted a federal
government.   From 1831 to 1861 there was a highly
centralized government, based upon the conservative
Constitution of 1833*.   Liberalism, with greater local
autonomy and individual freedom prevailed during the
years 1861 to 1891.   Parliamentary rule was established in Chile from 1891 to 1924.   The period from
1925 to the present has seen the growth of a relatively
stable and democratic nation, characterized by growing
industry, literacy, trade unionism, inflation, and the
nationalization of natural resources.   The entrenched
oligarchy is losing its traditional prerogatives, and is
beginning to give in to the growing demands for radical social and economic reforms.

There were three loci of opinion in 1810.   The reactionaries (Realista*) sought a return of monarchical
control; the moderates (Moderado*) would accept the
monarchy, granted certain reforms; the radicals (Exaltado*) desired immediate and complete independence.
Following the cabildo abierto* of September 1810, a
constituent congress was assembled.   The congress appointed a ruling junta, which was promptly deposed by
the Carrera Verdugo* brothers.   Military forces of the
new junta, under José Miguel Carrera Verdugo* and
Bernardo O'Higgins*, were defeated by the Spanish in

1814.   Radical sentiment grew from 1814 to 1817.   Independence came to fruition as José de San Martín's*
forces, having crossed the Andes, defeated the Spanish,
first at Chacabuco*, and irrevocably at Maipú*.   Independence was declared in February of 1818; San Martín
refused the offer of political leadership; the Carrera
brothers were shot; and O'Higgins established a brief
dictatorship.

Ruling for five years, O'Higgins created Chile as a
nation.   Though he promoted education, built a navy,
attempted land and ecclesiastical reforms, and ruled
efficiently, O'Higgins alienated the oligarchy.   He was
overthrown in 1823 as a result, and went into voluntary
exile to Peru.   The most important development between 1823 and 1830 was the establishment of two major and divergent political parties: the Conservative
Party (Partido Conservador*) and the Liberal Party
(Partido Liberal*).   The Conservatives, constituted by
the oligarchy, stood for centralized government, order,
and the status quo.   The Liberals sought constitutional
government, land and Church reforms.   These two
parties dominated Chile during the remainder of the 19th
century.   Between 1830 and 1861, three Conservative
presidents ruled Chile, each for a ten-year period.

The first dominant figure was Diego Portales Palazuelos* who, though he never occupied the Presidential
chair, ruled "over the President's shoulder" until as-
sasinated in 1837.   He engineered the Constitution of
1833*, which established a highly centralized government, and stood till 1925.   He superintended a re-marriage of Church and State, promoted trade, and sought
foreign investment.   He was the guiding hand behind
President (1831-41) Joaquín Prieto Vial*, under whom
the successful war against the Bolivian dictator Andrés
Santa Cruz was begun in 1837.   The President during
the 1840's was Manuel Bulnes Prieto*, under whom the
first American investment capital entered Chile; mining
developments created prosperity for the wealthy.   The
first influx of German immigrants resulted from the
disturbances of 1848, and brought new liberal ideas into Chile.

In the 1850's, Manuel Montt Torres* ruled as an
"enlightened despot," promoting and improving agriculture, trade, communication, and education.   Andrés
Bello López* completed his codification of civil law.
Montt's moderate innovations antagonized both landowners and the Church.   The liberals ruled from 1861

to 1891.   This period saw a fragmentation of the two
major parties, and the establishment of the Radical
Party (Partido Radical*).   The Liberal parties were
largely dominant, and were successful in reducing the
old prerogatives of the Church and in curtailing Presidential and central governmental power.

The national educational system provided the basis
for today's highly literate (by Latin American standards)
population.   A technical revolution benefited agriculture,
though a depression in the mid-1870's halted economic
growth for a time.   A notable event was the War of
the Pacific from 1879 to 1883 (Guerra del Pacífico*),
in which the rich nitrate deposits of the Atacama desert were taken by Chile, and Bolivia was deprived of
its border on the Pacific.   Growing industry, a mush-
rooming nitrate plutocracy, and the incipient growth of
labor unions resulted; an optimistic nationalism prevailed.   The last Liberal President, José Manuel Balmaceda Fernández*, came to power in 1886.   From
honest concern for the lower classes, he initiated social, economic, and infrastructural programs which of-
fended the landowners and the Church.   Congressional
opposition and later an armed revolt and civil war
brought down Balmaceda's government.   This last
strong President finally sought asylum in the Argentine
legation, and shot himself.

The period from 1891 to the present has seen the
growth of genuine democracy in Chile.   President
(1891-96) Jorge Montt Alvarez* relieved the bitterness
of the civil war by declaring a general amnesty.   During the period up to 1920, Chile enjoyed unprecedented
prosperity based upon booming sales of its nitrates and
copper.   But prosperity benefited only the wealthy oligarchy and the small plutocracy of new rich in business,
and it begat political corruption, from the highest officials to the impoverished citizen who sold his vote.
The Conservatives were joined by the now-wealthy Liberals.   The Radicals included both progressive busi-
nessmen and lower middle class office workers, united
in opposition to the oligarchy.   But Radical economics
did not satisfy the laborers who in 1912 established the
Socialist Workers' Party (Partido Socialista de Trabajadores*).   It became the Communist Party (Partido
Comunista*) in 1921.

During this period, the common man had no part in
the booming economy.   The illiteracy rate was about
50%, and nine-tenths of the population was impoverished.

Popular unrest led to a demand for reforms, and to
the election in 1920 of Arturo Alessandri Palma* (1920-
24).   President Alessandri promised land, tax, and social reforms, but Conservatives in Congress blocked
his legislation.   This forced the President to resign in
1924.   After two military coups, however, Alessandri
was recalled in 1925 and secured the passage of the
Constitution of 1925*.   The new constitution strengthened the Presidency, separated Church and State, established religious freedom, and gave public welfare
theoretical priority over property rights.   Damned by
the right and left for what he had done, or failed to do,
Alessandri was again deposed, and from 1925 to 1931,
Carlos Ibáñez del Campo* ruled as dictator.   The
Ibáñez's regime lasted through the boom of the late
1920's, sustained in a free spending program of U.S.
loans totaling $300,000,000.   The Great Depression
precipitated renewed unrest; Ibáñez was forced into
exile.

There followed two years of disorder, under many
short-lived administrations.   In 1932, Alessandri, now
a convert to economic conservatism, was returned to
the Presidency.   His finance minister, Gustavo Ross,
brought order to Chile's financial house, but in the
process established an oppressive regime.   He promoted building activity, tightened tax collection procedures, and increased the government's share of nitrate
profits to 25%.   An understandably ungrateful electorate
in 1938 turned to the Popular Front (Frente Popular*)
and elected Pedro Aguirre Cerda*.   The latter restored civil liberties and promised national economic
planning.   The Chilean Development Corporation (Corporación de Fomento de la Producción*), perhaps the
major achievement of the Popular Front Government,
was established as a result.

In the elections of 1942, the Conservatives nominated the discredited Ibáñez, while the Radicals, by
now the strongest party in Chile, nominated and easily
elected Juan Antonio Ríos Morales*.   The new President signed a treaty with the United States in 1943 to
fight the Axis powers.   As a result, Chile benefited
from the Lend-Lease program.   The Development Corporation received loans from the Export-Import Bank
of Washington, D.C., and embarked upon an ambitious
program to promote industrial growth, emphasizing
steel, water power, and a search for oil which met
with limited success.   The government enlarged the

public school system, extended public health facilities, and made a small beginning in low-rent housing and urban renewal.

Another radical, Gabriel González Videla*, assumed the Presidency in 1946. At first friendly towards Chile's 30, 000- to 50, 000-member Communist Party, he was later antagonized by the obstructionism of Communist ministers; eventually, in 1948, González Videla cleared the cabinet and the legislature of communists, banned the party, and broke diplomatic relations with Russia and Yugoslavia. González Videla too pursued the elusive goal of industrialization. Additional Export-Import Bank loans helped to build a steel mill near Concepción. Hydroelectric development continued, and a sugar beet industry was established. But copper prices fell after World War II, and agricultural productivity declined. Inflation, a problem in Chile for decades, continued, aggravated by excessive government issues of paper currency. Worker discontent rose as the election of 1952 approached.

With the Radicals badly divided, the Conservatives elected Ibáñez. Faced with economic decline, Ibáñez surprised many by ruling moderately. He reorganized and economized within government while continuing the industrialization program, yet nearly managed to balance the budget. A Conservative coalition in 1958 nominated and elected Jorge Alessandri Rodríguez*, son of the earlier president of the same name. Conservative and capitalist in economics, Alessandri nonetheless represented a move to the left in that he believed that government management of the economy was necessary. He urged the landowners to reinvest profits and produce more food. He selected an able, honest cabinet, secured the first balanced budget since 1950, and finished 1959 with a foreign exchange balance of $40 million. Given emergency economic powers, he trimmed the government civil staff by 5%, paid delinquent government debts, and took to the courts to prosecute income tax evaders.

This more promising economy was then shaken, in May of 1960, by a series of devastating earthquakes and tidal waves which killed thousands, upset the working of nearly half the nation's farmland, and caused damage estimated at $500 million. In 1961, a grant from the United States of $100 million helped to repair the damage. Also in 1961, the Alessandri administration initiated a ten-year development program

(1961-70), which called for the investment of some
$10 billion, and sought a 70% increase in mining pro-
duction, a 76% increase in industrial production, a
growth of 62% in agricultural production, and an incre-
ment of 97% in hydroelectric power capacity.   IBRD
(World Bank) experts in 1961 evaluated the plan, and
pronounced its goals feasible.   The Alessandri administration made some progress in tax reform, housing
development, water and sanitation development, but
little or no progress in land reform and education.
Laws enacted in 1962 and 1963 streamlined government
administration, broadened the tax base, and provided
for conversion to a single progressive income tax.

In September 1964, Eduardo Frei Montalva*, leader
of the Christian Democratic Party (Partido Demócrata
Cristiano*), was elected President for a six-year term.
The congressional elections of March 1965 gave the
Christian Democrats a majority in the Chamber of
Deputies, and increased strength in the Senate.   As a
result, Frei Montalva was able to fulfill in part his extensive and expensive platform promises: accelerated housing
construction, land reform for some 100,000 peasants,
and extended health and educational services.   Frei
Montalva was also able to "Chileanize" copper, which
meant that his government would have tighter regulations on all phases of the U.S.-owned copper industry
--i.e., pricing, production and marketing.

On September 4th, 1970, Chilean voters went to the
polls to elect a new President.   In the month that
marked the 160th anniversary of their independence,
the Chileans elected the first Marxist government in
the Western Hemisphere.   Socialist Salvador Allende
Gossens* received 36% of the popular vote, enough to
edge former President (1958-64) Jorge Alessandri Rodríguez, who received 35% of the vote, and the Christian Democratic candidate, Radomiro Tomic Romero*,
who received 28% of the vote.   After he was sworn in,
Allende Gossens pledged to initiate the socialization of
Chile.   But he said that his administration would be
"neither Marxist nor a Socialist government Castro-
style."

Allende Gossens has said he aims to achieve four
major objectives by 1976: 1) to recuperate basic resources, meaning nationalization of copper (already
underway) and other minerals such as nitrate, coal and
iron; 2) to radically speed up agrarian reform by expropriating most of rural Chile for conversion into

rural farm cooperatives; 3) to nationalize bank and credit (also underway); and 4) to control exports and imports (The Popular Unity program calls for nationalization of domestic and external commerce). The capacity of the 1970-76 administration to provide effective leadership and to fulfill its platform goals will depend on such major and interrelated variables as continuing foreign assistance; the market and prices for copper, nitrate, and iron; the reciprocal relationship between the Chilean government and private foreign investment; the flight of domestic capital; the course and extent of continued inflation; and Chile's immense and growing foreign debt with the expansion-crippling service thereon.

Government: The Constitution of 1833* and the Constitution of 1925* represent the pillars upon which the present structure of Chilean government rests. Chile is a unitarian Republic, with a centralized form of government, and a division of power vested into three main branches: the executive, the legislative, and the judicial. The Comptrollership General constitutes a fourth branch, but this is considered to be an independent body. Although the Constitution of 1925 stresses a separation of power through a system of checks and balances, it is the President of the Republic who conducts legislative and judicial, as well as executive functions.

A. The Executive. The President of Chile is officially designated "Supreme Chief of the Nation," and controls the executive branch of government. Native citizenship, 30 years of age, and eligibility to membership in the Chamber of Deputies are the legal qualifications to hold the Presidential office. Moreover, the President must be elected by direct popular vote, for a term of six years, and cannot immediately succeed himself. The President of Chile enjoys broad executive powers. The Constitution of 1925*, to remedy the evils of parliamentary rule in the late 19th and early 20th centuries, specifies 17 areas in which the President has sole or primary rule. In general, the constitution allows the President to administer and govern the state, with an authority extending over any policy implemented to preserve internal order and external security, and the observance and enforcement of the constitution.

More specifically, the President has the power to: issue decrees, instructions and regulations he may deem

necessary for the execution of laws; supervise the administration of the judiciary; extend the time of the
regular congressional sessions (for no more than 50
days); call extraordinary sessions of Congress in times
of emergency; appoint his cabinet, diplomatic agents,
intendants (provincial governors), judges, and military
and civilian personnel; raise taxes, disburse money
and raise additional funds (not to exceed 2% of the
budget); maintain relations with foreign countries; and
declare a state of seige.

The President has also other legal and extralegal
privileges which allow him to participate in the legislative process through his power to introduce measures
and through his suspensive veto.   In the event of a
President's death, resignation, or disability, one of
the cabinet ministers becomes acting President with
full executive powers.   However, this new chief of
state must call new elections within 60 days.   The
Minister of the Interior is first in the line of succession, followed by the other cabinet ministers, the
Presidents of the Senate and of the Chamber of Deputies, and finally the Chief Justice of the Supreme Court.

B.   The Legislative.   Legislative powers are vested
in the National Congress, a bi-cameral body composed
of a Chamber of Deputies (147 members) and a Senate
(45 members).   The Constitution requires that members from both houses be elected by direct popular
vote, that each deputy represent at least 30, 000 inhabitants, and that senators be at least 35 years of age.
Deputies as well as senators must be Chilean citizens.
The entire Chamber of Deputies is renewed in 29 electoral districts every four years.   Senators are chosen
from nine electoral provinces, five from each province,
for a term of eight years, half the total membership
being renewed every four years.

Legislative powers are exercised by Congress as an
independent body, or in concurrence with the executive
branch.   As an independent body, Congress can give
permission to the President to leave the country, approve treaties, impeach and try government officials,
ministers of the cabinet, high magistrates, military
and civilian personnel, and governors.   Impeachment
procedures are carried out by the Chamber of Deputies,
while the Senate tries all cases.   Congress needs the
cooperation of the executive branch in order to tax and
spend, authorize the alienation of public and private
property, authorize the contracting of debts, approve

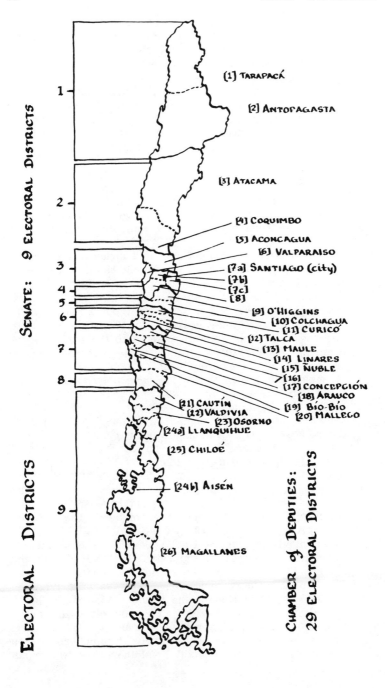

ELECTORAL DISTRICTS

SENATE: 9 ELECTORAL DISTRICTS

ELECTORAL DISTRICTS

CHAMBER of DEPUTIES:
29 ELECTORAL DISTRICTS

[1] TARAPACÁ

[2] ANTOFAGASTA

[3] ATACAMA

[4] COQUIMBO

[5] ACONCAGUA

[6] VALPARAISO

[7a] SANTIAGO (city)

[7b]

[7c]

[8]

[9] O'HIGGINS

[10] COLCHAGUA

[11] CURICÓ

[12] TALCA

[13] MAULE

[14] LINARES

[15] ÑUBLE

[16]

[17] CONCEPCIÓN

[18] ARAUCO

[19] BÍO-BÍO

[20] MALLECO

[21] CAUTÍN

[22] VALDIVIA

[23] OSORNO

[24a] LLANQUIHUE

[25] CHILOÉ

[24b] AISÉN

[26] MAGALLANES

the national budget, establish new currency, provide salaries for all branches of the armed forces, create employment services, restrict civil liberties in times of crisis, and grant pardon and amnesty.

Legislation may be initiated by any member of Congress. In special cases, the President may be called upon to take action. Only the President may initiate legislation to change the political or administrative division of the country, create new offices, change salaries of government employees, and cut the budget. The Congress can decrease the amount of money requested by the President, but cannot increase it. After a bill has been approved in both houses, it must be forwarded to the President who signs it into law, or vetoes it entirely or in part. A two-thirds vote in both houses is necessary to overrule the Presidential veto.

Congressional sessions are held annually from May 21 (Día de la Armada) to September 18 (Independence Day). Besides the President of the Republic, the President of the Senate can summon extraordinary sessions of Congress, upon written petition from a majority of the members of either house. The Constitution of 1925 does not grant any reserve powers to the central government, specifically stating that "no person or groups of persons is empowered to assume any other authority or rights other than those that have been expressly conferred upon them by the laws."

C. The Judiciary. The judiciary branch of the central government is composed of the Supreme Court, the highest court in the land, and various subordinate courts. There are 13 judges on the Supreme Court. They are appointed by the President of the Republic, who selects them from lists presented by the lower courts. To be eligible for the Supreme Court, a judge must be 36 years of age, and must have 15 years of legal experience. The members of the Supreme Court themselves choose the Chief Justice.

Primarily a court of final appeals, the Supreme Court has the power to supervise the lower courts and declare the application of certain laws unconstitutional. The Supreme Court, however, cannot declare a law, per se, unconstitutional, and hence it can excercise only limited judicial review. Immediately below the Supreme Court are the courts of appeal. These courts have jurisdiction over cases involving members of Congress. On the next judicial level there are two courts:

tribunals of major and minor quantities. As their designation indicates, these courts hear cases dealing with different sums of money. The courts also hear various criminal cases involving various offenses and fraudulent electoral cases.

D. The Comptrollership General. This independent branch of the government controls revenues and expenditures, and generally deals with the fiscal aspects of the nation's economy. Only the accounts of Congress are exempt from this control. The Comptroller General is appointed by the President of the Republic, with the approval of the Senate, and can only be removed by impeachment. In recent years, the Comptrollership General has grown into a powerful administrative court, with power to excercise judicial control, as well as to check the authority of the President of the Republic. For these reasons, the Comptrollership General has been alluded to as "the guardian of the Constitution."

E. Provincial Government. Chile is divided into 25 provinces, subdivided into departments, subdelegations, and districts. The 1925 Constitution provides two types of local administrations, one appointed, the other elected. The appointed officials are: the intendants, who govern the 25 provinces for a three-year term, governors, who administer departments; subdelegates, at the head of subdelegations; and, inspectors, who administer districts. Provinces generally have three to four departments each, with the exceptions of Santiago with six, and Aysén with one.

Locally elected officials are provincial assemblymen and municipal councilmen. Provincial assemblymen have never been up for election, thus leaving the municipal councilmen (elected by a geographical division known as a commune) as the only organs of locally elected government. If elected, councilmen must serve for a period of one year with no pecuniary renumeration. The powers of the councilmen are limited, and they deal primarily with community developments. Councilmen are subordinate to the intendants, who in turn give account of their local government to the President of the Republic. The intendants can veto the ordinances of the councilmen. However, a two-thirds majority of the councilmen present can override the intendant's veto.

CHILENO. Chilean.

CHILLAN.   Capital city of the province of Nuble*, in south-
    ern Chile.   During the struggle for Chilean indepen-
    dence, the city was in royalist hands.   On August 3,
    1813, Chillán was besieged by the troops fighting for
    Chilean independence led by José Miguel Carrera Ver-
    dugo*, then ruler of Chile.   Due to bad weather con-
    ditions, there was a stalemate between the Spanish
    royalists and the Chilean patriots.   The latter had to
    lift the seige and retreat to Concepción.   But before
    departing, the Chileans sacked the city.   Atrocities
    were committed on both sides, and many inhabitants
    were brutally murdered.   The death count exceeded
    500.   During this century, Chillán has been a disaster
    area in the earthquakes of 1939, 1960, and 1964.   Pop-
    ulation: 98, 500 (1971 est.).

CHILOE.   An island off the southern coast of Chile.   From
    this island to Cape Horn, there is an almost uninhabi-
    ted archipelago, a wilderness of rocky terraine, fjords,
    scrub vegetation and tundra, glaciers, and ice-sheets.
    Chiloé was one of the last strongholds of the Spaniards
    during the Chilean struggle for independence.   From
    1824 to 1826, it was occupied by royalist troops, un-
    der the command of Antonio Quintanilla.   Ramón Freire
    Serrano*, Supreme Director of Chile at the time, led
    an expedition to free the island and incorporate the
    territory into the National domain.   For two years,
    his attempts were frustrated by Quintanilla.   Finally,
    on January 13 and 14, 1826, Freire Serrano was able
    to drive the Spanish out.   A treaty was signed (Tratado
    de Tantauco*) and Chiloé was incorporated within the
    national boundaries of Chile.   Province of Chiloé popu-
    lation: 109, 430 (1971 est.); area: 27, 013. 5 sq. km.;
    capital city: Ancud*.

CHUQUICAMATA.   The largest and best known of the Chilean
    copper mines is Chuquicamata, located between the
    Atacama* desert and the western Cordillera*, at an
    altitude of 10, 000 feet.   The leading copper-producing
    property in South America, and the largest copper de-
    posit in the world, Chuquicamata was acquired and de-
    veloped by the Guggenheim brothers, who later sold it
    to the Anaconda Copper Mining Company*.   Chuquica-
    mata is an open pit mine and from 1915 to the present,
    output has been exclusively from upper oxide ores.
    Practically no underground working exist.   The ore is
    quarried, rather than mined, by blasting and power-

shovel work. Over a period of 50 years, the face of
the ore-bearing mountain has been blasted off and ter-
raced at various levels that reach a depth of about
1000 feet. Over 80 miles of railroad tracks run along
the terraces to the bottom of the vast crater. To the
close of 1969 some 380 million tons of ore have been
produced and treated, averaging 1.86% in copper content. Copper produced at this mine, in a period covering four decades, has been more than 6 million
metric tons.

CHURCH, THE. Chile, like other nations of Latin America,
is predominantly Roman Catholic (nominally, 95%).
During the colonial period, political and ecclesiastical
authority were virtually coextensive. Indeed, Church
authority came to exceed secular authority in the colonial period. Dominicans, Franciscans, and later Jesuits and Augustinians spread the faith. The Spanish
feudal system, with all its political and religious rami-
fications, was transplanted in Chile. Where normal
devotion was insufficient to secure Church authority,
the Holy Office (Inquisition) and the threat of excommu-
nication sufficed. Popular piety declined somewhat
during the colonial period, and the early monopoly of
the Church in education was gradually limited by a
growth in secular education, especially among the
wealthy.
    The Church became very rich; the Jesuits alone,
prior to their expulsion in 1767, controlled 50 hacien-
das. Church ministrations were largely ineffective
among the Indians, but were a strong civilizing influence among the largely illiterate mestizo masses. The
Church today, despite its official separation from the
State in the Constitution of 1925, enjoys continued success. Both clergy and laity are educated as never before. Theological exclusiveness is no longer basic to
the personality of the Chilean Catholic. Changed atti-
tudes among the clergy are nowhere better seen than
in the fact that high Church officials are sponsoring,
with Church lands, a program of agricultural education
and land reform. The Christian Democratic movement
reflects a renewed lay concern with the social and economic application of Christian theological beliefs. Also see RELIGIOUS PRACTICES.

CHURRO. A nice person; good-looking, agreeable.

CIENFUEGOS ARTEAGA, JOSE IGNACIO, 1762-1847. A
   priest from Talca who participated in the struggle for
   Chilean independence, and who had a distinguished political and diplomatic career. He belonged to the Federalist Party (Partido Federalista*), and took part in
   the formation of the government junta of 1811 (Junta de
   Gobierno de 1811*). After the battle of Rancagua* and
   the defeat of the Chilean patriots, he was exiled to the
   island of Juan Fernández*. When San Martín* and
   O'Higgins* won the battle at Chacabuco* (1817), he returned to Chile and was elected deputy, then senator,
   from 1818 to 1826. In 1826, he was appointed President of Congress. Among his many diplomatic posts,
   he was named Chilean plenipotentiary minister to the
   Vatican. In 1832, Rome named him Bishop of Concepción, an honor he refused in order to retire to Talca,
   where he spent the last years of his life rebuilding the
   church Matriz de Talca.

CIVIL RIGHTS [of the Chilean people]   see HUMAN RIGHTS.

CLARIN, EL   see THE PRESS.

CLARO VELASCO, BENJAMIN. President of the Political
   Party known as the Unión Republicana*. When in 1937
   the Unión Republicana fused with the Acción Nacional*
   to become the Acción Republicana*, Claro Velasco became President of the newly-formed party. In the
   same year he was elected deputy to Congress. On
   four occasions he was appointed Minister of Education
   (Ministro de Educación Pública), in 1942, 1943, and
   twice in 1946. He has held high office in the Ministry
   of National Defense (1943), and in the Ministry of Justice (1944). In 1950, he was named, by President
   (1946-52) Gabriel González Videla*, Minister of the
   Economy and Commerce.

CLUB DE LA REFORMA. A society founded in 1849 for
   members of the Liberal Party (Partido Liberal*).

COAL. Chile is one of the leading coal producers of South
   America, but coal has only been used for domestic
   consumption and has never been involved in foreign
   trade. Like the coal in most Latin American countries, Chilean coal is low grade. More than a fourth
   of the coal produced is absorbed by the Chilean railways, the remaining being used for industrial needs.

About 2.2 million tons of coal were mined in 1950.
Ten years later, this figure had dropped to 1.5 million
tons, with about the same yearly production during the
sixties. The opening of a large steel mill in Huachipato* in 1950 has increased the demand for coal.
Since that time, the plant has been operating using
65% domestic coal and importing the remainder from
the United States. The shortage of coal, especially of
high grade coal, has not been a serious problem, however, due to importation and also due to the fact that
since 1960 the Chilean economy has become increasingly dependent on oil and hydroelectric power instead of
coal.

COALICION. A rightist coalition of many parties founded in
1891 and dissolved in 1919. It received greatest support from the Conservative Party (Partido Conservador*). This political combination and others were
needed in the age of parliamentarism in Chile, which
began with the victory of Congress over the executive
powers vested in the President, in the Civil War of
1891 (Guerra Civil de 1891*). A majority was needed
in Congress to make national policies, and parties saw
the advantages of grouping together to achieve such
majority. The Coalición was opposed to the Liberal
coalition, the Alianza Liberal*.
    In 1901 the Coalición backed as Presidential candi-
date Pedro Montt Montt*, who was defeated by the Liberal Party candidate Germán Riesco Errázuriz*. In
1906, the Coalición candidate for the Presidency lost
again. It wasn't until 1915 that the Coalición managed
to back the winner in the Presidential elections of that
year. He was Juan Luis Sanfuentes Andonáegui*,
President of Chile from 1915 to 1920. During the
first three years of his government, members of the
Coalición formed the cabinet. In 1918, however, the
Alianza Liberal won a majority in the parliamentary
election of March 15, and the President was forced to
form a new cabinet which included many liberals. A
year later, the Coalición was dissolved and many of
its members joined the Unión Liberal*, which came
into existence in the same year.

COCHRANE OF DUNDONALD, ADMIRAL LORD THOMAS
ALEXANDER, 1775-1860. A British seaman of extra-
ordinary ability who fought for the independence of
Chile, Peru and Brazil, and is revered in all these

countries. He was born in Scotland in 1775 and joined the British Navy early in his youth. Because of a false accusation, he was dismissed in dishonor from the British Navy in 1814, fined, and sent to prison for two years. He escaped, appealed his sentence but was recaptured and sent back to prison where he finished his sentence. In 1818, he fought on behalf of Chile and Peru against Spain. In 1819, he was in command of the Chilean fleet and occupied the southern city of Valdivia*, held by the Spaniards. He was able to capture the Spanish prize vessel "La Esmeralda," which was later incorporated into the Chilean fleet.

In 1822, Lord Cochrane fought on behalf of Brazil and after independence was achieved in that country, he was named Marquis of Maranhão by Emperor Dom Pedro I. In 1827, he fought in Greece to help that country eradicate piracy. In 1832, the British Navy recognized his international repute and pardoned him. In 1847, King William IV named him rear admiral and he was soon after promoted Vice-admiral. In 1848, he commanded the British fleet in North America and the Antilles. Three years after, he was named Admiral. In 1854, the King of England named him Admiral in Chief of the British fleet. Because of the services he rendered in Chile, he is hailed as one of the country's heroes of independence and as the father of the Chilean Navy. The Spaniards called him "El Diablo," (The Devil). Lord Cochrane published a book on the liberation of Chile, Peru, and Brazil called: Narrative of Services in the Liberation of Chili, Peru and Brasil (2 vols.; 1859). He died in Kensington, England.

COLCHAGUA. A province of central Chile, located south of Santiago; population: 182,152 (1971 est.); area: 8,326.8 sq. km.; capital city: San Fernando*.

COLECTIVO. A taxi carrying from four to six persons from a determined point in a city to another.

COLLADO NUÑEZ, MODESTO, 1916- . He was born in Argentina and became a Chilean citizen in 1940. Member of the Christian Democratic cabinet of President (1964-70) Eduardo Frei Montalva*, first as Minister of Public Works and Communication (1964), and later as Minister of Housing and Urban Renewal (1965).

COLOCOLO, 1515-1561. An Araucanian chieftain who fought
valiantly against Pedro de Valdivia* and the Spaniards
who came to conquer Chile. He distinguished himself
during the years 1551 and 1553, and, with the aid of
Caupolicán*, defeated the Spaniards at the battle of
Tucapel*. Colocolo continued to fight in 1554 against
Valdivia's successor, Francisco Villagra*. When the
Spaniards retreated to the city of Concepción, Colocolo
occupied the city and burned it, wounding Villagra who
managed to escape. In 1555, the Spaniards, led by
Villagra, counter-attacked, and this time it was Colocolo who escaped. A year later, Colocolo was defeated
by the Spaniards on the shores of the river Bío-Bío*,
but returned to fight under Caupolicán two years later.
In 1559, Colocolo signed the first peace treaty with the
Spaniards, but in 1561 found himself fighting the Conquistadors once again. It was in that year that the
aging Indian chief lost his life at the battle of Lumaco*.

COMANDOS POPULARES. A political party of the Right
formed in 1958 and reformed in 1963. Twice dissolved.
In 1958 the Comandos Populares backed the Presidential candidacy of Jorge Alessandri Rodríguez*. The
party was dissolved in 1961 when it failed to win representation in Congress. In 1963, the party was
formed again to back the candidacy of Julio Durán Neumann* in the Presidential elections of 1964. In 1965,
the party participated in the parliamentary elections,
but once again failed to win representation thus dis-
solving itself.

COMERCIO Y ABASTECIMIENTO, MINISTERIO DE. The
Ministry of Commerce and Provision was created by
statute No. 5149 on October 6, 1941. Its main functions were to supervise the internal and external economy of the country. A year later, it ceased to exist
and was replaced by the Ministry of the Economy and
Commerce (Ministerio de Economía y Comercio*).

COMMUNICATIONS see THE ECONOMY: Internal: J.
Transportation....

COMPAÑIA DE ACERO DEL PACIFICO see CAP.

COMPAÑIA DE SALITRE DE CHILE see COSACH.

COMPAÑIA SUDAMERICANA DE VAPORES. A vapor boat

company run first with British, then American capital.
Its main office is in the port city of Valparaíso*.

COMPTROLLERSHIP GENERAL, THE see CHILE: GOV-
ERNMENT.

COMUNA. A unit of municipal government.

CONCENTRACION NACIONAL. A political fusion of four
major parties: the Radical, Conservative, Liberal,
and Democratic (Partido Radical*, Conservador*, Liberal*, Democrático*). It was organized in 1948 during the government (1946-52) of Gabriel González Videla* to pass a law in Congress which would have outlawed the Communist Party (Partido Comunista*). The
law went into effect and the Concentración Nacional continued to work as a coalition until 1950. In that year,
Congress passed another law to fix wages and prices
and there resulted a split within the coalition: Liberals and Conservatives siding together against the other
two parties, which had backed striking workers for
better wages. The Radical and Democratic parties
were accused of conspiring to create a revolutionary
syndicate with the labor unions. The Radicals were
also accused of bringing violence in the streets. When
demonstrations ensued, the Concentración Nacional dissolved.

CONCEPCION. 1) A province of central Chile, located
south of Santiago; population: 662, 679 (1971 est.);
area: 5, 681. 1 sq. km. ; capital city: Concepción*.
2) The third largest city in Chile. The port of
Talcahuano, only nine miles away, and the Bay of San
Vicente, just outside the city, provide excellent harbors for the commercial needs of the entire province.
Concepción has sufficient raw materials, water, coal
and hydroelectric energy to operate its own steel mill.
The Huachipato integrated Steel and Iron Industry* is
capable of satisfying the basic needs of the country.
With the construction of a new petroleum refinery now
finished, the city promises to become the industrial
center of Chile. Population: 202, 400 (1971 est.).

CONCHA CERDA, MELCHOR DE SANTIAGO, 1799-1883.
Graduate of law from the University of San Marcos in
Lima, Peru. In 1820, he returned to Chile, where he
had a distinguished political career. He held elective

office from 1823 to 1876. In 1828, with the Spaniard
José Joaquín Mora, he drafted the Chilean Constitution
(Constitution of 1828*).

CONCHA ORTIZ, MALAQUIAS, 1859-1921. Member of the
Radical Party (Partido Radical*) who in 1877 found the
Partido Democrático*, a splinter of the Radical Democratic Party. The members of the new party criticized the Radicals for siding with the workers during
the mining strikes of the 1870's, and for being anti-
clerical. Concha Ortiz became the Secretary General
of the Democratic Party, and in the Civil War of 1891
(Guerra Civil de 1891*), he sided with President (1886-
91) José Miguel Balmaceda Fernández*. The fall of
President Balmaceda Fernández contributed to his de-
tention by the forces of Congress. He was jailed in
1891, then freed shortly after.
    Three years later, he was framed by the military
authorities with the pretext that he was organizing an
uprising in one of the military posts in Santiago. The
charges later proved to be false; they were only a pretext to call a state of siege in the Santiago province to
rig the parliamentary elections of 1894. In that year,
Concha Ortiz wrote a controversial book about the
democratic process in Chile, El programa de la democracia. He also wrote a treatise on economic policies,
Tratado de economía experimental. In 1896, he was
named president of the Democratic Party, a post he
held until 1909. Until his death, he was very active
in politics, having held elective office from 1900 to
1921, first as a deputy, then as a senator. In 1915,
he was president of his party once again. From 1917
to 1918, and again from 1919 to 1920, he was Minister
of Industry and Public Works.

CONCHA QUESADA, MIGUEL, 1910- . Active member of
the Communist Party until 1955. He studied economics
in Mexico, and in Chile he became the vice-president
of a workers union known as the Workers in Private
Industry (Trabajadores en la Industria Privada). In
1946, he was appointed by President (1946-52) Gabriel
González Videla* as Minister of Agriculture, a post
he had to leave when González Videla outlawed the
Communist Party in 1948. In the government (1952-
58) of Carlos Ibáñez del Campo*, he was named Superintendent of Prices and Wages (1953-54). In 1955,
Concha Quesada was sent as honorary Chilean consul

to Milan, Italy. It was then that he renounced membership in the Communist Party.

CONCHA SUBERCASEAUX, CARLOS, 1863-1917. Lawyer by profession and member of the Conservative Party (Partido Conservador*). He was an enemy of President (1886-91) José Manuel Balmaceda Fernández* during the Civil War of 1891 (Guerra Civil de 1891*). From 1894 to 1906 he was a deputy to Congress and held various diplomatic assignments. In 1903, he was President of the Chamber of Deputies. From 1898 to 1899 he was Minister of War in the cabinet of President (1896-1901) Federico Errázuriz Echaurren*. From 1900 to 1903, he was Chilean minister to Argentina.

CONCON. A small town near Valparaíso*, and site of a bloody battle fought in the Civil War of 1891 (Guerra Civil de 1891*). The army supporting the rebellious Congress counted 9,248 men, and was under the leadership of Colonel Estanislao del Canto Artigas. The troops supporting President (1886-91) José Manuel Balmaceda Fernández* had some 8,000 men, and were under the leadership of two generals, Orozimbo Barbosa Puga and José Miguel Alcérrea. The army loyal to President Balmaceda Fernández was routed, losing 2,000 men killed or wounded; the congressional troops' losses were estimated at 50% of those of the loyalists.

CONFEDERACION NACIONAL DE TRABAJADORES (CNT) see LABOR.

CONFEDERACION REPUBLICANA DE ACCION CIVICA (C.R.A.C.). A political organization backing the rightist government (1927-31) of Carlos Ibáñez del Campo*, organized in 1930 and dissolved in 1931. Made up mostly of white-collar workers, its membership was always relatively small. In the Parliamentary elections of 1930, C.R.A.C. elected 14 deputies but no senators to Congress. When the Ibáñez del Campo government fell in 1931, C.R.A.C. dissolved.

CONFIN. Acronym for Consejo de Fomento e Investigaciones Agrícolas (Agricultural Extension Services).

CONGRESISTA. A term used in 1891 to designate a partisan of the rebellious Congress which was at war with President (1886-91) José Manuel Balmaceda Fernández*.

CONGRESO NACIONAL.   The Chilean National Congress.   It
is made up of a Chamber of Deputies and a Senate
(see CHILE: GOVERNMENT (B. The Legislative)).
The first National Congress was established with much
solemnity on July 4, 1811.   It was convened by the
junta government of 1810 (Junta de Gobierno de 1810*)
and was elected by a cabildo*.   There were three loci
of opinion in the first congress.   The reactionaries
sought the return of monarchical rule (Realista*); the
moderates would accept the monarchy, granted certain
constitutional reforms (Moderado*); and the Radicals
desired immediate and complete independence (Exaltado*).
The Congress of 1811 appointed a ruling junta, which
was promptly deposed by the Carrera Verdugo brothers,
José Miguel*, Juan José*, and Luis*.   As a result, the first National Congress came to an abrupt
end on December 2, 1811.

CONGRESO TERMAL.   A Congress convened in 1930, during
the presidency (1927-31) of Carlos Ibáñez del Campo*.
Called "Termal" because it took palce in Chillán*, a
summer resort with thermal baths.   This Congress was
elected by an electoral arbitration (Arbitraje electoral)
to avoid any political repercussions on the part of the
parties that composed it.   The basis for such a Congress was that when the number of candidates equals
the number of seats up for elections, a direct popular
vote is not necessary.

CONQUISTADOR.   Conqueror; specifically those Spaniards
who conquered the New World.

CONSEJO DE LAS INDIAS.   The supreme governing council
for the Spanish American colonies, known as "El Real
y Supremo Consejo de las Indias," was established in
1524 as a body independent of any other Spanish institution.   It controlled all functions of government in
Spanish America, and it was responsible for preparing
the laws, writing the royal decrees, and drawing up
royal ordinances by which the colonies were administered.   Among its many important functions were those
of supervising the treatment of the Indians, granting
permission for new expeditions of discovery, erecting
bishoprics and universities, and providing military defense for the Spanish colonies in America.   The council enjoyed wide powers throughout the Hapsburg period
(1514-1700).   In 1714, however, the Bourbon King

Philip V instituted the Secretariat of the Indies, with
the council subordinated to it. By 1790, the power of
the council was that of an advisory body. It was
abolished in 1812, re-established in 1814 for a period
of 20 years, and then finally ended.

CONSEJO DIRECTORIAL. A provisional government established on November 13, 1825, when the Supreme Director (1823-26) Ramón Freire Serrano* appointed Miguel
Infante Rojas* to subrogate his term of office. General Freire Serrano took the leave of absence from office to lead an expedition for the purpose of annexing
Chiloé* into the national territory. As a result of this
action, in 1826 Chile was divided into eight provinces:
Coquimbo*, Aconcagua*, Santiago*, Colchagua*, Maule*,
Concepción*, Valdivia*, and Chiloé*. On March 6,
1826, Freire Serrano returned to Santiago to take over
the duties of Supreme Director once again.

CONSEJO EPISCOPAL LATINOAMERICANO (CELAM). The
Latin American Episcopal Council was established in
1955 by Catholic bishops in Latin America. The main
concern of this institution has been the role of the
Catholic Church in Latin America. The following functions are undertaken by CELAM: 1) to study matters
of interest to the church in Latin America; 2) to coordinate activities; 3) to promote and assist Catholic ini-
tiatives; and 4) to prepare other conferences of the
Latin American episcopate to be convoked by the Holy
See. CELAM has a general secretariat and five under-
secretariats. Each undersecretariat assumed a different responsibility to the council, to be designated as
follows: 1) the preservation and propagation of the
faith; 2) the supervision of diocesan clergy and religious institutes; 3) the dissemination of religious education for the youth; 4) the increased role of apostolate
of the laity; and 5) social action and social assistance.

CONSTITUCION. The constitution of Chile is that of 1925
(Constitution of 1925*). Chile has had nine constitutions since its inception as an independent state. They
are listed below, enumerated chronologically.

CONSTITUCIONALISTA. A constitutionalist was a person
who backed the efforts of President (1886-91) José
Manuel Balmaceda Fernández* in his constitutional
struggle against the rebellious congress of 1891 (Guerra
Civil de 1891*).

CONSTITUTION OF 1811. It was drafted by the National
Congress, which in turn had been selected by the ca-
bildos*. At the time, there was still indecision whether to declare a "Magna Carta" for independent Chile
or to follow the Spanish King Ferdinand VII. The only
important clause was that it provided for the appointment
of a ruling junta (Junta de Gobierno de 1811*).

CONSTITUTION OF 1812. A provisional constitution drafted
by José Miguel Carrera Verdugo* to give legitimacy to
his rule (1812-13). It was necessary for establishing
diplomatic relations between Chile and the United States.

CONSTITUTION OF 1814. Another provisional constitution
to give legitimacy to the ruling junta in Santiago, after
the disastrous battle of Rancagua*.

CONSTITUTION OF 1818. The first constitution of independent and sovereign Chile. It delegated executive powers
to the Supreme Director (Director Supremo*), without
specifying how many years he was to rule and thus establishing a quasi-dictatorship. The legislative power
was delegated to a conservative Senate, consisting of
ten appointed members, and to a representative chamber, to be elected. The judicial power was greatly
modified from the days of Spanish colonial rule, and
it was vested in a Court of Appeals (Corte de Apelación),
which replaced the Real Audiencia*. A Supreme Court was
also established (Tribunal Superior), replacing the Consejo
de las Indias*. The Constitution of 1818 lasted four years.

CONSTITUTION OF 1822. This new Constitution was an attempt by Chilean Liberals to adopt the Spanish liberal
Constitution of 1812 (Cádiz). The Chilean constitution,
however, did not vest the executive power in a mon-
arch--as the Spanish did--but in a Supreme Director,
thus providing for a semi-republican form of government. The judicial branch of government was organized
on the same structure as that of the Constitution of 1818*.

CONSTITUTION OF 1823. This constitution was a modifica-
tion of that of 1818. According to its charter, Chile
was to be a unitarist republic, and the Supreme Director was to rule for four years, with the privilege of
being re-elected once. He had to be a Chilean by
birth, or a foreigner with Chilean nationality and with
a minimum of 12 years' residency in the country. The
executive power was greatly limited by this constitution

through a system of checks and balances. The Supreme Director was responsible to a State Council (Consejo del Estado), composed of nine members appointed by the Supreme Director. The executive power was to be also checked by a Senate, the elected chamber of representatives, and by an assembly of prominent citizens. The senate was composed of nine members elected every six years. The chamber of representatives consisted of 50 and up to 200 members, elected every eight years. The assembly of prominent citizens had a representative for each 200 people. This constitution did not have much success, and only two of its articles were implemented in later constitutions: the article which established a tribunal of justice for the land, and the article which secured individual rights.

CONSTITUTION OF 1828. The new constitutional proposal was made up of 134 articles and served as a basis for the Constitution of 1833*, which remained in effect for 92 years. The constitution of 1828 called for the indirect elections of a President, who would remain in power for five years and could be re-elected only after a lapse of one or more terms from the time he held office. The Vice-President, also elected by indirect vote, would succeed the President in case of death or disability. The executive branch of government did not dispose of extraordinary powers but had a veto. The legislative power was vested in a congress made up of a Senate and a Chamber of Deputies. The Senate was made up of two representatives from each province, elected indirectly by the provincial assemblies for a period of four years. The Chamber of Deputies was made up of representatives elected by direct vote for a period of two years. The judicial power was vested in a Tribunal of Justice. Ministers to the Supreme Court were appointed by Congress.

CONSTITUTION OF 1833. This constitution was drafted during a period (1831-61) of conservative rule in Chile. Based on the Constitution of 1828*, it had 168 articles and embodied Diego Portales'* belief that power should be concentrated in a highly centralized government. Chile was to be a unitarist republic, and Roman Catholicism was the official religion enjoying full partnership with the state. The President was to be elected by indirect vote for a period of five years, with the privilege of one re-election. The qualifications for the highest office were that the President had to be

native-born, and not less than 30 years of age. Suffrage was limited to literate males over 25, or literate
married men over 21, with the specification that the
voters be property owners.

There was no vice-president, and the Minister of the
Interior would succeed the President in case of death
or disability. Senators were also to be elected by indirect vote, for a period of six years. The Chamber
of Deputies, on the other hand, was to be elected with
direct vote, for a period of three years. Provincial and
municipal authorities were subjected to presidential control. Any foreigner could become a Chilean citizen if he
was literate and owned property, or the equivalent thereof.
Ministers had to be native-born. This constitution remained in effect, with a few modifications, until 1925.

CONSTITUTION OF 1925.   On August 30, 1925, a new constitution was adopted to replace that of 1833. The document was proposed by President (1920-24; 1925) Arturo
Alessandri Palma*, and it embodied the liberal ideals
of President (1886-91) José Manuel Balmaceda Fernández*, who had presented a similar proposal to Congress in 1890.   Unlike the Constitution of 1833*, the
new "Magna Carta" provided for a Presidential term
of six years with no immediate re-election. The President was to be elected by direct popular vote.   Congress could no longer unseat a member of the President's cabinet.   As a result, Presidential powers were
increased and the President alone was responsible for
his cabinet.   The age of parliamentarism had come to
an end.   Church and state were separated, and individual rights were guaranteed.   There was also a change
in the electorate, now made up of literate males over
21.   These were among the most significant provisions
of the constitution of 1925, presently in effect.

CONSTRUCTION AND HOUSING   see THE ECONOMY:
Internal: G. Housing Construction.

CONTRAGOLPE.   A newspaper published in Tierra del
Fuego*, since 1960.   It is the official organ of the
Socialist Party in southernmost Chile.

CONTRERAS LABARCA, CARLOS, 1899- . Lawyer by
profession and active member of the Communist Party
(Partido Comunista*).   In 1931, he was named secretary general of the Party.   From 1926 to 1941 he has

held elective office as deputy, and from 1941 to 1949, as senator. In 1946, he was appointed Minister of Public Works and Communications in the government (1946-52) of Gabriel González Videla*, who had been elected President of Chile with the help of the Communists and had to appoint members of that party to his cabinet. In 1961, Contreras Labarca was elected senator once again for a period of eight years. During that time, he was the head of the Chilean Delegation on Human Rights.

CONTRERAS TAPIA, VICTOR. Active member of the Communist Party. He has held elective office from 1945 to the present. From 1946 to 1947 he was Minister of Lands and Colonization, in the government (1946-52) of Gabriel González Videla*. In 1961, he was elected senator for a period of eight years. Contreras Tapia backed Salvador Allende Gossens* in the Presidential elections of 1952, 1958, 1964, and 1970.

CONVENCION PRESIDENCIAL DE IZQUIERDA. An assembly of leftist delegates convened by the Popular Front (Frente Popular*) in 1938 to organize a strategy for victory in the Presidential elections of that year. There were 1030 delegates who participated: 400 Radicals; 330 Socialists; 120 Communists; 120 Democrats; and 60 delegates from the workers union, the Confederación de Trabajadores de Chile (CTCh). After many ballots, the Popular Front backed the Radical Party's candidate Pedro Aguirre Cerda*, who went on to win the elections.

CONVENTILLO. (Literally, "little convent.") A single story housing of the lower classes. Derives its name from its U-shape and central courtyard, which resembles a convent patio.

COOPERATIVES see THE ECONOMY: Internal: O. Cooperatives.

COPERE. Acronym for Comité de Programación Económica y de Reconstrucción (a government Agency for Economic Programming and Reconstruction).

COPIAPO. Capital of the northern province of Atacama*; population: 48, 700 (1971 est.).

COPIHUE. The national flower of Chile.

COPPER. Chile has been described as a single gigantic
copper mine encrusted within a beautiful and varied
geography. Perhaps no other region in the world has
been more abundantly endowed with the mineral than
the Chilean Andes. The major mining towns are located in the western cordillera, extending from the
Atacama* desert region (in the northern province of
Antofagasta*) into central Chile, south of Santiago*.
In Chuquicamata*, El Salvador*, and Sewell*, more
than 90% of Chile's copper is produced. This mineral
has been mined in Chile since before the beginning of
the present century.

The industry, as it is known today, was developed
mainly by two United States-owned firms, the Anaconda
Copper Mining Company* and the Kennecott Copper
Corporation*. Their subsidiaries, the Chile's Exploration Company and the Andes Mining Company (Anaconda), and the Braden Copper Company (Kennecott), constitute what the Chileans call Gran Minería, composed
of large scale production with a minimum output of
25,000 tons annually. The rest of the copper industry
is divided into Mediana Minería and Pequeña Minería,
medium and small scale production made up of a handful of medium size enterprises and small ones. In
1932, when Chilean nitrate* lost its importance in
world markets, copper replaced it as the nation's
principal export.

Today Chile is the world's second largest copper
producer after the United States. Her output in 1960
constituted 14.3% of the world's production of copper.
The present copper production in Chile reached almost
700,000 metric tons (1 metric ton = 2,204 lbs.),
which accounts for: a) 2/3 of all exports; b) 1/4 of
all the copper moving in the free world; c) 1/8 of the
free world copper production; and d) 1/6 of the copper
the United States uses. New plans outlined by the
government of Salvador Allende Gossens* aim to raise
copper output to 1.2 million metric tons a year by
1975. But this is not all the Chilean government
wants. Upon being sworn into office on November 3,
1970, Allende Gossens pledged that he will nationalize
Chilean copper, with compensation to the U.S.-owned
firms.

Chilean copper resources, which have been primarily in the hands of foreigners since 1905, have a considerable impact on the national economy in at least
four main areas: first, as a contribution to the balance

of payments: in 1969, of the $900 million U.S. exports to Chile, $685 million originated with copper, and $535 million of this came from the Gran Minería. Since 1932, the copper exports through the Gran Minería have represented around 50% of Chile's total exports, reaching 64.5% in 1955 and dropping to 45.3% in 1965 (the reason for the 1965 drop was an increase in other exports rather than a decrease in copper exports). The returns from the Gran Minería, including the legal cost of production, taxation, importation of the companies themselves, custom duties, etc., have represented an average of about 52% of receipts collected in U.S. dollars by the country for its exportation.

Second, in participating in fiscal receipts: the amount of taxes collected from the Gran Minería has been variable within the total of the ordinary fiscal receipts, ranging from a high of 47.4% in 1955 to a low of 7% in 1954. It is usually in the area of 15 to 18%. Third, as an influence on employment: based on the supposition that each worker supports four other persons in addition to himself, a little more than one per cent of the total population lives directly from the copper industry, not to mention those employed by and dependent on business resultant from the copper enterprises. The fourth impact has been as an influence on the rate of technological advancement: the operation of extraction and refining installations in the country represents a significant contribution to technological progress. In addition, copper-related activities have contributed to an increasing demand for industrial goods, resulting in a stimulation of production of materials of a more and more advanced technical nature.

When President (1964-70) Eduardo Frei Montalva* was elected, he pledged to "chileanize" the nation's copper industry. Chileanization meant tighter government regulations over copper pricing, production, and marketing. On December 21, 1964, after less than two months in office, Frei announced that negotiations with the Kennecott Copper Corporation, the Anaconda Company, and the Cerro Company (a new copper concern which began in 1964) had resulted in an agreement. The pact which was signed aimed at doubling copper production by 1970 (from 617,000 metric tons to 1.2 million metric tons) and more than tripling Chile's refining capacity (from 200,000 tons to 700,000 tons). Most importantly, it made the Chilean government a

part owner of the North-American companies, which
meant that the government would participate decisively
in the administration, financing, exploitation, and com-
mercialization of the Chilean copper.

Separate agreements were signed with each of the
three U.S. firms: 1) the Cerro Corporation agreed to
a joint venture of a 75/25% proportion in the development of the Río Blanco mine. The cost of development
was predicted to be $81 million. 2) The Kennecott
Corporation agreed to give ownership of El Teniente*
mine to the Chilean government, on a 51/49% basis.
The Chilean government promised to pay Kennecott $80
million over a 20-year period. Kennecott, in turn,
agreed to use the money to expand production. Jointly,
they would obtain $100 million in loans from interna-
tional sources to expand El Teniente's output from
180,000 tons to 280,000 tons per year. 3) The Anaconda Corporation insisted on retaining sole ownership
of its operating mines. A newly-formed company, to
be owned 51% by Anaconda and 49% by the Chilean
government would be developed near Chuquicamata, and
any additional mines developed would be jointly owned.

In return for the cooperation by the U.S. companies,
Frei made two concessions: the management of the
companies, despite the government's share in ownership, would remain under American control; and company profits would be taxed at lower rates than previously. By 1970, the Frei administration insisted
that Chile should own at least 51% of the stock of the
American companies and new agreements were drawn
up. The Chilean Left opposed the Chileanization program. Economist Mario Vera argued that Chileanization (or "nacionalización pactada") would cost the
Chilean government $1,195 million. In his calculations
he took into account all the possible variables, using a
copper price of 52 cents per pound as his basis. He
came to the conclusion that on this basis of calculations
outright nationalization would cost the Chilean government only $347 million.

In his study, economist Vera presents refutations
for all the arguments against nationalization: he states
that the possibility of copper being replaced by a substitute is almost non-existent; that the complicated
technology in the extraction and refining of copper is
no more than a myth and that the Chilean technicians
are just as capable to run their mining operation as
their North American counterparts; that the financial

situation could not be any worse with nationalization
than it was under Frei's new agreements and would
more than likely be better off.   Upon evaluating the
perspectives for Chilean copper, Vera predicts that
with the nationalization of the mining resources, a
copper exchange in Santiago would be created so that
the production of the red metal in Chile would make
up 19% of world production by 1972.

Socialist President (1970-76) Salvador Allende Gossens agrees with economist Vera.   As a result,
Chilean copper is undergoing a process of nationalization.   President Allende sent to the Congress a draft
constitutional reform having as its basic objective the
nationalization of copper and other minerals vital to the
interests of the state.   First and foremost the reform
draft reiterates a principle already embodied in the
Mining Code, namely that the state has absolute, exclusive, inalienable and imprescriptible ownership of
all mines.   All of Chile has been in favor of nationalization.   All three Presidential candidates in the elections of 1970 pledged and proposed various drafts for
the nationalization of the copper mines.   The price for
copper has decreased from 88 cents per pound in 1970
to 48 cents per pound in 1971.   This significant drop
could represent a serious setback for the economic
programs set by Allende in his socialization campaign.
The following table (in U.S. dollars) shows that North
American companies' profits in Chile have been excessive, whereas the output increases have been meager:

INVESTMENTS:	A. Worldwide	B. Chile	B as % of A
Anaconda	$1, 116, 172, 000	$199, 030, 000	16. 64
Kennecott	$1, 108, 155, 000	$145, 877, 000	13. 16

PROFITS:	A. Worldwide	B. Chile	B as % of A
Anaconda	$ 99, 313, 000	$ 78, 692, 600	79. 24
Kennecott	$ 165, 395, 000	$ 35, 338, 600	21. 37

(See also: ANACONDA and KENNECOTT.)

COQUIMBO.   A province of north-central Chile.   Population:
372, 897; area: 39, 647 sq. km. ; capital city: La Serena*.

CORA.   Acronym for Corporación de la Reforma Agraria.
A Chilean governmental agency whose interests have
been the implementation of President (1964-70) Eduardo
Frei Montalva* agrarian reform proposals.   Frei's

agrarian reform proposed a fundamental change of the latifundio system, reapportionment of the land, and the application of a more advanced technology to increase the production of the land.   Such reforms affected some 100, 000 farmers.   President (1970-76) Salvador Allende Gossens* plans to change the Christian Democrats' goals of organizing land ownership and farm operations on a private basis, and is in favor of organizing a cooperative system of land cultivation insisting on collective ownership.

CORCHAC.   The Chilean Airport Authority.

CORDILLERA.   Mountain range.   Usually referring to the South American ridge of mountains known as the Andes.

CORDOVEZ DEL CASO, GREGORIO, 1783-1843.   A colonel in the army fighting for Chilean independence, he became involved in politics after 1810, taking part in the armed struggle against Spain.   After Chile officially became an independent state in 1818, he became mayor of La Serena*.   In 1822, he was elected deputy to Congress representing the province of Coquimbo*   In 1824, he moved that the Constitution of 1823* be nullified, but Congress voted down his motion.   He continued to be a representative to Congress until shortly before his death.

CORFO.   Acronym for Corporación de Fomento de la Producción, The government-controlled Chilean Production Development Corporation.   In 1939 the Chilean government created CORFO to promote industrial growth. The principal aim of this agency was to establish a comprehensive economic development plan which was to include hydroelectric power, oil development and refinery, and steel manufacturing.   The ostensible purpose of CORFO was to augment productivity so that Chile could pay off the debts contracted after the earthquake of 1939, but this was merely an excuse.   Actually, the unstable Chilean economy needed some form of government intervention to stimulate industrial development, but the congress opposed any form of government intervention in economics.

The Popular Front government which won the Presidential elections in 1938, on the other hand, espoused a doctrine of collectivism in economic growth.   The United States also favored governmental intervention in

Chile in order to guarantee loans it made for purposes of development. CORFO has come to be used as a model for other government development organizations in all parts of the developing world. It has created a mixed economy in Chile--i. e., a system which combines private and state ownership and control of the economy. The Corporation is largely responsible for industrial expansion in Chile since World War II, but has declined in strength and activity since 1950.

CORPORACION DE FOMENTO DE LA PRODUCCION see CORFO.

CORPORACION DE LA REFORMA AGRARIA see CORA.

CORPORACION DE LA VIVIENDA see CORVI.

CORREA FUENZALIDA, GUILLERMO, 1900- . Lawyer by profession and member of the Liberal Party (Partido Liberal*). From 1930 to 1937 he has held elective office as deputy to Congress. From 1937 to 1947 he was appointed to various ministries. He was Minister of Education (1937-38); Minister of Justice (1938); Minister of Foreign Affairs and Commerce (1938); and once again Minister of Justice (1946-47). He was also president of the Chilean Bank (Banco Central) as well as vice-president of the Liberal Party, and professor of law at the University of Chile.

CORREA LETELIER, HECTOR, 1915- . Lawyer by profession and member of the Conservative Party (Partido Conservador*). From 1941 to 1965 he has held elective office. He was also Vice-President, then President, of the Chamber of Deputies. In 1965, he became Chilean ambassador to Brazil.

CORREA MORANDE, MARIA. Chilean writer, and member of the Liberal Party (Partido Liberal*). She was the head of the feminist section of the Party, and for a brief period, director general of the Party (1950). From 1957 to 1961, she has held elected office as deputy to Congress. She was very active for the Liberals in the presidential campaigns of 1958, 1964, and 1970.

CORREGIDOR. Administrator in colonial times responsible to collect local taxes, maintain peace by instituting a police force, and supervise the work of Indians in the economic development of his district. Since the Corregimiento* was an administrative unit governing remote villages, it was easy for the corregidor to become rich unscrupulously. The corregidores were responsible for many scandals in colonial times. They were known especially for their maltreatment of Indians. In 1790, the Bourbon King Charles III reformed the colonial system by abolishing the office of corregidor and replacing it with the Intendentes*.

CORREGIMIENTO. Administrative unit in colonial times subordinated to the viceroyalty and the captaincy-general, devised to protect the Indians and govern remote communities by maintaining peace and collecting taxes.

CORTES. The Spanish Parliament.

CORUÑA. A northern mining town where striking nitrate miners clashed with the police in 1925. The miners were protesting the precarious working and living conditions provided for them and their families. They occupied a building and refused to leave it. Guards were called on the scene and many miners were shot to death. A group of rebellious strikers were taken prisoners, brought to a field, and executed. The blood bath had repercussions in other mining towns in Chile.

CORVALAN, LUIS, 1916- . A journalist, university professor, and militant member of the Communist Party (Partido Comunista*). He is considered a traditionalist. That is, he supports the Soviet international policy as opposed to the Red Chinese line, and cautions the most fervent admirers of Fidel Castro. He has been a leader in the Communist-controlled workers union, Central Unica de Trabajadores de Chile* (CUT), and has been named secretary general of the party on four occasions. In 1961, he was elected senator for a period of eight years. In every Presidential election from 1952 to date, he has backed the leftist candidate Salvador Allende Gossens*.

CORVI. Acronym for Corporación de la Vivienda. A governmental Corporation instituted to provide low-income housing for the Chilean middle class and poor. It came into existence during the second administration

(1952-58) of Carlos Ibáñez del Campo*.

COSACH.   Acronym for the Compañía de Salitre de Chile,
    the government-controlled Chilean Nitrate Company. It
    was created during the administration (1927-31) of
    Carlos Ibáñez del Campo*, with Chilean and American
    capital, and had a monopoly on nitrates and their by-
    product iodine.   The company proved to be a failure
    because there were not enough sales on the internation-
    al market to pay dividends to the government and the
    stockholders.   In 1932, COSACH was replaced by a
    new government company, the Chilean Nitrate and Io-
    dine Sales Corporation, which had monopoly control of
    all sales and exports.   But nitrate, which had been
    for many decades the principal among Chilean mineral
    exports, continued to decline in importance as the pro-
    duction of artificial nitrates increased all over the
    world.   Since the decade of the 1930's, Chilean ex-
    ports of nitrates have steadily declined, and there is
    little hope for the resurgence of this industry.

COVENSA.   (Corporación de Ventas de Salitre y Yodo).   The
    Central Sales Agency for nitrates and iodine.

CREOLE.   American-born Spaniard descendant of Conquista-
    dors and subsequent immigrants usually excluded from
    high-ranking official positions in the government of the
    Spanish colonies in America.   The Creoles made up
    the bulk of the white population in South America.   They
    were responsible for the most part for building colonial
    Spanish and Portuguese America and were the force be-
    hind the movement for independence in the 19th century.
    Although the law put the Creoles on an equal footing
    with the Peninsulares*, the former suffered discrimina-
    tion and disadvantages due mainly to their American
    birth.

CRUCHAGA TOCORNAL, MIGUEL, 1869-1949.   Lawyer, pro-
    fessor of international law, diplomat, and politician.
    He had a long distinguished career as a public servant.
    From 1900 to 1906 he was deputy to Congress.   He
    was Minister of the Treasury in 1903; Minister of the
    Interior in 1905; Minister of Industries and Public
    Works in 1905; Minister of Foreign Affairs and Com-
    merce in 1932.   He was also named subrogate Minis-
    ter of the Interior in 1935; of Health in 1935; and of
    the Treasury in 1936.   As a diplomat, he held many

important offices, first as Chilean Minister to Argentina, Uruguay and Paraguay, during the years 1907 through 1913, and then to Germany, from 1913 to 1920. During the next two years he was Chilean ambassador to Brazil, and three years later, in 1925, he became ambassador to England. In 1931 he was named ambassador to the United States. He also represented Chile in international meetings, and was an arbiter in the border dispute of 1915 between Mexico and the United States. In 1937 he was elected senator, and in the same year, President of the Senate. From that time until his death he was a senator.

CRUZ COKE LASSABE, EDUARDO, 1899- . He received a degree in medicine in 1921 and as a student became a member of the Conservative Party (Partido Conservador*). In 1937 he was named Minister of Health and Social Welfare. From 1941 to 1957 he held elective office as a senator. During that time he was responsible for introducing a bill in Congress sponsoring socialized medicine. The bill became law. In 1946, he was the Conservative Party's candidate for President, but lost to Gabriel González Videla*. In 1948, when González Videla proscribed the Communist Party (Partido Comunista*), Cruz Coke opposed the measure in Congress.

CRUZ GOYENECHE, LUIS DE LA, 1786-1829. Chilean patriot who participated in the campaign for independence, fighting in all the major battles against Spain (Rancagua*, Maipú*, Chacabuco*). He was a member of the Federalist Party (Partido Federalista*). After the battle of Chacabuco, in 1817, there was news that another Spanish invasion was going to take place. José de San Martín* and José Ignacio Zenteno* named Cruz Goyeneche Supreme Director of Chile, while Bernardo O'Higgins*, who had been wounded at Chacabuco, was trying to reorganize the armies fighting for independence. Cruz Goyeneche remained in power until the return of O'Higgins, who in 1818 was proclaimed Supreme Director with the founding of the Chilean Republic.

CUADRILATERO. A political fusion of four parties, the Partido National*, the Partido Radical*, and two splinters of the Liberal Party (Partido Liberal*), the Partido Liberal Doctrinario*, and the Partido Liberal

Mocetón*. It took its name ("quadrilateral" in English) from the four parties that formed it. Its position was to oppose the constitutional program of President (1886-91) José Manuel Balmaceda Fernández*. After the fall of Balmaceda, the Cuadrilatero instituted the Parliamentary rule in Chile that was to last until 1925.

CUECA. The national folk dance of Chile. During the first years of the republic, the cueca was part of the celebration in commemoration of the defeat of the Spanish. It has now become the traditional dance to celebrate Independence Day (September 18, 1810) and other festive occasions.

CUERPO DE CARABINEROS. The Chilean national police. Established in 1927 during the first government (1927-31) of Carlos Ibáñez del Campo*, the Cuerpo de Carabineros numbers today 30, 000 men and is equipped with heavy and modern armaments. The general director of the Chilean police receives his orders directly from the Minister of the Interior or the President of the Republic. In 1960, a special police force was organized known as the Grupo Móvil de Carabineros*. Its main activities were to break up workers' strikes as well as student and peasant demonstrations. The Chilean Left called this special force "a brutal force" which had managed to become in the short period of ten years (1960-70) the most repressive arm of the governments of Conservative Jorge Alessandri Rodríguez* (1958-64) and Christian Democrat Eduardo Frei Montalva* (1964-70). As soon as Socialist President Slavador Allende Gossens* came to power on November 3, 1970, he abolished the Grupo Móvil de Carabineros.

CUEVAS MACKENNA, FRANCISCO, 1910- . Graduated as a civil engineer in 1933, in 1953 he was named Minister of Mines, a post he resigned in 1954 to become President of the National Bank (Banco del Estado). In 1955, he was appointed Minister of the Treasury, leaving the Banco del Estado. In the government (1964-70) of Eduardo Frei Montalva*, he was appointed president of the National Mining Society (Sociedad Nacional de Minería).

CURALI. Site of a battle during the struggle for indepen-
dence against Spain. It was fought on May 1, 1819,
between the Chilean patriots and the Spanish royalists.
The first were under the command of Colonel Ramón
Freire Serrano*; the second, under the command of
Vicente Benavides*. The royalists were defeated and
Benavides had to escape to save his life.

CURAPALIHUE. Site of a battle during the campaign for
Chilean independence, fought on April 4, 1817, near
the city of Concepción*. The Chilean patriots were
led by José Gregorio de la Heras, while the Spanish
royalists were under the command of lieutenant colonel
Juan José Campillo. The royalists attacked by surprise but were repelled just the same by the Chileans.
Casualties were light on both sides.

CURICO. 1) A province of central Chile located south of
Santiago; population: 123, 600 (1971 est.); area: 5, 266. 3
sq. km.
2) Capital city of the central province of Curico;
population: 60, 400 (1971 est.).

CUSTOMS AND DUTIES see THE ECONOMY: External:
C. Customs and Duties.

-D-

DAVILA ESPINOZA, CARLOS, 1887-1955. Lawyer, newspaperman, and provisional President of Chile for 100
days; his government was known as the "gobierno de
los 100 días." In 1928, he obtained a law degree
from Columbia University. He also did post-graduate
work at the University of Southern California, and the
University of North Carolina. When the government
(1931-32) of Juan Esteban Montero* was dissolved on
June 16, 1932, Dávila Espinosa participated in the junta government that succeeded Montero. In July of the
same year, Dávila Espinosa became provisional President of Chile, and his government lasted until September 13, 1932. Member of the Radical Party (Partido
Radical*), and later a Conservative, Dávila Espinosa
had a distinguished career as newspaperman and diplomat. He worked on the Mercurio*, a daily published
in Santiago, and became director of the conservative

organ, La Nación*. As a diplomat, he held important posts overseas. From 1927 to 1931, he was Chilean ambassador to the United States. In 1946, he was the Chilean representative on the Economic Council of the United Nations. In 1954, he became Secretary General of the Organization of American States (OAS), a post he held until his death in Washington, D. C.

DECLARACION DE SANTIAGO, LA. In 1962 Chile, Ecuador, and Peru signed a multilateral agreement affirming their rights over 200 miles of territorial waters. Other Latin American countries that claim such an extension are Uruguay, Brazil, Argentina, Costa Rica, Nicaragua, and El Salvador.

DEFENSA NACIONAL, MINISTERIO DE. The National Defense Ministry was created to replace the Ministry of War and the Navy. This new Ministry only lasted a month. From it, two new ministries were created: the Ministry of War, and the Ministry of the Navy. In 1932, the Ministry of National Defense was created again by statute No. 5077. It included the Ministry of War, of the Navy and the undersecretariat of the Air Force. Shortly after, two new ministries were created once again, the Ministry of War and Aviation, and the Ministry of the Navy. But their existence was short-lived, and in December, 1932, the Ministry of National Defense was created for the third time, comprising the other two. It has lasted to the present.

DE LA CRUZ PRIETO, JOSE MARIA, 1799-1875. A career army officer who participated in the campaign for independence against Spain. In 1813 he was leader of a battalion during the battle of Chillán*, and in 1814 he escaped to Mendoza, Argentina, after the disastrous defeat of Rancagua*, suffered by the Chilean troops. He came back to Chile with the frontier army of the liberator José de San Martín* (Ejército de los Andes*), and in 1817 fought at the battle of Chacabuco*, Maipú*, and Pengal*. From 1824 to 1830 he held elective office. In 1830, he was named Minister of War. In 1838, he participated in the war against the Peru-Bolivia Confederation*. After this campaign, he was promoted to general. In 1851, he participated in the civil war (Guerra Civil de 1851*) against President (1851-61) Manuel Montt Torres*, who had defeated him at the polls. From 1846 to 1855, backed by the Libe-

ral Party (Partido Liberal*), Cruz Prieto was a senator.

DE LA CRUZ TOLEDO, MARIA.   The first woman to be
elected to the Chilean Senate in 1953.   She had attempted
to win a senate seat in 1950, but received very few
votes.   She organized, and became president of the Partido Feminista de Chile*, a party responsible for extending the suffrage to women in 1952, and for defending women's rights.   In the Presidential election of
1952, the party supported the candidacy of Carlos
Ibáñez del Campo*, who won the elections.   During the
Presidential campaign, De la Cruz Toledo had traveled
throughout Chile to win votes for Ibáñez del Campo.
In 1953, when a Senate seat was vacated in Santiago,
De la Cruz Toledo was urged by the President to run
for it.   She did and she won.   But her Senate career
was short-lived.   She soon antagonized her colleagues,
who forced her to resign in the same year.

DEPARTAMENTO.   A subdivision of the Chilean province.
Also see CHILE: GOVERNMENT (E. Provincial Government).

DEPENDENCIES   see CHILE.

DIAGUITAS.   Indians who came to Chile from western Argentina before the arrival of the Spaniards.   With the
Atacameños*, they settled in the semi-desert provinces
of Atacama* and Coquimbo*.   Both tribes are now extinct.

DIARIO ILUSTRADO, EL.   A daily newspaper published in
Santiago and organ of the Conservative Party (Partido
Conservador*).   When the Conservative Party formed
a coalition with the Liberals, in 1966, (Partido Nacional*), the El Diario Ilustrado became the organ of
the new party.   Also see THE PRESS.

DIARIO OFICIAL DE LA REPUBLICA DE CHILE.   A newspaper published in Santiago from 1877 to 1891.   During the Presidency (1886-91) of José Manuel Balmaceda
Fernández*, the newspaper was the official organ of
government.

DIARIO OFICIAL DEL VERDADERO GOBIERNO, EL.   A
newspaper published in Santiago during the Civil War

of 1891 (Guerra Civil de 1891*). It was the official
organ of the rebellious Congress and opposed the government (1886-91) of José Manuel Balmaceda Fernández*.

DIEGO RAMIREZ ISLANDS.   Dependencies of Chile.   A
small archipelago located at 56° 36' south latitude and
68° 43' west longitude, about 60 miles southwest of
Cape Horn.

DIRECTOR SUPREMO.   The Constitution of 1818*, the first
constitution of independent Chile, provided that the executive power should be relegated to a Supreme Director (Director Supremo), without specifying for how
many years he should rule and thus establishing a
quasi-dictatorship.   Bernardo O'Higgins* was Chile's
first Supreme Director (1817-23).

DOLORES.   A hillside in the province of Santiago, and site
of a battle fought on February 15, 1891, between troops
loyal to President (1886-91) José Manuel Balmaceda
Fernández* and troops siding with the rebellious Congress during the Civil War of 1891 (Guerra Civil de
1891*).   The loyalist army was defeated.

DONOSO, JOSE.   Novelist and short-story writer.   He
studied at the British Primary School in Santiago, and
was a classmate of Carlos Fuentes, noted Mexican
novelist.   Donoso went on to the University of Chile*
and in 1949 was awarded a scholarship to study at
Princeton, where he received his B.A. degree in 1951.
From that time, he has held high offices in the Ministry of Education.   From 1965 to 1967, he was a
writer-in-residence, and lecturer at the University of
Iowa.   Among his better known novels are Este domingo and El lugar.   Both works portray the decadence of
Santiago's society.   Two of his short-stories have received wide acclaim in Latin America, "Paseo" and
"Santelices."   In "Paseo," the author satirized the
routine of every day life in a Chilean household, and
depicts the world of inner feelings as viewed by a
child, who feels that he is less important than a dog
found in the street, or than the billiard game that his
uncles play.   In "Santelices," the author criticized the
routine life of a boarding house.   His hero becomes
fascinated by wild animals, rejects the monotony of
his office work, and thinks that he can escape society

by contemplation. Little by little he becomes alienated
from the world surrounding him, until his escapism becomes total when he commits suicide.

DUHALDE VAZQUEZ, ALFREDO, 1888- . Member of the
Radical Party (Partido Radical*). Elected representative to Congress from 1927 to 1937 as a deputy, and
from 1937 to 1945 as a senator. In 1942, he was
named Minister of National Defense, and in 1945, Minister of the Interior. On September 26, 1945, he was
named Vice-President of Chile. He became acting
President of the Republic with the death of President
(1942-46) Juan Antonio Ríos Morales*. Duhalde Vázquez was in office until November 4, 1946, when the
new President-elect, Gabriel González Videla*, was
inaugurated. Duhalde Vázquez was a candidate in the
Presidential elections of that year, but did not receive
too many votes. During his brief term, the country
was plagued by labor trouble and he lost the electoral
support he needed to win the elections of 1946.

DURAN NEUMANN, JULIO ANTONIO, 1918- . Lawyer by
profession and active member of the Radical Party
(Partido Radical*). Presidential candidate in the elections of September 4, 1964, he lost to Eduardo Frei
Montalva*, obtaining a mere 4.9% of the votes, as opposed to Frei Montalva's 55.6%. From 1945 to 1953,
Durán Neumann held elective office as a deputy, and
in 1957 he was elected senator for an eight-year term.
From 1952 to 1964, he was the leader of the Radical
Party. In the elections of 1964, Durán Neumann was
backed by the Radicals and by the political party known
as the Comandos Populares*.

-E-

EASTER ISLAND. Easter island, a volcanic projection
about 10 by 15 miles in extent, and also called Rapa-
Nui (large island), is Chile's most famous dependency.
Located 2,300 miles west of Chile, at 27° 3' to 12'
south latitude and 109° 14' to 25' west longitude, Easter island supports a population of about 600 Polyne-
sian-speaking natives. Food crops for domestic consumption include bananas, potatoes, sugar cane, taro
roots, and yams. Famed for its mysterious carved
stone monuments, the island was discovered by the

English pirate Edward Davis, named Easter Island by
the Dutch explorer Jacob Roggenveen in 1722, and
claimed by Spain in 1770.   Chile took control of the
island in 1888, and now administers the territory as
part of Valparaíso* Province.

ECHAVARRI ELORZA, JULIAN, 1911- . Accountant by
profession, and member of the Agrarian Labor Party
(Partido Agrario Laborista*).   From 1937 to 1953 he
held elective office as a deputy in Congress.   In 1954,
he was the leader of a splinter group within his party
which joined what was later to become the National
Popular Party (Partido Nacional Popular*).   In 1957,
he became vice-president of the new party and was
elected a senator.   In the Presidential elections of
1964, he supported the candidacy of Eduardo Frei
Montalva* and in 1966, Frei Montalva named him Ambassador to Spain.

ECHEVERRIA LARRAIN, JOAQUIN, 1774-1835. Lawyer by
profession, and deputy to the first National Congress
formed in 1811.   He was named Governor of Santiago
in 1813, and participated in the first junta government
of Chile (Junta de Gobierno de 1813*).   In 1817, because of his activities for the cause of independence
he was exiled to Peru, where he was held prisoner until 1818.   In that year, he returned to Chile, and was
named Minister of Foreign Relations by Bernardo
O'Higgins*, a post he held for five years.   During the
government (1823-36) of Ramón Freire Serrano* he
was elected senator, and in the same year he was
named rector of the University of San Felipe.   From
1820 to 1822, he assisted O'Higgins, who was Supreme
Director of Chile (1817-23), in governing the province
of Santiago*.

ECHEVERZ, SANTIAGO, 1792-1852.   Lawyer by profession
and member of the Conservative Party (Partido Conservador*).   He was Secretary of the Intendency of
Santiago in 1819 (Intendencia*), deputy to Congress in
1823 and 1825, and provincial judge in 1824.   In 1826,
he was named Minister of the Court of Appeals, and
two years later he was in charge of the constitutional
reform to the written Constitution of 1828*.   In 1831,
he was named Vice-President of the Chamber of Deputies, and in 1833 he signed the new Constitution (Constitution of 1833*), which remained in effect until 1925.

In 1843, he was Minister of the Supreme Court of Justice. Active in politics, he was elected senator in 1834 and held that office until 1843. He was again elected to the Senate in 1849, holding office until his death. As part of the Martial Court of Chile, in 1836 he commuted the sentence of Ramón Freire Serrano* from the death penalty to exile. This action caused him to be arrested, but he was later acquitted.

ECLA see CEPAL.

ECONOMIA, MINISTERIO DE. The Ministry of the Economy was created by statute No. 88, in 1953, and lasted until 1960. It changed the structure of the Ministry of the Economy and Commerce (Ministerio de Economía y Comercio*), which it replaced. Two subsecretariats were included in the new ministry: the secretariat of commerce, and that of industry and transports. In 1960, the Ministerio de Economía was changed to the Ministerio de Economía, Fomento y Reconstrucción*.

ECONOMIA, FOMENTO Y RECONSTRUCCION, MINISTERIO DE. The Ministry of the Economy, Development and Reconstruction was established in 1960 to replace the Ministry of the Economy (Ministerio de Economía*). President (1958-64) Jorge Alessandri Rodríguez* decreed it by statute No. 14171. The new ministry was created after the disastrous earthquake of 1960, which left more than 60,000 dead and hundreds of thousands homeless. It comprised two subsecretariats, that of the Economy, Development and Reconstruction, and that of Transport. It incorporated most of the departments of the old Ministry of the Economy and Commerce (Ministerio de Economía y Comercio*), and its main purpose was to alleviate the terrible damages left by the earthquake. The Chilean economy was on the verge of collapsing; the national currency had been devalued from 119 pesos to the dollar in 1953 to 1,000 pesos to the dollar in 1960; some 300,000 house units were needed to accommodate the poor and all the earthquake victims. In the face of this national disaster, President Alessandri Rodríguez used the Ministry of the Economy, Development and Reconstruction to channel the aid coming mostly from the United States, but also from many countries around the world.

ECONOMIA Y COMERCIO, MINISTERIO DE. The Ministry
of the Economy and Commerce was created in 1942 by
statute No. 6-4817, and it replaced the Ministry of
Commerce and Provisions (Ministerio de Comercio y
Abastecimientos*). Within the new ministry, there
were various departments divided into the following
classifications: Transport and Navigation; Industrialization; Mines and Petroleum; Hunting and Fishing; Statistics; Prices; and Control of Exports. In 1953, this
ministry ceased to exist and it was changed to the
Ministry of the Economy (Ministerio de Economía*).

ECONOMY, THE. Chile is a country which has a "peripheral"
economy. The term is used to designate a country
which is not fully developed and depends on the world
centers of economic power, such as the United States
or Russia, for its survival. Chile sells its major export, copper, without being able to control its price,
and purchases its major imports without any real bargaining power in the international markets. To under-
stand more clearly the economy of Chile we shall di-
vide it into two major categories: the Internal Economy and the External Economy. Each category will be
subdivided into sectors.

The Internal Economy: A. National Income. The
following table sets forth Chile's national income (NI)
and gross national product (GNP) in millions of escudos:

	1960	1964	1965	1966	1967	1968
NI	3,885	11,920	14,118	19,631	25,408	33,905
GNP	4,974	14,015	17,956	25,045	32,881	44,209

The current (1970) distribution of national income is:
agriculture, forestry, fishing, 15%; mines, 6%; manufacturing, 17%; construction, 4%; electricity, gas and
water power, 1%; transportation, 8%; trade, 23%; all
other, 26%.) Unfortunately, this picture of rapid
growth in the chart above is not a true one; inflation
accounts for most of the apparent gain. The cost of
living rose 17.3% in 1957 and almost 50% in 1970. In
September 1962 a dollar bought 1.5 escudos*; in September 1971 it buys 14.3 escudos. Prices of consumer goods in Santiago and Valparaíso are noticeably
higher than in other South American principal cities.
Real national income has grown, but only modestly.
Annual growth from 1960 to 1970 has averaged from
3.2% to 5.2%, and between 2.5% and 3.3% per capita,

with population growth reducing the per capita economic
expansion.   National income per capita is estimated between 450 and 600 dollars.

B.   Agriculture.   Since 1940 agricultural production
has fluctuated and domestic production of foodstuffs provides no more sustenance now than it did 30 years ago.
Presently, agriculture employs 28% of the nation's work
force and provides for 9% of the national income.   The
Central Valley is the most fertile region in Chile and
contains approximately half the land under cultivation.
Of Chile's total area of 74,177,000 hectares (2.471
acres = one hectare), between five and six million hectares are under cultivation, including 1.4 million hectares that are irrigated.

A near colonial land ownership pattern has characterized Chile's arable land since the time of the colonial period.   In 1965 1.5% of the landowners owned more
than 70% of the land.   While there are over 300 large
farms (fundos*) with more than 4,900 hectares, there
remain 500,000 peasants subsisting on fewer than two
hectares per family, with land holdings of less than 1%
of the total arable land.   Inquilinos* work the fundos
and are aided during the harvest season by afuerinos*.
Sharecropping has also been important in the cultivation
of the land.   Frequent absentee ownership, combined
with implementation of old, familiar methods, has
limited production growth.   Many technical problems
arise also from the inappropriateness of crops to the
size of the farms on which they are grown.   Leading
crops include wheat, barley, beans, rice, potatoes,
and citrus fruits.

Chilean vineyards produced more than 500 million
liters of wine in 1970, much of which is exported.
Peaches, nectarines, and plums are also exported.
Prior to 1940, Chile was a net exporter of agricultural
products.   The nation's heavy emphasis on industrial
development since then has made the country import
more foodstuffs each year.   In the decade of the 1960's,
food imports absorbed approximately half of all investments in imports.   Natural problems have also troubled
Chilean agriculture.   Serious droughts reduced farm
production in the years 1961-62, 1964-65, 1966-67, and
1968-69.   Chile produces domestically about two-thirds
of its meat needs, importing some 50,000 tons of meat
annually from Argentina.   In the decade of the 1960's,
Chile has emphasized stock raising in the Central Valley (beef) and in the far south (sheep).   In 1968 there

were some 3.5 million heads of cattle and some 6.5
million heads of sheep.

The Agrarian Reform Law passed by the Christian
Democratic government (1964-70) of Eduardo Frei Montalva* permitted the expropriation of certain inefficient
holdings for cash, and provided for the consolidation of
the minifundia* and for some experiments in cooperative farming. Frei's promise to create 100,000 new
landowners in Chile was carried out slowly; by 1970
that goal had not quite been reached. A much more
ambitious Agrarian Reform Law was recently sent to
Congress by President (1970-76) Salvador Allende Gossens*. In his message of November, 1970, President
Allende promised the campesinos* decisive advances in
the Agricultural Reform. The bill sent to Congress
would increase agricultural development by means of a
price policy, credits, fertilizers, technical assistance,
improved marketing methods, the redistribution of the
land and of water rights, the creation of cooperatives,
and the raising of the living standards of farm workers.
All arable land not under cultivation would be expro-
priated with a 10% deposit and payments for the land
with interest over a 20-year period. Well-managed
large estates, unless exceptionally large, would not be
reduced in size. Strengthened by the results of the
March 1971 elections, President Allende was seen as
having a very good chance of securing passage of his
new farm legislation.

C. Forestry. Of Chile's 741,767 square kilometers
(one km. = 0.62137 mile) about 22% of the national area
(160,000 sq. km.) is forested. "Forest Chile," the
primary timber area, lies between Concepción* and Punta Arenas*. Income from lumber exports exceeds $12
million per year. Little of the commercially usable
timber is as yet reached by Chile's limited system of
roads. Commercial timber cutting is carried on by
some 600 sawmills and 9,000 workers on both sides of
the Bío-Bío river in the provinces of Concepción and
Bío-Bío*. Chile's lumber production has not grown
very much in recent years; production in million cubic
meters was 6.5 in 1963 and 6.6 in 1969. Paper production in the 1960's averaged some 100,000 tons annually, more than enough for domestic needs.

Leading customers for Chile's lumber exports are
Argentina, Brazil, Bolivia, and Mexico, and some West-
ern European nations, especially Germany and England.
Important softwoods include alerce, araucaria, manio,

and pine.   Pine is by far the most important softwood;
a forest census showed 277. 7 million pine trees in
1953.   Hardwoods include alamo, beech, laurel, lenga,
and olivillo.   While Chilean law provides a 30-year tax
exemption on timber in forest preserves, conservation
of forest resources has not been adequate.   Most harvested forests have not been reseeded or replanted in
a systematic way.   Timber losses each year resulting
from fire or other natural hazards surpass replacement
growth.

Foreign investments in Chile until 1970 include loans
to the timber industry from the Export-Import Bank
(Eximbank) and from the Inter-American Development
Bank (IDB).   With the realization of a Marxist Government in Chile for the period 1970-76, foreign investment in the timber industry has dwindled to practically
nothing.   There is a great potential in the Chilean lumber industry and the government of Socialist Allende
wants to reap the profits.   The publicly-owned Compañía Manufacturera de Papeles y Cartones, largest
paper, pulp, and box manufacturer in Latin America,
has pioneered a growing export business for Chile in
recent years.

D.   Fishing.   Chile's fishing industry has grown
very much in the past two decades.   The total catch
in 1950 was 57, 000 metric tons; in 1960, more than
300, 000 metric tons.   By 1970 the catch had surpassed
700, 000 metric tons.   Approximately half the total catch
was whiting.   Other important seafoods are anchovies,
haddock, herring, lobster, oysters, sardines, sword-
fish, and tuna.   Chile's whaling fleet caught 2, 338
whales in 1962; from these 6, 600 metric tons of whale
oil was produced.   Most of the fish caught is consumed
domestically and is sold fresh.   There are some 60
fish canneries in Chile, employing a total of 4, 000 men,
and some 10, 000 fishermen.   Chile's fast-growing fishmeal industry in 1970 produced more than 100, 000
metric tons of fishmeal, largely for export.   Chile
claims the fish-rich coastal waters for 200 miles off-
shore, as do Peru and Ecuador.   Foreign vessels may
not fish these waters without an official permit.   Like
the lumber industry, the Chilean fishing industry has a
great potential for growth.

E.   Mining.   Chile is known as a country of mines.
The importance of nitrates in the past has yielded to
the prime importance of copper today.   Chile is the
second copper-producing nation in the world and the

Chilean government wants to increase production so
that it can become the first.   (For an analysis of Chilean mining see also COAL; COPPER; IRON: NITRATES;
PETROLEUM; STEEL.)

F.   Manufacturing.   Manufacturing produces one-
fourth of the GNP and employs about 20% of the work
force.   Industrial production has increased rapidly in
the 1960's, with a growth of about 5% annually for the
decade 1960-1970.   The Corporación de Fomento de la
Producción* (CORFO) has promoted the expansion of
manufacturing, power, and agriculture, while the Compañía de Acero del Pacífico* (CAP) has established the
basis for heavy industrial development.   Chile is one
of the few Latin American countries that has both iron
and coal in quantities sufficient to supply its iron and
steel industry.   Nearly all of Chile's manufacturing is
for domestic consumption.   The leading manufactured
goods by production and income are 1) beverages, food
and tobacco; 2) textiles; 3) metal and metal products;
4) chemicals; and 5) leather and rubber commodities.
Chile satisfies domestically its needs for cement, cellulose, explosives, glass, newsprint, paper, shoes,
wool textiles, and most consumer goods.   The leading
center for manufacturing is Santiago.   The Socialist
government of Salvador Allende Gossens favors diversi-
fication in manufacturing, with special emphasis on
iron and steel, cellulose, newsprint, petroleum, cement, fisheries, and chemicals.

G.   Housing Construction.   The housing deficit in
Chile in 1964 was estimated at 500,000 units.   To
keep up with Chile's expanding population an estimated
50,000 units per year are needed.   More than 70% of
working class families live in homes having only one
room.   Previous to the Jorge Alessandri Rodríguez*
administration (1958-1964), new homes were built at a
rate of only 5,000 per year.   Alessandri was able to
build 200,000 new homes, largely for those of the
lower-middle class.   The subsequent administration
(1964-70) of Eduardo Frei Montalva* kept its promise
to build 300,000 units by 1970.   Most of this housing
progress was accomplished under the guidance of the
government's housing office, the Corporación de la
Vivienda* (CORVI).   Some 200,000 units are needed for
the period 1971-75 and President Allende has promised
to earmark almost 9% of the 1971 budget to housing
development.

H.   Public Health.   Chile has made considerable progress in public health.   For example, while the death rate in 1920 was 30. 7 per 1, 000, by 1970 it had fallen to 11. 5 per 1, 000.   The infant mortality rate has also decreased, though it is still very high.   It fell from 163. 6 per 1, 000 live births in 1945 to 100 in 1970.   Life expectancy at birth is now a little over 50 years, one of the highest in Latin America.   The leading causes of deaths are heart diseases, pulmonary diseases and tuberculosis.   Deaths from cancer are increasing.   Significantly, the death rate is much lower in the dry northern provinces.   Chile graduates about 230 doctors each year; but each year the population increases by more than 200, 000 or nearly 900 for each new doctor.   The ratio of doctors to inhabitants is 1 for each 1, 900.

In Santiago, there is one doctor for every 900 persons, and the figures for Valparaíso and Concepción are also favorable.   But in the other provinces, the ratio is approximately one doctor per 5, 000 persons, with some rural areas having a ratio of one doctor per 10, 000 persons.   In 1960, there were 224 hospitals in Chile, with 33, 358 beds, or five beds per 1, 000 persons.   Since then, the National Health Service has provided hospital beds and treatment for about 75% of the population.   In 1970, the government spent about 9% of its budget on public health improvements.   Chile has a comprehensive and compulsory social insurance program for its workers and their families.   Workers pay 5% of their wages for coverage, with their employers contributing 10%, and the state an additional 5. 5%.   The program covers medical needs from birth to funeral expenses.   It also covers unemployment and retirement benefits as well as life insurance.

I.   Manpower and Employment.   In 1970, Chile's labor force numbered approximately 3 million workers, including more than a half million women.   Of these, 28% were employed in agriculture, 20% in manufacturing, 9% in transportation, and 7% in mining.   Approximately half a million were white collar workers.   By law, the regular work day is eight hours, and the regular work week forty-eight hours.   Workers are entitled to a two-week paid vacation annually, provided they have completed 288 days of employment.   Overtime work must by law be paid at a rate of time and a half. Neither minors nor women may legally work at night, and minors can work only with parental consent.   Women employees are entitled to six weeks' pre-natal and six weeks' post-natal leave with pay.   Also see LABOR.

J.   Transportation and Telecommunication.   In 1971, Chile had 56,412 kilometers of highways, of which 2,315 formed part of the Pan American Highway.   Of total roads, 2,442 kilometers were first-class paved roads, 21,840 were second-class paved roads, and 31,772 were earth.   There were also 9,172 kilometers of railraods, most of which are state-owned.   There are nine international airports, 13 seaplane bases, and 89 registered landing strips.   Chile's national airline Línea Aérea Nacional (LAN*) serves important domestic routes as well as international routes.   In 1970, LAN served 48 cities and 7 countries.   Because of its long coastline, Chile's coastal shipping is important. Ten of Chile's 20 ports are used primarily for coastal shipping.   Most coastal vessels are Chilean and are run by the Compañía Sudamericana de Vapores*.

The nation's merchant marine also plays an important role with its 98 vessels.   Important ports are Antofagasta (which also serves the country of Bolivia), Arica, Coquimbo, Iquique, Punta Arenas, San Antonio, Talcahuano, Tocopilla and Valparaíso.   Telephones in 1970 numbered 312,042, mostly in the Santiago-Valparaíso-Concepción areas.   In 1970, there were 1.5 million radio sets in Chile and with more than 80 privately-owned radio stations.   Ninety per cent of all Chileans had at least one radio in their homes.   Television sets numbered 200,000 in 1970, a great increase since 1962 when there were only 4,000 sets.   In 1968, Chile built the first telecommunication T.V. station in Longovillo, able to receive programs from all over the world via satellite.

K.   Energy and Power.   Among the nations of Latin America, Chile ranks second (to Brazil) in hydroelectric power potential, having an estimated reserve of 10 million kilowatts.   In 1970, installed hydroelectric capacity in Chile was 986,000 kilowatts, or 9.86% of the potential.   Production of electricity by water power has grown in recent years; electric power is produced by 17 plants, of which 10 are hydroelectric.   Industries, largely copper, consume a large percentage of all electricity produced.   Government-owned plants produce most of the power for industrial and non-industrial uses.   Chile is well suited to develop its hydroelectric resources.   The bulk of its potential is located near its population center in central Chile.   Moreover, the narrowness of the country makes distribution economical and efficient.   Also see: COAL and PETROLEUM.

   L.   Banking.   During the 1920's, the Chilean government established a number of banking institutions to promote various sectors of the economy, the most important of which was the Central Bank of Chile (Banco Central de Chile).   Today, the Central Bank is the only institution allowed to issue notes.   Its other functions include extending credit to governmental agencies and controlling interest rates, credits, commissions, and banking charges.   Other important banking institutions in Chile are: the State Bank (Banco del Estado), the Mining Credit and Development Bank (Caja de Crédito Minero), the People's Savings Bank (Caja de Crédito Popular), the Agricultural Colonization Institute (Caja de Colonización Agrícola), and the Amortization Institute (Caja Autónoma de Amortización de la Dueda Pública).

   The State Bank was established in 1953 through the merger of four institutions.   In addition to its main office in Santiago, it has 146 branches throughout the nation.   The Bank is empowered to act through savings, loans, mortgages, and industrial planning.   It may also engage in domestic and foreign trade.   The Mining Credit and Development Bank, founded in 1927, is concerned primarily with mining operations.   The Agricultural Colonization Institute was created in 1928 to deal with the problem of land distribution in the Central Valley.   In 1959, its structure was reorganized and the Institute was called the Corporación de la Reforma Agraria (CORA*).

   The People's Savings Bank, founded in 1921, mainly serves the small borrower.   It does 85% of all the legal pawn-brokering in Chile.   The Amortization Institute, established in 1932, services the internal and foreign public debt.   There are 30 commercial banks in Chile, of which three are branches of foreign banking firms.   The largest private commercial bank in Chile is the Banco de Chile, which controls 40% of all commercial banking capital.   In 1960, the government of (1958-64) Jorge Alessandri Rodríguez* established a system of 22 savings and loan associations.   In 1970, there were 6,526 million escudos in Chile (one dollar = 14.3 escudos), with a gold reserve of $47 million.

   According to the government of President (1970-76) Allende, Chilean banking practices have been monopolistic.   The main problem has been the concentration of credit. That is, a group of monopolistic enterprises with strong ties in the banking system obtain the largest percentage of the credit, while a large number of medium size and small size enterprises have no access to this source of financing. In addition, the charge has been that the conditions under which credit is obtained are discriminatory, as the interest is lower for the dominating monopolistic groups. Among the private national banks in 1970, three represented 44.5% of the deposits, obtained 55% of the profits, and participated in 44.3% of the loans. All this has led the Allende government to the conclusion that it is necessary to establish State control over the banks. And this is what Allende plans to do in the near future.

M. Insurance. The number of Chilean insurance firms doubled between 1930 and 1960, from 75 to 155. Foreign-owned insurance firms number 25 within that total. In 1927, the insurance business was reserved to Chilean firms by law (although foreign firms which existed prior to that year were not affected). Private insurance operations are supervised by the government, and the Chilean Reinsurance Institute (Caja reaseguradora de Chile) has a monopoly of all foreign reinsurance. The state-owned Insurance Institute (Instituto de Seguros del Estado) carries out all fire and casualty insurance of the central government, and it was established in 1953. Seventeen firms write life insurance. The two leading firms are the Compañía Chilena de Seguros la Previsión and the Compañía de Seguros la Chilena Consolidada. Due to inflation, life insurance has steadily declined in popularity as a form of protection. The total value of life policies in force has declined by half in the past ten years.

N. Securities. Chile's securities market has been one of the most active in Latin America until 1970, when the Chileans elected the first Marxist government in the Western Hemisphere. Socialist President Salvador Allende Gossens* promised to initiate a process of structural transformation in the Chilean economy and, as a result, there has been a flight of Chilean capital overseas with a decline in the volume of stock transactions. The first stock exchanges to be established in Chile were the one in Valparaíso (1892) and the one in Santiago (1893). Since then, as corporate business increased, so did the stock market. The Chilean securities market has dealt in about 350 stocks, as well as Government mortgages, and industrial bonds in gold and in foreign exchange. Commodity trading has been carried out in the Bolsa de Santiago, Santiago Stock Exchange.

Mining and industrial shares have accounted for more than 30% of the total value in stock transactions, with another 10% of the total transactions in marine, banking, and agricultural stocks. Stock transactions have accounted for 90% of the total value of trading, with bonds accounting for the remaining 10%. Chilean investment abroad has been largely flight capital, and in 1965 was estimated at about 900 million escudos (then, one dollar was worth 4.5 escudos). Following the election of Allende, there was a panic among stock-holders and there resulted much flight of capital. As Allende proceeds to nationalize the copper mines and other large business firms, as well as the banks, the Bolsa de Santiago is likely to close in the near future.

O. Cooperatives. By comparison with Scandinavian countries, Chile's cooperative organization is still in the formative stage. Yet the government of President Allende has promised to break up the latifundia and the minifundia and to establish cooperatives that will affect the lives of more than 100,000 farmers who thus far have had little influence on agricultural policies. Under Eduardo Frei Montalva's administration, the dairy and grape growers' and wine-makers' cooperatives were very successful. Today the leading dairy cooperatives are the Cooperativa Agrícola Lechera del Norte, the Cooperativa Agrícola Lechera de los Andes, and the Cooperativa de Productores de Leche de Aconcagua. Recently, several grocery cooperatives were established in the Santiago area in order to reduce the cost of food. There have also been cooperatives to regulate the marketing of grain products, sheep raising, poultry farms, and fishing.

P. Taxes. Laws of 1962 and 1963 broadened the tax base, and provided for conversion to a single progressive income tax. Chile's tax administration, already among the most efficient in Latin America, is rapidly becoming more strict. Income tax evasion is now punished as a crime, whereas in recent years about 40% of those who should have paid taxes did not do so and got away with it. Income taxes bring in about 30% of government revenue, sales taxes about 30%, and import and export taxes the remaining 40%. In the decade of the 1960's, the base income tax for unincorporated copper firms was 22.5% and 19.5% for

incorporated copper firms. Foreign-owned copper
firms paid a 50% tax on basic production plus a surtax
of 25% which was progressively reduced as the firm
increased its production. The non-mining corporate
income tax was 23.4%.

There is a progressive personal income tax of 8%
to a maximum of 50%. Minimum property taxes are
about 1.5% of assessed valuation. Inheritance and gift
taxes are scaled progressively up to 50%. There is a
base sales tax of 6%, and a 10% tax on luxury goods
such as cigars, cigarettes, grain alcohol, beer, matches,
and wine. There is also a tax on electric power consumption, rail fares, telegraph messages, pharmaceuticals, and gasoline. Most legal documents require
government tax stamps. A special tax of 200% by
value is levied on all motor vehicles. This tax is ap-
plied whether the vehicles are imported or assembled
and manufactured in Chile.

Q. Internal Trade. United Nation's data, using
1958 as the base year and 100 as the base figure, give
the following indications of the magnitude of internal
trade in Chile: 1959, 145; 1960, 170; 1961, 205; 1962,
258; 1963, 380; 1964, 575; 1965, 724; 1966, 847; 1967,
1,032; 1968, 1,320. These yearly increases, however,
reflect the run-away inflation that has been endemic in
Chile during the last decades. The principal production
center for commerce, finance, and industry is the
Santiago-Valparaíso area. Owing to Chile's great length,
coastal shipping plays an important role in Chile's internal trade. Valparaíso is the port for the Santiago
area. The central manufacturing region reaches northern markets through Antofagasta and souther markets
through Concepción, which itself is a growing center
for manufacturing.

Principal cities have both refrigerated and unrefrig-
erated storage warehouses, as do the leading ports.
Typically, the small entrepreneur sells specialized
goods in a small retail store. There are only a few
chain stores, mostly in the grocery business. While
production and consumption of processed and packaged
foods is increasing, most staples are still purchased
from bulk supplies. There is little credit buying in
Chile. In urban areas, business advertising is done
through billboards, radio, television, and in movie
houses. Magazines and newspapers also play an important role in advertising.

R.   Planning.   Chile was one of the first nations in
Latin America to establish a National Economic Development Plan.   The government agency responsible was
the Corporación de Fomento de la Producción* (CORFO).
CORFO was established in 1939 to spearhead the government's economic planning efforts.   The ten-year
plan proposed by CORFO in 1960 was reviewed by experts of the International Bank for Reconstruction and
Development (IBRD) and the Agency for International
Development (AID).   It was found to be a feasible plan,
calling for the attainment of an annual average increase
of 5.5% in the GNP, and for total investment of nearly
$10 billion from 1961 to 1970.   The plan was success-
ful in its first three years, and growth in the GNP exceeded the goal by 2%.   Consumption of goods and services rose 5% above the goal, but total investment fell
short of the goal by 4%.

For the remainder of the decade, achievement under
the plan was uneven.   While mining, construction, and
services exceeded the goals by more than 18% each,
agriculture fell 11% below the goal, and industry 32%.
Local and regional planning were assisted by the activities of the Central Planning Bureau, the Economic
Planning Center of the University of Chile, and the
Chilean Society for Planning and Development.   In 1970,
President Allende not merely proposed a new Economic
Plan, but stated that "the economic policy of the Unidad
Popular Government, in its fundamental approach, aims
substantially at the replacement of the present economic
structure with another one, which will allow the reali-
zation of a socialist and pluralistic society to begin."

He further stated that "to attain this aim, the government will promptly start to develop the three major
areas of ownership: state, mixed, and private."   By
that, he meant that the state area will be made up by
the existing state enterprises plus the one that will be
set up in the future, especially in the economic sectors that deal with basic natural resources, large domestic and foreign monopolies, banking, foreign commerce, and the fields that have strategic importance
to the nation's development.   The mixed area will be
made up of companies which combine private and state
capital, and which are to be administered and managed
jointly.   The private area will consist of existing companies set up as stock corporations, partnership, and
institutions having commercial or industrial private
ownership.

ECONOMY, THE.   The External Economy.
    A.   Foreign Trade.   Approximately one-seventh of
Chile's gross national product is exported, and import
and export taxes account for about one-third of the
state's tax revenue.   Historically, Chile has been an
exporter of minerals, and copper and its by-products
account for almost 70% of the foreign exchange.   Im-
port-Export relationship since 1964 is shown in the
following table, in million of dollars:

	1964	1965	1966	1967	1968	1969	1970
Imports	608	604	757	868	835	934	1,020
Exports	625	688	881	913	911	1,129	1,143

    In 1970, Chile's major exports were: copper and
its by-products, 68%; iron ore and other metals, 13%;
cellulose paper, fishmeal, cattle and agricultural products, 10%; saltpeter, iodine, and sodium nitrate, 6%;
and other industrial products, 3%.   Chile's major imports were capital goods (machinery and transport
equipment mainly for copper production), 44%; consumer goods, 28%; semi-processed goods (chemicals,
raw cotton, crude petroleum, railroad equipment), 28%.
The principal nations receiving Chile's exports in 1970
were: United States, 34%; United Kingdom, 14%; West
Germany, 11%; the Netherlands, 7%; and, Japan, 7%.
The principal suppliers of Chilean imports for the same
year were: United States, 35%; West Germany, 12%;
Argentina, 8%; United Kingdom, 7%; France 5%; and,
Japan, 4%.
    Marxist President Salvador Allende Gossens stated
that "the foreign trade policy of the popular government
must be considered as a part of the national development plan and most particularly within the context of
the general foreign policy of the nation."   And he
pledged to strengthen economic relations with all countries of the world, regardless of their international
system, the only limitation being that the national interests of Chile must be served and that the development must be in agreement with Chile's international
policy.   President Allende had in mind particularly
Cuba, Red China, and the countries of the Eastern
European block.
    B.   Balance of Payments.   Chile's balance of pay-
ments has shown favorable tendencies during the last
three years.   The compensating balances for the period
1964-1970 show the following results, in millions of

dollars:

1964	1965	1966	1967	1968	1969	1970
+ 9	+ 6	+ 10	-49	+ 134	+ 182	+ 120

Part of this result is due to the development of exports
during the last three years.   There has been a favorable situation in the price of copper; and new products
have entered the international market.   Outside of copper exports, however, the gains have been modest.   In
the 1968-70 period, exports reached an average of US$
1, 061 millions.   This figure compares with that of the
period 1960-64 of $507. 6 millions.

Chile's largest balance of payments deficit is with
Argentina, from whom the country imports large
amounts of live animals and cereals and exports relatively little.   Chile's position as a supplier of raw materials is not an advantageous one.   If the price of copper drops on the international market there is likely
to be a balance of payments deficit.   Moreover, the
country must sell its natural resources at a modest
profit, but purchase the finished goods necessary for
its industrialization at a high cost.   In the past, and
as recently as 1967, Chile has been aided to minimize
balance of payments deficits by the Agency for International Development (AID), the Inter-American Development Bank (IDB), the Export-Import Bank (Eximbank),
and the International Monetary Fund (IMF).   Whether
these credit agencies will continue to support Chile's
Marxist government in the future remains to be seen.

C.   Customs and Duties.   Chile is a signer of the
Treaty of Montevideo, which established the Latin
American Free Trade Association (LAFTA).   This
agreement was ratified on May 2, 1961.   By the treaty
provisions, the member nations mutually provide
"favored treatment."   Other member nations include
Argentina, Brazil, Colombia, Ecuador, Mexico, Paraguay, and Uruguay.   Chile has bilateral trade treaties
with ten European countries: Austria, Denmark, Fin-
land, West Germany, Norway, Portugal, Spain, Sweden,
Switzerland, and Yugoslavia, and is expected to formulate other treaties with East European countries.   Chile
has also bilateral trade agreements with ten American
countries: Argentina, Bolivia, Brazil, Canada, Colombia, Cuba, Ecuador, Mexico, Peru, and the United
States.   A bilateral trade treaty with Cuba was signed
just recently, at the end of 1970.   Since the early

1930's, Chile's trade policy has been restrictive and protectionist. Originally, restrictive trade policies resulted from fluctuations in the prices of nitrates.

Current goals of the government are to end, or at least minimize, the balance of payments deficits, conserve foreign exchange, and provide a major source of revenue. Favorable treatment is given to essential imports, while luxury goods, and goods that compete with the domestic industry are taxed heavily. The most basic import duty is based upon weight and volume. An additional charge is based upon the value of the commodity and its necessity. Essential imports are only taxed 3% by value; general merchandise is subject to a charge of 30% by value; and, luxury goods are taxed at a minimum rate of 62% by value. Besides these import duties, a law of April 1959 established an additional charge of up to 200% of the commodity value, according to the need for the product. Exemptions from this form of import duty include certain imports of the large copper companies, Chilean Airlines (LAN*), the University of Chile, imports from the LAFTA countries, and goods entering through duty-free ports.

Arica*, Punta Arenas*, and Chiloé* were exempted from import duties and most import taxes in 1956, and were declared free ports. These cities were not exempted from paying import duties on luxury goods. Payment of import duties on machinery, industrial products, and other specified capital goods may be deferred, with prior approval of the Central Bank (Banco Central). All but minimal charges are to be paid on antibiotics, drugs, catgut, farm machinery, highway machinery, sugar, fresh pineapples, surgical sutures, lubricants, combustibles, books, and magazines. Most goods may be freely exported from Chile, although many agricultural and animal products are limited by export quotas, in order to supply the country with its domestic needs. With the exception of the copper, iron and nitrate firms, export earnings must be deposited in an authorized bank within ten days of receipt.

D. Foreign Investments. Foreign investments in Chile have come mainly from the United Kingdom and the United States. In 1970, foreign investments in the country totalled approximately $1.0 billion. British investments, which reached a peak of $410 million in 1940, have since declined to about a fourth that number. U.S. investments, on the other hand, have in-

creased to almost $1.0 billion, largely in the copper
and nitrate industries.   Two U.S. copper firms, Anaconda* and Kennecott*, produced 90% of Chile's copper
until 1965.   The nationalization of the copper mines,
pledged by President Allende as he was sworn into office in November, 1970, will inevitably result in a
drastic cut in U.S. investments in Chile.   Foreign investors have been subjected to the same legal conditions as domestic investors.

Today, any firm wishing to invest in Chile must obtain clearance from the office of the President of Chile
through the Committee on Foreign Investment of the
Ministry of the Economy.   Arrangements with individual
companies specify what privileges and encouragements
to invest will be accorded.   In establishing plants for
the processing of Chilean raw materials, foreign investors may bring in capital equipment free of customs and
duties.   The government guarantees the applicable taxes
will not be collected discriminately to the exclusive det-
riment of the foreign firm.   Taxes may, of course, be
increased for all foreign and domestic producers of
given products.   Depreciation allowances are provided,
and the government may grant the right to re-export
capital.   Profits and interest on investment may be
remitted to other nations.

E.   Foreign Aid.   Loans and grants to Chile under
the Alliance for Progress reached a total of $350 mil-
lion as of June, 1964.   While it is difficult to distin-
guish accurately the uses to which all funds were ap-
plied, at least the following amounts were authorized
in the areas indicated:

Education	US$ 5,300,000
Homes	9,000,000
Business and Industry	46,000,000
Sanitation, Potable Water	11,000,000
Agriculture	17,000,000
Infrastructure	87,000,000
Currency Stabilization	120,000,000

International agencies which have been active in
Chile include the Agency for International Development
(AID), the Inter-American Development Bank (IDB), the
Export-Import Bank of Washington (Eximbank), and the
Development Loan Fund (DLF).   Important recent projects
of the AID include the building of 23 primary schools, fi-
nancing health clinics, and building port facilities at San

Vicente.   IDB projects include loans to farm credit,
irrigation projects, low-income housing, college facilities, city water supplies improvement, and equipment
for a new refinery at Concepción.

Eximbank loans provided for steel mill equipment at
Huachipato*, and machinery for industrial development.
The DLF loan projects include a savings bank system,
and the new city airport at Pudahuel, in Santiago.
These agencies have also subscribed numerous infrastructural projects.   In 1961, Chile was among the
first nations in Latin America to request Peace Corps
volunteers.   Peace Corps projects have dealt with
rural education and urban and town planning.   For the
decade 1960-1970, Chile has received two-thirds of all
U.S. development assistance.   U.S. assistance to Chile
has been reduced drastically with the advent of the first
elected Marxist government in the Western Hemisphere.

F. Tourism.   The capital city, Santiago*, was
founded in 1541 by Pedro de Valdivia*.   Of interest to
the tourist are: La Moneda*, the Presidential Palace,
built by the Spaniards in the 17th century; the church
of San Francisco*, a 16th century structure and the
oldest church in Chile; the Cathedral*, originally a
colonial building now located at the Plaza de Armas;
the National Museum of Fine Arts*, located in the
Parque Forestal, the oldest museum of painting in
South America; the Historic Museum, with a good collection of pre-historic ceramics and colonial furniture;
the Museum of Contemporary Art, exhibiting the works
of Contemporary Chilean painters; the Santa Lucía Hill*,
a park centrally located with a colonial fortress at the
summit, now turned into a museum; and the San Cristóbal Hill*, at the top of which there is a statue of the
Virgin.

The main street, the Alameda, is 108 yards wide,
and is ornamented with historic statues of San Martín*
and O'Higgins*.   A one-day tour from Santiago* to the
port of Valparaíso*, 90 miles away, gives the tourist
the opportunity to see small towns and farms typical
of rural Chile.   The trip over the coastal range provides great views of Chilean beaches with the snow-
capped Andes mountains in the background.   A five-
minute drive from Valparaíso to Viña del Mar* is well
worth taking. Viña del Mar has been called the South
American Riviera, with lovely homes, quaint fishing
boats, and luxurious hotels and casinos.   Portillo*,
Farellones*, and other spots in the Chilean Andes are

becoming popular ski resorts.   There are fine beaches
in the northern cities of Iquique* and Antofagasta*, also
noted for their fine deep-sea fishing.

Very popular is the Chilean lake region in the south,
often compared to the lake regions of Switzerland and
northern Italy.   A five-day trip from Santiago to Buenos
Aires by way of the Lake region is a most rewarding
experience.   Most hotels in the capital make tour arrangements and offer excursions to Valparaíso, Viña
del Mar, the ski resorts, and the Lake region.   Good
roads and rail facilities extend nearly the length of the
country.   Interesting to visit are Arica*, the northern-
most Chilean city, Puerto Montt*, a city south of the
Lake region with mostly a German population, and Punta Arenas*, the southernmost city in the world, in
Tierra del Fuego*.   In 1970, there were some 76,000
tourists entering Chile, an increase of 10,000 over a
decade ago.

EDUCACION PUBLICA, MINISTERIO DE.   The Ministry of
Public Education was created by statute No. 7912 on
November 30, 1927.   The new ministry changed its
name from Public Instruction to Public Education.   Its
functions were to perform the supervision of the state's
education and to create and maintain primary educational services, and special and professional establishments
such as museums, libraries, archives, astronomical
observatories, etc.   The historical antecedents of the
ministry go back to 1837, when the Ministry of Justice,
Religion and Public Instruction (Ministerio de Justicia,
Culto e Instrucción Pública*) was created.   In 1887, the
branch dealing with Religion was incorporated in the
Ministry of Foreign Affairs, and in 1889, the Ministry
of Justice was separated from that of Public Instruction; it is from the latter that the present Ministry derives.   The following autonomous institutions are incorporated in the Ministry of Public Education and are
under the authority of the President of the Republic:
The University of Chile; The Technical University in
Santiago; the Board of Scholarships and Fellowships;
and the Educational Society of Chile.   Among its many
functions, the Ministry is responsible for the censorship of cinema.   Also see the following entry.

EDUCATION.   The Chilean educational system is based on
the French model.   Primary education is given through
the first six grades; it is compulsory and free.   Second-

ary education, given through grade 12, is divided into
two groups: one, to further education and prepare students to enter the universities; the other, to technically
prepare students to enter a trade.   In 1971, there were
11 universities in Chile, two state institutions and nine
private.   The state universities were the Universidad
Técnica del Estado, in Santiago, and the Universidad
Técnica del Estado, in Antofagasta.   The nine private
universities were: the Universidad de Chile, and the
Universidad Católica de Chile, in Santiago; the Universidad de Chile, the Universidad Católica, and the Universidad Técnica Federico Santamaría, in Valparaíso;
the Universidad del Norte, and the Universidad de
Chile, in Antofagasta; the Universidad de Concepción,
in Concepción; and, the Universidad Austral, in Valdivia.

Chile has a literacy rate of more than 80%, one of
the highest in Latin America.   Out of every 1, 000
persons that enter the primary schools, 115 go on to
secondary schools and 59 to vocational training schools;
16 enter the universities.   In 1970, there were 59, 000
teachers for the approximately two million primary and
secondary school students.   In the same year, about
56, 500 students were enrolled in the 11 universities.
This distribution clearly indicates that there is a lack
of primary and secondary school teachers, and that the
school system does little to promote social mobility.
University students, on the average, come from the
wealthy class or from middle class families.   Very few
students from the lower strata of society reach the university system.   Like elsewhere in Latin America,
Chilean students are active politically (see FECH and
UFUCH).

EGAÑA FABRES, MARIANO, 1793-1846.   Lawyer by profession and active in politics since the establishment of
the Chilean Republic.   In 1813, he was Secretary of
the Interior in the junta government of José Miguel
Carrera Verdugo*, and a year later, after the defeat
of the Chilean patriots at Rancagua*, he was exiled by
the Spaniards to the island of Juan Fernández*.   After
the Chilean victory at the battle of Chacabuco* in 1817,
he returned to Chile, and occupied various high offices
in government: mayor of the police department of Santiago; member of the Tribunal of Justice; Secretary of
Economy; collector of revenues.   In 1823, he was appointed Secretary of the junta government, and in 1824

he was sent to London as Chilean plenipotentiary minister.

Egaña Fabres was attorney general of the Supreme Court of Justice in 1830, and in the same year he was Minister of the Interior and later of Foreign Affairs. He was on the editorial staff that drafted the Constitution of 1833*, and in 1834 he was elected senator. Two years later, he was sent to Peru as plenipotentiary minister of Chile, returning to Chile after a few months to assume the post of Minister of Justice. In 1840, he returned to Peru as plenipotentiary minister. Three years later, he was named Vice-President of the Senate and received the honorary title of Official of the Legion of Honor of the Republic, for his many services rendered to his country.

EGAÑA RISCO, JUAN, 1769-1836.   Bachelor of canons and laws, lawyer, and professor of Latin and rhetoric at the University of San Felipe.   Active in the struggle for independence, he took part in the first junta government of 1811 (Junta de Gobierno de 1811*).   He was a deputy to the first National Congress, and with Camilo Henrique*, he edited a newspaper, La Aurora de Chile*. After the battle of Rancagua*, in 1814, he was persecuted by the royalists (Realista*), and exiled to the island of Juan Fernández*.   He returned to Chile after the battle of Chacabuco*, in 1819, and became a member of the Municipal Council of Santiago.   After the fall from power of Bernardo O'Higgins*, he participated in drafting a constitutional ordinance.   In 1823, he was named plenipotentiary representative from the province of Santiago*, meeting with the representatives from Concepción* and Coquimbo* to reconstitute the Republic.   Politically, he belonged to the Federalist Party (Partido Federalista*), and was elected senator in 1824, and deputy in 1825.   In 1827, he was President of the Provincial Assembly of Santiago.   When he died, he left behind many literary works, covering a multitude of subjects.

EJERCITO DE LOS ANDES.   The Army of the Andes was organized by José de San Martín* in 1817 to fight for the liberation of Chile.   Assembling his forces in western Argentina for the final blow against the Spaniards, and choosing Bernardo O'Higgins* instead of José Miguel Carrera Verdugo* as his second-in-command, San Martín made the historic cross over the Andes and de-

feated the Spaniards at Chacabuco* (1817) and Maipú*
(1818). With the help of the Army of the Andes, Chile
was able to formally declare itself independent of Spain
in 1818.

ELQUI. A fertile valley north of Santiago* and east of La
Serena*. The town of Vicuña, where Gabriela Mistral*
was born, is located in this valley.

EMPLEADO. White collar employee.

EMPLOYMENT see THE ECONOMY: Internal: I. Manpower and Employment.

EMPREMAR. (Empresa Marítima) Port Authority.

EMPRESA. The State Railways, officially known as Ferrocarriles del Estado, and frequently abbreviated F. F. E.
E., but commonly referred to as the Empresa.

ENAMI. State Mining Enterprise (Empresa Nacional de
Minería).

ENAP. (Empresa Nacional de Petróleo). State oil monopoly.

ENCOMENDERO see ENCOMIENDA.

ENCOMIENDA. A system of forced labor whereby a group
of Indians was "commended" to a Spanish overlord for
meritorious services. The overlord supposedly was to
be the material and spiritual guardian of the Indians,
and he was to collect tributes from them for providing
this protection. Since most of the time the Indians
could not afford to pay the royal tithe, this obligation
was transmitted into service. Encountering a stubborn
resistance to work on the part of the Indians, the encomendero often turned from guardian to torturer, re-
sorting to violence. Like the Repartimiento*, the encomienda system failed in Chile because the Araucanians* for over 300 years refused to be subjugated by
the Conquistadors*.

ENDESA. Acronym for Empresa Nacional de Electricidad,
S. A., or National Electricity Co., Inc. The gigantic
electrification program undertaken by ENDESA has remained entirely under state control, very much like
the U. S. Tennessee Valley Authority. ENDESA is a

subsidiary of the Chilean Development Corporation
(CORFO*).

ENERGY AND POWER see THE ECONOMY: Internal: K.
Energy and Power.

ENRIQUEZ FIODDEN, HUMBERTO, 1907- . Lawyer by
profession and active member of the Radical Party
(Partido Radical*). Professor of political economics
and public finances at the University of Concepción*,
and professor of political economics at the Law School
of the University of Chile*. In 1946, he was Minister
of Education in the administration (1946-52) of Gabriel
González Videla*. He held elective office from 1949
to 1961, as a deputy to Congress, and from 1961 to
1969 as a senator. In 1965, he was president of the
Radical Party.

ENRIQUEZ FIODDEN, INES. Lawyer by profession, and the
first woman to be elected (1951) to the Chilean Congress as a deputy. During her studies at the University of Concepción*, she was elected president of the
Women's Association. Active in the Radical Party
(Partido Radical*), she became president of the Femi-
nine Organization of the party. Her term in congress
expired in 1969.

ERCILLA see THE PRESS.

ERCILLA Y ZUÑIGA, ALONSO DE, 1533-1594. A career
military officer, poet, and diplomat, Ercilla y Zúñiga
is renowned for his epic poem La Araucana* and for
his participation in the Spanish wars against the Araucanian Indians of Chile. Coming from a noble Spanish
family, Ercilla y Zúñiga was able to obtain a good university education and to travel widely in Europe. He
was in England on the occasion of Prince Philip's marriage to Queen Mary, daughter of Edward VI, when he
heard of the civil wars in Peru and Chile. In London,
he met Jerónimo de Alderete, who was embarking for
the New World. The young poet decided to go along
and in 1557 joined García Hurtado de Mendoza* on an
expedition to Chile against the Araucanians. It was in
the course of the war that Ercilla y Zúñiga wrote the
first and second parts of the Araucana.
    At first, he was a friend of Hurtado de Mendoza.
They were both young and had known each other in

Spain. Soon, however, their relationship deteriorated, and when Ercilla y Zúñiga drew his sword to duel in the presence of his superior, Hurtado de Mendoza, he was sentenced to death for his act of disrespect and insubordination. The sentence was later commuted. Ercilla y Zúñiga was exiled from Chile and on his return trip to Europe he married doña María de Barzán (1570) from Panama. It was in Spain that Ercilla y Zúñiga was able to complete and publish La Araucana (1590) perhaps the greatest epic poem in Spanish. In 1594 the poet-warrior died in Madrid.

ERRAZURIZ ALDUNATE, FERNANDO, 1777-1841. Councilman at the cabildo* of 1810, and deputy to the first National Congress (Congreso Nacional*) of 1811. He actively participated in the struggle for Chilean independence and suffered persecution after the battle of Rancagua*, in 1814. In 1823, he was a member of the junta that succeeded Bernardo O'Higgins. He was also a member of the convention of 1822 and for many years a senator. In 1824, he became President of the Senate, and for the next two years acted as President of the Provincial Assembly of Santiago. He served three different times as President ad interim of the Republic: in 1824, when Supreme Director (1823-27) Ramón Freire Serrano* absented himself from the capital; in 1831, when as Vice-President he succeeded President (1830-31) José Tomás Ovalle* who had just died; and, again in 1831, when President (1831-41) Joaquín Prieto Vial* left the capital to undertake an armed campaign to secure his power as ruler of Chile. It was a period of civil strife and Freire Serrano was attempting a return from exile to assume the Presidency once again. Those supporting him were arrested and Errázuriz Aldunate demanded that the prisoners be tried by a military court. As acting President of Chile, Errázuriz Aldunate was responsible for initiating the drafting of a new constitution (Constitution of 1833*). During that period, international relations were established with France, and Chile's independence was recognized by England.

ERRAZURIZ ECHAURREN, FEDERICO, 1850-1901. Lawyer by profession, and President (1896-1901) of Chile. He began his political career as a deputy in 1876, and in 1890 he became Minister of the Navy and of War. During this time, Chile was experiencing a period of political instability, and cabinets were formed and dissolved in matter of months or sometimes weeks. Errázuriz Echaurren became involved in the Civil War of 1891 (Guerra Civil de 1891*), and opposed the government (1886-91) of José Manuel Balmaceda Fernández*. In 1894, Errázuriz Echaurren was elected senator, and two years later, backed by a Conservative-Liberal-National coalition, he was elected President of Chile. A surprising contrast to the ministerial instability during this time was the relatively peaceful and normal succession of presidents. Errázuriz Echaurren gave amnesty to many balmacedistas*, and allowed the followers of the overthrown President to form part of his cabinet. During his administration, Errázuriz Echaurren promoted education, established a nursing school, and various commercial and technical institutes. He undertook many public works, and was responsible for increasing the streetcar service in Santiago. In 1901, Errázuriz Echaurren resigned as President, and died a few months later.

ERRAZURIZ ERRAZURIZ, ISIDORO, 1835-1898. Lawyer, newspaperman and writer. In 1858, he was imprisoned when he tried to reform the Constitution of 1833*. He was exiled to Argentina, and later allowed to return to Chile with a pardon in 1861. Member of the newspaper staff of El Mercurio*, he founded his own paper, La Patria, which was published until 1896. Active in politics, he was elected deputy in 1870, 1882, and 1891. He also took part in the War of the Pacific (Guerra del Pacífico*) in 1881. In the Civil War of 1891 (Guerra Civil de 1891*), he sided with the rebellious Congress against President (1886-91) José Manuel Balmaceda Fernández*. Two years before, he had founded the political coalition known as the Cuadrilatero*. With the defeat of President Balmaceda Fernández, he was named temporary Minister of the Interior (1891). In 1893, he was named Minister of the Navy and of War. Three years later, he became Chilean plenipotentiary minister to Brazil.

ERRAZURIZ ZAÑARTU, FEDERICO, 1825-1877. Descendent of one of the most aristocratic families in Santiago, Errázuriz Zañartu was a very active member of the Liberal Party (Partido Liberal*) and became President of Chile, for a five-year term, in 1871. Lawyer by profession, he was persecuted politically during the

government (1851-61) of conservative Manuel Montt
Torres*. He participated in an attempt to prevent
Montt Torres from taking office and, as a result, was
exiled to Peru. By 1861, Errázuriz Zañartu had returned to Chile and was elected deputy to Congress.
From 1865 to 1868 he was Subrogate Minister of the
Navy and War, and in 1867 he was elected senator--an
office he maintained until he became President. His
term in office was marked by public reforms: he extended the railways, expanded the universities, beautified the streets and boulevards of the capital, and made
the Cerro Santa Lucía* a national park. Errázuriz
Zañartu was the first Chilean President to have one
term of office. He amended the Constitution of 1833*
to prevent Presidential re-elections and thus secure
that the ruling party would not turn the presidency into
a dictatorship.

During his government, there were fervid religious
struggles, regarding the abolition of clerical privileges,
the separation of Church and State, the elimination of
ecclesiastical courts of law, and the burial of non-
Catholics in the cemeteries. All of these questions
proved to be a dividing factor between liberals and conservatives. The liberals, not able to push for a separation of Church and State, won some of the points:
priests were liable in civil courts, and the cemeteries
sectioned off parcels of land for non-Catholic burials.
In the last year of his administration, Errázuriz
Zañartu's economic policies experienced an inflationary
crisis. The beautifying of Santiago, under the direction of Benjamín Vicuña Mackenna*, cost the government quite a bit of money. It was the price to trans-
form the city from a provincial center into a modern
metropolis. At the end of his term, Errázuriz Zañartu threw his support to Aníbal Pinto Garmendía*, who
was elected as the next President (1876-81) of Chile.

ESCUDO [E°]. The official Chilean monetary unit. One
escudo is the equivalent of 1, 000 pesos. The escudo
was introduced in 1960, when Chile devalued its monetary unit, the peso. At that time, the escudo was on
the par with the U. S. dollar. By 1970, however, there
were 14. 3 escudos to the dollar on the official exchange.
After the elections of Marxist President (1970-76) Salvador Allende Gossens*, the escudo dropped as low as
55 to the dollar on the Santiago black market. In February, 1970, there were 6, 526 million escudos in Chile.

ESCUELA MILITAR.   The Chilean military academy.   Located in Santiago, the school trains cadets to become
officers in the army.   It corresponds to the U.S. West
Point.   Every year, a selected group of cadets is sent
to the United States to learn more advanced military
tactics.

ESCUELA NORMAL.   The first "normal school," or School
of Education in Latin America was inaugurated in Chile
on June 14, 1842, two years after the first school of
education was founded in the United States.   Its main
function is to train young men and women to become
teachers in the elementary and secondary schools.   The
noted Argentine writer and statesman Domingo Faustino
Sarmiento* became its first director.

ESTADO, MINISTERIO DEL.   The Ministry of State was
created in 1818 by the Constitution of the same year
(Constitution of 1818*).   It replaced the Secretariat of
the Government, and its main functions were to keep
a record of all governmental affairs.   In 1822, the
Ministry of State was renamed Ministry of the Government, also incorporating the Department of Foreign
Affairs, thus becoming the Ministry of Government and
of Foreign Affairs (Ministerio de Gobierno y Relaciones Exteriores*).

ESTANCO.   A government store for monopolized goods.
Established in Chile during the government (1823-26)
of Ramón Freire Serrano* to alleviate the precarious
economic situation of the country following the armed
struggle for independence.   Tobacco, cards, tea, and
liquors were some of the goods sold in the store, and
the store-keeper had to receive a concession from the
government to operate the enterprise.   The first con-
cessionary was Diego Portales Palazuelos*, who became a leading political figure in Chile for the next
35 years as the strong man in the Conservative Party
(Partido Conservador*).   A political group known as
the estanqueros* was formed around the figure of
Portales Palazuelos.   Their doctrine was to maintain
a strong centralized government.

ESTANQUEROS.   Literally the term refers to store-keepers
who in 1824 were given a government concession to
sell monopolized goods, such as tobacco, tea, and
liquors (Estanco*).   In 1824, the meaning of the term

was extended to political supporters of Diego Portales
Palazuelos*, whose objective was to establish a strong
centralized government which would prevent anarchy
and preserve law and order.   Since most of the adherents of this group had associations with the Estanco,
they became known as the estanqueros.   The group was
never formally constituted in a political party.

ESTATUTOS DE GARANTIAS CONSTITUCIONALES.   The
Statute of Constitutional Guarantees was sent to both
houses of Congress after the presidential elections of
September 4, 1970 showed that none of the three candidates had received a majority.   Socialist Salvador
Allende Gossens* had topped Conservative Jorge Alessandri Rodríguez* and Christian Democrat Rodomiro
Tomic Romero*.   Allende had received 36% of the vote
to Alessandri's 35% and Tomic's 28%.   In exchange for
congressional confirmation, the Christian Democrats,
whose votes Allende needed to become President, demanded that Allende sign the Estatuto de Garantías
Constitucionales after its approval by both houses of
Congress.   The document was a political amendment
to the Constitution of 1925*, which provided for the
following: freedom of all political parties to operate
within the Chilean system of government; freedom of the
press; the right to assemble; freedom in education; no
censorship of the mail; and professionalization of the
armed forces and the police.   Allende signed the amendment and was declared President of Chile by a vote of
153 to 36.   He only opposed one clause, which stated
that the Chilean armed forces would take power to see
that the amendment was observed to the letter.   The
clause was dropped.

ESTRELLA, LA   see THE PRESS.

EXALTADO.   The radicals, or exaltados, were a political
group which was organized with the first National Congress (Congreso Nacional*) in 1811.   Their aims were
to end the absolute colonial rule of Spain, and to establish a federalist republic.   Politically, they sided
with Liberalism, and were in a minority within the
government (1812-13) of José Miguel Carrera Verdugo*.
Among the most notable members of this group we find
Bernardo O'Higgins*, Juan Martínez de Rozas*, and
Manuel Salas*.   When the first junta government was
established, the exaltados* only counted 12 deputies.

In their exasperation for fear of being excluded from
the junta, they were driven into an extreme federalist
and even separatist agitation which provoked all sorts
of disturbances in the provinces and almost threw them
into a state of anarchy. In the first National Congress,
the moderates were in the majority (Moderado*), and
the exaltados were defeated in their goals to rouse the
south to rebellion. José Miguel Carrera Verdugo*, who
assumed the directorship of the nation in 1812, did so
with the help of the exaltados who rallied around his
figure when they saw a possible leader. It seems that
what Joaquín Nabuco said about the exaltados in Brazil
also applies to the exaltados in Chile: "It is impossible
to achieve a revolution without the radicals, and it is
impossible to govern with them." The exaltados should
not be confused with members of the Radical Party
(Partido Radical*), which was organized in 1857.

EXECUTIVE, THE see CHILE: GOVERNMENT.

EYZAGUIRRE ARECHEVALA, AGUSTIN, 1768-1837. Active
in the revolutionary struggle for Chilean independence.
He was deputy to Congress in 1811 and in 1825, as a
"moderate" (Moderado*). In 1814, he formed part of
the governing junta in favor of sovereignty. In 1818
he was elected a senator, and from 1823 to 1824 he
became President of the Senate. In 1823, once again
he formed part of the governing junta. When President (1826) Manuel Blanco Encalada* resigned, Eyzaguirre Arechevala became provisional President of
Chile, a post he filled until 1827. His government
had all sorts of difficulties, especially with the rebellious provinces in the south. In finances, there was
total chaos and there was no money in the treasury.
Faced with a bankrupt government, Eyzaguirre Arechevala tried to sell church-owned properties but his plan
failed. Soldiers were not paid nor deputies received
their salaries. This caused trouble with the army as
well as with the politicians. In 1827, after a troubled
year in office, Eyzaguirre Arechevala was deposed and
congress named Ramón Freire Serrano* as President.

-F-

FALANGE CONSERVATIVA. A political organization formed
to mobilize conservative youth. It became a political

party in 1938, known as the Falange Nacional*. In the
Presidential elections of that year, it backed conservative candidate Gustavo Ross Santa María, who lost.

FALANGE NACIONAL. A political party created in 1938
    and dissolved in 1957. It originated as a conservative
    party inspired in the papal encyclicals Rerum Novarum
    and Quadrogesimo Anno. The political antecedent of
    the Falange Nacional was the Falange Conservativa*.
    In the Presidential elections of 1938, it supported Gus-
    tavo Ross Santa María. In the parliamentary elections
    of 1941, the Falange elected three deputies; in those
    of 1945 it elected four; in those of 1949 it elected
    three deputies and a senator; and, in 1957, it elected
    14 deputies and one senator. In 1957, the Falange
    Nacional was dissolved to form the new Christian Demo-
    cratic Party (Partido Demócrata Cristiano*).

FALANGE RADICAL AGRARIA SOCIALISTA. Political com-
    bination organized in 1948 with the Falange Nacional*,
    the Agrarian Labor Party and the Radical Democrats.
    Its main purpose was to oppose the government (1946-
    52) of Gabriel González Videla*, who had been elected
    with the help of the Communists. In 1949, it was dis-
    solved into the various parties that formed it originally.

FARELLONES. A ski resort just outside of Santiago*.

FECH. Acronym for Federación de Estudiantes de Chile.
    The older of the two leading student organizations in
    Chile (the other is UFUCh*), FECH was founded in
    1906 as a protest movement. Its primary function was
    to unite local groups within the University of Chile. Its
    members today include both undergraduates and grad-
    uate students in the various professional schools. Since
    1962, FECH has been largely dominated by young mem-
    bers of the Christian Democratic Party (Partido Demó-
    crata Cristiano*). With the recent election of Socialist
    President Allende it is expected that student members
    of the far leftist coalition Unidad Popular* will control
    FECH during the next six years.

FEDERACION DE ESTUDIANTES DE CHILE see FECH.

FEDERACION DE IZQUIERDA. A political combination of
    several leftist groups formed in 1932 after the fall of
    President (1927-31) Carlos Ibáñez del Campo*. It got

its support mainly from the Liberal Democratic Party
(Partido Liberal Democrático*), and the Socialist Republican Party (Partido Socialista Republicano*).   The
Party elected as its spokesman Arturo Alessandri
Palma*, who later renounced.   His renunciation marked
the end of the coalition and the party dissolved after only one month of existence.

FEDERACION NACIONAL POPULAR.   A political coalition
of various minor parties of the Right and the Center,
founded in 1956 and dissolved after a few months.   Its
doctrinary principles were to withdraw from the class
struggle advocated by the Left and follow a middle-of-
the-road course.

FEDERACION OBRERA DE CHILE (FOCH).   A workers' union formed in 1909 by Luis Emilio Recabarren Serrano*
to represent the interest of the railroad employees.   In
1916, the union broadened its base to represent the interests of the entire Chilean working class.   In 1921,
the union adhered to the principles of the Communist
International Syndicate of Workers, which aimed to end
the suppression and exploitation of the working man.
The union's ideology was reflected in a class struggle
that would result in the fall of capitalism and would
establish a social organization that advocated the control and ownership of industry, capital and land by the
community as a whole.   By 1924, the union had a membership of 140,000 men.   In 1931, the union was outlawed by rightist President (1927-31) Carlos Ibáñez del
Campo*.

FEDERACION SOCIAL CRISTIANA.   A political coalition
formed in 1955 to unite the National Falange (Falange
Nacional*) and the Christian Social Conservative Party
(Partido Socialista Conservador*).   In 1957, the party
became the Christian Democratic Party of Chile (Partido Demócrata Cristiano*).

FEDERALISMO.   A system of government whereby a union
of provinces or states is created, with each member
state delegating its powers to a central authority.   In
order to oppose the authoritarian rule (1817-23) of
Bernardo O'Higgins*, Chile became a federalist republic in 1826.   As early as 1822, the provinces in the
south had rebelled against O'Higgins.   Revolts broke
in Concepción*, in the south, and in La Serena*, in

the north, and in the province of Santiago* there rose
a spirit of rebellion against the Chilean liberator. In
1823, O'Higgins resigned and went into exile. The
South proclaimed General Ramón Freire Serrano* as
caudillo, and the latter ruled Chile until 1826, proclaiming it a federalist republic to be modelled after
that of the United States of America.

FEDERALISTA. An adherent to the establishment of federalismo* in Chile. When Benardo O'Higgins resigned in
1823, the federalistas organized themselves into a political party, supporting President (1823-26) Ramón
Freire Serrano*. Freire Serrano was at the time
fighting against the realistas* to incorporate the island
of Chiloé* into the national territory of Chile, a feat
he accomplished in 1826. The aim of the federalistas
was to organize their country with a Republican form
of government whereby each province (state) would be
semi-autonomous, with their own government and funds.
For matters of national interests, the provinces would
become subordinated to the province of Santiago, the
central seat of government. As a political party, the
Federalistas were very strong, as they proved in the
parliamentary elections of 1826, when they elected 56
deputies. After the elections, Chile was divided into
eight provinces, with each province establishing a provincial assembly and a Governor to be elected by popular vote. In 1827, the Federalista party disappeared.
Its legacy was to have established a federalist republic in Chile.

FERNANDEZ ALBANO, ELIAS, 1845-1910. A lawyer by
profession since 1869, he entered Congress as a deputy in 1884, beginning a long and distinguished political
career. For ten years he directed the Mortgage Bank
(Caja Ipotecaria). He was named Minister of the In-
terior--the equivalent of the office of vice-president in
the United States--in the cabinet of President (1896-
1901) Federico Errázuriz Echaurren*, and in the cabinet of President (1906-10) Pedro Montt Montt*. On
both occasions he became acting President of Chile.
The first time, in 1900, during a three-month absence
of President Errázuriz Echaurren; the second time, in
1910, when President Montt Montt went to Europe on
a trip and died there. Fernández Albano died in office
as acting President of Chile.

FERNANDEZ LARRAIN, SERGIO, 1901- . Lawyer by pro-
    fession and active member of the Conservative Party
    (Partido Conservador*). Between 1937 and 1957 he
    held elective office as a deputy to Congress. He be-
    came known for his repressive measures dealing with
    the Chilean Communists, and was one of the members
    of Congress who urged President (1946-52) Gabriel
    González Videla* to outlaw the Communist Party (Par-
    tido Comunista*). As a result, he became a member
    of the executive junta of his party. From 1959 to
    1962 he was ambassador to Spain in the government
    (1958-64) of Jorge Alessandri Rodríguez*.

FIGUEROA GAJARGO, ANA. Born in Santiago. Professor
    of English in 1928, and one of the most active women
    in Chile to promote the universal suffrage. In 1948,
    she became the president of the Chilean Federation of
    Feminine Institutions (Federación Chilena de Institu-
    ciones Femeninas). Among other things, the Federa-
    tion promoted and obtained the voting rights for women,
    promulgated as law in December, 1948. Between 1950
    and 1952, she was Chilean plenipotentiary minister to
    the Third General Assembly of the United Nations;
    delegate to the Commission on Human Rights; president
    of the Social, Cultural and Humanitarian Commission;
    and the first woman on the Security Council and Dis-
    armament Committee of the U.N. From 1952 to 1959
    she held many important posts at the United Nations;
    for example, she was the representative at the U.N.
    for refugees from all over the world.

FIGUEROA LARRAIN, EMILIANO, 1866-1931. Lawyer by
    profession, and active member of the Democratic Par-
    ty (Partido Democrático*). He was named acting Pres-
    ident of Chile in 1910, when acting President (1910)
    Elías Fernández Albano* died, and was President (1925-
    27) of Chile after Arturo Alessandri Palma* renounced
    the office in 1925. As President, Figueroa Larraín
    named Carlos Ibáñez del Campo* as Minister of War;
    the first important post held by the latter on his way
    to the Presidency. After two hectic years in office,
    Figueroa Larraín resigned, and in May 1927 Ibáñez
    del Campo emerged as head of the government (1927-
    31).

FISHING see THE ECONOMY: Internal: D. Fishing.

FLECHA ROJA, LA see THE PRESS.

FLORA AND FAUNA see CHILE.

FOCH see FEDERACION OBRERA DE CHILE.

FOMENTO, MINISTERIO DE. The Ministry of Development
    was created by statute No. 7912 in 1927 and included
    the departments of Agriculture, Industry, Colonization,
    Public Works, Commerce and Communications. In
    1930, the Department of Agriculture became a Secre-
    tariat and was separated from the Ministry of Develop-
    ment. In the same year, Public Works became a sep-
    arate entity. In 1942, the Ministry of Development
    was dissolved and it became the Ministry of Public
    Works and Communication (Ministerio de Obras Públicas
    y Vías de Comunicación*).

FOREIGN AID see THE ECONOMY: External: E. Foreign
    Aid.

FOREIGN INVESTMENTS see THE ECONOMY: External:
    D. Foreign Investments; etc.

FOREIGN RELATIONS. Chile is one of the few genuinely
    democratic nations of Latin America. In the Cold War
    polarization of nations, Chile has been staunchly pro-
    Western. This situation, however, may change with
    the first election of a Marxist government in the West-
    ern Hemisphere. While devoted to the Organization of
    American States, in which it plays a leading role,
    Chile nonetheless adheres strongly to the doctrine
    of non-intervention. Both attitudes were seen in the
    OAS move to impose sanctions against Cuba. While
    Chile voted against the move, later it followed the
    majority decision by breaking diplomatic and trade re-
    lations with the Castro regime. With yet another na-
    tion, Chile's relations have been less than cordial: in
    1948, owing to disruptive Communist political activities,
    the Chilean government broke diplomatic relations with
    the Soviet Union. President (1964-70) Eduardo Frei
    Montalva*, however, restored diplomatic relations with
    the U.S.S.R.
        With other nations, Chile's relations have been
    typically friendly and cordial. Chile-U.S. relations
    have in recent decades been amicable. The Good
    Neighbor Policy, World War II, and the Alliance for

Progress have helped promote harmonious relations between the two nations. Chile's friendship with Great
Britain is of long standing. The Scottish officer Lord
Cochrane* helped to found the Chilean Navy, and today
most vessels in Chile's navy are British-made. British
naval missions have helped to train officers of the
Chilean navy. Trade between the two nations was substantial before World War II, and is still important,
though smaller than before. While both nations claim
identical portions of Antarctica, the disagreement has
never become a serious problem. When Chile's boundary dispute with Argentina threatened war in 1902, the
quarrel was arbitrated and settled by England's Edward
VII.

Despite obvious historical ties, Chile's relations with
Spain have been less than fully cordial. Most of the
original Spanish settlers of Chile were independent-
minded Basques; there has since been no significant
Spanish emigration to Chile. Since the Spanish Civil
War, a majority of the Chilean people have clearly
been unhappy with the Franco regime. Still, diplomatic
relations are proper, and trade between the two nations
is growing. Germans have had somewhat the same influence upon Chile's Army that the British have had upon the navy. Prior to World War II, there was substantial trade between the two nations, though this commerce has not regained its pre-war eminence. Chile
has retained a small but sometimes vocal Nazi movement. Chile's relations with other nations of Western
Europe have been friendly and without incident, but
little has been done to promote trade or cultural relations with the nations of Eastern Europe.

With neighboring nations of South America, Chile
maintains congenial relations, although this was not
always so. With regard to Argentina, Chile feels less
than fully amicable. Chileans distrust Argentine nationalism, and fear economic domination by their larger neighbor. In recent decades, as in the early 1900's
(see above), the pattern in cases of border disagreement has been one of arbitration. Chile's relations
with Peru and Bolivia, exacerbated following the War
of the Pacific (Guerra del Pacifico*), have moved toward normality, although Chile does not have deep ties
with either nation. Both nations diverge from Chile in
geography and political development. Following belated
negotiations in 1904 and 1929, Peru retained Tacna,
Chile gained Arica, and Bolivia, the weakest of the

three, got the consolation prize: the use of Antofagasta as a free port, and a rail line from Antofagasta to La Paz. Of the three nations, Bolivia remains, understandably, the least satisfied.

Chile's relations with other nations in Latin America, as with the rest of the world, correlate strongly with political affinity. Relations with Uruguay, Venezuela, Mexico, and with Brazil, prior to the 1964 military coup, have been especially cordial. Its relations with other nations, if less cordial, are nonetheless satisfactory. On November 13, 1970, President Salvador Allende Gossens* (1970-76) recognized the government of Fidel Castro and resumed diplomatic relations with Cuba. President Allende is known to favor a restoration of diplomatic relations with Red China and with the Eastern European countries.

FOREIGN TRADE see THE ECONOMY: External: A. Foreign Trade; etc.

FORESTRY see THE ECONOMY: Internal: C. Forestry.

FRAP see FRENTE DE ACCION POPULAR.

FRAS see FRENTE RADICAL AGRARIO SOCIALISTA.

FREIRE SERRANO, RAMON, 1787-1851. Very active in the Chilean struggle for independence and twice (1823-26; 1827) Supreme Director of Chile. He fought in all major battles against Spain, distinguishing himself in the battles of Rancagua* (1814) and Chacabuco* (1817). A career army officer, Freire Serrano was acclaimed caudillo in the south after a spirit of rebellion had risen against the authority of Bernardo O'Higgins*, who was forced to resign in 1823. At the time, the creole leaders in Santiago had formed a junta government to succeed O'Higgins. Because of the disturbances in the capital, Freire Serrano was marching from the south and soon reached the capital, where he refused to recognize the existing junta and named a new one. The new junta lost no time in proclaiming Freire Serrano Supreme Director.

Congress produced a constitution (Constitution of 1823*), drawn up by the eminent Chilean statesman Juan Egaña Risco*. The constitution was enforced only for six months. Freire Serrano upset the regime by a coup d'état and proclaimed himself dictator. As

Erratum

[The following entry was omitted from page 140 of the
Historical Dictionary of Chile, by Salvatore Bizzarro]

FREI MONTALVA, EDUARDO, 1911-   Lawyer and former
university professor, one of the founders of the Christian Democratic Party (Partido Demócrata Cristiano*),
and President of Chile for the term 1964-70.   Active
in politics since his university days, Frei took his law
degree at the age of 22, graduating with honors.   Between 1932 and 1935 he was secretary and then president of Chile's Catholic youth organization, Asociación
Nacional de Estudiantes Catolicós y Juventud Católica
de Chile.   In 1934 he went to Rome to attend the University Youth Congress as a delegate from Chile.   A
year later, he helped organize the youth faction of the
Movimiento Nacional Conservador, which in 1938 became known as the Falange Nacional*.   (Chileans insist
that the Falange Nacional had no connection with the
Spanish Falange, but it is a strange coincidence that the
name was chosen in the year when the Falange tri-
umphed in Spain.)   In 1957, the Falange Nacional became the Christian Democratic Party of Chile.

Frei was Minister of Public Works in the administration of President (1942-46) Juan Antonio Ríos*.
Three years later, he was elected senator from the
region known as the "Norte Chico" (the provinces of
Atacama and Coquimbo).   In the congressional elections of 1957, he was elected senator from Santiago,
with the largest plurality received by any candidate in
that election.   In 1958 he was a candidate for the Presidency, finishing third behind President (1958-64) Jorge
Alessandri Rodríguez*, who had defeated Socialist
Salvador Allende Gossens* by some 35,000 votes.   In
1964, Chileans chose Frei as President by an over-
whelming majority.   With over 2. 5 million votes cast,
Frei polled over 1. 4 million votes, or 55. 6%.   His
nearest opponent, Senator Allende, polled 975,210 votes,
or 38. 6%.

Among his accomplishments as President, Frei
has enacted into law an agrarian reform program, which
proposed a fundamental change of the latifundio system,
reapportionment of land with compensation to the owners,
and the application of more advanced technology to

increase production; has introduced an education bill which made it mandatory for children to go to school until age 16; has called for the "Chileanization" of the copper mines-i. e., tighter government control over copper pricing, production and marketing; and has created the Ministerio de la Vivienda*, a new Ministry whose aims have been to provide low-income housing for the Chilean middle class and the poor. Frei also re-established diplomatic relations with the U. S. S. R., Poland, Czechoslovakia, Hungary, and Rumania, which had been severed during the administration of President (1946-52) Gabriel Gonzáles Videla*.

Under Frei's leadership, the Christian Democrats have not remained a unified party. Even before the presidential elections of September 4, 1970, the left-wing faction within the party split and formed a new party called MAPU*. After the elections, another left-wing faction splintered, forming the Christian Left (Izquierda Cristiana). Frei, however, has remained the number one man in his party. In mid-1972, he and Sergio Onofre Jarpa, who has emerged as the leader of the right-wing Nationalist Party (Partido Nacional*), formed a coalition with two other parties of the right known as the Confederación Democrática (CODE). Their aim was to stop Allende's socialization of Chile with a clear victory in the congressional elections of March 4, 1973. Both Frei and Onofre Jarpa had confidently predicted CODE would win a two-thirds majority in the Senate and control of the Chamber of Deputies. Had this come to pass, the Confederación Democrática would have been able to block most of Allende's program and to begin a motion to impeach the President. But when the final votes were counted, Allende's own coalition, the Unidad Popular*, had picked up six new seats in the Chamber of Deputies and three new seats in the Senate. Both Frei and Onofre Jarpa won Senate seats, however, and they may be challenging each other with an eye on the presidential elections of September 4, 1976. From this may depend the continued cooperation between Christian Democrats and Nationalists.

a sympathizer of the liberal political group known as the Pipiolos*, Freire Serrano took strong measures against the Church and the Conservatives, known as Pelucones*. Among his accomplishments were the initiation of the internal organization of a new congress, appointment of a committee to draw up another constitution; and many public works such as the building of roads and schools and the beautification of urban centers. These reforms were costly and the precarious state of the Chilean economy was severly hampered. In order to alleviate the economic situation, Freire Serrano instituted the estanco*, giving the government taxation rights on monopolized goods.

In 1824 Freire Serrano unsuccessfully attempted to annex the island of Chiloé* in the south, still a Spanish possession. In 1826 he returned south with an expedition and this time his campaign was successful. Chiloé was included within the national boundaries. In the same year, Chile was proclaimed a federalist republic and divided into eight provinces, each governed by a general assembly. Soon, there arose antagonism between the capital and the other provinces. Unable to cope with the situation, Freire Serrano resigned. Early in 1827, Colonel Enrique Campino* led a revolt in Santiago. He dispersed congress, but was himself abandoned by his own supporters. Freire Serrano was then recalled as Supreme Director. He accepted, but was unable to formulate a workable frame of government and resigned within a few months. Congress accepted his resignation and Francisco Antonio Pinto* attempted to organize a new government.

FRENAP see FRENTE NACIONAL DEL PUEBLO.

FRENTE DE ACCION POPULAR (FRAP). A coalition of leftist parties formed in 1956 and dissolved in 1969. The member parties were the Communist Party (Partido Comunista*), which operated underground until 1958, the Socialist Party (Partido Socialista*), the National Democratic Party (Partido Democrático Nacional*), and the People's Vanguard Party (Partido Vanguardista del Pueblo*). Both the Communist and the Socialist Parties, the strongest members within the coalition, followed a Marxist ideology. Their fundamental postulates were nationalization of the country's natural resources and centralized state control. In the parliamentary elections of 1957, the FRAP elected 17

deputies and 8 senators.   In the Presidential elections
of the following year, the FRAP's candidate was Socialist Salvador Allende Gossens*.   Jorge Alessandri Rodríguez*, the conservative candidate, defeated Allende
by a mere 33, 000 votes.   Encouraged by such showing,
the FRAP intensified its campaign with an eye on the
Presidential elections of 1964.

Shortly before the elections of 1964, the People's
Vanguard Party broke away from FRAP to support
Christian Democrat Eduardo Frei Montalva*.   Allende
was defeated at the polls by the Christian Democratic
candidate.   But this time, by some 430, 000 votes.   In
1968, FRAP began to lose its power and a year later
it was dissolved.   The major member parties formed
a new leftist coalition with other minor parties known
as the Unidad Popular*.

FRENTE DEL PUEBLO.   Political combination of leftist parties organized in 1951 to back the Presidential candidacy of Salvador Allende Gossens*.   It was made up of
the Communist Party (Partido Comunista*), the Socialist Party (Partido Socialista*), and the Popular Socialist Party (Partido Socialista Popular*).   Allende Gossens lost the election to rightist candidate Carlos
Ibáñez del Campo*.   The coalition lasted until 1955.
A year later, the leftist parties in Chile were grouped
into a new coalition known as the Frente de Acción
Popular* (FRAP).

FRENTE DEMOCRATICO DE CHILE.   A political combination of parties from the Center and the Right formed
in 1962 to nominate a Presidential candidate for the
elections of 1964.   The member parties were the Radical Party (Partido Radical*), the Conservative Party
(Partido Conservador*), and the Liberal Party (Partido
Liberal*).   The coalition was formed mainly to stop
the Communist threat in Chile.   In 1964, the Radical
Party candidate Julio Durán Neumann* was the choice
of the Frente Democrático de Chile.   In the same year,
however, Durán resigned and decided to run as a Radical, and the Frente Democrático de Chile was dissolved.

FRENTE NACIONAL DEL PUEBLO.   A political combination
of leftist parties organized in 1955 to present a united
front at the Presidential elections of 1958.   Its candidate was Salvador Allende Gossens*.   Socialists, Communists, and Radicals made up the bulk of the mem-

bership. In 1956, however, the coalition was dissolved, and a new coalition was formed, called the Frente de Acción Popular* (FRAP).

FRENTE NACIONAL DEMOCRATICO. Political party organized in 1949 to oppose the government of President
(1946-52) Gabriel González Videla*. Most of the membership was made up of Communists who in 1948 had to
go underground as a result of the measures taken by the
President to outlaw the Communist Party (Partido Comunista*). In the Parliamentary election of 1949, the
Frente Nacional Democrático only elected two deputies.
In early 1950, there were grave incidents with striking
members of the labor unions and the police, resulting
in various deaths. The party, having instigated the
confrontations, was held responsible. As a result, it
lost its popular support and was dissolved in that year.

FRENTE POPULAR. A political coalition made up of several
left-of-center parties which included the Communists,
the Socialists, the Radicals, the Radical Socialists and
the union organization known as the Confederation of
Workers of Chile. It was formed in 1936 as a measure
to keep in check the widespread fascist ideology prevalent in Europe at the time. The basic tenets of this
new coalition were to safeguard the interests of the
workers and to fight fascism and imperialism in the
name of democracy. When events in Europe pointed
to a rise in fascism, especially when the Spanish Republic fell in 1939 and World War II was imminent, the
Frente Popular consolidated its forces and became one
of the most powerful parties in Chile. In the Presidential elections of 1938, the Frente Popular backed the
Radical candidate Pedro Aguirre Cerda*, who won. By
1941, the Socialists had pulled out of the coalition presenting their own candidates for the parliamentary elections of that year. Soon the Communists abandoned the
coalition as well, and when in 1941 President Aguirre
Cerda died in office, the coalition was dissolved.

FUENZALIDA CORREA, OSVALDO, 1894- . Lawyer by
profession and member of the Radical Party (Partido
Radical*). He was general auditor of the body of
Carabineers, the Chilean Police, from 1927 to 1929.
During that time, he was also a member of the Liberal
Doctrinary Party (Partido Liberal Doctrinario*). When
this dissolved, he became a Radical. In 1943, he was

Minister of Land and Colonization in the government
(1942-46) of Juan Antonio Río Morales*. From 1945
to 1947, he was Chilean Ambassador to Italy. He has
remained active in the Radical Party.

FUENZALIDA ESPINOZA, EDMUNDO, 1905- . Journalist
by profession who early in his life entered politics as
a member of the Liberal Party (Partido Liberal*), and
has since held elective office. He has also had a long
distinguished diplomatic career. From 1932 to 1941
he was deputy to Congress, and was appointed Vice-
President of the Chamber of Deputies (1935). After
World War II, he was consul of Chile in Milan and
Bilbao. From 1959 to 1961, he was Chilean ambassador to Guatemala. Also, in 1961, he was ambassador
to Austria, and permanent delegate before the International Organization of Atomic Energy. He was ambassador to Uruguay from 1963 to 1964, and in 1965
was ambassador to Switzerland.

FUNDO. Rural property; large landed estate or hacienda.

FUSION LIBERAL-CONSERVADORA. A political union between the Liberal and the Conservative parties, both
representing conservative interests in Chilean society,
organized in 1857 during the conservative government
(1851-61) of Manuel Montt Torres*. In 1851, the
Liberals had proclaimed the elections of Montt Torres
as fraudulent, instigating an armed revolt which lasted
three months and cost a total of some 2,500 lives.
While Montt Torres was unable to mollify the Liberals,
he had even more problems with the Conservatives.
The Conservatives' chief protest was against the elimination of the mayorazgos* (the entailed estates), and
also against the indignity suffered by the Church when
Montt Torres became involved in a dispute with the
Archbishop of Santiago over the removal of a sacristan
from the diocese of Santiago. Montt Torres threatened
to expel the archbishop, and this provoked a very strong
reaction on the part of the Conservatives.
    The difficulties of both parties with the President
produced the coalition Fusión Liberal-Conservadora.
As the elections of 1861 came close, it was evident
that the Conservatives had to reckon with the power of
the Liberals. The latter wanted to reform the Constitution of 1833*, and demanded a single term for the
office of President, separation of Church and State,

and religious freedom for non-Catholics. Montt Torres
wanted a Conservative to succeed him, but threatened
with another armed revolt, he had to accept a more
moderate candidate who was backed by the Liberals,
José Joaquín Pérez*, who came to power in 1861
through 1871. The election of Pérez ended a 30-year
Conservative rule in Chile and marked the beginning of
a 30-year Liberal rule. The Fusión Liberal-Conservadora lasted until 1875, when disagreements between the
Conservatives and Liberals over matters of Church and
State brought about its dissolution.

-G-

GALVARINO. Legendary Araucanian chieftain who was reported to have been born around 1557. The year of
his death is unknown. Galvarino became famous for
his exceptional bravery. He was captured in Lagunilla,
and the Spanish governor requested that both his hands
be cut off. Galvarino placed his right hand on the
block, and when it had been removed, he, without a
word, placed his left hand on the block. At the conclusion of the sentence, he placed his head on the
block, but his life was spared so that he might serve
as an example to those who would disobey the Spaniards.
Galvarino left swearing to avenge himself. He spent
the rest of his life inciting Indian uprisings but was
captured again and executed. Some Chilean historians
believe that he killed himself in order not to give his
enemies the satisfaction of killing him.

GANDARILLAS GUZMAN, MANUEL JOSE, 1789-1842. A
lawyer by profession who participated in the struggle
for Chilean independence with the Carrera Verdugo*
brothers. In 1814, he was named secretary of the
Town Council of Santiago. After the battle of Rancagua*, he went into exile to Mendoza and from there to
Buenos Aires. After the battle of Chacabuco*, he returned to Chile. He went into voluntary exile to Argentina when Bernardo O'Higgins* took power, and returned to Chile once again after the overthrow of
O'Higgins. In 1825, he formed part of the governing
council which took power in the absence of President
(1823-26) Ramón Freire Serrano*. In 1826, he was
Chancellor of the Exchequer, and helped organize the
Estanquero party*. In 1828, he was elected a deputy

to Congress but resigned. From 1831 to 1842 he was a senator; he died in office.

GANDARILLAS LUCO, JOSE ANTONIO, 1839-1913. Lawyer by profession and member of the Liberal Doctrinaire Party (Partido Liberal Doctrinario*). From 1870 to 1875 he was Minister to the Court of Appeals. In 1876 he was elected a deputy to Congress. In 1879, he occupied the Ministry of Justice and Public Instruction. He was also subrogate Minister of the War and Navy. From 1869 to 1895, he formed part of the commission for the revision of the Penal Code. In 1888 he was elected a deputy to Congress, and a senator in 1891. In 1892, he was named President of the Senate. He unsuccessfully ran for President in 1886, backed by the Liberal Doctrinaire Party.

GANDARILLAS LUCO, PEDRO NOLASCO, 1839-1891. A parliamentarist who was elected a deputy to Congress in 1876. In 1883, he was the fiscal treasurer and administrator of the Estanco*. In 1885, he was named Chancellor of the Exchequer. A year later, he was Director of the Treasury and President of the Tribunal of Accounts. From 1882 to 1894 he was a senator. In 1889, he was subrogate Minister of the Interior. He also assisted in the ministries of Justice and Public Instruction, of the War and Navy, and of Industry and Public Works. In 1890, he was subrogate Minister of Foreign Affairs. He also worked with other members of Congress to bring down President (1886-91) José Manuel Balmaceda Fernández* (see Guerra Civil de 1891). He was persecuted by government officials for his activities and in 1891 took his own life.

GARCIA CARRASCO DIAZ, FRANCISCO ANTONIO, 1742-1813. He had a long career within the military. He was twice temporary governor of Valparaíso*, and in 1808 he was named temporary governor of Chile. In 1809, he became governor of Chile and his one-year term was shaken by internal and international difficulties. There was a movement in Chile to declare independence and not to recognize Napoleon's brother Joseph Bonaparte as King of Spain. The governor had to sustain a repressive attitude against all those who wished the French to win in Spain. In 1810, the people of Santiago rejected the role played by the governor to aid the independence movement in Chile. García Carrasco

Díaz lost support and left for Callao, Peru, in 1811.

GENTE DECENTE.   (Literally, "decent people.")   Middle-
class persons.

GENTE HONESTA.   (Literally, "honest people.")   People of
the lower class.

GENTE HUMILDE.   Poor or "humble people."

GEOGRAPHY, CHILEAN   see CHILE.

GOBIERNO, SECRETARIA DE.   The Secretariat of State was
founded in 1814 and provided three secretariats within
the provisional government of 1814:   that of government,
that of the Exchequer, and that of War.   The Constitution of 1818* changed the name Secretaría de Gobierno
to Ministry of State (Ministerio de Estado*).

GOBIERNO Y RELACIONES EXTERIORES, MINISTERIO DE.
The Ministry of Goverment and of Foreign Affairs was
created by law in 1822, and approved by the Chilean
Constitution of that year.   The ministry lasted until
1824, when it changed its name to Ministerio del Interior y de Relaciones Exteriores*, or the Ministry of
the Interior and Foreign Affairs.

GODOY ALCAYAGA, LUCILA   see MISTRAL, GABRIELA.

GOMEZ MILLAS, JUAN, 1900- .   Professor of history and
geography at the University of Chile, where in 1931 he
became secretary general of the university.   He was
later named Dean of the Faculty of Philosophy and Education.   In 1953, he was named Minister of Education
in the cabinet of President (1952-58) Carlos Ibáñez del
Campo*.   In the same year, he was elected president
of the University of Chile, and was re-elected to that
position in 1958.   In 1964, he was once again named
Minister of Education in the cabinet of President (1964-
70) Eduardo Frei Montalva*.

GONZALEZ ROJAS, EUGENIO, 1903- .   A university professor, and member of the Socialist Party (Partido
Socialista*), who in 1927 was Secretary of the Department of Labor.   Five years later, he was named Minister of Education in the government (1932-38) of Arturo Alessandri Palma*.   He has served in Congress

as a senator from 1949 to 1957, and from 1948 to
1950 he was Secretary General of the Socialist Party.
After his senate term, he was invited by the Venezuelan Government to organize a Pedagogic Institute in
that country. He returned to Chile in 1959, and abandoned politics to dedicate himself to education. In that
year, he was appointed Dean of the Faculty of Philosophy and Education at the University of Chile*. In
1963, he was elected president of the same university.

GONZALEZ VIDELA, GABRIEL, 1899- . Lawyer by profession, active member of the Radical Party (Partido
Radical*), and President of Chile from 1946 to 1952.
From 1930 to 1941, he held elective office as a deputy
in Congress. In 1933, he was named president of the
Radical Party, in the same year, he was President of
the Chamber of Deputies. During the government
(1938-41) of Pedro Aguirre Cerda*, he was Chilean
ambassador to France. In 1941, he was appointed ambassador to Brazil by President (1941-46) Juan Antonio
Ríos Morales*. In 1945, González Videla was elected
senator for an eight-year term. In 1946, he ran for
President as the candidate of the Radical Party, and
was elected with the backing of the so-called Popular
Front (Frente Popular*), a coalition of several parties
of the Left which included the Communists and the
Socialists. As a gesture of gratitude, the new President appointed three Communists to his 11-man cabinet.
Inaugurated on November 4, 1946, he had to cope
with many internal problems, among which the most
serious were inflation on the one hand, and a serious
lag in production on the other. Not able to woo the
Communists who controlled the labor unions, and who
demanded better pay for the workers, González Videla
alienated the three Communist members of his cabinet
who resigned after only five months. Anti-inflation
laws were passed by Congress. The workers, however,
threatened to strike and disrupt the economy even further unless they received better pay. With his back
to the wall, González Videla had to sign into law an
increase in the national minimum wage at least 25%
over that of the preceding year. In 1948, feeling that
the Communists were becoming too powerful in their
control of the labor segment of Chilean society, and
urged by the conservative Liberal Party (Partido Liberal*), González Videla outlawed the Communist Party
and broke relations with Russia. The 15 Communist

deputies and the five Communist senators were allowed
to finish their terms in office, but some of them were
persecuted.

One of those persecuted was the poet Pablo Neruda*,
senator from Tarapacá. Neruda had denounced the
steps taken by President González Videla to outlaw the
party which had helped him achieve power. In a famous discourse read to an open session of Congress,
Neruda said "Yo acuso, " "I accuse." He then went on
to criticize the President calling him a "traitor."
President González Videla took Neruda to court, and
the poet was found guilty by a kangaroo court. As a
result, he lost his seat in the Senate and was given a
prison sentence, which he avoided by going into hiding
for a year. It was during that time that Neruda wrote
the poem "Yo acuso," published in the collection Canto
general (1950) and banned in Chile.

The government of González Videla had problems
not only with the intellectuals. Strikes and a growing
inflation, which ranged from 25% to 30% yearly, seriously hindered any economic progress made in those
years. In 1949, there was a sharp decline in the
price of copper, a commodity which accounted for approximately 60% of the nation's foreign exchange. The
cost of living had risen 40% in the meantime over that
of the previous year. People became restless. The
announcement that bus fares would go up touched off a
series of riots which left seven persons dead and hundreds wounded. The runaway inflation continued through
1952, when González Videla's term expired, and Carlos
Ibáñez del Campo* was elected President (1952-58) of
Chile.

GONZALEZ VON MAREES, JORGE, 1900-1962. Lawyer by
profession and leader of the Chilean Nazi Party, the
Movimiento Nacional Socialista de Chile*, which he
helped organize in 1937. The party elected three deputies and González Von Marées was one of them. At
the opening session of congress, González Von Marées
opposed the passage of Social Security for workers, a
bill which was defeated. In 1938, he helped the candidacy of President (1938-41) Pedro Aguirre Cerda*, who
won also receiving the help of the Chilean Left. González Von Marées became the leader of a revolutionary
movement to establish a fascist state in Chile. He
caused many disturbances involving Communists and
Radicals on the one hand, and the Nazis on the other.

Several of these disturbances resulted in deaths. He, himself, always carried a gun, and once fired a shot at an opening session of congress, for which he was detained. He was later submitted to a medical examination, but was released. He served as deputy until 1949, then joined the Liberal Party (Partido Liberal*). Not in agreement with the candidacy of Jorge Alessandri Rodríguez*, he left politics in 1951.

GOVERNMENT see CHILE: GOVERNMENT.

GOVERNORS OF CHILE during the colonial period.

Pedro de Valdivia (1541-1553)

García Hurtado de Mendoza (1557-1561)

Francisco de Villagra (1561-1563)

Melchor Bravo de Saravia (1567-1575)

Rodrigo de Quiroga (1575-1580)

Alonso de Sotomayor (1583-1592)

Martín García Oñez de Loyola (1592-1598)

Alonso de Rivera (1601-1605)

Alonso García Ramón (1605-1610)

Lope de Ulloa y Lemus (1618-1620)

Luis Fernández de Córdova y Arce (1625-1629)

Francisco Laso de la Vega (1629-1639)

Francisco López de Zúñiga (1639-1646)

Martín de Mujica y Buitrón (1646-1649)

Antonio de Acuña y Cabrere (1650-1655)

Pedro Porter de Casanate (1656-1662)

Francisco de Meneses (1664-1668)

Diego de Avila Coello y Pacheco (1668-1670)

Juan Henríquez (1670-1682)

Marco José de Garro (1682-1692)

Tomás Marín de Poveda (1692-1700)

Francisco Ibáñez de Peralta (1700-1709)

Juan Andrés de Ustáriz (1709-1717)

Gabriel Cano de Aponte (1717-1733)

José Antonio Manso de Velasco (1737-1745)

Domingo Ortiz de Rozas (1746-1755)

Manuel Amat y Junient (1755-1761)

Antonio Guill y Gonzaga (1762-1768)

Agustín de Jáuregui (1773-1780)

Ambrosio de Benavides (1780-1787)

Ambrosio O'Higgins y Ballenary (1788-1796)

Gabriel de Avilés (1796-1799)

Joaquín del Pino (1799-1801)

Luis Muñoz de Guzmán (1802-1808)

Antonio García Carrasco (1808-1810)	Mariano Osorio (1814-1815)
Mateo de Toro y Zam- brano y Ureta (1810)	Casimiro Marcó del Pont (1815-1817)

GRAN FEDERACION OBRERA DE CHILE. A workers' union, founded in 1909 by railroad employees, which became a syndicate. The Marxist leader Luis Emilio Recabarren* changed its name, also in 1909, from the Gran Federación Obrera de Chile to the Federación Obrera de Chile* (FOCH).

GROVE VALLEJO, MARMADUKE, 1879-1954. An Air Force career officer who led two coups d'état in Chile. The first, in 1925, was engineered to bring back from Italy President (1920-24) Arturo Alessandri Palma*, who had been forced by the Army to resign in 1924. The second, occurred in 1932, when Marmaduke Grove Vallejo was chief of the Chilean Air Force, shortly after the fall of President (1927-31) Carlos Ibáñez del Campo*. A proclaimed nationalist, Grove Vallejo led a revolt to try to establish a Socialist Republic in Chile. His success was short-lived. Twelve days later he, in turn, was ousted by Carlos Dávila Espinoza*. From 1933 to 1949, Grove Vallejo was an elected deputy to Congress as a member of the Socialist Party.

GRUPO MOVIL DE CARABINEROS. A special police force organized in 1960 for the purpose of breaking up workers' strikes and student and peasant demonstrations. See also CUERPO DE CARABINEROS.

GUERRA, MINISTERIO DE. The Ministry of War was created in 1818. It was previously known as the Secretariat of War. In 1822, the Ministry of War was dissolved and the Chilean Constitution of that year formed a new Ministry, known as the Ministry of War and Navy. In 1923, the Ministry of War was created once again by statute No. 153, and separated from the Ministry of the Navy. In 1927, both the Ministry of War and the Ministry of the Navy were combined to form the new Ministry of National Defense.

GUERRA, SECRETARIA DE. The Secretariat of War was created in 1814 to draft provisions for a provincial government independent of Spain. The Secretariat proclaimed that a Supreme Director would be in charge of

government, the office of Chancellor of the Exchequer
was also created. In 1818, the Secretariat of War
changed its name to Ministry of War.

GUERRA A MUERTE. A "war to the death" fought during
the years between 1819 and 1822 between royalists
(Realista*) and independents (Independiente*). All prisoners taken during this internal war were shot. The
royalists were under the command of Vincente Benavides*.
After the victory at Maipú* for the Independents (April
5, 1818), Benavides organized the forces loyal to the
King of Spain into guerilla units, waging war on those
who had declared the independence of Chile. Many
battles were fought in central Chile, in Curalí, Tarpellanca, Trilaleu, Hualqui, Pangal, all between 1819 and
1822. Then in 1822 Benavides was captured as he attempted to reach Peru, and was shot. The war to the
death was momentarily over, but another royalist, Juan
Manuel Picó, continued to fight for another two years.

GUERRA CIVIL DE 1829-1830. The first civil war in Chile
was fought during the years 1829 and 1830. It was
caused by the Congress electing Joaquín Vicuña* as
Vice-President in spite of the fact that Vicuña had
come in fourth in the Presidential election of 1829.
President (1827-29) Francisco Pinto Díaz*, in order to
maintain the peace, resigned, but Congress refused to
accept his resignation. Pinto resigned once again the
same year and Congress named Francisco Ramón Vicuña Larraín* as President. But the chief of the rebellious troops, José Joaquín Prieto Vial*, commissioned Manuel Bulnes Prieto*, a colonel, to mobilize
troops in the south.
   On November 9, 1829, Bulnes Prieto occupied the
city of Rancagua*, and all the territory encompassed
between the rivers Bío-Bío and the Maule. The newly-
appointed Vicuña Larraín summoned Ramón Freire Serrano* to come to his aid, but Freire Serrano refused
because he was opposed to the President. The rebellious troops, encountering little resistance on the part
of government troops, forced the President to leave
the capital and take refuge in Valparaíso*. But the
government refused to come to terms with the rebels,
and the Battle of Ochagavía* ensued between government
troops under the command of Francisco Lastra y de la
Sotta* and the rebel forces under the command of General Prieto Vial.

Lastra y de la Sotta realized the impossibility of defeating Prieto Vial, and a treaty was signed between
the two men, which placed both armies under the command of Freire Serrano, who was to supervise the new
elections for a junta government. But the treaty was a
failure since both armies were disposed to fight. The
rebellious army then occupied the city of Coquimbo,
capturing the President. Freire Serrano broke with
the rebels and pledged to help the government troops.
A new battle ensued at Lircay. Freire Serrano was
defeated and the number of dead and wounded was well
over 1000 men. Prieto Vial, as victor, put an end to
the civil war, and José Tomás Ovalle Bezanilla became President (1830-31). The event marked the beginning of 30 years of Conservative control in Chile.

GUERRA CIVIL DE 1851. The Civil War of 1851 was the
result of liberal malcontent with the continuation of
conservative rule under Presidents (1841-51) Manuel
Bulnes Prieto* and (1851-61) Manuel Montt Torres*.
On September 7, 1851, and on September 13, 1851,
the liberals staged two small uprisings in the cities of
La Serena* and Concepción*. After the election of
1851, they attempted by violence and revolt to prevent
the inauguration of Montt Torres, but they were defeated in December in the Battle of Loncomilla*. La
Serena continued to be a center for revolutionaries but
the strong conservative men of Montt Torres kept a
close watch on developments there, sending government troops more than once to quell uprisings.

GUERRA CIVIL DE 1859. The Civil War of 1859 was begun
on January 5th with the aim of overthrowing the government of Manuel Montt Torres* (1851-61). On that day,
the rebellious army occupied the police headquarters
in the city of Copiapó, and were hoping that military
uprisings would occur simultaneously in the north and
south of Chile. Already toward the end of 1858 the
liberal forces in Chile were strengthened by a coalition with certain conservatives who desired to end the
long dominance of their party. President Montt Torres
favored as his successor an ultra-conservative, Antonio Varas de la Barra*, who was opposed by the Liberals and members of his own party. As a result,
there were agitations followed by imprisonments. Then,
at the end of 1858, martial law was declared to prevent the convening of an assembly. At this, the libe-

rals and radicals rose and there ensued the civil war
which lasted for four months costing an estimated
5000 lives. The government was victorious and could
proceed with order to prepare for the coming elections
of 1861.

GUERRA CIVIL DE 1891. The Civil War of 1891 was the
result of a conflict between the executive and the legislative powers within the Chilean government. On the
one side, President (1886-91) José Manuel Balmaceda
Fernández*, a Liberal, wanted to unite the badly split
Liberal Party; on the other hand, a group of liberals
opposed the President and were in favor of parliamentary rule. When the presidential elections of 1891 approached, Balmaceda Fernández backed Enrique Salvador Sanfuentes Andonaegui*, but the liberal groups
within Congress refused to back the presidential choice.
The Liberals were joined by the Conservatives, whom
Balmaceda Fernández had driven to the opposition by
his anti-ecclesiastical legislation.
     During his years in power, the President had brought
general prosperity to the country, but a controversy had
ensued over congressional criticism of government spending. The President was accused of being extravagant,
and of attempting to free himself from Congress so that
he could rule dictatorially. By the time of the elections, Balmaceda counted with a few political supporters. His cabinets were characterized by ministerial
crises and did not last very long. Congress challenged
his cabinet choices and refused to approve his budget.
Balmaceda played into the hands of his enemies when,
in January, 1891, without convening Congress, he appropriated funds for the new fiscal year.
     A week later, Congress met in a National Assembly,
deposed the President, and created a governing junta,
appointing Jorge Montt*, a naval officer and son of the
late President (1851-61) Manuel Montt Montt* to head
the provisional government. Balmaceda, exercising
dictatorial powers, refused to yield. Although the army remained loyal to the President, the rebellious
junta, with the support of the Navy, which controlled
the ports, defeated the government forces in two encounters: the Battle of Concón*, near Valparaíso*,
and that of La Placilla*, near Santiago*. Both battles,
which left more than 10,000 dead, occurred in August
1891. The defeated Balmaceda found asylum in the
Argentine Embassy, refusing to resign until the expira-

tion of his term, on the 18th of September, 1891.

GUERRA DEL PACIFICO.   The so-called "War of the Pacific" began in 1879 and ended in 1883.   It was also
   called the "Nitrate War" and it was waged by Chile
   against Peru and Bolivia to take possession of the Atacama Desert, rich in nitrate deposits.   The Atacama
   Desert stretched 600 miles from Chilean Copiapó* to
   Peruvian Arica* and was divided among three countries:
   Peru, Bolivia, and Chile.   Peru claimed the province
   of Tarapacá*, whose port was Iquique*; Bolivia, the
   province of Atacama*, whose port was Antofagasta*;
   and Chile, the province of Copiapó.   Up to the outbreak of the war, Bolivian territory was fixed at 25°
   south latitude.   An aggressive Chile, however, claimed
   that its boundaries reached as far as 23° south latitude.
   During the government of Bolivian President Mariano
   Melgarejo, a compromise was reached in 1866 fixing
   the Chilean-Bolivian border between the two claims,
   at 24° south latitude.
      But while both Chile and Peru exploited the rich ni-
   trate fields, Bolivia remained pretty much inactive.
   Chile was conceded the right of mining in both Bolivian
   and Peruvian territory, paying a royalty for Chilean
   operations north of Copiapó.   In 1873, Peru and Bolivia, interested in limiting the operations and expansion of their southern neighbor, signed a secret treaty
   to protect themselves from Chilean imperialism.   A
   year later, Chile demanded that Bolivia sign a formal
   treaty fixing their common boundary at 24° south latitude, just below the port of Antofagasta.   In the treaty,
   there was the stipulation that Chilean mining north of
   the new border would be favored by a reduction in roy-
   alties that Chile was to pay to Bolivia.
      In 1875, Peru took steps to prohibit any furthering
   of Chilean operations in Tarapacá.   Three years later,
   a new Bolivian government raised the taxes on Chilean
   exports using the port of Antofagasta.   Chilean companies operating in the area protested and demanded
   that their government take adequate steps against the
   Bolivian demands.   Faced with an acute economic
   crisis at home, Chilean President (1876-1881) Aníbal
   Pinto* sent a fleet north on February 4, 1879.   The
   fleet seized the port of Antofagasta and Bolivia declared war on Chile, on March 1, 1879.   The Peruvian government immediately assembled an army to
   protect Bolivian interests, offering to arbitrate the

question.   Chile refused the Peruvian overture, and
demanded that Peru remain neutral.   Moreover, Chile
demanded that Peru abrogate its former treaty with
Bolivia.   When Peru refused to do so, on April 5,
1879, Chile declared war.   Thus Chile was at war with
two nations, with double its population.   Chile's pre-
paredness was responsible for its aggressive attitude.
The Chilean army and navy were by far superior to
those of Bolivia and Peru combined.

After the occupation of Antofagasta, the Chileans
seized the port of Iquique in 1879.   In the same year,
the Chileans moved north, and in 1880 they occupied
Tacna and Arica.   In 1881, the Chilean navy blockaded
the port of Lima, and an army marching from the south
occupied the Peruvian capital and remained there until
1884.   The Peruvian and Bolivian nitrate fields were
now open and Chile took possession of them.   The disaster overturned the governments of both Peru and Bolivia.   In 1883, Chile dictated the terms of peace.
Chile obtained Antofagasta from Bolivia, and Tarapacá
from Peru.   Tacna and Arica were assigned to Chile
for a period of ten years, at the end of which a refe-
rendum would decide the nationality of both cities,
whether they were to be Peruvian or Chilean.   But the
time came, and Chile refused to abide by the former
treaty, remaining in possession of the two northern
cities.

This led to a bitter quarrel between Chile and Peru
that was not resolved until 1929, through the intervention of the United States as arbiter.   In that year,
President Herbert Hoover proposed a settlement which
both countries were willing to accept: Tacna would be
assigned to Peru, and Arica would go to Chile.   The
results of the war were consequential for the three
countries involved: Bolivia was deprived of its territory on the Pacific, losing the port of Antofagasta,
its only access to the sea, and the entire province of
Atacama; Peru lost part of its southern territory, including Arica and the province of Tarapacá; Chile enlarged its territory to extend north of 18° south latitude, entering upon a period of economic prosperity
from the sales of nitrate, copper, and other by-products.

GUERRA Y AVIACION, MINISTERIO DE.   The Ministry of
War and Aviation was created by statute No. 173 on
July 8, 1932.   Shortly after, in December, it changed

its name to the Ministry of National Defense (Ministerio de Defensa National*), and it included the Departments of War, Aviation, and the Navy.

GUERRA Y MARINA, MINISTERIO DE.   The Ministry of War
and the Navy was created by the Constitution of 1822*,
which united under one ministry the Departments of
War and the Navy.   This ministry lasted until 1924,
when by Statute No. 153 it was separated into two ministries, that of War and that of the Navy.

GUERRAS DE ARAUCO.   A series of wars against the Araucanian* Indians which lasted for more than three centuries.   The saguinary subjugation of the Araucanians
began when Diego de Almagro* led the first expedition
into Chile in 1535, and lasted until the close of the
19th century.   What has been described as the "blood-
iest of all conquests" was finally ended peacefully in
1883 when the Chileans signed a treaty with the Indian
chieftains assigning certain lands to the Araucanians in
perpetuity (reservations).

GUMUCIO VIVES, RAFAEL AGUSTIN, 1909- . Councilman
for the province of Santiago from 1938 to 1941.   He
was general director of the Department of Statistics
(1945), and Under Secretary of the Treasury (1946-52).
He became president of the National Falange Party
(Falange Nacional*), and in 1955 he was President of
the Socialist Christian Federation (Federación Social
Cristiana*).   In 1957 he was elected a deputy to Congress in a special election, and was re-elected from
1961 to 1965, with the backing of the Christian Democratic Party (Partido Demócrata Cristiano*).   In 1965
he was elected senator running as a Christian Democrat.   In 1969, he was one of the founders of the
Movimiento de Acción Popular Unitaria* (MAPU), a
splinter group of the Christian Democratic Party which
supported Socialist Salvador Allende Gossens* in the
Presidential elections of 1970.

GUTIERREZ ALLIENDE, JOSE RAMON, 1899- . A lawyer
by profession and a member of the Conservative Party
(Partido Conservador*).   He was Secretary of the
Senate and a member of the Court of Appeals of Santiago.   From 1926 to 1930 he was a deputy in Congress.
From 1937 to 1938 he was named by President (1932-
38) Arturo Alessandri Palma* as Minister of Foreign

Affairs.   In 1959, he presided over the Chilean delegation to the 14th General Assembly of United Nations in
New York.

-H-

HACIENDA.   Large estate or ranch.

HACIENDA, MINISTERIO DE.   The Ministry of the Treasury
was established in 1817 from the Under Secretariat of
the Treasury, previously established in 1814.   The
functions of the Ministry have been to manage the finances of state, public rent, monetary and fiscal laws,
banks and credits, and income taxes.   The following
services are also provided by the ministry: the impo-
sition of internal taxation; the issuing of money; the
regulating of customs and duties, stocks and commerce.
Various autonomous organisms, such as the Central
Bank of Chile (Banco Central de Chile), the State Bank
of Chile (Banco del Estado de Chile), and the Loans
and Savings Association (Caja Central de Ahorros y
Préstamos), are connected to the government through
the Ministry of the Treasury.   In 1837, the Ministry
was responsible for internal and external commerce,
mining, industry, and agriculture.   In 1887, a new
Ministry of Industry and Public Works (Ministerio de
Industrias y Obras Públicas*) was created, which supervised agriculture, industry, and public works, re-
lieving the Ministry of the Treasury of these tasks.   In
1927, a Ministry of Mining was created (Ministerio de
Minería*), and the Ministry of the Treasury was relieved of its supervisory duties over mining.

HALES JARMARNE, ALEJANDRO.   A lawyer by profession,
he was a member of the Executive Committee of the
Student Federation (Federación de Estudiantes de Chile*).
From 1946 to 1947, after graduating from law school,
he served as secretary of the Agrarian Labor Party
(Partido Agrario Laborista*), becoming its vice-president in 1949.   In 1953 he was appointed Minister of
Agriculture in the government (1952-58) of Carlos
Ibáñez del Campo*.   From 1954 to 1958, he was Chilean ambassador to Bolivia.   In 1960, he was named
president of the Chilean delegation to the Congress held
by the Economic Commission for Latin America* (ECLA);
and in 1966 he became Minister of Mines (Ministerio

de Minería*) in the government (1964-70) of Eduardo
Frei Montalva*.

HENRIQUEZ GONZALEZ, CAMILO, 1769-1825. Known as
the precursor and patriarch of Chilean journalism,
Camilo Henríquez in 1812 founded the first national
newspaper in Chile, La Aurora de Chile*. When Henríquez was born, Chile was still a dependency of the
Spanish empire in America. When Chile fought from
1810 to 1818 to obtain complete independence, it was
Camilo Henríquez who insisted that the Chileans should
fight the Spanish yoke. As early as 1783, he had entered the religious order of San Camilo de Lelis in
Lima, Peru. On more than one occasion, Henríquez
was admonished by the Holy See not to take part in
political squabbles. But in 1810, knowing of the country's struggle for independence, Henríquez returned to
Chile and wrote fervent articles and speeches to aid
the cause of independence using the pseudonym Quirino
Lemanchez.

On January 6, 1811, he wrote a proclamation of
Independence, which was published in Buenos Aires and
London, and made him famous overnight. Henríquez
was also a good preacher and used the pulpit to insti-
gate revolutionary fervor in young Chileans. He participated in various junta governments, having been a
deputy in 1811 and a senator from 1812 to 1814. In
1813, he had the honor of being named President of
the Senate. After the defeat of the Chilean patriots at
the Battle of Rancagua* (1814), Camilo Henríquez was
exiled to Argentina, where he remained until 1822. In
that year, he was re-elected to Congress, and died
while holding office.

HERALDO, EL. A newspaper published in Valparaíso from
1888 until 1953. It was considered to be the Valparaíso official organ of the Liberal Party (Partido Libe-
ral*). In 1890, it opposed the government (1886-91)
of José Manuel Balmaceda Fernández*, and, as a result, was placed under censorship. Among its most
distinguished collaborators was the renowned Nicara-
guan poet Rubén Darío.

HERNANDEZ JAQUE, JUVENAL, 1899- . Lawyer by profession and active member of the Radical Party (Partido Radical*). From 1928 to 1932, he was deputy to
Congress. He taught at the University of Chile, where

he was also Dean of the Law School, and President of
the University from 1932 to 1952. In 1940, he was
named Minister of National Defense in the government
(1938-41) of Pedro Aguirre Cerda*. After the death of
Aguirre Cerda, he was renamed Minister of National
Defense by acting President Jerónimo Méndez Arancibia.
In 1947, he was once again named Minister of National
Defense in the cabinet of President (1946-52) Gabriel
González Videla*. A year later, he presided over the
Chilean Delegation to the Ninth Panamerican Conference
held in Bogotá, Colombia. From 1959 to 1964, he was
Chilean ambassador to Venezuela.

HERRERA LANE, FELIPE, 1922- . A lawyer by profession
and professor of political and constitutional law at the
University of Chile. He has also taught in the Department of Economics and Business Administration. He
became well-known in Chile and in many other countries
for his banking abilities. In 1943, he was an executive
in the Central Bank of Chile (Banco Central), and from
1953 to 1958, he served as its president. Active as a
student, in 1945 he was elected president of the Federation of Students (FECH*) of the University of Chile.
He was appointed Minister of the Treasury in 1953 in
the cabinet of President (1952-58) Carlos Ibáñez del
Campo*. In 1958, he became executive director of the
International Monetary Fund, spending a year in the
United States. He was named president of the Inter-
american Development Bank (Banco Interamericano de
Desarollo--BID) in 1960. He has been an active member of the Socialist Party (Partido Socialista*), and
later, of the Christian Democratic Party (Partido
Demócrata Cristiano*). He considered entering the
1970 Presidential race as a Christian Democrat or an
Independent, but never became a candidate.

HERRERA PALACIOS, OSCAR, 1907- . A career military
officer who attained the rank of major in the Chilean
armed forces. He also taught physical education, history and geography in the military school in Santiago
(Escuela Militar*). In 1952 he received a law degree
from the University of Chile, and a year later was
named Minister of Labor in the cabinet of President
(1952-58) Carlos Ibáñez del Campo*. In 1954, he was
appointed Minister of Education, and a year later became the Minister of the Economy and the Treasury,
a post he renounced in 1956.

HEVIA LABBE, HORACIO. One of the founders of the Socialist Republican Party (Partido Social Republicano*),
and its first president, Hevia Labbe served as Minister of the Interior in 1931, and again from 1932 to
1933. As a member of the first cabinet of President
(1932-38) Arturo Alessandri Palma*, he considered the
right-wing political group Milicia Republicana* as too
extreme, and, as a result, a danger to the public order. When a parade permit was issued to the Milicia
Republicana, Hevia Labbe resigned as Minister of the
Interior. For a short time in 1933, he was also
Minister of Public Health.

HIDALGO. Nobleman; military officer in the Spanish wars
against the Moors.

HIDALGO PLAZA, MANUEL, 1882-1956. Member of the
Chilean Revolutionary Workers Movement, and later of
the Radical Party (Partido Radical*). He was president of the Workers Congress held in 1910, and one of
the founders of the Socialist Labor Party (Partido Socialista de Trabajadores*). In 1925, he helped to
draft the new constitution (Constitution of 1925*), and
joined the Radical Socialist Party (Partido Radical
Socialista*). For the next eight years, he served as
a senator. In 1931, he directed the Trotskyite wing
(Izquierda Comunista*) of the Communist Party (Partido Comunista*), and ran for the Presidency. Two
years later, he was re-elected senator for a four-year
term. From 1939 to 1943, he served as Chilean ambassador to Mexico. When he returned to Chile in
1943, he was appointed Minister of Public Works. He
also held the post of Minister of the Economy and Commerce in 1946. From 1950 to 1953, he was ambassador to Panama.

HIGIENE, ASISTENCIA Y PREVISION SOCIAL, MINISTERIO
DE. The Ministry of Hygiene, Social Security and
Assistance was created by Statute No. 44 on October
14, 1924. Two weeks later its name was changed to
Ministry of Hygiene, Social Security and Assistance,
and Labor (Ministerio de Higiene, Asistencia y Previsión Social y Trabajo*).

HIGIENE, ASISTENCIA Y PREVISION SOCIAL Y TRABAJO,
MINISTERIO DE. The Ministry of Hygiene, Social
Security and Assistance, and Labor, was created by

Statute No. 66 on October 27, 1924. The functions of
this Ministry were to coordinate all aspects of sanitation and hygiene, and all programs of public welfare
and social security. This Ministry lasted three years,
and in 1927 its name was changed to Ministry of Social
Welfare (Ministerio de Bienestar Social*).

HIRIART CORVALAN, OSVALDO, 1895- . Lawyer by profession, and active member of the Radical Party (Partido Radical*). From 1937 to 1945, he served as a
senator. In 1943, he was named Minister of the Interior in the cabinet of President (1942-46) Juan Antonio Ríos Morales*. In 1944, he was Subrogate Minister of Labor. A year later he became executive director of ENDESA*, the Chilean National Electric Company. He has also held important posts in the Chilean
Development Corporation (Corporación de Fomento de
la Producción*).

HISTORIC MUSEUM. Located at 50 Miraflores Street, in
Santiago, the museum contains a good collection of pre-
historic ceramics, stones, woods and mummies, as
well as a colonial furniture collection, a collection of
religious objects, and a collection of 19th century furniture.

HISTORY see CHILE: HISTORY.

HOLIDAYS. The Labor Code specifies May 1 and Sundays
as legal holidays. Paid vacations, ranging from 15 to
25 days, are provided for by the Labor Code. Other
national and religious holidays are usually treated as
legal holidays, even though they are not specifically
mentioned in the law. The most important Chilean
holiday is Independence Day. To commemorate the
event, Chileans celebrate the 18th and the 19th of
September (Independence was declared on September
18, 1810). During these two days, public meetings
are held, and many eminent speakers are called upon
to revive the glory of the past and emulate the days of
the cabildo abierto*. José de San Martín* and Bernardo O'Higgins* are honored everywhere, and the universities in Santiago celebrate the "Semana Universitaria, " a week of parading, festivities, and jubilation.
On January 1, the New Year is celebrated. May 1 is
Labor Day. Union leaders usually organize parades
and public meetings for the laboring classes.

May 21 is Armed Forces Day, or Día de la Armada.
Chileans pay particular homage to Captain Arturo Prat*,
a hero of the War of the Pacific (Guerra del Pacífico*).
It is on this day that the Chilean President delivers his
State of the Nation address, before the National Congress.   October 12 is Columbus Day, or Día de la
Raza ("Day of the Race").   It is also the day of the
"Big Game."   The two rival universities in Santiago,
the University of Chile and the Catholic University,
play a soccer match in front of huge crowds.   Religious holidays in Chile are celebrated according to the
dictates of the Roman Catholic Church.   The following
are legalized holidays: June 29 (Day of Saints Peter
and Paul); August 15 (Day of the Assumption); November 1 (All Saints' Day); December 8 (Day of the Im-
maculate Conception); and December 25 (Christmas Day).
The following are movable religious holidays: Good
Friday; Holy Saturday; the Ascension; and Corpus
Christi.   Many workers in special occupations or in
seasonal work are not granted these unofficial holidays.

HUACHIPATO.   An integrated iron and steel plant (that is,
a plant whose facilities cover the whole gamut of steel-
making operations, from the mining and quarrying of
raw materials to the manufacture of finished products)
located at the Bay of San Vicente.   San Vicente is near
Concepción*, 360 miles south of Santiago*, and two
miles south of Talcahuano*, one of Chile's finest harbors.   Several advantages were envisioned in choosing
this site for the plant: the Bay of San Vicente is
sheltered and has deep waters (a necessary prerequi-
site to bring in heavy shipments of iron ore from
mines located some 500 miles to the north); hydroelectric power is obtainable from the Abanico Plant, located on the Río Laja, in the Andes; the coal mines
at Lota and Schwager are only 25 miles to the south;
fresh water to operate the plant is supplied by the
nearby Bío-Bío River, five miles south of the bay (an
estimated 30 million gallons per day are required);
there are good rail and road communications with the
consuming centers of the north; and lastly, the prox-
imity of cities like Talcahuano and Concepción provides
an adequate supply of labor and minimizes transportation and housing problems.
      Construction of the Huachipato Plant was actively
started in 1947 by the Compañía de Acero del Pacífico*
(CAP).   With domestic and foreign capital (the major-

ity of which came from the United States), CAP began
partial operation of the plant in 1949, and full operation in 1950.   Since the time of its inception, the
Huachipato Plant has played a significant role in Chile's
rapid industrial development.   As a result of successive
improvement, modernization and expansion programs,
steel ingot production has increased from 178, 000 metric tons in 1951 to over 600, 000 metric tons annually
in the period 1965-70.

HUALQUI.   Site of a battle fought on November 20, 1819
during the Chilean wars of liberation.   The antagonists
were the Spanish royalists and the Chilean patriots.
The royalists were under the leadership of Vicente
Benavides*, and attacked the town of Hualqui on the
right shoulder of the Bío-Bío River with 50 men.   The
town was defended by José Tomás Huerta, who with a
force of 25 men was able to offset the attack and defeat Benavides.   A day later, three royalist prisoners,
an officer and two soldiers, were publicly executed in
the town's plaza.   This was the custom with prisoners
during the so-called War to the Death (Guerra a Muerte*).

HUARA.   Site of a battle during the Civil War of 1891,
fought between troops loyal to the government (1886-
91) of José Manuel Balmaceda Fernández* and troops
loyal to the parliamentary system of government which
was backed by the rebellious Chilean Congress (Guerra
Civil de 1891*).

HUASO.   The Chilean counterpart of the Argentine "gaucho, "
a horseman of the plains.

HUELGA GENERAL DE ANTOFAGASTA.   A strike of railroad workers which took place on February 6, 1906,
in the northern city of Antofagasta*.   The workers demanded a one and one-half hour lunch break, as opposed to the one hour allotted to them.   The strikers
clashed with the police and various workers and police-
men were killed and wounded.

HUERTA MUÑOZ, JOSE MIGUEL, 1919- .   Lawyer by profession and active member of the Liberal Party (Partido Liberal*).   He was elected deputy to Congress
four times, from 1949 to 1965.   In 1962, he served
as Vice-President of the Chamber of Deputies.

HUIDOBRO, VIDENTE, 1893-1948. A Chilean poet who has
achieved notoriety for his poetic manifestoes. Huidobro
lived for many years in Paris, and was greatly influenced by the French poets Rimbaud, Reverdy, Cocteau,
Cendrars, Verlaine and Mallarmé. It was in France
that he founded his school of creacionismo, declaring
that "the first duty of the poet is to create" and that
"the poet is a small god." His most important works
are: El espejo del agua (1916-18), Horizón carré
(1917), Manifestes (1925) and Vientos contrarios (1926).
In his Arte poética, (Art of Poetry), included in the
collection El espejo del agua, and in his Manifesto of
1917, Huidobro explained his conception of what a poet
should be and what poetry is. His theories attracted
wide attention in Latin American and French letters,
but his creacionismo did not attract many followers.

HUINCAS. An expression used by the Mapuche* Indians of
Central Chile to designate the white man.

HUMAN RIGHTS. Article X of the Constitution of 1925 provides the following rights and guarantees for all Chileans: equality before the law (in Chile there exists no
privileged class, nor any slave class); freedom of religion, liberty of conscience, and freedom of worship;
freedom of speech and of the press; freedom of lawful
assembly; freedom of lawful association; freedom to
petition any constituted authority; academic freedom in
state and private schools and universities; inviolability
of private property; labor laws for the protection of
the worker; and, freedom of movement, to settle and
travel in any part of the Chilean territory.
    Articles VII, VIII, and IX deal with "universal suf-
frage" and specifically state that all literate Chileans
at the age of 21 have the legal right and the legal duty
to vote. The list of persons who cannot vote include
members of the armed forces, and the national police
force, as well as those citizens who are physically or
mentally disabled. Any eligible person who fails to
register is subject, according to the law, to a period
of 60 days in jail, and a fine. In 1952 Chilean women
voted in a Presidential election for the first time in
the history of their country; until 1949 they had only
been allowed to vote in municipal elections. In the
same year, however, a new electoral law gave women
the right to vote, provided they were at the age of 21,
and were literate.

Women under 18 years of age are not permitted to
work in unhealthful or dangerous occupations, and may
not work from 8 p. m. to 7 a. m., unless special permission is granted them by the Ministry of Labor.
Women must be paid half their salaries for the six-
week periods before and after childbirth and their jobs
must be kept open.   An employer of 20 or more women must provide a nursery where women can leave
their children, and where babies under one year of age
can be nursed.   A female over 12 and a male over 14
can lawfully marry, provided they have the consent of
their parents or guardians, and that they notify the official of the Civil Register.   In Chile what is termed
"divorce" does not dissolve the marriage but merely
separates the parties.   A divorced mother, regardless
of whether she was the guilty party or not, is given
custody of all male children under 14, and of daughters
of any age.

Children under 14 years of age who have not completed their compulsory education may be employed only in industrial establishments operated by members of
the same family, i. e., in any small factory operated
by no more than one family unit.   Children between the
ages of 14 and 18 who have not completed their compulsory elementary education must go to school at least
two hours per day, until such time that their school
requirements are fulfilled.   Children under 18 years
of age are not permitted to work from 8 p. m. to 7 a.
m.   All children under 21 must be under the care of
a parent or a guardian.   School age for all children is
6 to 15 years of age.

In Chile there are no more than 300, 000 Araucanians* and other related Indian groups.   They live mainly in southern Chile and are granted by the 1925 Constitution full rights as citizens.   However, most Indians still live separated from the rest of the community.   Hardly any Indians meets, or cares to be
bothered with, voting requirements, and the Government interferes very little in the life of the Indian
community.   As for Negroes, slavery in Chile never
reached major proportion, as in the case of Brazil
and Cuba.   Only a few thousand Negroes arrived in
Chile during the days of colonial appendage.   Since
that time, Negroes have been assimilated into the rest
of the population.   Immigrants have arrived in Chile
always in small numbers.   The Constitution of 1925
grants them rights and guarantees similar to those

granted to Chilean-born inhabitants of the land. In recent years foreigners were allowed to vote in municipal
elections. In order to become Chilean citizens, all
immigrants must reside in Chile for a period of five
years.

HUMAY, MARIA. Organizer of the Partido Progresista
Femenino*, which was formed in 1952 as a splinter of
the Partido Femenino de Chile*. She was named president of the newly formed party.

HUNEEUS GANA, JORGE, 1866-1926. Lawyer by profession
and active member of the Radical Party (Partido Radical*). He was also a professor of constitutional law
and editor of The Law Review. He backed Congress
in the dispute with President (1886-91) José Manuel
Balmaceda Fernández*, and was elected a deputy in
1897, 1900, and 1907. In 1909, he was named Minister of Education, and from 1912 until his retirement
in 1918, he was Chilean minister to Belgium and Hol-
land.

HURTADO DE MENDOZA, GARCIA, 1535-1609. Son of the
viceroy of Peru, the Marqués de Cañete, García Hurtado de Mendoza was named governor of Chile in 1557
and led an expedition into that country to subdue the
Araucanian Indians and conquer the land in the name
of the King of Spain. During the rest of 1557, the
young governor was able to push the Indians as far
south as the river Bío-Bío. The new native leader,
Caupolicán*, was captured, tortured, and killed. Early in 1559, Hurtado de Mendoza had to surrender the
governorship to his rival Francisco de Villagra*, but
left Chile with a record of fine achievement. Spanish
control of the northern and central parts of Chile had
been established, and explorations to the Magellan
strait, which was also claimed in the name of the King
of Spain, continued. In 1562, he became viceroy of
Peru.

-I-

IBAÑEZ AGUILA, BERNARDO. School teacher by profession
and active member of the Socialist Party (Partido Socialista*). In 1935, he organized a teacher's union
called Unión de Profesores, and later joined the Work-

er's Union, Confederación de Trabajadores de Chile, of which he became secretary general in 1939. In 1941 he was elected a deputy in Congress for a four-year term, and in 1946 ran as a candidate for the Presidency of Chile, losing to Gabriel González Videla*. Since then, he has remained active in the labor organizations and has served on the Commission for the International Organization of Labor.

IBÁÑEZ DEL CAMPO, CARLOS, 1877-1960. After graduation from the Military School (Escuela Militar*) in 1896, Ibáñez del Campo became a career military officer and served twice as President of Chile (1927-31; 1952-58). He participated in two uprisings as a major in the Chilean armed forces: one on September 5, 1924, the other on January 23, 1925. Both uprisings were conducted by the military to secure two things: substantial changes in the constitution, and the return from exile of President Arturo Alessandri Palma*. Alessandri returned, and the Constitution of 1833* was amended (see CONSTITUTION OF 1925). In 1925, Ibáñez del Campo, whose political ideology was conservative, was named Minister of War by Alessandri. There followed a period of instability in Chile, and new elections returned Emiliano Figueroa Larraín* to the Presidency (1925-27). But after two hectic years in power, the well-meaning but weak Figueroa Larraín resigned, and Ibáñez del Campo, who had been appointed Minister of the Interior, succeeded him.

Ibáñez del Campo immediately called for new Presidential elections presenting himself as a candidate. He was acclaimed the unanimous victor. The army was behind him and he was able to impose a rigid discipline upon lawmakers and public workers. Congress went along with his decisions. He launched an expensive campaign of public works, increased the pay of the military and provided new guns and battleships for them, and established a new Chilean Nitrate Company at a time when Chile's principal export, nitrate, was in serious trouble on the world market because of the production of artificial nitrates (see COSACH). Ibáñez del Campo was able to undertake all these ambitious programs with the help of some $300 million in loans from New York bankers. The coming of the world Depression, however, created problems for Chile which Ibáñez del Campo could not solve, and this foreshadowed his ouster in 1931. Popular discontent increased. Stu-

dents rioted and when the police opened fire, four were
killed, as were several faculty members.   General
strikes were called throughout the nation.   The Chilean
President, unable to stop the unrest, was forced to
leave office and cross the border into Argentina.

His second term (1952-58) as President saw the har-
dy 75-year-old promising the Chileans to "save the nation from the false democracy of Gabriel González Videla*." Ibáñez del Campo had several counts against
him: his dictatorial rule from 1927 to 1931; his re-
peated plots as an army officer; his conservatism with
fascist overtones; and, his admiration for the Argentine
dictator Juan Perón.   In spite of these drawbacks,
Ibáñez del Campo was elected President for a second
time.   Even the Chilean left, disenchanted with the repressive policies of González Videla, supported him.
The President's anti-liberal, even anti-democratic views
were well-known, and Congress kept him in check giving him a troubled first year in office.   But Ibáñez del
Campo did not revert to his dictatorial role, and he was
conciliatory with his opposition.

The close of the Korean War in 1953 brought a sharp
decline in the price of copper, which hindered the progress of the Chilean economy.   The Chilean President,
as a result, blamed the United States, saying that the
Chileans were the servants of American imperialism.
Perón had become famous for attacking the United States
and for instilling a sense of nationalism in Argentina.
Ibáñez del Campo, who truly admired him, wanted to
do the same in Chile.   But if the Chileans went along
with their President's anti-Americanism, they did not
appreciate the enthusiastic official reception given to
Perón when the latter visited Chile in 1953.   When Perón was finally overthrown in 1955, the news was received joyously by the Chileans.

In 1956, the Chilean left united to oppose the President and his conservative policies, and was reorganized
under the Frente de Acción Popular* (FRAP).   Ibáñez
del Campo was able to finish his second term in office,
stepping down in 1958.   By this time, because of the
President's conciliatory policies, the Communist Party
(Partido Comunista*) was once again operating legally
in Chile.   The Ibáñez del Campo administration had
been responsible for the continuation of the democratic
process, and for a certain degree of economic progress.
A new Ministry of Mining was created, a housing project was initiated (see CORVI), the State Bank of Chile

(Banco del Estado) was established, and a Social Security Institute came into existence.

IGLESIA DE SAN FRANCISCO see SAN FRANCISCO CHURCH.

IGLESIA CATEDRAL DE SANTIAGO see THE CATHEDRAL.

INDAP. Acronym for the Instituto de Desarrollo Agropecuario. The functions of this institution, which is a department within the Ministry of Agriculture (Ministerio de Agricultura*), are to improve the science of farming, soil cultivation, crop production, and the raising of livestock.

INDEPENDENCIA, DECLARACION DE. The Declaration of Independence. On September 18, 1810, Chilean patriots proclaimed a junta government to rule in the name of King Ferdinand VII of Spain. Eight years later Chile formally declared itself independent of Spain. The Supreme Director Bernardo O'Higgins* ordered that in each Chilean city there was to be a registry with the names of all those favoring independence and those opposing it. The Chilean citizenry voted almost unanimously for independence. The official proclamation took place in Santiago on February 12, 1818, a date which marked the first anniversary of the Battle of Chacabuco*. Chileans today celebrate their independence on September 18, in commemoration of the first junta government established in the country.

INDEPENDIENTE. A person who favored independence during the Chilean struggle for emancipation with Spain (1810-22). Usually, the independiente belonged to the political group known as exaltados*.

INDUSTRIA Y OBRAS PUBLICAS, MINISTERIO DE. The Ministry of Industry and Public Works was established by law on June 21, 1887. The functions of this ministry were to supervise the industrial and agricultural growth of the country, hunting and fishing, and textiles and mines. The ministry was also responsible for the regulation of public works. In 1912, it changed its name to Ministerio de Industria, Obras Públicas y Ferrocarriles*, with the addition of the railway network under its supervision.

INDUSTRIA, OBRAS PUBLICAS Y FERROCARRILES, MINIS-
    TERIO DE. The Ministry of Industry, Public Works
    and Railways was created by Statute No. 2613 on Jan-
    uary 17, 1912. Its previous name was Ministerio de
    Industria y Obras Públicas*. In 1924, the ministry
    split into the Ministry of Public Works (Ministerio de
    Obras y Vías Públicas*) and the Ministry of Agricul-
    ture, Industry and Colonization (Ministerio de Agricul-
    tura, Industria y Colonización*).

INFANTE ROJAS, JOSE MIGUEL, 1788-1844. Lawyer by
    profession, and a distinguished career politician dur-
    ing and after the Chilean struggle for independence.
    He was elected Secretary of the First National Congress
    in 1811. He belonged to the Partido Moderado* and the
    Partido Federalista*, and, in 1814, formed part of the
    junta government of that year. He was in Argentina on
    a special mission when the Chilean patriots suffered a
    setback at the battle of Rancagua*. He returned to
    Chile after the battle of Chacabuco*, and was named
    Minister of the Treasury by Bernardo O'Higgins*. In
    1821, to defend his federalist ideas, he founded the
    newspaper El Valdiviano Federal. Two years later,
    he helped organize the Federalist Party. When Ber-
    nardo O'Higgins was forced to leave office in 1823,
    Infante Rojas was one of three men who succeeded him
    in power. He also served as Vice-President, and later
    President of Congress, having been elected a deputy
    and then a senator. When, in 1825, the Supreme Di-
    rector (1823-26) Ramón Freire Serrano* left Santiago
    to fight the Spaniards in Chiloé and include that island
    within the national territory of Chile, Infante Rojas
    succeeded him in power. During the absence of Freire
    Serrano, Infante Rojas tried to impose the Federalist
    system in Chile, but only succeeded in doing so for a
    short period of time. In 1843, Infante Rojas was
    named Minister of the Supreme Court of Chile and a
    member of the Law Faculty at the University of Chile.
    He renounced both commissions and died a year later.

INQUILINO. Tenant; specifically a tenant farmer.

INSTITUTO DE DESARROLLO AGROPECUARIO see INDAP.

INSTRUCCION PUBLICA, MINISTERIO DE. The Ministry of
    Public Instruction (education) was created by Statute no.
    1296 in 1899. Its antecedent, the Ministry of Justice
    and Public Instruction (Ministerio de Justicia e Instruc-

ción Pública*), was divided into two departments on that
date, both administered by the newly created ministry.
The Department of Justice and the Department of Public
Instruction each had an undersecretariat but were both
served by a single minister, the Minister of Public Instruction.   The functions of the new ministry were to
provide justice and education for all Chileans, establishing fair courts of law as well as public elementary,
junior and senior high schools all over the country.
The Ministry of Public Instruction lasted until 1927,
when another statute (no. 7912) changed its name to
that of Public Education (Educación Pública*).

INSURANCE   see THE ECONOMY: Internal: M. Insurance.

INTENDENCIA.   An administrative division of viceroyalties
in the late 18th century designed to relieve the functions of the viceroys in such matters as the supervision
of the affairs of finances and of war.   The competence
of the Intendencia extended to the departments of justice, finance, war, and police.   The coming of royally-
appointed intendentes* into the administrative process
of the districts made possible the elimination of corrupt
alcaldes mayores* and corregidores*.   Since the intendants were salaried officers of the crown, the tempta-
tion for graft and corruption was alleviated.   Among
their many duties, the intendants were charged with
the overseeing of districts, collection of taxes, promotion of business and trade, and the organization of the
local militia.   Some viceroys regarded the new reforms
as inimical to their own power and angrily protested
to the crown, but to no avail.   This system lasted well
into the next century.

INTENDENTES.   Intendants; see INTENDENCIA.

INTERIOR, MINISTERIO DE.   The Ministry of the Interior
was created on December 9, 1871 as a separate entity
from the Ministry of Foreign Affairs.   It is the most
important appointed office in the ministerial cabinet,
and is responsible for the internal security of the country and for the maintenance of law and order.   The
Minister of the Interior is first in line to succeed the
President in the event of the latter's disability or
death.   All of the following services are with the jurisdiction of the Ministry of the Interior: the electoral
registry; the post office; telegraphs; social security;
electrification; police; zoological gardens; and the ad-

ministration of the San Cristóbal Park (Cerro San
Cristóbal). In 1814, the Ministry of the Interior was
called Ministry of Government. In 1824 it became the
Ministry of the Interior and Foreign Affairs, and, since
1871, it has been the Ministry of the Interior.

INTERIOR Y RELACIONES EXTERIORES, MINISTERIO DE.
The Ministry of the Interior and Foreign Affairs was
created on August 14, 1824. Its functions were many.
In addition to being responsible for the internal security of the country, the ministry was in charge of all
diplomatic and consular activities in and out of the
country. In 1871 the Ministry split into two new entities: the Ministry of the Interior and the Ministry of
Foreign Affairs.

INTERNAL TRADE see THE ECONOMY: Internal: Q. Internal Trade.

INTERNATIONAL ASSISTANCE see THE ECONOMY: External: E. Foreign Aid.

IQUIQUE. Capital city of the northern province of Tarapacá*.
Population: 61, 700 (1971 est.).

IRIBARREN CABEZA, JUAN ANTONIO, 1885- . A lawyer
by profession and member of the Radical Party, Iribarren Cabeza spent many years of his life teaching
in the Law School at the University of Chile. In 1940
he was named Minister of Education in the government
of President (1938-41) Pedro Aguirre Cerda*. In 1946
he became Minister of the Interior, and served for a
short time as interim President of Chile, succeeding
Alfredo Duhalde Vázquez* who resigned. Iribarren Cabeza has been an advisor of CORFO* and is the author
of a book, Historia general de derecho.

IRISARRI ALONSO, ANTONIO JOSE DE, 1786-1868. He was
born in Guatemala and came to Chile, where he was a
participant in the struggle for independence. He was
regidor* of the cabildo* in Santiago (1811), and was
Minister of Government for seven days (1814). Because of his political participation in the struggle
against Spain, he was exiled to Argentina in 1814. In
1818 he returned to Chile and sided with Bernardo
O'Higgins* in the dispute with the Carrera Verdugo*
brothers. After the exile of O'Higgins, Irisarri Alonso
returned to Guatemala, where he remained until 1830.

In that year, he returned to Chile, once again becoming involved in politics. In 1834 he was named governor of Curicó*. He then participated in the war against Peru and Bolivia (see PERU-BOLIVIA CONFEDERATION), and went to Peru to sign the treaty of Paucaparta on behalf of Chile. The Chilean government, however, rejected the treaty which was unfavorable to Chile. Irisarri Alonso was accused of having been a traitor during the negotiations and was ordered to return to Santiago. Refusing to do so, he was tried in absentia and sentenced to death. In light of these events, Irisarri Alonso returned to Guatemala where, in 1855, he was named plenipotentiary minister to El Salvador and the United States.

IRON. During the first half of this century, Chile exported iron ore to the United States. Then, in the early 1950's, a domestic steel industry was established at Huachipato*. As a result, the Chilean demand for domestic consumption of iron ore increased and the export of the mineral ceased. In 1951, 3.2 million long tons of iron ore were produced (1 long ton = 2,240 lbs.), but production fell to less than half that amount in 1955 as some of the major iron ore deposits in south-central Chile became exhausted. In 1959, Algarrobo*, the largest and newest of the Chilean iron mines was purchased by the Compañía de Acero del Pacífico* (CAP), and partial operation of the mine began. It was not until 1962-63 that a full-scale operation was begun. In that period, the mineral extracted from the open-pit mine amounted to 2.3 million long tons. A year later (in the period 1963-64) production increased to 2.7 million long tons. By the late years of the last decade, production was up to 5.2 million tons, almost double what had been produced in 1956. Chilean deposits of iron ore have reserves on some 150 million tons, with additional probable reserves of 75 million tons.

IRRARAZAVAL ALCALDE, JOSE MIGUEL, 1801-1848. Lawyer by profession and member of the Law School and Political Science Department at the University of Chile. A delegate to the assembly called by the junta government in 1823, he also served as a deputy in Congress and as regidor* to the cabildo* held in Santiago in 1825. In 1827 he was Vice-President of Congress, and, three years later, participated in the Plenipotentiary Congress called in Santiago. From 1834 to 1848 he served in the Senate, having been one of the drafters

of the Constitution of 1833*. He was also a member
of the Commission on Higher Education, and sat as a
judge on the Supreme Court in 1836. Five years later,
he was appointed Minister of the Interior and Foreign
Affairs by President (1831-41) Joaquín Prieto Vial*.
Just before his death in 1848 he was elected President
of the Senate.

IRRARAZAVAL ALCALDE, RAMON LUIS, 1809-1856. A
lawyer by profession and member of the Conservative
Party (Partido Conservador*). From 1834 to 1839 he
was deputy to Congress, and served as Vice-President
of the Chamber of Deputies in 1840. Irrarázaval Alcalde held many high positions in the government (1841-
51) of Manuel Bulnes Prieto*. In 1841, he was subrogate Minister of Foreign Affairs, a post he again occupied in 1844. From 1844 to 1845 he served as Minister of the Interior and acting President of Chile, because of the President's illness. From 1845 to 1851
he was Chilean plenipotentiary minister to Rome [the
Papal State].

IRRARAZAVAL LARRAIN, MANUEL JOSE, 1835-1896. A
life-long politician who was a member and later became President of the Conservative Party (Partido
Conservador*). In 1863 he founded the Conservative
newspaper El Bien Público, and a year later founded
another paper, El Independiente. He was deputy to
Congress from 1864 to 1870, and in 1873 was elected
senator, a post he held until 1882. In 1874, he became known as the champion of the Catholic cause
during the virulent dispute with Chilean liberals. Many
of the liberals belonged to the Masonic Lodges and
wanted to have a separation of Church and State with
secularized education. After the overthrow of President (1886-91) José Manuel Balmaceda Fernández*,
Irrarázaval Larraín became Minister of the Interior
and Secretary of the Junta government of Iquique*.
For reasons of health, he abandoned his political activities and emigrated to the United States, dying five
years later in New York.

IRRARAZAVAL LECAROS, RAUL, 1906- . Lawyer by
profession and member of the Conservative Party
(Partido Conservador*). From 1941 to 1949 he was
a deputy to Congress. In 1950 he was named Minister of the Treasury in the cabinet of President (1946-

52) Gabriel González Videla*. During the early 1950's, he served as vice-president of the Conservative Party, and was named ambassador to the Vatican by President (1952-58) Jorge Alessandri Rodríguez*. From 1957 to 1965, he was a member of the Senate. He has also been a member of various law guilds and has written several articles in the Law Review of Chile.

IRRARAZAVAL ZAÑARTU, ALFREDO, 1867-1934. Member of the Liberal Party (Partido Liberal*), and a distinguished career diplomat and politician. In 1891, he collaborated with Congress to overthrow President (1886-91) José Manuel Balmaceda Fernández*, taking part in the battles of Concón* and Placilla*. Two years later, he was named Secretary of the Chilean Delegation to Berlin. In 1900, with the backing of the Liberal and Democratic Parties, he was elected a deputy to Congress, holding elective office until 1912. For the next 14 years he held ambassadorial posts to Japan (1911), to Brazil (1913), to Germany (1920), and to Ecuador (1925).

ISLA DE PASCUA   see EASTER ISLAND.

IZQUIERDA COMUNISTA. (Literally, "the Communist Left.") A political party formed in 1931 when Carlos Ibáñez del Campo* was ousted from the Presidency. A splinter of the Communist Party (Partido Comunista*), the Izquierda Comunista was headed by Manuel Hidalgo Plaza*. The group was Trotskyite in its orientation, and participated in the 4th International. In the Presidential elections of 1931, the Izquierda Comunista ran Manuel Hidalgo Plaza as their candidate, but, with the latter's defeat, the party dissolved and its members joined the Socialist Party (Partido Socialista*).

IZQUIERDA NACIONAL. A political party known as the Nationalist Left, formed in 1964 as a splinter of the Radical Party (Partido Radical*). During the Presidential elections of that year, the Radical Party supported Julio Durán Neumann*, while the Izquierda Nacional supported Salvador Allende Gossens*. Following the elections, the party dissolved.

-J-

JUAN FERNANDEZ ISLANDS. Dependencies of Chile. Located 360 miles west of Valparaíso, at 33° 48' south
latitude and 78° 45' to 80° 47' west longitude, the islands are rugged, volcanic, and wooded. The two
principal islands of the Juan Fernández group, spaced
100 miles apart, are Más Atierra, 36 square miles in
area, and Más Afuera, 33 square miles in extent.
Named for their discoverer in 1574, the islands' chief
fame comes from their association with Daniel Defoe's
novel, Robinson Crusoe, which was inspired by the experience of Alexander Selkirk on Más Atierra Island
from 1704 to 1708. The Juan Fernández Islands are
inhabited by native people whose main occupation is
lobster fishing. During the struggle for independence,
many Chilean patriots were exiled to the Juan Fernández Islands by the Spanish Crown. After independence
was achieved, many political prisoners were sent into
exile to the islands.

JUDICIARY, THE see CHILE: GOVERNMENT.

JUNTA DE GOBIERNO (1810). On September 18, 1810,
Chilean patriots proclaimed a junta government to rule
in the name of King Ferdinand VII. Five persons
were named to participate in the junta government:
Mateo de Toro y Zambrano*, President; the Bishop of
Santiago, Don José Antonio Martínez Aldunate y Garces,
Vice-President; Fernando Márquez de la Plata, first
secretary; Juan Martínez de Rojas Correa*, second
secretary; and Ignacio de la Correa Cuevas*, third
secretary. The junta immediately voted to form a
Chilean army and to open trade with all friendly nations. Eight years after the first junta government
was established, Chile formally declared itself independent of Spain. Chileans celebrate their independence on September 18.

JUNTA DE GOBIERNO (1811). On September 4, 1811, there
was a military coup in Chile, and another junta government was established. The cabildo* was temporarily
abolished, and all offspring of slaves were considered
free.

JUNTA DE GOBIERNO (1812). The junta government of 1811
was abolished by José Miguel Carrera Verdugo*, who

organized the new junta government of 1812 and became
its president.   The issue at hand was whether or not
Chile should continue to be a Spanish colony.

JUNTA DE GOBIERNO (1813).   A new junta government was
established in Chile when José Miguel Carrera Verdugo*
left Santiago as the head of the Chilean army for independence.   His brother Juan José* succeeded him as
president of the new junta.   Total separation from
Spain was sought; and a Supreme Director of Chile,
equivalent to a head of state, was elected, summoning
a cabildo abierto*.   Francisco de la Lastra y de la
Sotta* was unanimously chosen to lead Chile toward independence.

JUNTA DE GOBIERNO (1891).   From 1823 to 1891, Chile
experienced an autocratic form of government, with
conservatism prevailing from 1831 to 1861, and liberalism from 1861 to 1891.   No junta governments appeared
during this period, and the Supreme Director of Chile
enjoyed wide powers.   In 1891, however, a rebellious
Congress forced President José Manuel Balmaceda
Fernández* to resign after a brief civil war, setting
up a junta government to rule in the name of the people.
Jorge Montt Alvarez* was its President, assuming
power on August 31, 1891, and again on September 3,
1891, when a new junta was formed.   Participating in
the new junta were Waldo Silva Algüe*, Vice-President
of the Senate, and Ramón Barros Luco*, President of
the Chamber of Deputies.   A new law of municipalities
was decreed, establishing local autonomy and electoral
freedom.   These reforms introduced a "parliamentary
regime" in Chile, very much like that of England, under which the executive was subject to the will of the
majority of Congress.   After the victory of Congress,
new Presidential elections were called in 1891, electing
Jorge Montt Alvarez* (1891-96).

JUNTA DE GOBIERNO (1932).   In June-July 1932, four junta
governments came into existence to establish a Socialist
Republic in Chile.   On June 4, 1932, a military revolt
broke out and the government was overthrown.   The
first junta government was established with General Arturo Puga Osorio as President, ruling with Carlos
Dávila Espinoza and Eugenio Motte Hurtado.   On June
13, the first junta was dissolved and another established,
with Puga Osorio assuming the executive power once

again.   Three days later, a third junta government was
established, as plots and coups d'état succeeded one
another.   Marmaduke Grove Vallejo*, who insisted on
establishing a Socialist Republic, was exiled to Easter
Island* and accused of being a Communist.   This time,
Carlos Dávila Espinoza* became President of the new
junta.
    On June 30, a fourth junta government was estab-
lished, with Dávila Espinoza as President.   This junta
lasted only one week.   Because of the failure of these
four junta governments, established and dissolved within a period of less than two months, the Armed Forces
demanded a return to constitutionality.   On October 2,
1932, Abraham Oyanedel Urrutia, the President of the
Supreme Court in Chile, assumed temporary powers as
President and called a new Presidential election.   As
a result, Arturo Alessandri Palma* was elected President (1932-38) for a second term.

JUNTA DE GOBIERNO DE IQUIQUE (1891).   A junta govern-
    ment was established on August 31, 1891 in the city of
    Iquique* by a rebellious Chilean Congress who went to
    war against President (1886-91) José Manuel Balmaceda
    Fernández* (see GUERRA CIVIL DE 1891).   The junta
    was composed of Jorge Montt Alvarez*, Ramón Barros
    Luco*, and Waldo Silva Algüe*, who assumed the ex-
    ecutive power.   The junta organized an army which was
    victorious at Placilla*, and set up a temporary govern-
    ment until elections could be held in that year.

JUNTA DE GOBIERNO PROVISIONAL (1823).   A provisional
    junta government was set up on January 28, 1823 when
    Bernardo O'Higgins* resigned as Supreme Director of
    Chile and went into exile.   The junta was composed of
    Agustín Eyzaguirre Arechavala*, José Miguel Infante
    Rojas*, and Fernando Errázuriz Aldunate*, who as-
    sumed the executive power.   This junta lasted until
    March 29, 1823, when it was dissolved and a new jun-
    ta was established, known as the Junta de Represen-
    tantes* (following entry).

JUNTA DE REPRESENTANTES (1823).   This junta govern-
    ment, established on March 29, 1823, replaced the
    Provisional Junta Government (Junta de Gobierno Pro-
    visional*) which had been ruling since January 28, 1823.
    Three representatives from different cities assumed the
    executive power: Juan Egaña Risco*, from Santiago*,

Manuel Vásquez de Novoa, from Concepción*, and
Mariano Antonio González, from Coquimbo*. The junta immediately called an assembly to elect a constituent Congress. There would be a nine-member Senate,
a governor for each of the six departments, and local
administrators. The Supreme Director would be elected
by Congress. Two days after the junta came into
power, Congress chose Ramón Freire Serrano* as Supreme Director of Chile.

JUNTA MILITAR DE GOBIERNO (1924). This junta government was formed by the military when President (1920-
24) Arturo Alessandri Palma* resigned on September
10, 1924. A conflict had developed between the President and the military over the devaluation of the national currency to alleviate the economic crisis. The military wanted Alessandri to devaluate the currency at
once, and his refusal was a cause for his resignation.
The military junta which assumed governing powers
over the country was composed of General Luis Altamirano Talavera*, Vice-Admiral Francisco Nef Jaras,
and General Juan Pablo Bennet Argadoña. A few
months later, however, the military junta, which had
vowed a return to constitutional rule, was overthrown
by army officers in the capital, and a new junta was
formed (see following entry).

JUNTA MILITAR DE GOBIERNO (1925). On January 23,
1925, a second military junta came into power under
the pretext that Luis Altamirano Talavera* had not
carried out the reforms he had promised when his
military junta was established on September 11, 1924
(see preceding entry). This new junta, which remained
in power only six days, wanted President (1920-24) Arturo Alessandri Palma* to return to Chile to govern
the land. On January 27, 1925, a third military junta
was formed with the sole purpose of inviting President
Alessandri back from his self-imposed exile in Italy.
Alessandri arrived in Santiago* on March 20, 1925,
and was widely acclaimed by the people and by Emilio
Bello Codesido*, who had presided over the third military junta.

JUSTICIA, CULTO E INSTRUCCION PUBLICA, MINISTERIO
DE. The Ministry of Justice, Worship and Public Education was established by law in 1837 and lasted until
1887, when it became known as the Ministry of Justice

and Public Education (Ministerio de Justicia e Instrucción Pública*). The functions of this Ministry were to
administer the law of the land, grant religious freedom
to the people, and be in charge of public education.

JUSTICIA, MINISTERIO DE.   The Ministry of Justice was
established in 1899 by Statute no. 1296.   The functions
of the Ministry of Justice are to maintain a balance
between the executive and the judicial power, and to
administer the law of the land.   The Under Secretariat
of Justice controls the following organisms: the civil
registry, the legal medical service, the Council for the
National Defense, pensions, and the budget of state.

JUSTICIA E INSTRUCCION PUBLICA, MINISTERIO DE.   The
Ministry of Justice and Public Education was established
by law in 1887 and lasted until 1899.   The functions of
this Ministry were to administer the law of the land
and to provide public education for all Chileans.

JUVENTUD CONSERVADORA.   A group of young conservatives which organized itself after the collapse of Carlos
Ibáñez del Campo's* government (1927-31).   Later, the
group became known as the Falange Conservadora* and
subsequently as the Falange Nacional*.

-K-

KENNECOTT COPPER CORPORATION.   The rise of Chile's
modern copper industry dates from 1905, when William
Braden purchased El Teniente mine at Sewell*, 75
miles southeast of Santiago.   El Teniente, one of the
great underground mines in the world, is located at an
elevation of 8, 000 feet.   Large capital investments by
the Guggenheim brothers, followed by the sale of the
mine, in 1915, to the Kennecott Copper Corporation,
made possible the mechanization of El Teniente and
its spectacular production.   Block-carving extraction
of the ore is carried on at various levels within the
mountain, which is connected by aerial tramway with
the smelter at Caletones, four miles away in the can-
yon of El Teniente river.   The smelter is operated by
the Braden Copper Company*.
    After extraction, the ore is crushed and treated;
the resulting concentrate is brought to the smelter,
and the finished product is transported by rail to the

Pacific Coast of Chile and, subsequently, shipped abroad.
Since it began operation, the annual copper production
of El Teniente--with the relative price of copper on the
U.S. markets, and the percentage of copper in the ore
extracted--is given in the following chart.

Year	Copper price (¢ per lb.)	Short tons produced	Copper percentage
1906-11	----	6,769	2.33
1921	----	13,702	----
1931	----	103,572	----
1941	11.7	141,071	----
1945	11.6	164,000	2.26
1950	21.0	158,000	2.09
1951	24.4	171,129	2.11
1955	36.6	155,000	2.40
1956	41.6	180,000	2.01
1957	28.9	173,000	1.96
1958	25.4	192,000	1.94
1959	30.0	184,000	1.93
1960	31.0	176,000	1.99
1961	29.3	168,000	1.90
1962	31.0	154,000	1.95
1963	32.5	160,000	1.93
1964	35.0	180,000	1.93

In 1966, during the Vietnam War, Chileans were com-
pelled to sell 90,000 tons of copper at a price of 36¢
per pound (on the London Metal Exchange Market the
price for copper was set at 50¢ per pound), and in
1969, when negotiations were arranged to "chileanize"
the copper industry--i.e., tighter government regulations over copper pricing, production, and marketing--
the price for copper was set at 42.5¢ per pound (as
opposed to 52.5¢ on the London Metal Exchange Market). El Teniente mine has been the largest taxpayer
in Chile. It produces approximately 40% of Chilean
copper, and four out of every five dollars earned by
the Braden Copper Company have gone back to the
Chilean economy. Normally Kennecott paid 70% of its
profits to the Chilean government, but in 1961 the conservative President (1958-64) Jorge Alessandri Rodríguez* increased the tax to about 75%.

In 1962 taxes were raised again to 82%, and the trend
has continued in 1963 (86%) and in 1964 (87.5% tax). In
1965, and again in 1969, taxes were lowered as the result of an agreement between the Chilean government

and Kennecott (see COPPER). The reason why copper taxes have been heavier on the lot of the Braden Copper Company has been that for the last two decades Kennecott has not increased its production (whereas Anaconda* has). Since Kennecott has been interested mainly in its total earnings from copper, the corporation has increased copper output in Utah (open pit mine), since the metal is easier to extract, rather than from El Teniente. With the chileanization of copper first, and nationalization as the next step, Kennecott's output in Chile will eventually terminate.

KRAUSISMO. A neo-Kantian pantheistic philosophy which did not have much success in Germany where it was originated by Karl Christian Friedrich Krause (1781-1832), but which gained a wide following in Spain and Latin America. One of the tenets of this philosophical system was that humanity would arrive at an organic completeness which represented the maturity of the human race. This, in turn, would bring about the unification of all mankind. In Chile, Krausismo was widely spread among the Free Masons. But, like Positivism*, Krausismo was never very strong in Chile and soon lost its appeal.

-L-

LABOR. Chile's trade unions grew out of the mutual aid societies which were organized during the 19th century. But in 1903, union membership totaled only 63, 000, and was largely limited to workers in ship-loading, manufacturing, and mining. The first labor federation was formed in 1909; almost from the beginning, the Federación Obrera de Chile* (FOCH) was under the control of the Socialist Workers' Party (Partido Socialista de Trabajadores*). In 1921, the FOCH was affiliated with the Red Trade Union International; in 1922 it established official liason with the Chilean Communist Party (Partido Comunista de Chile*). By 1928, the FOCH claimed 136, 000 members. Growing slowly in the decades prior to 1930, organized labor became very influential politically during the 1930's. Labor growth was stimulated by the founding in 1933 of the Socialist Party of Chile (Partido Socialista de Chile*).

The decade of the thirties saw the bifurcation of the labor movement into Socialist and Communist-oriented

unions. Socialist-Communist rivalry led to such extensive labor unrest that the government in 1948 passed
the Defense of Democracy Law, which outlawed the
Communist Party. Ironically, this law, which also
gave the government the right to intervene in union
affairs, provoked a re-marriage of convenience between the Communist and Socialist forces; the result
was a new national labor organization, the Central Unica de Trabajadores de Chile* (CUT). This new union
was sponsored by the government in order to frustrate
Communist influence, yet it remained strongly Marxist
in its orientation. The growing power of the Christian
Democratic Party (Partido Demócrata Cristiano*) led
to the formation in 1958 of a rival national labor organization, the Confederación Nacional de Trabajadores*
(CNT), which has since succeeded in attracting dissi-
dent CUT unions to its fold.

Labor thus was polarized into two camps: the Marxist, larger but disunited, affiliated with international
Communism, and the Christian Democratic, smaller but
more united, democratic and anti-Communist, and growing rapidly. By 1960, total union membership was
230,000, while the nation's labor force had reached
2.75 million, or about 35% of the population. Agriculture, forestry, and fishing engage 27% of all workers;
service and government occupations, 20%; commerce,
11%; mining and quarrying, 5%; and construction, 8%.
About 45% of the work force engages in manual labor,
while some 24% are classified as white-collar workers.
Whereas worker productivity in industry and construction has increased, it has in other areas either failed
to improve or actually declined. As a result, per
capita income has declined since 1957.

Demographically, labor is an urban phenomenon;
90% of its organized membership is in the four largest
cities: Santiago, Valparaíso, Concepción, and Antofagasta. Agricultural unions are small, weak, and
poorly organized, while the conservative landholders
are united and strong. Actual unemployment has remained low in the decade of the 1960's. The total of
registered unemployed for that period was less than
20,000. However, there is substantial hidden under-
employment, workers whose occupations provide less
than full-time employment. After Socialist Salvador
Allende Gossens* became President of Chile in 1970,
unemployment has increased at a drastic rate, reaching an all-time high of 9.8%. See also THE ECONOMY.

LAFTA see LATIN AMERICAN FREE TRADE ASSOCIATION.

LAN-CHILE.   Linea Aérea Nacional de Chile.   Chile's Airline Agency.

LANGUAGE.   The official language of the Chilean people is
Spanish.   There still remain 50, 000 pure-blooded
Araucanians, and another 200, 000 of closely related
stock, who speak Indian tongues.   There are also German and Italian immigrants who are, for the most part,
bi-lingual.   The purity of the Castilian tongue has been
somewhat adulterated in its new environment by other
European languages and by English.   In conversation,
most Chileans drop their final "s".   In Atlantic Chile
many words have been anglicized, whereas in the
northern territories formerly held by Peru and Bolivia,
linguistic characteristics inherited from those two
countries are still used in every day language.

LARRAIN GARCIA MORENO, JAIME.   A career politician
who belonged to the Agrarian Labor Party (Partido
Agrario Laborista*).   He was elected a deputy to Con-
gress in 1921, and a senator in 1945.   After the death
of Juan Antonio Río Morales* in 1946, a new Presiden-
tial election was called and Jaime Larraín García
Moreno became the candidate of the Agrarian Labor
Party, losing the election to Gabriel González Videla*.
In 1951, opposed to his party's Presidential candidate,
and not wanting to support Carlos Ibáñez del Campo*,
Larraín and other dissenters fromed a new party, the
Movimiento de Recuperación Doctrinaria*.   When the
National Party (Partido Nacional*) was formed in 1956,
Larraín joined the new political party.

LARRAIN VIAL, BERNARDO, 1914- .   Lawyer by profession and active member of the Conservative Party (Partido Conservador*).   In the late 1930's he became president of the Juventud Conservadora*.   In 1949 he was
elected a deputy to Congress, an office he held until
1957.   In that year, he became a senator for an eight-
year term.   In 1965 he was elected president of the
Conservative Party of Chile.

LA SERENA.   Capital city of the north-central province of
Coquimbo*; population: 71, 200 (1971 est.).

LASTARRIA SANTANDER, JOSE VICTORINO, 1817-1888.
Lawyer by profession and active member of the Liberal
Party (Partido Liberal*). Lastarria Santander was an
educator and a scholar. He was also one of the most
spirited protagonist of a Positivist philosophical school
known as the "religion of humanity." This school reflected an enthusiasm for free inquiry and scientific
method. In 1837, Lastarria Santander became the
secretary of the Law Academy, and the following year
published various books on law. After he graduated
from Law School in 1839, he became the intellectual
leader of the Liberal Party. In 1842 he founded the
Literary Society of Santiago, and figured prominently
with the Chilean intellegentsia.

His major works are in the field of law and literature: Teoría del derecho penal, Elementos de derecho
penal, Bosquejo histórico de la constitución del gobierno
de Chile, and Estudio sobre los primeros poetas es-
pañoles, to mention a few. He also founded a newspaper, El Seminario de Santiago, which became the organ of the Liberal Party. In 1843 he worked with the
Ministry of the Interior and with the National Institute
of Law (Instituto Nacional). In the same year he was
elected a deputy to Congress, an office he held until
1861. During that time he founded a literary review,
La Revista de Santiago, and defended the romantic
ideas of the Argentine exile Domingo Faustino Sarmiento*. Sarmiento had denounced Andrés Bello's* devotion to classicism and argued for the creation of an indigenous American literature. Lastarria added his
voice in favor of a total break with colonial habits and
tradition.

In 1862 Lastarria was named Chilean plenipotentiary
minister to Peru, Argentina and Brazil. From 1867
to 1873 he was again elected deputy to Congress. In
1872, after a trip through the Atacama Desert, he
wrote his Rural Code, Código Rural. In 1873 he
founded the Fine Arts Center of Santiago (La Academia
de Bellas Artes). He became Minister of the Court
of Appeals of Santiago, and in 1876 was elected senator. In the same year, he was named Minister of the
Interior in the cabinet of President (1876-81) Aníbal
Pinto Garmendia*. From 1879 to 1885, he once again
served as a senator. Because of a disagreement with
the President of the Liberal Party, Domingo Santamaría González*, Lastarria and a group of dissidents
left the party and formed a new political entity called

the Partido Liberal Doctrinario*. Lastarria became its
president. During the last years of his life, he served
as a judge on the Supreme Court.

LASTARRIA VILLAREAL, DEMETRIO, 1846-1891. Lawyer
by profession and member of the Liberal Party (Partido
Liberal*). He travelled throughout Europe and became
a diplomat in Chile, forming part of the Chilean delegation to Peru in 1863 and to Argentina in 1864. From
1876 to 1891 he was a deputy to Congress, assuming
other high official posts during this period of liberal
rule in Chile. In 1879 he served as Vice-President of
the Chamber of Deputies; in 1880 he was Chilean plenipotentiary minister to Brazil; in 1883, attorney general
of the municipality of Santiago; in 1885, provisional
President of the Chamber of Deputies; in 1888, Minister of Foreign Affairs; and in 1889 he served as Minister of the Interior. In the Civil War of 1891 (Guerra
Civil de 1891*), he sided with President (1886-91) José
Manuel Balmaceda Fernández*, and when the latter resigned and later committed suicide, Lastarria Villareal
left the country to go to Argentina, but died on the way.

LATCHMAN ALFARO, RICARDO A., 1903-1965. Teacher
by profession and a successful diplomat and politician
who wrote many books on history and literature. He
was an active member of the Socialist Party (Partido
Socialista*) and, in the 1940's, helped found the Unión
Socialista*. He was a deputy to Congress from 1937
until 1941, and for the following seven years he was
assigned to many diplomatic posts in Argentina, Uruguay and Colombia. He was the Chilean delegate to
the ninth American Conference in Bogotá, and served
as Chilean ambassador to Uruguay from 1959 to 1963.
In 1963, his last year in public life, he was head of
cultural affairs in the Ministry of Foreign Affairs.

LATIFUNDIA. Vast landed uncultivated or poorly cultivated
estate, of 1000 acres or more in size, belonging to a
single proprietor.

LATIFUNDISTA. Large landowner.

LATIN AMERICAN FREE TRADE ASSOCIATION (LAFTA).
Chile is a member of the Latin American Free Trade
Association, also known by its Spanish nomenclature
Asociación Latinoamericana de Libre Comercio (ALALC).

The aims of LAFTA are to stimulate the economic integration of the Latin American countries. To date,
this goal has achieved only limited results.

LATORRE BENAVENTE, JUAN JOSE, 1846-1912. A career
naval officer and member of the Liberal Party (Partido
Liberal*). He distinguished himself in the War of the
Pacific*, and in his attempts to modernize the Chilean
Navy by introducing electricity on board ship and
modern fire arms. During the government of President (1886-91) José Manuel Balmaceda Fernández* he
was sent to England to supervise the construction of
modern naval vessels for Chile. In 1890 he was in
Spain when a rebellious Congress demanded the resignation of the Chilean President. He returned to Chile
and remained sympathetic to the President while the
Navy defected in favor of Congress. With the fall of
the Balmaceda government, Latorre Benavente was dismissed by the Navy and exiled. He returned to Chile
in 1894 and was reinstated by the Navy. In the same
year, he decided to run for the Senate, backed by the
Liberal Democratic Party (Partido Liberal Democrático*), and was elected for a six-year term. He ran
again in 1900 and was re-elected for another six-year
term. In 1908, the Navy promoted him to Vice-Admiral. Before his death, he received the insignia of
Commander of the Foreign Legion from the French
government.

LATORRE GONZALES, ORLANDO, 1916- . Lawyer by
profession and member of the Socialist Party known
as Vanguardia Popular Socialista*. He served as a
cabinet member during the government of (1952-58)
Carlos Ibáñez del Campo, first as Minister of Justice
(1952), and later as Minister of Public Works (1953).
He was one of the creators of CORVI*, a government-
sponsored housing project. In 1954 he joined the
Agrarian Labor Party (Partido Agrario Laborista*),
becoming President of the party in 1955.

LATORRE, MARIANO, 1886-1955. Noted Chilean novelist
who headed a literary school known as criollismo or
"novel of the land." Primarily a short-story writer,
Latorre has written about the rural regions of his native land. His major works are: Cuna de cóndores
(1918); Zurzulita (1920); Chilenos del mar (1929); and
Hombres y zorros (1937). For his detailed descrip-

tions, Latorre has often been compared to the Spanish
novelist José María de Pereda.

LAUCA. A river in the northern province of Tarapacá*,
which crosses the border between Chile and Bolivia and
has been the cause of a continuing dispute between the
two countries since 1953. In 1939, with permission
from Bolivia, Chile used the waters of the Lauca to
irrigate the Valley of Azapa, near Arica*. Shortly
after, Bolivia also began to use the waters of the river
to irrigate land adjacent to the Chilean border. For a
little over a decade, the irrigation projects of the two
countries proceeded amicably. Then, in 1953, Bolivia
accused Chile of having altered the course of the river,
which resulted in more water for irrigation for the
Chileans. The Chileans, in turn, accused the Bolivians
of using the Lauca River as a pretext to obtain a port
on the Pacific. Bolivia had lost the port of Antofagasta*
in the War of the Pacific (Guerra del Pacífico*). Unable to find an amicable solution to the dispute, Bolivian President Víctor Paz Estensorro broke diplomatic
relations with Chile in 1962. As of 1971, the two
countries had not resumed diplomatic relations.

LAUTARO, 1535-1557. An Indian chieftain who fought brave-
ly to expel the Spaniards from Chile. In 1550, he was
captured by Pedro de Valdivia* and was forced to serve
as a scout for the Spaniards for the next three years.
During his captivity, the successful Lautaro maintained
contacts with the Araucanians*, waiting for the propi-
tious moment to annihilate the Spanish camp. Such an
opportunity presented itself in the battle of Tucapel*,
where Pedro de Valdivia* and his men were killed by
Lautaro, who had joined the Araucanians under the
command of Caupolicán* and Colocolo*. Lautaro participated in the siege of Concepción in 1554, which saw
the defeat of the Spaniards under Francisco de Villagra*.
In 1557, at the battle of Mataquito, Villagra and his
men were able to surprise the Indian camp, annihilat-
ing their force and killing Lautaro.

LAZCANO ECHAURREN, FERNANDO, 1848-1919. Lawyer
by profession, and active member of the Liberal Party
(Partido Liberal*). He served as a deputy to Congress
from 1873 to 1879, and was elected a representative
to the Constituent Congress held in Santiago in 1891.
From 1894 to 1919 he served as a senator. He was

Vice-President, and later President of the Chilean
Senate, and in 1906 ran for the Presidency of the Republic, losing to Conservative Pedro Montt Montt*.

LEBU.   Capital of the province of Arauco* in south-central
Chile; population: 14, 000 (1971 est.).

LEGISLATIVE, THE   see CHILE: GOVERNMENT.

LEIGHTON GUZMAN, BERNARDO, 1909- . Lawyer by
profession and one of the founders of the Christian
Democratic Party (Partido Demócrata Cristiano*).   As
a student, he became president of the Juventud Conservadora*, and later was an active participant in the
formation of the Falange Nacional*.   Very active in
politics, he became Minister of Labor (1937-38) in the
cabinet of President (1932-38) Arturo Alessandri Palma*.
From 1950 to 1952 he served as Minister of Education
in the cabinet of President (1946-52) Gabriel González
Videla*.   After the Chileans elected Eduardo Frei
Montalva* in 1964, the first Christian Democratic
president in the Western Hemisphere, Leighton was
immediately named Minister of the Interior, assuming
the Presidency for a short time in 1965 while Frei
was on a European junket.   Leighton still figures
among the most influential Christian Democrats in the
hierarchy of the party.

LEMACHEZ, QUIRINO   see CAMILO HENRIQUEZ GONZALEZ.

LEY DE DEFENSA DE LA DEMOCRACIA.   The "law for the
defense of democracy" was sponsored by President
(1946-52) Gabriel González Videla* with the purpose of
outlawing the Communist Party (Partido Comunista*).
The law was passed on September 3, 1948.   It remained in effect for a decade and was finally rescinded
on August 6, 1958.

LIEBRE.   A microbus which can carry up to 17 persons.

LILLO, BALDOMERO, 1867-1923.   Short-story writer whose
themes of social protest began a new period of "realist
literature" in Chile.   His literature was concerned with
man's struggle in an industrially growing country, the
injustice of a stratified society, the hardship of the
coal miners, and the tragedy of individual lives drawn
into poverty and degredation.   Lillo's most effective

works of social protest were Sub terra (1904) and Sub
sole (1907). In these stories, Lillo sympathizes with
the worker's struggle for better working conditions,
and with the plight of the poor, especially the roto*,
the Indian, and the huaso*.

LILLO ROBLES, EUSEBIO, 1826-1910. A newspaperman
who became famous after 1847 for writing the lyrics
for the Chilean National Anthem. He was a reporter
for El Mercurio and El Comercio, both printed in Valparaíso. In 1850, with Francisco Bilbao Barquín, he
founded the Sociedad de la Igualdad. In 1851, he took
part in the civil war (Guerra Civil de 1851*) against
conservative President (1851-61) Manuel Montt Torres*,
was arrested and exiled to Peru. He returned to Chile
in 1852 and was editor of La Patria, another newspaper. In 1858, he returned to Peru and moved on to
Bolivia, where he spent the next couple of years in
mining towns. He returned to Chile to become the
president of the University of Chile (1872), a post he
held for six years. During the War of the Pacific*,
he became Chilean minister to Peru. In 1866, he was
named Minister of the Interior by President (1886-91)
José Manuel Balmaceda Fernández*. He was elected
senator with the backing of the Liberal Party (Partido
Liberal*) and became Vice-President of the Senate.
When President Balmaceda committed suicide, Lillo
Robles was entrusted with the President's political
testament which he made public. In 1896, Lillo Robles
became president of the political party known as the
Alianza Popular*.

LINARES. 1) A province of central Chile located south of
Santiago; population: 197, 541 (1971 est.); area: 9413. 8
sq. km. ; capital city: Linares*.
2) Capital city of the province of Linares*; population: 60, 400 (1971 est.).

LINDEROS. Site of a battle in the plains near Copiapó*,
fought on January 8, 1852, between troops loyal to the
government and Liberals who were attempting to overthrow Conservative President (1851-61) Manuel Montt
Torres*. The government forces, led by Victorino
Garrido, defeated the Liberals under the command of
Bernardino Barahona.

LIRCAY. Site of a battle fought on the shores of the River
Lircay, near the city of Talca*, between troops loyal
to interim President (1830) Francisco Ruiz Tagle Portales* and troops loyal to ex-President General Ramón
Freire Serrano*. This battle occurred during the
Civil War of 1829-30 (Guerra Civil de 1829-30*), and
the antecedents were the following: the Treaty of
Ochagavía* stipulated that a junta government be formed
and that the army be put under the command of Ramón
Freire Serrano. The troops of General Joaquín Prieto
Vial* refused to abide by the treaty, however, and with
permission from President Ruiz Tagle Portales, they
waged war on Freire Serrano. Prieto Vial was aided
by Colonel Manuel Bulnes Prieto*, and their army was
too powerful for the forces of Freire Serrano. The
latter called a retreat, but many of his troops were
surrounded and killed. Freire Serrano was able to
escape and Prieto Vial returned to Santiago, where a
year later he was declared President of Chile.

LLANQUIHUE. A province of south-central Chile; population:
201, 823 (1971 est.); area: 18, 205.1 sq. km. ; capital
city: Puerto Montt*.

LO CAÑAS. Site of a planned sabotage against the government (1886-91) of José Manuel Balmaceda Fernández*.
The rebellious junta of Iquique (Junta Revolucionaria de
Iquique*) had dispatched some 60 men to blow up bridges
on the River Maipú. Government troops discovered the
plot and killed all the saboteurs except eight. The prisoners were then brought to Santiago and after a mass
trial were all sentenced to death and executed.

LONCOMILLA. Site of the last battle fought during the
Civil War of 1851 (Guerra Civil de 1851*). General
José María de la Cruz Prieto* and his rebellious
troops waged this battle on December 8, on General
Manuel Bulnes Prieto* and his troops loyal to President (1851-61) Manuel Montt Torres*. The battle took
place on the shores of the River Loncomilla and lasted
four hours. Many losses were inflicted on both sides.
Cruz Prieto decided to march south with his army,
but two days later, after all the rebellious forces had
surrendered at Purapel*, Cruz Prieto capitulated and
submitted his forces to the government.

LOROS. Site of a battle fought in 1859 between troops loyal
to President (1851-61) Manuel Montt Torres* and rebellious troops loyal to General Pedro León Gallo*.
The rebellious troops defeated the government troops
who were under the command of José María Silva
Chávez. Pedro León Gallo himself led the rebel army
(see also GUERRA CIVIL DE 1859).

LOS ANGELES. A city in south central Chile and capital of
the province of Bío-Bío*; population: 85,700 (1971
est.). Also, the site of the battle during the so-called
"War to the Death," fought in 1819 between the royalists
(Realista*), who favored the Spanish crown, and the independents (Independientes*), who favored total separation from Spain. The royalists were defeating the independent army until Marshall Andrés de Alcázar y
Zapata came to the latter's defense and was able to
disperse the royalist troops.

-M-

M.I.R. see MOVIMIENTO DE IZQUIERDA REVOLUCIONA-
RIO.

MAC-IVER RODRIGUEZ, ENRIQUE, 1845-1922. Lawyer by
profession and member of the Radical Party (Partido
Radical*). After serving as a deputy to Congress for
a three-year term (1876-79), he became a journalist
and was a contributor to the paper El Heraldo de Santiago, the official organ of the Radical Party. In 1880
he was re-elected to the Chamber of Deputies, this
time serving as its Vice-President. He was a deputy
to Congress until 1900, when he became a senator
(1900-1922). In 1890-91, he participated in the congressional rebellion against President (1886-91) José
Manuel Balmaceda Fernández*. In 1891, during the
civil war of that year, he left for Argentina, but returned when Balmaceda resigned. The next year, he
was named Minister of the Treasury by President
(1891-96) Jorge Montt Alvarez*. In 1894 he was
Minister of the Interior, and a year later he once
again became Minister of the Treasury. In 1919 he
was elected Advisor of State and a member of the
Chilean Academy of Law. A mason, from 1883-1894
he was the Serene Grand Master of the Masonic Lodge
in Santiago.

MACKENNA, JUAN, 1771-1814. Born in Ireland, at the age
of 13 Mackenna left for Spain, where he studied mathematics and engineering. He participated in the Spanish-
African campaigns of 1787, and then was assigned to
go to Peru and to Chile. During the government of
Viceroy Ambrosio O'Higgins, Bernardo O'Higgins'*
father, Mackenna was named governor of the southern
Chilean province of Osorno* (1797). He was subsequently sent to Santiago de Chile (1808), and three
years later became governor of Valparaíso*. During
the struggle for Chilean independence he sided with
Spain and wanted to foment a counterrevolution to stop
the Carrera Verdugo* brothers from taking power.
Later, Mackenna became a follower of Bernardo O'Higgins and denounced Spain for its colonial policies in
the New World. In 1814, after the Spanish victory at
Rancagua*, Mackenna was exiled to Argentina. There
he met again with the Carrera Verdugo brothers, who
hated him for his participation in the counterrevolution
of 1811. José Miguel Carrera Verdugo* defied
Mackenna in Buenos Aires, and killed him in the subsequent duel.

MACKENNA ASTORGA, JUAN EDUARDO, 1846-1929. Lawyer by profession, politician, and member of the Liberal Party (Partido Liberal*). He was regidor* of
Santiago in 1873 and was elected to the Chamber of
Deputies three years later. He participated in the de-
bate over the separation of Church and State, which
he favored. He was secretary general of the Chilean
army during the War of the Pacific* in 1879. In 1890
he served as Minister of Foreign Affairs in the cabinet of President (1886-91) José Manuel Balmaceda
Fernández*. In 1891 he was elected to the Senate and
served as its Vice-President. With the fall of the
Balmaceda government and the triumph of the rebellious Congress, Mackenna Astorga emigrated to the
United States. All his possessions were confiscated
in Chile. When he later returned to his country, he
began a long legal process to recuperate his property.
From 1905 until 1915 he served again as a senator,
and in 1913 was elected president of the Liberal Democratic Party (Partido Liberal Democrático*). He also
worked in the Ministry of Public Education as an advisor, retiring in 1920.

MAGALLANES. A province of southern Chile; population:
    85, 341 (1971 est.); area: 132, 033. 5 sq. km. ; capital
    city: Punta Arenas*.

MAIPON. A river near the city of Chillán in southern-cen-
    tral Chile, and the site of a battle fought on August 3,
    1813 between troops loyal to Spain and troops fighting
    for Chilean independence. Antonio Pareja* led the
    royalist troops (Realista*), while José Miguel Carrera
    Verdugo* led the troops fighting for independence (In-
    dependiente*). This battle foreshadowed the siege of
    Chillán. The Chilean patriots arrived in Chillán and
    looted the city, getting drunk in the process. The
    royalist troops, who had withdrawn to the outskirts of
    the city, returned with great power and almost suc-
    ceeded in destroying the Independent Army. In light
    of the great danger facing them, Carrera Verdugo or-
    dered his men to retreat. This withdrawal cost them
    many casualties.

MAIPU. One of the most important battles in the struggle
    for Chilean independence, fought on April 5, 1818, on
    the plains of Maipú just south of Santiago*. José de
    San Martín*, who had routed the Spaniards at Chaca-
    buco*, met them again at Maipú. The two armies had
    some 5000 men on either side. The Spaniards, under
    the command of Mariano Osorio*, were forced to fight
    San Martín and his troops. The engagement began at
    noon and lasted approximately two hours. In spite of
    the fact that San Martín lost 35% of his men, the
    Spaniards were forced to retreat and take refuge in
    the houses of a country estate, from which they were
    subsequently driven. Their losses were heavy, and
    the victory went to the side fighting for independence.
    San Martín sent word to Santiago that practically all
    of the south of Chile had been liberated, and the city
    burst into a delirium of joy. San Martín was offered
    10, 000 pesos for his services, but he refused all gifts.
    Most of Chile was then free.

MALLECO. A province of central Chile located south of
    Santiago; population: 193, 161 (1971 est.); area:
    14, 095. 1 sq. km. ; capital city: Angol*.

MANPOWER see THE ECONOMY: Internal: I. Manpower
    and Employment. See also LABOR.

MANUFACTURING see THE ECONOMY: Internal: F. Manufacturing; etc.

MANZANO DE LA SOTTA, ESTEBAN, 1793-1830. When the
struggle for Chilean independence began, Manzano de
la Sotta decided to join the Chilean army. In 1813, he
was promoted to colonel, and for the ensuing nine years
he formed part of the junta government that ruled without the consent of Spain. In 1822 he was elected a
deputy to Congress as a member of the Pipiolo* Party.
In 1830 he participated in the civil war (Guerra Civil
de 1829-30*), but was taken prisoner by government
troops. He died in jail in Valparaíso*.

MAPU see MOVIMIENTO DE ACCION POPULAR UNITARIA.

MAPUCHE. A nomadic tribe of Indians who lived in Central
Chile for about 400 years. They were conquered by
the Chileans in 1881, after three centuries of open
struggle. Since then, they settled in the province of
Cautín*, where they live in poverty.

MARIN ESQUIVEL, JOSE GASPAR, 1772-1839. Doctor of
theology and secretary of the first junta government
that ruled Chile independently of Spain (1811). He also participated in the Provisional Junta Government of
1811 and became a follower of Bernardo O'Higgins*.
In 1812 he was elected to the Senate, and in 1823 sat
on the Supreme Court. Elected deputy in 1825, he
was chosen to be Vice-President of the Chamber of
Deputies. When O'Higgins was exiled, Marín Esquivel
tried to arouse the populace in favor of the deposed
Supreme Director. As a result of his actions, Supreme Director (1823-26) Ramón Freire Serrano*
persecuted him. In 1828 he was re-elected to the
Senate, and four years later served again as Vice-
President of the Chamber of Deputies.

MARINA, MINISTERIO DE. The Ministry of the Navy was
created by Statute No. 163 on December 19, 1924.
In 1927 this ministry was dissolved and a new Ministry of National Defense was created. In the same
year, the Ministry of National Defense was divided
into two ministries: the Ministry of War and the
Ministry of the Navy. In 1932 a new law was decreed
which once again united these two ministries, and the
Ministry of Aviation, into a new ministry: the Minis-

try of National Defense (Ministerio de Defensa Nacional*).

MARTINEZ DE ROZAS CORREA, JUAN, 1759-1813. Lawyer by profession and army officer during the struggle for Chilean independence. In 1790 he was promoted to colonel in the army in Concepción*. He became a member of the Exaltado* Party, and took part in the first junta government in Santiago in 1811, becoming president of the junta when Mateo de Toro y Zambrano Ureta* died in that office on May 2. When José Miguel Carrera Verdugo* came to power as president of the junta in 1812, Martínez de Rozas returned to Concepción, where he organized an army and set up the provisional junta government of Concepción. To keep a united front, Carrera Verdugo sent Bernardo O'Higgins* to make a pact with the army in Concepción. In spite of this effort, Martínez de Rozas and Carrera Verdugo came to blows on July 8, 1812. Carrera Verdugo wanted Santiago to be the center of revolutionary activities against Spain, while Martínez de Rozas wanted the provinces to play the major role in the struggle. The provisional junta of Concepción was dissolved as Carrera Verdugo triumphantly marched into the city. Martínez de Rozas was arrested and exiled to Mendoza, Argentina, where he died a year later.

MARTINEZ SOTOMAYOR, CARLOS, 1930- . Lawyer by profession and active member of the Radical Party (Partido Radical*). From 1953 to 1957 he was president of the Radical Youth Movement. After he graduated from the University of Chile, Martínez Sotomayor began a diplomatic career as Chilean representative to the International Congress in Buenos Aires (1955) and Stockholm (1957). He was a delegate to the American Conference of Democratic Parties held in Venezuela in 1960, and was also ambassador to the United Nations in that year. In 1963 he was named subrogate Minister of the Interior by President (1958-64) Jorge Alessandri Rodríguez*. In 1962 he traveled to the U.S. and Mexico, and was president of the Chilean delegation to the Punta del Este meeting in Uruguay. From 1963 to 1965, he served again as ambassador to the U.N., taking a trip to Geneva in 1964 as a representative to the World Conference on Trade and Development. He occasionally teaches law and economics at the University of Chile.

MATTA GOYENECHEA, GUILLERMO, 1829-1899.   A Chilean
poet and diplomat who was also very active in politics.
In 1858 he was exiled for taking part in anti-government manifestations, but returned to Chile in 1862 under an amnesty law.   In 1870 he was elected to the
Chamber of Deputies with the backing of the Liberal
Party (Partido Liberal*), and in 1874 served as its
Vice-President.   From 1875 to 1881 he was governor
of the province of Atacama*, and in 1881 was sent to
Germany as Chilean minister to that country.   He returned to Chile in 1887, and was named plenipotentiary
minister to Uruguay.   In 1891 Matta Goyenechea was
serving as minister to Argentina when the civil war
(Guerra Civil de 1891*) broke in Chile.   He was loyal
to President (1886-91) José Manuel Balmaceda Fernández* and resigned his diplomatic post.   Later as a
supporter of Congress, he was appointed governor of
Concepción.   In 1894 he was elected to the Senate.

MATTA GOYENECHEA, MANUEL ANTONIO, 1826-1892.
Brother of Guillermo Matta Goyenechea*, he studied in
Germany.   Upon his return to Chile, he became the
ideological leader of the Radical Party (Partido Radical*).
He was jailed for his anti-government demonstrations
and sentenced to death, but President (1951-61) Manuel
Montt Torres* commuted the sentence to exile.   He returned to Chile in 1862 with an amnesty law and founded
the newspaper La voz de Chile.   From 1855 to 1876 he
served as a deputy to Congress, and was President of
the Chamber of Deputies in 1876.   From 1876 to 1892
he served in the Senate.   He was against the government (1886-91) of José Balmaceda Fernández* during
the Civil War of 1891 (Guerra Civil de 1891*).   With
the victory of the rebellious Congress, he was named
Minister of Foreign Affairs.

MATTE LARRAIN, ARTURO, 1893-   .   Lawyer by profession and member of the conservative party known as
Partido Agrario Laborista*.   In 1943 and 1944, he was
Minister of the Treasury in the government of President (1942-46) Juan Antonio Ríos Morales*.   In 1950
he was elected to the Senate, and two years later was
the candidate of the right for the Presidency of Chile.
He was defeated by another conservative, Carlos Ibáñez
del Campo*.

MAULE. A province of central Chile located south of Santiago; population: 94,925 (1971 est.); area: 5696.9 sq. km.; capital city: Cauquenes*.

MAYORAZGO. An entailed estate.

MAZA FERNANDEZ, JOSE, 1889- . Lawyer by profession and one of the most distinguished Chilean diplomats. He was President of the Liberal Party (Partido Liberal*). Elected deputy in 1921, he served in Congress until 1924, leaving that body to become Minister of the Interior. He was the principal drafter of the Constitution of 1925*. In that year, he was elected to the Senate, where he served until 1953. In 1945 he was the Chilean Delegate to the U.N. Conference in San Francisco, California. He held ambassadorial posts in Uruguay (1943), Peru (1945), and Argentina (1958). In 1954 he was elected President of the General Assembly of the United Nations, the only Chilean to receive such an honor.

MEDICINE AND HEALTH PROGRAMS see THE ECONOMY: Internal: H. Public Health.

MEJIAS CONCHA, ELIECER, 1895- . Lawyer by profession and active member of the Radical Party (Partido Radical*). In 1919 he was president of the Chilean Student Federation (Federación de Estudiantes de Chile*). The following year he served as secretary general of the Radical Party. Elected deputy to Congress in 1930, he served almost continually until 1953. In 1942 he was president of the Radical Party, and three years later was named subrogate Minister of the Interior in the cabinet of President (1942-46) Juan Antonio Ríos Morales*.

MENSAJE see THE PRESS.

MERCURIO, EL see THE PRESS.

MESTIZO. An offspring of a European and an Indian, whose share of white blood placed him on a higher social level than the pure Indian or the Black slave.

MICRO. A bus.

MILICIA REPUBLICANA.   A conservative group which was
organized in 1932 with the purpose of overseeing the
constitutionality of the government in power in Chile.
Eulogio Sánchez Gutiérrez* was the founder of the
militia, which increased its membership to 50,000
within the first year.   In 1933 the Militia asked permission to parade in the streets of the capital.   Horacio Hevia*, the Minister of the Interior, considered
the militia a danger to the country.   When permission
to parade was granted, Hevia resigned.   The militia
was dissolved in 1935, when the danger of dictatorship
had disappeared in Chile.   Some of its members then
formed a new political party known as the Acción Nacional*.

MINAS, MINISTERIO DE.   The Ministry of Mines was created by Statute No. 16 in 1953.   The same year the
name was changed to Ministerio de Minería*.

MINERIA, MINISTERIO DE.   The Ministry of Mining was
created by Statute No. 231 in 1953.   The functions of
this ministry are to supervise mining in Chile, and to
handle the marketing operations of minerals both in
Chile and abroad.   The most important sectors of this
ministry are the National Mining Enterprise (Empresa
Nacional de Minería), the Nitrate and Iodine Sales
Corporation (Corporación de Ventas de Salitre y Yodo),
the National Petroleum Enterprise (Empresa Nacional
de Petróleo), and the Copper Department (Departamento del Cobre).   At one time, the Ministry of Mining
was a department within the Ministry of the Treasury
(1837-87).   In the year 1887, the Department of Mining was included in the Ministry of Industries and Public Works.   In 1927 the Department of Mining became
part of the Ministry of the Treasury.   In 1953, as already stated, mining became a new ministry, and it
continues to function today as such.

MINIFUNDIA.   A small farm or plantation of less than 1000
acres in size.   Division of the large landed estate.

MINING see THE ECONOMY: Internal: E. Mining. See
also: COAL, COPPER, IRON, NITRATES, PETRO-
LEUM, STEEL.

MISTRAL, GABRIELA, 1889-1957.   Born as Lucila Godoy
Alcayaga, she adopted the pseudonym Gabriela Mistral.

The first South American poet to win the Nobel Prize
for literature (1945). In recognition of her poetic gifts,
the Chilean government appointed her to high positions
in the consular service of her country and in the
League of Nations. In her youth she worked for a
decade as a rural schoolteacher in the north and south
of Chile. She was then invited by the Mexican government to reorganize the primary and secondary school
systems of that country. Early in life, she fell in
love with a young man from Santiago, but lost him
when he committed suicide. To him she dedicated
many love poems included in Los sonetos de la muerte,
or Sonnets of Death (1914), and in Desolación, or Desolation (1922).

In her later writings, she turned towards a humani-
tarianism with religious overtones, pleading with Christ
that he save a corrupted humanity, as well as the soul
of her dead lover. She bemoans the fate of the Jewish
race, of the poor, and shows pity and understanding
towards the unmarried mother of forlorn children. But
in her writings there is very little social content of a
political or economic nature. Her poetry is very sub-
jective and personal. The main themes of her writings
are love and death, desolation and solitude. In her
poems, there is an idealism which is soft and tender
when it deals with love, but becomes a harsh cry when
confronted with injustice and cowardice. Her greatest
works are considered to be Desolación, and Tala, or
Thorny Tree (1938). They both evoke images of burning sands, barren horizons, and death.

MODERADO. A moderate during the Chilean struggle for
independence. The first national Congress of Chile
was established on July 4, 1811. Three loci of opinion were represented at this congress: the reactionaries or royalists (Realista*) sought the return of
monarchical rule; the moderates (Moderado*) were determined to maintain the political status quo, accepting the monarchy with certain constitutional reforms;
and the radicals (Exaltado*) desired complete and immediate independence. The moderates were in the
majority in Congress. Their material interests in
many cases had been bound up with the Spanish colonial regime. They wanted a continuation of such a regime with some modifications. They insisted, for example, that the creoles* be given as much say in the
governance of Chile as the peninsulares*. The Mode-

rados also wanted a free hand in commerce and the right to choose their own candidates to be representatives to the Spanish Court. The moderates, with the help of the realistas were able to exclude the exaltados from the Junta Government of 1812, choosing José Miguel Carrera Verdugo* as their President.

MOLINA SILVA, SERGIO, 1928- . Received a degree in economics and became dean of the Economics Department at the University of Chile, where he also taught courses in statistics and micro-economics. In 1952 he worked with the United Nations as an economic expert on Latin America. A year later, he was Chilean delegate to the Fiscal Commission of the U.N. In 1954 he was the Director of Income Tax and Finances in the Ministry of the Treasury, and represented Chile on an International Finance Conference held in Rio de Janeiro, Brazil. In 1955 he took an active part in the development of the Economic Commission for Latin America* (ECLA), and returned to teach at the University of Chile. In 1964 he was named Minister of the Treasury in the cabinet of President (1964-70) Eduardo Frei Montalva*.

MONAP   see MOVIMIENTO NACIONAL DEL PUEBLO.

MONEDA, LA.   The mint; the Chilean presidential palace in Santiago. Built by the Spaniards in the 17th century. In the first patio there is a beautiful 17th century copper fountain and two 18th century cannons.

MONTE PINTO.   Site of a battle in the hills of Concepción* fought between the Spaniards and the Araucanian Indians in 1557. The Spaniards, led by García Hurtado de Mendoza*, easily defeated the Indians, whose losses were reported in the thousands. The struggle between the Conquistadors and the aborigines, however, lasted over 300 years.

MONTERO RODRIGUEZ, JUAN ESTEBAN, 1879-1959. Active member of the Radical Party (Partido Radical*) and Minister of the Interior in the quasi-dictatorial government (1927-31) of Carlos Ibáñez del Campo*. On July 26, 1931, Ibáñez was forced to resign and go to Argentina after a series of student strikes and a revolt of the business interests in Chile had broken out. Chile was experiencing a troubled economy as

the national treasury was depleted and the large revenues which had formerly come from the nitrate and
copper industries had declined to a trickle.   The effects of the world Depression had contributed to a loss
of foreign market.   With the fall of President Ibáñez,
Montero Rodríguez, then Minister of the Interior, succeeded him.   Montero Rodríguez lasted less than a
month in office, and was succeeded by Manuel Truco.
When the latter threatened to cut salaries for all government employees and the armed forces in the interest
of the economy, a revolt broke out which was quelled
by the army.   Rioting continued until Presidential elections were held.   Juan Montero Rodríguez became
President, and lasted seven months in office (from
December 4, 1931, until June 4, 1932).   Discontent
continued in Chile and demonstrations and strikes
forced the President to proclaim martial law.   On
June 4, 1932, the Socialists, under the leadership of
Carlos Dávila Espinoza*, overthrew the President.
The situation became more stable with the election of
Arturo Alessandri Palma* to a second term as Presi-
dent (1932-38) of Chile.

MONTT ALVAREZ, JORGE, 1845-1922.   Distinguished naval
officer and Commander of the Chilean Navy; key figure
in the overthrow of José Manuel Balmaceda Fernández*;
and President of Chile from 1891 to 1896.   As a naval
officer, ·Montt Alvarez participated in the post-indepen-
dence (1818-64) fight against Spain.   The latter was trying
to recover its lost colonies and the Chilean territory of
Chiloé*.   He also fought in the War of the Pacific*, and
participated in the Chilean blockade of the Peruvian part
of Callao in 1880.   The Congressional rebellion which
brought Montt Alvarez to power also brought about the
collapse of the political system which had prevailed in
Chile since 1831.   It marked the end of the unitarist presidency with its almost dictatorial powers, and the establishment of a parliamentary system very much like that
functioning in England at the time.
    Montt Alvarez presided over the junta government
of August 31, 1891, and on December 26 of that year,
he was duly elected President with the backing of the
Conservative Party (Partido Conservador*).   The Presidential powers were limited, and the ruling cabinet
became responsible to the party or coalition of parties
which represented the majority in Congress.   President Montt Alvarez immediately granted partial amnesty

to the followers of Balmaceda Fernández, and stabilized
the electoral system in Chile.   One of the most important reforms of his administration was to see that Congress would be chosen by popular election.

In spite of congressional reforms, Chile entered into a period of ministerial instability which lasted until
approximately 1920.   During Montt Alvarez's term in
office there were eight complete cabinet changes and
11 partial changes within the cabinet.   Some of the
President's accomplishments were to embark upon a
program of public works and to strengthen the Chilean
Navy.   At the end of his term in office, Montt Alvarez
traveled widely in Europe, stopping in England where
he received high honors from the English government.
On his return to Chile in 1898, he was named honorary
mayor of the city of Valparaíso*.   A few years later
he retired from public life.

MONTT MONTT, PEDRO, 1846-1910.   Lawyer by profession,
member of the Liberal Democratic Party (Partido Liberal Democrático*), and President of Chile from 1906
to 1910.   In 1886 Montt Montt was named Minister of
Justice and Public Education by President (1886-91)
José Manuel Balmaceda Fernández*.   In 1889 he served
as Minister of the Treasury, but later resigned in opposition to President Balmaceda Fernández.   Montt
Montt participated in the Civil War of 1891 (Guerra
Civil de 1891*), siding with the rebellious Congress.
He was elected President of Chile in 1906, after having served in Congress both as a deputy and a senator.
Ministerial instability characterized his four years in
office.   In 1907 there were labor problems in the north
which almost caused the President to resign.   His administration embarked upon an ambitious program of
public works, which included programs to beautify the
cities and build roads, bridges, and various edifices.
Montt Montt was responsible for finishing the Fine Arts
Museum in Santiago, and many new schools were inaugurated during his term in office.

MONTT TORRES, MANUEL, 1809-1880.   Lawyer, university professor, general in the armed forces, active
member of the Conservative Party (Partido Conservador*), and President of Chile from 1851 to 1861.   Before becoming President, Montt Torres served in Congress as a deputy and senator, and held various cabinet posts in the two previous conservative governments

of Joaquín Prieto Vial* (1831-41) and Manuel Bulnes
Prieto* (1841-51). Montt Torres had become prominent
under the Bulnes regime and had supported the President against recurrent liberal uprisings. In the elections of 1851, which returned Montt Torres to the Presidency, the Liberals staged another uprising declaring
the ballots fraudulent and trying to prevent Montt Torres
from being inaugurated. The armed revolt lasted some
three months, costing an estimated 3000 lives (see
GUERRA CIVIL DE 1851).

Montt Torres ruled with a heavy hand, exiling liberal leaders, imprisoning agitators who sought to disrupt
the peace, and stifling many of the free voices he had
earlier encouraged. During his two terms in office,
Montt Torres failed to mollify the Liberals, and also
got in trouble with the Conservatives. The latter accused him of eliminating the mayorazgo (the entailed
estates), and of running a railroad through their lati-
fundias*. But Montt Torres became even more unpop-
ular when he tried to intervene in Church matters. He
asserted the right of patronage over ecclesiastical appointments and came into open conflict with the Archbishop of Santiago. The Archbishop wanted to remove
a sacristan from his parish and Montt Torres threatened
that he would remove the Archbishop himself if he took
such an action. The incident aroused an immense crisis, but the matter was finally resolved amicably.

The President's ten years in office proved to be an
enlightened despotism as he improved agriculture, gave
Chile its first good railroad system, increased the number of schools and libraries, and published the Civic
Code of the land, which had been prepared by Andrés
Bello*. Toward the end of his second term (1856-61),
the Liberals formed a new opposition to the conservative rule of Montt Torres. In 1858 there were agitations and imprisonments, and when martial law was
imposed on the land the Liberals and Radicals rose up
in arms. There was another civil war that lasted four
months (see GUERRA CIVIL DE 1859), leaving an estimated 5000 dead. The government once again was victorious but the coming Presidential elections brought a
close to the 30-year conservative rule in Chile.

MOVIMIENTO DE ACCION POPULAR UNITARIA (MAPU).   A
splinter of the Christian Democratic Party (Partido
Demócrata Cristiano*) founded in 1969 by Rafael Agustín Gumucio Vives* and Jacques Chonchol*. The prin-

cipal objective of this left-wing party is to bring about
a structural transformation in Chile by fighting capitalism, imperialism, and the exploitation of the Chilean
worker.   In 1970, the MAPU joined five other left-of-
center parties to form the Unión Popular*, a group
which supported the Presidential candidacy of Socialist
Salvador Allende Gossens*.   Allende was elected President and Jacques Chonchol, who had become the Secretary General of Mapu, was named Minister of Agriculture.   The basic program of MAPU consists of seven
points: 1) to limit the consumer's aspirations, and
market, to basic needs; 2) to recuperate the national
mineral wealth from foreign hands; 3) to accelerate the
Agrarian Reform Program; 4) to include the workers in
shaping the national destiny; 5) to nationalize banking in
Chile; 6) to accelerate the process of industrialization;
and 7) to reform the educational system of the country
by opening up the schools to all Chileans and not only
to a privileged few.

MOVIMIENTO DE IZQUIERDA REVOLUCIONARIO (M. I. R).
The Movement of the Revolutionary Left is made up of
Chilean terrorists who have been trying to force the
Chilean government since 1967 to adopt more extreme
policies to bring about a socialist society.   The majority of its members are leftist students operating underground.   The MIR is strongest in the city of Concepción*.

MOVIMIENTO DE RECUPERACION DOCTRINARIA.   The
Doctrinarian Recuperation Movement was formed in 1951
and was made up of dissidents within the Agrarian Laborist Party of Chile (Partido Agrario Laborista*).
The main purpose of this political group was to oppose
the candidacy of Carlos Ibáñez del Campo* for the
Presidency.   In 1954 the group dissolved to form a
new party, the Partido Nacional Agrario*.

MOVIMIENTO NACIONAL DE IZQUIERDA.   The Leftist National Movement was organized in 1964.   It was formed
to back the Presidential candidacy of Eduardo Frei
Montalva*.   It was dissolved in September of the same
year, just before the elections, and integrated within
the Socialist Democratic Party (Partido Socialista Democrático*).

MOVIMIENTO NACIONAL DEL PUEBLO (MONAD). A conservative political party which tried to attract popular
   support. It was formed in 1952 to back the Presidential candidacy of Carlos Ibáñez del Campo*, and dissolved after the Presidential elections of 1958. In a
   manifesto published in October of 1952, members of
   the party announced their full support for President
   (1952-58) Ibáñez del Campo. In 1953, the party elected
   one deputy to Congress, and in 1956, it fused with the
   Federación Nacional Popular*. During the Presidential
   elections of 1958, MONAD backed conservative Jorge
   Alessandri Rodríguez*.

MOVIMIENTO NACIONAL SOCIALISTA DE CHILE. The National Socialist Movement was formed in 1932 and dissolved six years later. It became known as the Chilean Nazi Party and was organized by Jorge González
   Von Marées*. Its political models were the German
   and Italian fascist parties, and its aims were to fight
   the spread of international Communism. The party's
   basic doctrine was that the individual was a servant to
   the State, and that the government had to exercise total control over every facet of the national life. Violence would be stopped by violent means. The party
   received strong opposition in Chile, and its short existence was marred by many political incidents. There
   were public street fights and violent encounters with
   the police. The leader of the party, Von Marées, was
   arrested when he fired some shots in the Chilean Congress, wounding another deputy. He resigned from the
   leadership of the party in 1938 and the party was dissolved. Its members joined another political group
   known as the Vanguardia Popular Socialista*. In the
   1938 elections, the party supported the Presidential
   candidacy of Pedro Aguirre Cerda*, who was also
   backed by the Chilean left.

MOVIMIENTO NACIONALISTA DE CHILE. The Nationalist
   Movement was a party with fascist tendencies formed
   in 1941 by Guillermo Izquierd Araya and dissolved in
   1945. The main purpose of the party was to abolish
   the universal suffrage and bring about in Chile the formation of a corporate state very much like that of
   Mussolini in Italy. The defeat of fascism in Europe
   was one of the downfalls of the Chilean Nationalist
   Movement. Many of its members later joined the Partido Agrario Laborista*.

MOVIMIENTO REPUBLICANO. The Republican Movement
was a political party formed in 1956 to regroup the
conservative elements within Chilean society who had
backed the Presidential candidacy of Carlos Ibáñez del
Campo* in 1952. In the Presidential elections of 1958,
the Movimiento Republicano backed Jorge Alessandri
Rodríguez*. When the party failed to get representation in Congress in 1961, it was dissolved.

MOVIMIENTO REVOLUCIONARIO NACIONAL SINDACALISTA
(MRNS). The National Revolutionary Syndacalist Movement was formed in 1963 to back the Presidential candidacy of Jorge Prat Echaurren*, considered by many
as a man who was trying to revive Nazi activities in
Chile. The main objective of the party was to oppose
Communism in Chile and to create a corporate state.
In 1964 Prat Echaurren renounced a bid to run for the
Presidency and the party was dissolved by the Minister
of the Interior for its Nazi tendencies. In spite of
this, the party operated underground during the term
of President (1964-70) Eduardo Frei Montalva*.

MUHLEMBROCK LIRA, JULIO VON, 1913- . One of the
founders and leaders of the Agrarian Laborist Party
(Partido Agrario Laborista*). He was opposed to the
Presidential candidacy of Carlos Ibáñez del Campo* in
1952, causing a split within the party. Two years
later, Rafael Tarud* formed a new party, the Partido
Agrario Laborista Recuperacionista*, which was leftist
in orientation. Mühlembrock Lira left the party in
1960 and joined the Partido Liberal*. In 1961 he was
elected to the Senate for an eight-year term.

MUSEO DE ARTE CONTEMPORANEO see MUSEUM OF
CONTEMPORARY ART.

MUSEO DE ARTE POPULAR see MUSEUM OF POPULAR
ART.

MUSEO HISTORICO see HISTORIC MUSEUM.

MUSEO NACIONAL DE BELLAS ARTES see THE NATIONAL
MUSEUM OF ARTS.

MUSEO NACIONAL DE LA QUINTA NORMAL see NATIONAL
MUSEUM OF QUINTA NORMAL.

MUSEUM OF CONTEMPORARY ART. Located in the Quinta
Normal in Santiago, this museum exhibits modern Chilean paintings.

MUSEUM OF POPULAR ART. Located in the Cerro Santa
Lucía in Santiago, the museum contains an exhibit of
South-American folklore.

MUTINY OF CAMBIASO. This mutiny occurred during the Civil War of 1851 (Guerra Civil de 1851*) in the southernmost Chilean city of Punta Arenas*. The liberals had tried
to prevent the inauguration of President (1851-61) Manuel
Montt Torres* and had taken up arms. The mutiny was
just one of such incidents against the government. It was
led by lieutenant Miguel José Cambiaso*, who tried to
proclaim General José María de la Cruz Prieto* President of Chile. The mutineers failed to accomplish
this and Cambiaso left Chile.

MUTINY OF FIGUEROA. It took place in Santiago on April
1, 1811. The mutiny was organized and led by Colonel
Tomás de Figueroa Caravaca, who wished to re-establish a monarchy in Chile to rule under the Spanish
hegemony. The mutiny failed, however, and Figueroa
was captured and executed.

MUTINY OF QUILLOTA. This mutiny took place on June 3,
1837 in the town of Quillota. It was a mutiny which
had international overtones. According to Chilean historians, it was organized by the Bolivian Minister to
Chile, Manuel de la Cruz Méndez, with the purpose of
overthrowing the Chilean government and forming a
Peru-Bolivian Confederation* which extended to the
south of Chile. The mutiny failed, and the Bolivian
minister was assassinated in Santiago.

MUTINY OF SEPTEMBER 5, 1938 see SEGURO OBRERO,
MATANZA DE.

MUTINY OF URRIOLA. It took place on April 20, 1851,
forshadowing the civil war that was to occur in the
latter months of that year. The mutiny was organized
and led by Colonel Pedro Alcántara Urriola Balbontín*,
who wanted José María de la Cruz Prieto* to become
President of Chile instead of the government candidate
Manuel Montt Torres*. The mutiny terminated with
the death of Urriola. The incident divided the Chilean

people into two factions, the supporters of the government and the supporters of Cruz Prieto. This dichotomy precipitated events that led to the Civil War of 1851 (Guerra Civil de 1851*).

-N-

NACION, LA   see THE PRESS.

NATIONAL INCOME   see THE ECONOMY: Internal: A. National Income.

NATIONAL LIBRARY.   The National Library of Chile (Biblioteca Nacional) is located between Miraflores and Mac-Iver streets in Santiago.   The building was erected in 1924 and its interior has oil murals by the Chilean painters Arturo Gordon and Alfredo Helsby.   Some of the divisions of the library are the National Archives and State Museums; the General Directory of Libraries in Chile; and the Historical, Judicial, and Geographical Archives.   In the section called "Fondo General," one finds all foreign works; in the Chilean section, all that is printed in Chile; in the American section, works in Spanish edited and published in North and South America.   In special sections one finds the archives of the colonial period, those of the Real Audiencia*, of the cabildo*, of the Inquisition, and of the Jesuits and other religious orders.   The National Library was founded in 1813, and was formerly located where the present-day Municipal Theater is.   Some of its rarest manuscripts date back to 1475.   The famous Siete partidas of the Spanish King Alfonso el Sabio, dated 1491, are in the National Library, as well as the epic poem La Araucana*, by Alonso de Ercilla y Zúñiga*, dated 1597, and the Arauco Domado* by Pedro Oña*, dated 1605.

NATIONAL MUSEUM OF ARTS, THE.   Located in the Parque Forestal in Santiago, it is the oldest museum of painting in South America.   The museum contains a large collection of Chilean paintings by such artists as Juan Francisco González, Alfredo Valenzuela, Alberto Valenzuela Llanos, and other paintings by foreign artists such as Monvoisin, Murillo, Guido Reni, and Rembrandt.   The National Museum also has a large collection of barroque art.

NATIONAL MUSEUM OF QUINTA NORMAL, THE.   A museum of fauna, flora, archeology, and mineralogy,
founded in 1830. It's most famous exhibit is that of
the mummy of "Cerro Plomo," found in 1954, and
probably buried in the snow by an Inca.

NECOCHEA NEMEL, EDUARDO, 1898- . Civil engineer
by profession and one of the founders of the Agrarian
Party (Partido Agrario*). He was president of the
party, and in 1945 helped organize the Partido Agrario
Laborista*. He also became president of the new
group. In the 1950's, Necochea Nemel became vice-
president of the Chilean Steel Company, Compañía
Acera del Pacífico*.

NERUDA, PABLO. Born in 1904 as Neftalí Ricardo Reyes
Basoalto, legally adopting the pseudonym Pablo Neruda
in 1946. The son of a rail worker, Neruda became
famous as a poet while still a young man. Since 1936,
when he was in Spain as Chilean consul during the first
two months of the Spanish Civil War, Neruda has also
become a political figure of considerable importance.
In 1937, he became a member of the Frente Popular*,
a political coalition made up of several left-of-center
parties which included the Communists, the Socialists
and the Radicals; in 1939, he was Chilean consul for
Spanish emigration; from 1942 to 1944, he took part in
the organization of the second front to help Russia; in
1945, he was elected Communist senator from Antofagasta and Tarapacá; in 1948, he publicly accused the
Chilean President (1946-52) Gabriel González Videla*
of being a traitor and as a result, was persecuted by
the law and went underground; in 1950, he won the
Stalin Prize for literature. Because of his political
beliefs he has been denied admission to the United
States more than once.
     More recently, in December 1970, he was appointed
by President (1970-76) Salvador Allende Gossens* as
Chilean ambassador to France. Neruda had been the
Presidential candidate for the Communist Party in 1970,
but withdrew just before the September elections as
part of the coalition front Unidad Popular* that backed
Allende Gossens. On October 20, 1971 Neruda was
awarded the Nobel prize for literature, the second
Chilean poet to win such an honor (the other was
Gabriela Mistral*) and only the third Latin American
writer to be recognized by the Swedish Academy. Ne-

ruda was cited for "a poetry that with the action of an elemental force brings alive a continent's destiny and dreams." Considered as one of the best Hispanic poets today, he has been a very prolific writer. He wrote his first book at 15 and published it, La canción de la fiesta, when he was 17 years old (1921); he published his second, Crepusculario, two years later. His Veinte poemas de amor y una canción desesperada, published in 1925 made him famous immediately. In it, Neruda created an original landscape and a poetry which reflected his own personal experience.

Neruda's fame extended even more with the publication of Residencia en la tierra I-II (1925-31; 1931-35). These two books were published in Chile first, and then in Spain. Soon after their publication, they became widely acclaimed and Neruda's name figured prominently with that of Federico García Lorca and other renowned Spanish poets of the so-called "Generation of 1927." The themes of these last two books were anguish, solitude, and death, all expressed in an absurd world. This pessimistic view of the world was continued by Neruda in the first two sections of Tercera residencia (1934-43), but it ends with the last poem of "Las furias y las penas" (Section II of the book). From this point on, Neruda begins a new phase of his writings. Section III of Terca residencia represents the political conversion of Pablo Neruda, as a poet committed to social justice. His social themes, already present in Crepusculario (in poems such as "Barrio sin luz" or "El ciego de la pandereta"), abandon the pessimism of the earlier poems and begin to offer a solution to injustice and misery. The poet abandons the contemplation of the self in a chaotic world and begins to see order in things. His preoccupation is no longer with death but with life. He is willing to put his art at the service of social realism, being primarily concerned with the rights of his fellow men.

After 1936, Neruda's message becomes more political. Neruda's most important literary works since that time are: España en el corazón (1937), a collection of poems defending the legitimacy of the Spanish Republican government and accusing the loyalist forces of General Francisco Franco of bringing destruction to Spain; Canto general, another collection of poems expressing a clear political orientation, and narrating in an epic fashion the history of America, as it was in 1400, and as it evolved to the present; and Las uvas y el viento (1954), a book inspired mostly by the Chilean landscape and by the workers' struggle to improve their living conditions.

There are two main periods in the poetry of Pablo Neruda.   There is the lyrical assertion of the natural world and of the individual human being as part of it, reflected in the earlier poems (1921-36).   And there is the social participation of the poet who identifies himself with his fellow men, as well as an austere vision of the seer who knows that the world is full of tragedy and injustice, reflected in the "engaged poetry" (1936 to the present).   The first period is characterized by pessimism, the second by optimism.   With España en el corazón and with the last section of Tercera residencia, Neruda gives ua a poetry whose foundations rest on the doctrine of social realism.   The Canto general and Las uvas y el viento are an attempt on the part of the poet to interpret the destiny of America from a historical and a political perspective.

Since 1936, the change in orientation in Neruda's work is the product of two major events in his life: his witnessing of the Spanish Civil War and his adherence to the Communist Party.   As a result, he is the poet who, because of his political beliefs, has become the spokesman of the deprived and sings of their hope. Neruda's other major works are: three volumes of the Odas elementales (1954, 1956, 1957); Estravagario (1958); and, Memorial de isla negra (1964).   He has also written a play, Vida, fulgor y muerte de Joaquín Murieta (1966), a social documentary of a Chilean emigrant who went to work in the California gold mines during the gold rush of 1849.

NITRATES.   After the War of the Pacific*, Chile remained in possession of the disputed Atacama* desert, rich in deposits of mineral salts--chiefly sodium nitrate. These deposits had been worked since 1830, mainly by Chile, in order to export nitrates to the exhausted farm lands of Europe and North America.   In 1860, Alfred Nobel produced nitroglycerine, and Chile became the world's largest exporter of nitrate.   Since 1930, however, the mineral has declined in importance as the production of artificial nitrates has increased everywhere in the industrial world.   Ever since World War I, actually, the development of artificial nitrates by the Germans hindered the Chilean monopoly in the world.   During the last 20 years, world production of

artificial nitrates rose 230%, whereas Chilean nitrate
dropped 38 to 40% below the 1950 production.

NOTICIAS DE LA ULTIMA HORA, LAS   see THE PRESS.

NOVOA LOPEZ DE ARTIGAS, JOSE MARIA VAZQUEZ DE,
     1800-1886. Lawyer by profession and political follower
     of Ramón Freire Serrano*.   In 1824 he was in Peru
     and Ecuador and fought for the independence of these
     two countries.   He returned to Chile and was elected
     deputy to Congress, becoming Freire Serrano's advisor.
     In 1825 he was named Minister of War and the Navy
     by Freire Serrano, and a year later he was elected to
     the Senate.   In 1828 he became President of the Senate.
     While Freire Serrano was in exile in Peru in 1829
     Novoa López de Artigas tried to reinstate the Chilean
     leader.   His plans were frustrated, however, and
     Novoa López de Artigas was also exiled to Peru, where
     he remained until his death.

NOVOA VIDAL, JOVINO, 1822-1895.   Lawyer by profession
     and active member of the National Party (Partido Na-
     tional*).   In 1859 he was Minister of the Treasury in
     the cabinet of President (1851-61) Manuel Montt Torres*.
     A year later he became Minister of Justice.   In 1861
     he was accused by Congress of having spent more than
     a million pesos on railroads during the Civil War of
     1859 (Guerra Civil de 1859*) while he was Minister of
     the Treasury.   He was also accused of having sent to
     the gallows participants in the civil war who were
     against President Montt Torres.   Novoa Vidal was ab-
     solved and served in Congress first as a deputy, then
     as senator, until his death.   He was Chilean Minister
     to Peru during the War of the Pacific*, and when he
     returned to Chile he was a judge on the Supreme Court.
     In 1889 he was one of the founders of the political
     group called Cuadrilatero*.

ÑUBLE.   A province of central Chile, located south of San-
     tiago*; population: 328, 132 (1971 est.); area: 13, 951. 3
     sq. km.; capital city: Chillán*.

NUEVA ACCION PUBLICA.   The New Public Action Party
     was founded in 1931 by a group of socialist politicians
     when the government of (1927-31) Carlos Ibáñez del
     Campo* was overthrown.   Marmaduke Grove Vallejo*,
     the colonel who established a Socialist Republic in

Chile that lasted only 12 days, was among the founders of the party. In 1933 the party was dissolved and its members were among the organizers of the Chilean Socialist Party (Partido Socialista*).

NUEVA IZQUIERDA DEMOCRATICA. The new Democratic Left was a political group which tried to become a party in 1963, but failed to win representation in Congress and was dissolved a year later. Its organizers were members of Padena*, the National Democratic Party, and were unhappy with Padena's pledge to back Socialist Salvador Allende Gossens* in the Presidential elections of 1964. The New Democratic Left backed Christian Democrat Eduardo Frei Montalva* instead. When this entity was dissolved, its members joined the Agrarian Labor Party (Partido Agrario Laborista*).

-O-

O.A.S. see ORGANIZATION OF AMERICAN STATES.

OBLIGADO. (Literally, "the obliged one.") A peasant or agrarian worker.

OBRAS PUBLICAS, COMERCIO Y VIAS DE COMUNICACIONES, MINISTERIO DE. The Ministry of Public Works, Commerce, and Communications was created by Statute No. 408 on March 24, 1925. Its functions were to supervise public works, communications and the internal and external commerce. In 1927 this ministry was replaced by the Ministry of Development (Ministerio de Fomento*).

OBRAS PUBLICAS, MINISTERIO DE. The Ministry of Public Works was created by Statute No. 3770 on August 20, 1930, becoming a separate entity from the Ministry of Development (Ministerio de Fomento*). The new ministry was under the supervision of the General Director who would also serve as Minister of State. On August 28, 1931, the Ministry of Public Works once again became a branch of the Ministry of Development.

OBRAS PUBLICAS Y VIAS DE COMUNICACION, MINISTERIO DE. The Ministry of Public Works and Communications was created by Statute No. 6-4817 on August 26, 1942.

It was previously called the Ministry of Development (Ministerio de Fomento*). The functions of this Ministry are to plan urban and rural development and to facilitate communications in the land. It has an Under Secretariat in charge of the following services: architecture; urban development; road construction; irrigation programs; sanitation; maintainance of ports and airports. The historical antecedents of the present Ministry of Public Works and Communications date to 1887, when the Ministry of Industry and Public Works was created (Ministerio de Industria y Obras Públicas*). In 1912 the Department of railroads was added to this ministry, and in 1924 the ministry came under the supervision of the Department of Commerce. From 1927 to 1942, with a brief one-year interruption, the Ministry of Public Works and Communication was called the Ministry of Development.

OBRAS Y VIAS PUBLICAS, MINISTERIO DE. The Ministry of Works and Public Roads was created by Statute No. 43, on October 14, 1924. It was separate from the Ministry of Industry and Railroads, and its functions were to supervise the growth of railroads, the maintainance of ports, construction of roads and bridges, and public works. In 1925 this ministry was called Ministerio de Obras Públicas, Comercio y Vías de Comunicaciones*.

OBRERO. Blue-collar worker.

OCHAGAVIA. Site of the first battle of the Civil War of 1829-30 (Guerra Civil de 1829-30*), fought on December 14, 1829. The rebel forces were under the command of Joaquín Prieto Vial*, and were opposed by the government forces led by Francisco de la Lastra y de la Sotta*. After the fight an armistice was signed which lasted 48 hours. (See TRATADO DE OCHAGAVIA.)

OCHAGAVIA ERRAZURIZ, SILVESTRE, 1820-1883. Lawyer by profession and active member of the National Party (Partido Nacional*). In 1846 he was named Minister of Foreign Affairs. During the next few years he traveled to Europe, and on his return to Chile in 1852 was named Minister of Justice. From 1852 to 1858 he served as a deputy to Congress, also serving as Vice-President of the Chamber of Deputies, and served

in the Senate from 1858 to 1867. In 1861 he was of-
fered the conservative candidacy in the Presidential
elections, but refused. Up until the time of his death,
he continued to serve in the Chilean Congress.

O'HIGGINISTA. A loyal supporter of Bernardo O'Higgins*.

O'HIGGINS. A province of central Chile located south of
Santiago*; population: 303,565 (1971 est.); area:
7,105.5 sq. km.; capital city: Rancagua*.

O'HIGGINS, BERNARDO, 1778-1842. The son of an Irish
immigrant, Bernardo O'Higgins is considered by Chileans as their national liberator. The young O'Higgins
studied in Peru, where his father served as Viceroy,
and in England, where he learned about his Anglo-
Saxon background. In London he met the Venezuelan
Francisco de Miranda, who was the first advocate of
South American independence. After his father's death
in 1801, the young O'Higgins came under the tutelage
of Juan Martínez de Rozas*, a Liberal and a Free
Mason. Both men conspired to overthrow the Spanish
yoke in Chile. On September 18, 1810, Chilean patriots proclaimed a junta government to rule in the
name of King Ferdinand VII. It was another eight
years before Chile finally declared itself independent
of Spain, and O'Higgins played an important role during that stormy period. From 1811 to 1814, a royalist
plot to restore colonial rule was countered by O'Higgins
and José Miguel Carrera Verdugo*.
      The despotic rule of Carrera Verdugo incited the
first families of Santiago to revolt under the leadership of O'Higgins. Early in 1814, the latter was
named commander-in-chief of the Chilean Army. The
appointment angered Carrera Verdugo and the rivalry
between the two Chilean patriots brought disunity to
the armies fighting for independence. Only the Spanish
threat to re-establish its hegemony in Chile prevented
O'Higgins and Carrera from coming to blows. At the
Battle of Rancagua* (October 1, 1814), the Spanish
forces routed the troops of Carrera and O'Higgins.
They were both exiled to Argentina and the quarrel between the two Chilean patriots and their followers was
carried over into Mendoza. Carrera conducted himself
in such a manner that the Argentine liberator José de
San Martín*, who was preparing an army for the invasion of Chile, ejected him from the province of Cuyo.

San Martín welcomed his Chilean allies, picking O'Higgins rather than Carrera as his second-in-command.
On February 12, 1817, after a legendary crossing of the Andes mountains, O'Higgins and San Martín defeated the Spanish forces at Chacabuco*.

Three days after the victory, a cabildo abierto* summoned in Santiago proclaimed O'Higgins Supreme Director of Chile--a post San Martín had refused. During a stormy five-year rule, O'Higgins was able to expel the Spanish from Chile (except for one garrison on the Southern island of Chiloé*), and to create a modern navy with the aid of Lord Cochrane*. The latter accepted a commission from O'Higgins in 1818 to guard the long Chilean coast and raid Spanish shipping from Chile to Ecuador. O'Higgins aided both Lord Cochrane and San Martín in their campaign to achieve the independence of Peru. But the Chilean liberator's popularity waned as the wealthy class did not wish to pay high taxes in order to send Chilean soldiers to fight in Peru.

O'Higgins enforced several reforms which further angered the Conservatives: he abolished the titles of nobility, and proposed the abolition of the mayorazgos* (entailed estates passed intact from father to son); he organized a "Legion of Merit" which honored men of accomplishment without regard to social position. O'Higgins also insisted upon the state's right of patronage over ecclesiastical appointments. The Church felt threatened even more by the opening of cemeteries for non-Catholics and by the declaration that dissenters would be tolerated. O'Higgins proposed and carried out other reforms: he increased the number of public schools, encouraged the importation of books, improved roads, and beautified the city of Santiago.

The wealthy class, deploring increased taxes, sought to overthrow O'Higgins. The followers of the Carrera Verdugo brothers accused him of being responsible for the death of their heroes. The aristocracy became increasingly disenchanted with O'Higgins, and the first uprising against him was organized in southern Chile by Ramón Freire Serrano*. By 1823, revolt had spread throughout Chile, and aristocrats in Santiago forced O'Higgins to resign. Discouraged by the turn of events, O'Higgins left Chile in 1823 and went to Peru. For the next five years his followers tried to return him to power, but failed. Just before his resignation, O'Higgins had been elected to a ten-year term as Supreme

Director of Chile, but the Chilean liberator never returned to his homeland, dying in exile in 1842.

OÑA, PEDRO, 1570-1643.   Chilean epic poet who wrote
Arauco domado* to celebrate the deeds of Diego Hurtado de Mendoza* and the conquest of Chile.

ORDEN SOCIALISTA.   The Socialist Order was founded in
1931 by Arturo Bianchi Gundián and Luciano Kulczewski
García.   Two years later, the party participated in the
Socialist Convention which gave birth to the Partido
Socialista de Chile* (April 19, 1933).   The Orden Socialista ceased to be a party and its members joined
the Socialist Party.

ORGANIZACION DE ESTADOS AMERICANOS (OEA)   see
ORGANIZATION OF AMERICAN STATES (OAS).

ORGANIZACION LATINOAMERICANA DE SOLIDARIDAD
(OLAS).   The Latin American Organization of Solidarity
was established in Havana, Cuba, in 1966, to coordinate and support wars of national liberation on the
American continent.   Chile is one of 27 countries which
participated at the first Convention of OLAS held in
July, 1967, sending delegates from the Communist and
the Socialist parties.   When Socialist President (1970-
76) Salvador Allende Gossens* came to power, he
pledged continued support for OLAS.   Chile, however,
like the other Latin American countries that pledged
support, has not played an active role in the wars of
national liberation, though it has given verbal support
to such movements in Latin America.

ORGANIZATION OF AMERICAN STATES (OAS).   The Organization of American States, of which Chile is a
member, was established on April 30, 1948, at the
Ninth Conference of American States held in Bogotá,
Columbia.   The charter was signed by the 21 American Republics, including Cuba.   After Fidel Castro
came to power, however, Cuba was expelled from the
OAS (1961).   In the past, Chile has traditionally voted
with the United States, the most influential member
within the organization.   In 1961, however, Chile ab-
stained on the Cuban vote, though later it adhered to
the majority decision by breaking diplomatic and trade
relations with Cuba.   From 1965 to date, Chile has
followed a more independent course.   In April 1965,

Chile opposed the United States intervention in the
Dominican Republic, and in November 1970, Socialist
President (1970-76) Salvador Allende Gossens* resumed
diplomatic and trade relations with the Castro government. In his Presidential campaign, Allende pledged
that Chile would withdraw from the OAS if the Latin
American Republics continued to vote according to the
dictates of the United States, as most of them had
done in the past. The Chilean President is in favor
of establishing a Union of Latin American Republics
without the presence or the influence of the "Colossus
of the North."

OSORIO, MARIANO, 1777-1819. Born in Spain. He was a
career military man in the Spanish Army who fought
to retain Chile as a Spanish colony. In 1814, after
his victory against the army fighting for independence
at Rancagua*, he was named by the Viceroy of Peru
as Governor of Chile, holding that office from October
9, 1814, until December 26, 1815. Osorio sent many
Chilean patriots into exile to the island of Juan Fernández*, and ruled with an iron hand. Arbitrary arrests, repeals of the mild reforms introduced by Juan
Martínez de Rozas* and José Miguel Carrera Verdugo*,
and suppression of free speech were characteristic of
the Osorio government.
The attempts of the Crown to restore Spanish power
in Chile showed signs of brutal despotism and convinced Chilean patriots that the time had come for independence. At the end of 1815, Osorio returned to
Peru, and three years later he was put in charge of
the expeditionary army which disembarked in Chile on
January 4, 1818. Osorio was defeated at the Battle of
Maipu* (April 5, 1818), and left the country. On his
way back to Spain he contracted a contagious fever and
died in Havana, Cuba.

OSORNO. 1) A province of central-southern Chile; population: 170,409 (1971 est.); area: 9,236.3 sq. km.
2) Capital city of the central-southern province of
the same name; population; 116,900 (1971 est.).

-P-

PACTO ANDINO. A commercial treaty signed by five Andean countries: Colombia, Ecuador, Peru, Bolivia,

and Chile. Its objectives are economic integration.
There is a common rule about foreign investment: profits are to remain in the Andes Sub-region and not be
channelled outside the countries that have signed the
agreement. Preferential treatment is to be given to
Ecuador and Bolivia, recognizing their relatively lesser
economic development. There is a program of joined
or parallel production and an agreement was reached
among the signatories to eliminate inefficiencies and
produce a substitute for an import. The final agreements chartered in the Pacto Andino were made in
December, 1970, in Cartagena, Colombia.

PADENA see PARTIDO DEMOCRATA NACIONAL.

PALENA. A disputed territory situated between 43° 30' and
44° south latitude on the Chile-Argentina southern border. Both Chile and Argentina claimed the land, located in the region of the Palena, Encuentro, and Falso
Engaño rivers and Palena Lake. The dispute dates
back to 1902, and was legally solved in December,
1966, through the arbitration of Great Britain. Although Argentina received the greater acreage of land,
with the demarcation line passing through the Encuentro
River, Chileans were happy because their share of the
land could be cultivated. Argentina's share is located
high on the Andes mountains, and most of it is inac-
cessible and unproductive. From 1966 to date, occa-
sional disturbances over the disputed land have been
reported in the Palena region.

PALTA. Name given to the avocado pear.

PARRA, NICANOR. Born in 1914. Contemporary Chilean
poet and author of the following works: Cancionero sin
nombre (1937), Poemas y antipoemas (1954), La cueca
larga (1957), Versos de salón (1962), and Canciones
ruda (1966). In his early poems, Parra experimented
with surrealistic images. He was attracted by the
Chilean landscape and expressed a feeling of nostalgia
for the values of his land. In his later poems, he
creates an atmosphere of intense reality and writes
some verses of social protest, such as "Autorretrato"
and "Los vicios del mundo moderno, " both found in his
collection Poemas y antipoemas. Parra has declared
that in his early poems one only finds irony and humor,
and that a feeling of tenderness and a humanitarian ap-

proach to life can only be found in his later poems,
especially the ones dealing with social protest.

PARTIDO. . .   see POLITICAL PARTIES.

PELUCONES.   Another name for Chilean conservatives.
Literally, the term which came into use around 1823
meant "those who wear large bushy wigs," and was
used scornfully by the pipiolos*, or Liberals.   The
pelucones consisted of a small but powerful big-proper-
ty class that tended to accentuate the economic inequal-
ities existing in Chile.   This political group was an ally of the Church and it opposed the liberal, anticlerical
programs of the pipiolos, who were in power from 1823
to about 1830.   In 1830, the pelucones came into power,
and governed Chile for nearly 30 years.

PENINSULAR.   A Spaniard born in the mother country who
was usually at the top of the social ladder in the Spanish American colonies.   The peninsular class was
never very numerous, and it included high-ranking of-
ficials--viceroys, captains-general, governors, bishops,
archbishops, and other members of the high clergy.

PEREZ MASCAYANO, JOSE JOAQUIN, 1801-1889.   Member
of the National Party (Partido Nacional*), Pérez Mascayano served in the Chilean Congress as deputy and
senator from 1834 to 1861.   He also served in the
diplomatic corps as secretary of the Chilean delegation
to the United States, cultural attaché to France, and
ambassador to Argentina.   In 1861, he was elected
President of Chile with liberal and conservative support.   He remained in power for ten years, during
which time the country underwent a period of progress.
However, political and religious quarrels marred the
stability of the government.   A moderate Liberal,
Pérez Mascayano appointed to his cabinet members
from both the Conservative and Liberal parties.   He
worked for greater political and religious tolerance,
but because of a unitarist constitution the President
continued to enjoy wide powers.   In essence, the government was a ruling oligarchy, just as it had been
under the previous conservative rule (1831-61).   From
1865 to 1866 there was a war with Spain, and Chile
joined hands with Peru.   In 1869 there was another
war, this time against the Araucanian Indians* who
had never been completely conquered, even in colonial

days. During the Pérez administration both Conservatives and Liberals split; the segments of old parties
entered into new alliances and new parties emerged.
With Pérez, Chile entered a 30-year liberal rule.

PEREZ ROSALES, VICENTE, 1807-1886. A Chilean writer
of some importance, and one of the founders of the
city of Puerto Montt* in the south of Chile. In 1814,
his father was exiled to Argentina for his revolutionary
activities against Spain. The young Pérez Rosales went
with him and lived in Mendoza until 1848, the year he
returned to Chile. A Conservative, he was elected
deputy to Congress in 1861, and senator in 1876. Some
of his best-known works are Ensayos sobre Chile, and
Recuerdos del pasado.

PEREZ SALAS, FRANCISCO ANTONIO, 1764-1828. A Chilean patriot who participated in the struggle for independence against Spain. In 1810, he was one of those
who proclaimed a junta government to rule in the name
of King Ferdinand VII, and two years later collaborated
to draft the Chilean Constitution of 1812*. In 1813, he
became President of the junta government (April 13-
August 5), but was exiled a year later by José Miguel
Carrera Verdugo* because of his conservative views.
In 1817, he returned to Chile and was named president
of the Tribunal of Justice. The next year he was
elected senator to Congress, and became President of
the Conservative Senate. Later that year he became
a Minister of the Supreme Court of Justice.

PERU-BOLIVIA CONFEDERATION. When the Bolivian dictator Andrés Santa Cruz moved to federate his nation
with Peru, Chile declared war on both countries. The
war lasted three years, from 1836 to 1839. The cause
of the war was that Chileans interpreted the confederation of its two neighboring countries as a political and
economic threat to their country. The war was won
by Chile, the federation was broken up, and the Bolivian dictator was exiled.

PESO [$]. The official Chilean monetary unit until 1960,
when the peso was devalued and the escudo* [E°] was
introduced. One escudo is the equivalent of 1, 000
pesos. The peso was divided into 100 centavos. In
1931, 100 pesos were the equivalent of US $ 12. 71.
Twenty-five years later, 100 pesos were the equivalent

of 10¢ (U.S.).

PETROLEUM. All of Chile's oil comes from the province
of Magallanes* in the far south. Oil was discovered
and used for commercial purposes in 1949. In that
year, the initial production amounted to 8,800 cubic
meters. In the following year, 100,000 cubic meters
were produced. This figure was quadrupled in 1955
and by 1970 had been increased six-fold. The rate of
production continues to increase but, thus far, all Chilean oil has been absorbed by the domestic market.

PINTO DIAZ, FRANCISCO ANTONIO, 1775-1858. Lawyer
by profession and Chilean patriot who fought against
Spain during the struggle for independence, obtaining
the rank of brigadier general in the revolutionary army.
He was a follower of Bernardo O'Higgins* and held
various ministerial posts during the latter's administration from 1817 to 1823. Significant events took place
in Chile from 1823 to 1830, the most important being
the institution of the first two political parties in Chile,
the Conservatives (pelucones*) and the Liberals (pipiolos*). These two parties were to determine the national destiny for the rest of the century. Pinto Díaz
was a member of the pipiolos. In 1827, he became acting President of Chile when President (1826-27) Agustín Eyzaguirre Arechevala* resigned on February 13.
Pinto Díaz governed for two years, solidifying the Republican government in Chile with the implementation
of the Constitution of 1828*. In 1829, he was formally
elected President of Chile but resigned in the face of
a Conservative uprising organized by General Joaquín
Prieto Vial* in the southern city of Concepción*. A
civil war ensued (Guerra Civil de 1829-30*), and when
it was finally settled the nation was delivered into conservative control for the next three decades.

PINTO GARMENDIA, ANIBAL, 1825-1884. Pinto Garmendía
had a brief university career as a professor of philosophy and the humanities, but devoted his life mainly to
politics. Member of the Liberal Party (Partido Liberal*), he served as a representative to the Chilean
Delegation to Rome (1848); as a deputy and senator to
Congress (1852-76); as Minister of the Navy (1871);
and as President of Chile (1876-81). During his administration, Chile declared war on Peru and Bolivia
(see WAR OF THE PACIFIC*). Prior to this war, Chile

was experiencing a severe economic depression, due in part to over-extensions at home, an earthquake and subsequent floods, and the fluctuating world markets that were a result of the American Civil War and the Franco-Prussian War. The government of Pinto, confronted with this acute economic crisis, decided to fight Peru and Bolivia for possession of the Atacama Desert* with its rich deposits of mineral salts (chiefly nitrate). By the end of Pinto's term, Chile had occupied Peruvian Tacna and Arica, and Bolivian Antofagasta; the economic situation had improved; and the elections of 1881 had put another liberal in power.

PIPIOLOS. (Literally, "novice, rawhand, beginner.") A name given contemptuously to a political group formed in Chile in 1823, after the fall of Bernardo O'Higgins*. The pipiolos were inspired by the liberal and democratic ideals of the French Revolution. They were anti-clerical and characterized the devoiced elements of the aristocracy. It is said that the pipiolos were the political antecedent of the Liberal Party, although the two are separated historically and cronologically. Ramón Freire Serrano*, Supreme Director (1823-26; 1827) of Chile, became the champion of the pipiolo cause. During his government, he began what is known in Chile as the pipiolo era, characterized by economic instability and anarchy. In 1830, after one year of civil strife (see GUERRA CIVIL DE 1829-30), the pipiolos lost what political power they had, and Chile was ruled by the opposing party, the pelucones*, for about 30 years.

PLACILLA. Site of the last battle fought during the Civil War of 1891 (Guerra Civil de 1891*). The forces backing the rebellious Congress defeated the government forces of President (1886-91) José Manuel Balmaceda Fernández*. Balmaceda Fernández resigned and a junta government was established to rule until the election of a new President (see JUNTA DE GOBIERNO DE IQUIQUE).

POBLACION CALLAMPA. (Literally, "mushroom settlement.") Shantytown, city slums.

POLITICAL PARTIES. Chile's political structure has evolved from a one-party rule, at the time of independence, to the multi-party system prevalent today. Although in

1936 Chile had the incredible number of 36 parties,
seven parties have largely dominated the political arena
in recent years. Imitating the French and Italian political make-up, Chilean parties fall into a right-center-
left framework. The Right is represented by two parties which have the support of the Church, the landed
aristocracy, the wealthy industrialists, and the upper-
middle class: The Partido Conservador Unido* (PCU),
and the Partido Liberal* (PL). The Partido Radical*
(PR), the party of the middle class, and the Partido
Democrata Cristiano* (PDC), one of the strongest parties in Chile, constitute the Center. The Left is represented by a Socialist-Communist-dominated coalition
known as the Unidad Popular*. The three major parties
within the coalition are: the Partido Comunista Chileno*
(PCch), the Partido Socialista* (PS), and the Movimiento de Acción Popular Unitaria* (MAPU). All Chilean
political parties that now exist, or have existed, are
listed alphabetically below using their Spanish nomenclature:

Partido Agrario. The Agrarian Party was founded
in 1931 by a group of concerned agriculturists who belonged to the Agrarian Society of Concepción (Sociedad
Agrícola de Concepción). Their aim was to unionize
agriculture. They believed that agriculture should be
considered the principal national economic activity, and
that the State should be simply a co-ordinator of the
national economic forces. In 1945, the Agrarian Party merged with the Alianza Popular Libertadora* to
form the Agrarian Labor Party (Partido Agrario Laborista*).

Partido Agrario Laborista. The Agrarian Labor
Party was formed in 1945 by the merger of the Partido Agrario* with the Alianza Popular Libertadora*.
In 1952, the party supported the candidacy of Carlos
Ibáñez del Campo*, and was joined by elements of the
fascist-oriented Movimiento Nacionalista de Chile*.
The basic goals of the Agrarian Labor Party were to
form a syndacalist union for all agricultural workers
and to attempt to establish a corporate state in Chile.
In October 1958 the party merged with the Partido Nacional* to form the Partido Nacional Popular*.

Partido Agrario Laborista Recuperacionista. The
Agrarian Labor Recuperationist Party was founded in
1954 and was an offshoot of the Agrarian Labor Party
(Partido Agrario Laborista*). Although both parties
wanted to unionize agrarian labor, there were factional

differences between the two.   The Agrarian Labor Party was rightist-oriented, while the Agrarian Labor Recuperationist Party wanted to maintain more of a mid-
dle-of-the-road course.   The Agrarian Labor Recuperationist Party was dissolved in 1958.

Partido Carrerino.   A political party formed in 1812
by the followers of José Miguel Carrera Verdugo*.   In
that year, Carrera won forcible domination over Congress and set himself up as dictator of Chile.   A new
Congress was summoned, bereft of objectionable members, and Carrera was able to introduce some notable
reforms: the liberal Constitution of 1812* was drafted;
freedom of trade was declared; the Chilean flag was
designed with the national emblem; and relations with
the United States were established.   All these reforms
contributed to the popularity of Carrera and to the formation of the Partido Carrerino, which was in opposition to the Partido O'Higginista*, made up of followers
of Bernardo O'Higgins*.   The rivalry between these
two parties of independence increased during 1813 and
the years that followed.

The royalists (Realista*) were trying to reconquer
Chile as a Spanish colony and dispatched an army from
Peru which occupied the southern island of Chiloé*,
and made plans to fight the patriots in Santiago.   Early
in 1814, the governing junta in the capital appointed
Carrera as Commander of the Chilean Army, but later
rescinded its appointment and named O'Higgins Chief
of the Armed Forces for the defense of Chile.   Carrera
refused to accept the change.   O'Higgins, who was
south with an army of some 2000 men, decided to
march to the capital to rid Chile of the dictator Carrera.   Just before the two armies of independence
were to meet in battle, however, the news arrived in
Santiago that a new royalist expedition led by Manuel
Osorio* was marching on the Chilean capital.   Carrera
and O'Higgins, in light of the new danger, joined forces,
but only briefly.   At the battle of Rancagua* in December, 1814, the armies fighting for independence were
disunited, split between Carrerinos and O'Higginistas.
The battle was a defeat for both Chilean patriots, and
the rivalry between the two increased.   During the next
two years Carrera and his two brothers Luis* and Juan
José*, as well as Bernardo O'Higgins, went into exile
in Mendoza, Argentina, accompanied by their followers.

The quarrels of Chile were carried into Mendoza.
Carrera antagonized the Argentine liberator José de

San Martín*, who was training an army to invade Chile
and fight the royalists.   San Martín ejected Carrera
and his followers from the province of Cuyo and co-
operated with O'Higgins in forging the army of reconquest.   San Martín and O'Higgins were victorious at
Chacabuco* (February 12, 1817), and O'Higgins was
named Supreme Director of Chile.   After this, the
Carrera brothers were persecuted by the O'Higginistas.
Two of them, Luis and Juan José, tried to enter Chile
from Argentina to arouse public sentiment in their favor and overthrow O'Higgins.   Their plot was discovered, however, and they were taken prisoners and
returned to Mendoza, where they were tried, found
guilty, and executed.   José Miguel, who was in Uruguay at the time, went to Argentina surrounded by his
followers with plans of invading Chile and avenging his
brothers' deaths.   He, too, was captured by the followers of O'Higgins, summarily tried in Mendoza and
executed.   With the death of the last Carrera brother,
the Partido Carrerino was dissolved.

Partido Comunista Chileno (PCch).   The Chilean
Communist Party has characteristically lacked revolutionary fervor and it pretty much follows the dictates
of the "Communist International" (Comintern) and the
Moscow line.   The strongest Communist Party in South
America, it was founded in 1922 at a political labor
convention.   The historical antecedent of the PCch is
the Socialist Workers' Party (Partido Obrero Socialista*).
In 1937, when the Communist Party was outlawed in
Chile, its members joined a new party called the Partido Nacional Democrático*.   The Communist Party's
beginnings were endangered by divisions and inner
struggles, especially during the bitter Stalin-Trotsky
fight.   The early strategy concentrated on the destruction of social democratic parties, whose existence was
declared to be the major obstacle to the desired violent
revolution.   This focus of activism prescribed by Lenin
in the 1920's was rejected by the PCch in later years,
if it was ever adopted.

Since 1935, Russia has advocated a "popular front"
policy, abandoning the Lenin formula.   This approach
aimed at a broad alliance of Marxist and non-Marxist
parties for the sole purpose of obtaining power through
the electorate.   In 1938, Communist support through
the Popular Front (Frente Popular*) paved the way for
the election of Radical Pedro Aguirre Cerda*.   In 1946,
the Communists joined the first postwar government in

Chile, that of Gabriel González Videla*.   Three Communist ministers were designated, but they were dismissed from the cabinet in April 1947.   Their unseat-
ing coincided with a period of increasing friction between the United States and Russia.   Since the three
were militantly anti-American, González Videla did not
want to strain Chile-U. S. relations.

As a result, the Communists opened hostilities
against the González Videla administration by instigating a series of strikes.   This occurred at the same
time that Moscow announced an international policy of
class warfare.   In 1948, after thousands of party members had been arrested in Chile, the parliament passed
the Law for the Defense of Democracy, banning the
Communist Party and striking its members from the
voters' registration.   The ban lasted ten years.   But
PCch members continued to be active in politics under
the disguise of other political parties.   In 1958, the
party was reinstated once again by President (1952-58)
Carlos Ibáñez del Campo*.   In 1947, a year before the
party was outlawed, the PCch garnered 16.5% of the
vote, the third largest block after the Conservative
Party (Partido Conservador*) and the Radical Party
(Partido Radical*).   In 1960, the PCch listed candidates for municipal councils, but received only 9% of
the vote.   Its percentage, however, has continually increased since, with 11.3% of the vote in 1961, 12.7%
in 1963, 15.9% in 1970, and 17.3% in 1971.

In 1964, the Communists participated in the popular
front coalition, Frente de Acción Popular* (FRAP), to
back the candidacy of Socialist Salvador Allende Gossens*, who was defeated at the polls by Christian
Democrat Eduardo Frei Montalva*.   In 1969, the Communists joined another popular front coalition, the
Unidad Popular*, to back Allende for the Presidential
elections of 1970.   On September 4, 1970, the Russian
strategy was victorious for the first time in any country of the Western world.   Chileans went to the poll
to elect the first Marxist government in the Western
Hemisphere.

Partido Conservador (PC).   The Conservative Party
is one of the oldest parties in Chile.   Established immediately after the rise of the republic, it was known
at the time as the Pelucone* Party.   Historically, the
PC has been the party of the elite, the Church, and
the landed aristocracy.   Its name became officially the
Partido Conservador during the government (1851-61)

of Manuel Montt Torres*.   In 1949, the PC split into
two parties: the Partido Conservador Social Cristiano*
and the Partido Conservador Tradicionalista*.   Four
years later, the two parties combined to form the
United Conservative Party (Partido Conservador Unido*).

Partido Conservador Social Cristiano.   The Social
Christian Conservative Party, an offshoot of the Conservative Party (Partido Conservador*), was established
in 1949.   Its main ideology was to orient the party's
activities around a framework of Christian ethics.   The
party opposed all restrictive action against Communism.
In 1953, the party joined the other conservative splinter
party, the Partido Conservador Tradicionalista*, to
form the Partido Conservador Unido*.

Partido Conservador Tradicionalista.   The Traditional Conservative Party was created in 1949 when the
Conservative Party (Partido Conservador*) split into
two factions, the other being the Partido Conservador
Social Cristiano*.   The split came when both factions
presented a candidate for the Senate in the parliamentary elections of that year.   In 1953, the two factions
joined again to form the Partido Conservador Unido*.

Partido Conservador Unido (PCU).   Also referred
to as the Conservative Party (Partido Conservador),
the United Conservative Party was founded in 1953 by
the fusion of the Partido Conservador Social Cristiano*
and the Partido Conservador Tradicionalista*.   The
PCU is the party of the élite, the Church, and the
landed aristocracy.   Although markedly traditionalist
and right-oriented, the PCU differs from extreme-
rightist parties, such as the Fascist or Monarchist
parties of Italy, for example, or the John Birchers in
the United States of America.   The PCU has traditionally found its strength in rural Chile, where the most
orthodox adherents of Roman Catholicism are concentrated.   The party's 1961 platform declared that its
"fundamental doctrine was in keeping with the teachings
of the Church."   The PCU platform also called for
non-governmental intervention in business or agriculture and encouraged foreign investments in Chile.

The Conservative Party received strong support
during the decade 1940-50, polling 17% of the vote in
1941, 23% in 1945, and 25% in 1950.   Since then, the
Conservative Party's strength decreased steadily.   In
the 1963 municipal elections, the party polled a mere
11% of the vote, and in the congressional elections of

1965 PCU representation in the Chamber of Deputies
dropped from 17 to 4, with no representation won for
the Senate.   In 1966, two parties of the Right, the
PCU and the Liberal Party (Partido Liberal*) fused to
form a new party, the National Party (Partido Nacional*).
The last time the PCU elected a Presidential candidate
was in 1958, when Chilean voters chose conservative
Jorge Alessandri Rodríguez*.   Alessandri was the
National Party choice in the Presidential elections of
1970, but lost to Socialist Salvador Allende Gossens*.
In the municipal elections of 1971 the combined Con-
servative-Liberal strength was 18.5%.

Partido Corporativo Popular.   Political party of the
Right founded in 1932 and dissolved in 1938, when many
of its members joined the Falange Nacional*.   The basic doctrine of the party was to establish a corporate
state to be modelled after that of fascist Italy.

Partido Democracia Agrario Laborista.   A political
party of the Center which came into existence in 1963.
It was formed by the fusion of the Nueva Izquierda
Democrática* with the Partido Agrario Laborista*.   In
1965, the party was dissolved and many of its members joined the Christian Democratic Party (Partido
Demócrata Cristiano*).

Partido Democracia Radical.   The Radical Democracy Party was founded in 1969 as a splinter group of
the Radical Party (Partido Radical*).   It represented the
right-wing within the Radical Party and opposed the candidacy of Socialist Salvador Allende Gossens*, the Radical Party's choice, in the Presidential elections of 1970.
The leading theoritician in the Partido Democracia Radical is Julio Durán Neumann*.

Partido Demócrata.   A political party of the Right,
which came into existence in 1932 when the Partido
Democrático* split into two parties: the Partido Demócrata and the Partido Democrático.   The Partido
Demócratico sympathized with the Left and recognized
the class struggle.   The Partido Demócrata, on the
other hand, aligned with two parties of the Right, the
Conservative Party (Partido Conservador*) and the
Liberal Party (Partido Liberal*).   In 1941, the Partido Demócrata became reunited with the Partido Democrático.

Partido Demócrata Cristiano (PDC).   The Christian
Democratic Party was founded in 1957 through the
merger of two conservative parties, the Falange Nacional* and the Partido Social Cristiano*.   The his-

torical antecedents of the party date back to 1931, when
the youth organization of the Conservative Party (Juventud Conservadora*) was established. The Juventud Conservadora later became the Falange Nacional. Unlike
its predecessors, however, the PDC is a decidely anti-
oligarchic, left-of-center movement. In the short period of 14 years, the PDC has become the most powerful party in Chile. In the 1958 Presidential elections,
the PDC candidate, Eduardo Frei Montalva*, ran a
poor third to Conservative Jorge Alessandri Rodríguez*
and Socialist Salvador Allende Gossens* (Frei receiving
only 20.7% of the vote as opposed to Alessandri's
31.6% and Allende's 28.9%).

Six years later, however, Frei became the first
Christian Democratic President in the Western Hemisphere. He received an impressive 55.6% of the vote
as opposed to his nearest contender, Allende, who obtained 38.6%. In the municipal elections of 1963, the
PDC received the largest percentage of votes (22.7%).
Two years later, in the congressional elections of 1965,
the PDC elected 82 deputies out of 147 seats, while
raising its total number of senators from 1 to 12. In
the 1971 municipal elections, Allende's Popular Unity
(Unidad Popular*) coalition claimed 50.8% of the vote,
but the most popular single party in the country remained Frei's Christian Democrats, who polled 25.8%
of the vote, 3% more than Allende's Socialists. The
political philosophy of the PDC is based on the papal
encyclicals Rerum Novarum, Quadrogesimo Anno, and
Pacem in Terris. The PDC proposes to bring about
radical reforms in Chile's semifeudal economic and
social structure and achieve a readjustment of society
working within a framework of Christian ethics.

Partido Democrático. The Democratic Party was
established in 1887 and dissolved in 1960. It came into existence once again in 1961 but was dissolved in
1965 when it failed to win representation in Congress.
The party's basic program was centered around four
points: 1) civil equality for men and women; 2) land
reform program to convert the tenants into property
owners; 3) social security program for the workers,
the sick, the old, and 4) suspension of capital punishment. In 1960, the party became part of PADENA
(Partido Nacional Democrático*). During the period
1961-65, the party formed part of the Frente Democrático de Chile*.

Partido Democrático de Chile. A splinter of the
Partido Democrático* founded in 1952 to oppose the
candidacy of Carlos Ibáñez del Campo*. The orientation of the party was leftist and in 1956, the Partido
Democrático de Chile joined the Socialist-Communist-
backed coalition Frente de Acción Popular* (FRAP).

Partido Democrático Nacional (PADENA). The National Democratic Party was formed in 1960 through
the merger of the Partido Popular Nacional* and the
Partido Democrático* with a faction of the Partido Socialista Democrático*, and the Partido Radical Doctrinario*. In the same year, PADENA leaders voted
in favor of joining the Socialist-Communist-backed coalition Frente de Acción Popular* (FRAP). The
PADENA platform has been characterized by a moderate leftism with socialist tendencies, but absolutely
democratic. In the 1961 congressional elections,
PADENA elected 12 deputies but failed to win representation in the Senate. PADENA representation fell
from 6.9% in 1961 to 5.2% in 1963. In the 1965 congressional elections PADENA deputies were reduced
to three. In 1965, PADENA left the FRAP.

Partido Democrático Socialista. A middle-of-the-
road party formed in 1964 through the merger of the
Partido Democrático*, the Partido Socialista del
Pueblo*, and the Movimiento Nacional de Izquierda*.
When the party failed to win representation in the con-
gressional elections of 1965, it was dissolved.

Partido Federalista. See FEDERALISMO.

Partido Femenino de Chile. A political party organized in 1946 to defend the rights of women in Chile,
allow them to vote and participate in the electoral
process. In 1950, when there was a vacant seat in
the Senate, the party presented as candidate María de
la Cruz Toledo*, who obtained a very small number
of votes. As the presidential elections of 1952 approached, the party backed the candidacy of Carlos
Ibáñez del Campo*, who was elected President (1952-
58). In 1952, there was another vacancy in the
Senate and de la Cruz Toledo presented herself once
again as candidate. She won the elections. Soon after, however, the Chilean Congress declared the in-
ability of the lady senator to serve. After this, the
importance of the party declined and the Partido Femenino de Chile was dissolved in 1953.

Partido Liberal (PL). The Liberal Party is one of
the oldest parties in Chile. It was founded during the

government (1841-51) of conservative Manuel Bulnes
Prieto* by Victorino Lastarria Santander* to oppose
"the authoritarian and ecclesiastic bias of the Conservative Party" (Partido Conservador*). Basing their
philosophy on the French principle of laissez-faire,
the Liberals advocated a separation of Church and
State, limitation of executive authority, one presidential term of five years instead of two, civil rights,
and universal suffrage. Traditionally, the PL has
represented the wealthy industrialists and the upper
middle-class.

In contrast to the Conservative Party, the Liberal
Party has been more progressive and has emphasized
the need for education and social reforms. Its strength
is urban, as well as rural. But like the Conservative
Party, PL percentage in Congress has dropped con-
siderably in the last few years. In 1941, PL representation was 15%. In 1949, the party polled 18% of
the vote, the highest percentage it ever reached. In
1961, the party polled 16% of the vote, and in 1963, a
mere 12%. In the 1965 congressional elections PL
deputies had dropped from 28 to 5, and PL candidates
to the Senate were not able to win any seats. In 1966,
the party fused with the United Conservative Party
(Partido Conservador Unido*) to form a new party of
the Right, the National Party (Partido Nacional*). In
the 1970 Presidential elections the National Party candidate was Jorge Alessandri Rodríguez*, but he lost
to Socialist Salvador Allende Gossens*. In the 1971
municipal elections the combined Liberal-Conservative
strength was 18.5% of the vote.

Partido Liberal Democrático. The Liberal Democratic Party was founded in 1875 by Benjamín Vicuña
Mackenna* and dissolved at his death in 1886. The
party's ideology was that of other Liberal parties of
the epoch, based on a principle of laissez-faire. It
was anti-clerical and represented the wealthy industrialists. In the Presidential elections of 1876 the
Liberal Democratic Party backed the candidacy of
Vicuña Mackenna, but he withdrew his name a day before the elections. In 1892, the Liberal Democratic
Party was reorganized by Manuel Arístide Zañartu*.
Its objectives were: 1) to establish the independence
of the executive and legislative branches of government;
2) to decentralize governmental power; 3) to maintain
public order and protect the country's infant industry;
and 4) to re-establish administrative integrity in gov-

ernment.   In 1924 there was a split in the party and
two new parties emerged: the Partido Liberal Democrático Aliancista* and the Partido Liberal Democrático
Unionista*.   In 1932, the Liberal Democratic Party was
incorporated with the other two factions into the Liberal
Party (Partido Liberal*).

Partido Liberal Democrático Aliancista.   A splinter
of the Liberal Democratic Party (Partido Liberal Democrático*) formed in 1924 to support President (1920-24)
Arturo Alessandri Palma* who had gone into self-imposed exile in Italy.   In 1930, it united with several
other factions of the Liberal Democratic Party to form
the United Liberal Party (Partido Liberal Unido*).

Partido Liberal Democrático Unionista.   A splinter
of the Liberal Democratic Party (Partido Liberal Democrático*) formed in 1924 to oppose the government
(1920-24) of Arturo Alessandri Palma*.   In 1932, the
Partido Liberal Democrático Unionista reunited with
the Liberal Democratic Party and other smaller splinter groups to form the Liberal Party (Partido Liberal*).

Partido Liberal Doctrinario.   The Liberal Doctrinary
Party was founded during the government (1881-86) of
Domingo Santa María González*.   It sustained and advanced the liberal ideology of the epoch, represented
the wealthy industrialist class, and was anti-clerical.
In 1932, the Partido Liberal Doctrinario joined the political combination known as Federación de Izquierda*,
and shortly after fused with the Liberal Party (Partido
Liberal*).

Partido Liberal Independiente.   Another name used
by the Liberal Doctrinary Party (Partido Liberal Doctrinario*) in a manifesto published in 1885.   In the
manifesto, the government (1881-86) of Liberal Domingo Santa María González* was highly criticized.

Partido Liberal Progresista.   The Liberal Progressive party was founded 1944, committed to laissez-faire,
establishment of "authentic liberalism, " and the modernization of Chile.   In 1953 elections, it received no representation in Congress and was dissolved, most of its members joining the Liberal Party (Partido Liberal*).

Partido Liberal Unido.   The United Liberal Party
was the name adopted from 1930 to 1932 by the Liberal
Party (Partido Liberal*) to bring together all the splinter groups within the party.

Partido Nacional (PN).   The National Party was
established in 1857 by conservative President (1851-61)
Manuel Montt Torres*.   Its historical antecedents are

the Pelucone* Party and the Conservative Party (Partido Conservador*). Like the Conservative Party, the National Party represented the elite and the landed aristocracy. But while the Conservatives were the defenders of the Roman Catholic Church and its vested interests in Chile, the members of the PN were opposed to ecclesiastic supremacy and Church control over civil power. During the disturbances of 1891 (see GUERRA CIVIL DE 1891), the National Party sided with the rebellious Congress against President (1886-91) José Manuel Balmaceda Fernández*.

There followed a period (1891-1925) of parliamentarism in Chile, during which the PN formed part of the Alianza Liberal* and the Coalición*, two political coalitions of the Right. In 1930, the National Party joined the Liberal Party (Partido Liberal*) and other smaller parties of the Right to form the United Liberal Party (Partido Liberal Unido*). Two years later, this entity became known once again as the Liberal Party. In 1956, the National Party was re-organized by the merger of the National Agrarian Party (Partido Nacional Agrario*) with the Agrarian Labor Recuperationist Party (Partido Agrario Laborista Recuperacionista*). But this political organization lasted only two years.

Much more important, was the founding of the National Party in 1966, through the merger of the Liberal Party with the United Conservative Party (Partido Conservador Unido*). This new coalition of the Right proposed to incorporate all rightist elements within the society for the purpose of opposing the Marxist threat in Chile. In the Presidential elections of 1970, the PN chose Jorge Alessandri Rodríguez*. The 74-year-old Alessandri, who had already been elected President (1958-64) of Chile, was given a very good chance to beat Socialist Salvador Allende Gossens*. Allende won, however, even if by a narrow margin. In the 1971 municipal elections, the National Party received 18.5% of the vote, as opposed to Allende's leftist coalition, the Unidad Popular*, which received 50.8% of the vote.

Partido Nacional Agrario. The National Agrarian Party was formed in 1954 from two splinter groups of the Agrarian Laborist Party (Partido Agrario Laborista*). The National Agrarian Party was opposed to the class struggle advocated by the Chilean Left but was in favor of nationalism. In 1956, the party be-

came part of the Federación Nacional Popular*. Later
in the same year, it merged with the Agrarian Labor
Recuperationist Party (Partido Agrario Laborista Recuperacionista*) to form the National Party (Partido
Nacional*).

Partido Nacional Cristiano. The National Christian
Party was created in 1952 by some disenchanted members of the Conservative Party (Partido Conservador*)
who wanted to bring about social reforms working within a framework of Christian ethics. The party never
reached major proportions and in 1956 it was re-incorporated in the Conservative Party.

Partido Nacional Democrático. Name adopted by the
Communist Party (Partido Comunista*) in order to maintain its existence after law no. 6026 (February, 1937)
declared it illegal. The law was rescinded shortly after and the party reassumed its original name.

Partido Nacional Popular. The National Popular
Party was founded in 1958 and dissolved in 1960. It
was created by the fusion of the Agrarian Labor Party
(Partido Agrario Laborista*) with the National Party
(Partido Nacional*). The party's doctrine was right-of-
center and its platform called for the economic and social "modernization" of the Republic. In 1960, the
National Popular Party merged with the Democratic
Party (Partido Democrático*), the Social Democratic
Party (Partido Socialista Democrático*), and the Radical Doctrinary Party (Partido Radical Doctrinario*), to
form the National Democratic Party (Partido Democrático Nacional*).

Partido Nacionalista. The Nationalist Party was
founded in 1914 and was based on the positivist principle that science was the only valid knowledge and
that religion should be divorced from civil matters.
But the party went much further than that. It called
for the strengthening of the executive power in an age
of parliamentarism (1891-1925), the nationalization of
the country's basic mineral resources, reforms in
education and in the monetary system, and protection
for the Chilean working class. In 1920, unable to win
representation in Congress, the Nationalist Party was
dissolved.

Partido Nacionalista Socialista Obrero. The Nationalist Socialist Workers' Party was founded in 1964.
Its ideology was Marxist but the party was opposed to
the establishment of a militarist state in Chile. Unable to win representation in Congress, the party was

dissolved shortly after its inception.

Partido Obrero Revolucionario. The Workers' Revolutionary Party was founded in 1941 and dissolved shortly after for not being officially registered by law. The affiliations of the party were Communist-Trotskyists, and its basic doctrine was to wage a relentless class struggle against capitalism and to establish a socialist state in Chile. The party failed to win representation in Congress.

Partido Obrero Socialista. A Marxist-Leninist party founded in 1912. One of its founders was Luis Emilio Recabarren Serrano*, who also founded the Chilean Workers' Union. The basic tenents of the party were to fight capitalism and to establish a classless society in Chile. In 1920 the party adopted the resolutions of the Third International Communist Convention held in Europe, which concentrated on the destruction of social democratic parties. The existence of these parties was declared to be the major obstacle to the desired violent revolution of which Lenin had spoken. In 1922 the party elected two deputies to Congress and changed its name to the Communist Party of Chile (Partido Comunista Chileno*).

Partido O'Higginista. A political party formed in 1812 by the followers of Bernardo O'Higgins*. The aim of the party was to set up O'Higgins as Supreme Director of Chile and overthrow José Miguel Carrera Verdugo*, who was practically dictator of Chile by 1813 (see PARTIDO CARRERINO). After the armies fighting for independence were defeated at the Battle of Rancagua* (October 1, 1814), O'Higgins and his followers, and Carrera and his followers, were exiled to Mendoza, Argentina, where Carrera conducted himself in such a manner that the Argentine liberator José de San Martín*, who was preparing an army for the invasion of Chile, ejected him from the province of Cuyo. O'Higgins and his men remained, and were helped by San Martín in forging an army for the reconquest of Chile.

The royalist troops in Chile were defeated by San Martín and O'Higgins at the Battle of Chacabuco (February 12, 1817), and O'Higgins was named Supreme Director of Chile. The followers of Carrera Verdugo opposed O'Higgins, but they were exiled and persecuted. José Miguel and his two brothers Luis* and Juan José* were taken prisoner because of their plans to cross the border into Chile and foment a coup d'état. They were summarily tried and executed in Mendoza. The Partido O'Higginista had practically no opposition for some five years. Public opinion, however, was turning slowly against the Supreme Director, who was held responsible for the killing of the Carrera brothers. As a result, O'Higgins was overthrown and went into exile in 1823. During the next five years, the O'Higginistas tried to bring O'Higgins back from Peru and once again declare him Supreme Director of the land. They failed and the Partido O'Higginista was dissolved in 1830.

Partido Progresista Femenino. The Progressive Feminist Party of Chile was founded in 1952 as a splinter of the Partido Femenino de Chile*. Doctor María Humuy* became its president and supported the Presidential candidacy of Carlos Ibáñez del Campo*. When the party failed to win representation in the municipal elections of 1953, it was dissolved.

Partido Progresista Nacional. The Progressive National Party was the name used by the Communists in the parliamentary elections of 1941. The party was able to elect 15 deputies and 3 senators.

Partido Radical (PR). The Radical Party was founded in 1861 as a splinter of the Liberal Party (Partido Liberal*). The party's doctrine was oriented toward 19th-century Liberalism and laissez-faire, but evolved slowly toward a "collectivist orientation" becoming the party of the middle class. By the 1930's the Radical Party had greatly expanded its basis of support. It had evolved into the party of the white-collar workers, farmers, and other segments of what can be called the upper middle-class. More importantly, it had become the strongest political party in Chile. However, before the advent of the Popular Front (Frente Popular*), a Radical had never been elected President of Chile.

The victory of Pedro Aguirre Cerda* in 1938 enabled the Radicals to displace many of the Liberal and Conservative appointees to government positions; thus the Radical goal of controlling government patronage was reached. For the next 14 years the Radicals controlled Chile. However, in 1958, the PR Presidential candidate, Luis Bossay Leyva*, ran a poor fourth. Immediately after the elections, the left-wing of the party was overthrown and the right-wing remained in control. This division, coupled with internal dissention, has cost the party its leading role in Chilean politics. During the decade 1940-1950 the PR polled 20-25% of the vote. In 1953, the party suffered heavy losses, receiving a mere 13.5% of the vote, but in 1956 its percentage climbed right back to 22%.

During 1961-1963 the PR averaged 20% of the vote. In the congressional elections of 1965, however, the PR representation in the Chamber of Deputies dropped from 38 to 20. In 1969, there was a split in the Radical Party. This time the left-wing of the party emerged as the dominant faction, and the right-wing formed a splinter group known as Partido Democracia Radical*. In the 1970 Presidential elections, the PR joined the Communist-Socialist-backed coalition Unidad Popular* and supported the candidacy of Socialist Salvador Allende Gossens*. In the municipal elections of 1971, the Radical Party strength dropped to 8.1% of the vote, as opposed to 13% obtained the year before.

Partido Radical Democrático. The Radical Democratic Party was an offshoot of the Radical Party (Partido Radical*) and was founded in 1885. Its doctrine was left-of-center and its goal was to woo the laboring classes in Chile. When the party failed to accomplish this, it was dissolved shortly after. In 1946, the Radical Democratic Party was organized again. Its principle doctrine coincided with that of the Radical Party except for one major point: the Radical Democratic Party sustained an absolute anti-Communist position and refused to form a coalition government with the Communists. In 1949, the Radical Democratic Party was re-incorporated in the Radical Party.

Partido Radical Doctrinario. A splinter of the Radical Party (Partido Radical*) formed in 1938 and dissolved shortly after. The Radical Doctrinary Party refused to join the Popular Front (Frente Popular*) and support the Presidential candidacy of Pedro Aguirre Cerda*. Its doctrine was right-of-center and the party did not want to participate in a coalition government with the Communists and Socialists. Ten years later, in 1948, the Radical Doctrinary Party was formed again. This time the party followed a left-of-center course, accused the radicals of conspiring with the government (1946-52) of Gabriel González Videla* to outlaw the Communist Party (see LEY DE DEFENSA DE LA DEMOCRACIA), and to oppose legislation that would favor the working class. In 1958, the Radical Doctrinary Party joined the Socialist-Communist-backed coalition Frente de Acción Popular* (FRAP) to support the Presidential candidacy of Socialist Salvador Allende

Gossens*. A year later, the party split into two
groups: one remained within the FRAP, the other
joined the Alianza de Partidos y Fuerzas Populares*.

Partido Radical Socialista. The Radical Socialist
Party was founded in 1931. It was a splinter of the
Radical Party (Partido Radical*) which adopted a leftist platform calling for: 1) the total reform of the educational system; 2) the domestic exploitation of the
country's natural resources to be undertaken by collective ownership; 3) the redistribution of wealth, with
better pay for the laboring class; 4) the institution of
a state-controlled banking system to issue notes and
extend credit; 5) the recognition of the class struggle;
6) the opposition to imperialism; 7) civil rights; 8) the
separation of Church and State; 9) the economic integration of the Latin American countries; and 10) the
elimination of the existing unitarist form of government
and the establishment of a federalist republic in Chile.
The party lost importance in 1943 and was dissolved.

Partido Social Cristiano. The Social Christian Party was founded in 1958 and derived from the National
Christian Party (Partido Nacional Cristiano*). Its
orientation was rightist and its political philosophy was
based on the papal encyclicals Rerum Novarum and
Quadrogesimo Anno. Shortly after its inception, the
Social Christian Party became part of the United Conservative Party (Partido Conservador Unido*).

Partido Social Democrático (PSD). A relatively new
political party founded in 1968 to offer an alternative
to Chilean Socialists who did not profess Marxism.
Similar in doctrine to the German and Italian Social
Democratic parties, the PSD had its own candidate in
the Presidential election of September 4, 1970, Rafael
Tarud Siwady*, who was also supported by the Acción
Popular Independiente (see API). In December, 1969,
the PSD joined a coalition of six left-of-center parties
(see UNIDAD POPULAR*). A few months later, Tarud
Siwady withdrew from the race to support the candidacy
of Socialist President (1970-76) Salvador Allende Gossens*.

Partido Social Republicano. The Social Republican
Party was founded in 1931 after the fall of President
(1927-31) Carlos Ibáñez del Campo*. The principle
objectives of the party were to defend public liberties
and the democratic institutions of the Republic. Arturo
Alessandri Palma*, who was elected President of Chile
for the second time in 1932, was one of the founders

of the party.   With stability assured in the Chilean political institutions, the party was dissolved in 1935.

Partido Socialista (PS).   The Socialist Party was
formed in 1933 through the merger of various socialist
parties of the left: the Acción Revolucionaria Socialista*, the Orden Socialista*, the Partido Socialista
Marxista*, and the Partido Socialista Unificado*, with
the Nueva Acción Pública*.   In 1948, the Socialist
Party changed its name to Socialist Party of Chile
(Partido Socialista de Chile).   There has been no mass
infiltration of the Socialist Party by the Communists.
Many Communists joined the Socialist Party when their
own party was banned in 1948.   Most of them withdrew
from the Socialist Party, however, when the Communist Party (Partido Comunista*) regained its legality in
1958.   The history of relations between these two
Marxist parties has been one of hostility.

Despite this tradition of rivalry, however, the Socialists seem generally to favor maintaining their alliance with the Communists.   This has been the case
in the last four Presidential elections, when the candidate of the Left was Salvador Allende Gossens*, a
Socialist.   The original Chilean Socialist Workers'
Party (Partido Socialista de Trabajadores*), founded
in 1912, joined the Communist International (Comintern)
and changed its name to the Communist Party in 1922.
For the next ten years, the Communists more or less
monopolized the Marxist Left.   It was after the fall of
Carlos Ibáñez del Campo* in 1931 that independent socialist groups emerged.   These groups evolved as a
consequence of the dissatisfaction on the part of the
Left with Communist leadership, which was ultra-left-
ist and badly organized.

The military rising of June 4, 1932, marked the
birth of the present Socialist Party (even though the
party was not formally organized until a year later).
Marmaduke Grove Vallejo*, Chief of the Chilean air
force and a proclaimed nationalist, led the revolt
which established a 12-day Socialist Republic.   By
1935, the Socialist Party had obtained control of the
majority of the trade unions and had become the principal party of the Chilean working class.   In the Presidential elections of 1938 the Socialists backed Grove
Vallejo, while the Communists backed Radical Pedro
Aguirre Cerda*.   This provoked additional resentment
among the Socialists.   Just before the elections, however, the Socialists joined the Communists to support

Aguirre Cerda when it was evident that their own candidate did not have a chance.

Socialist political ideology has not been consistent. It began with a strong anti-Communist bias, but was quick to join the Communists in the Popular Front (Frente Popular*) once it was given the opportunity. Then it broke with the Popular Front in 1946 and adopted the Peronist line. Afterwards, the Socialists have favored Titoism, and during the last decade they have been partial to Peking in the Sino-Soviet conflict. The ideological flexibility of the Socialist Party since 1933, however, does not connote any lack of basic principles. Actually all the various doctrines to which the Socialists have adhered have contained the same fundamental concepts: nationalism, anti-parliamentarism, socialism, and proletarianism.

Chilean Socialism may thus be defined as a nationalistic party of the left, Marxist in ideology, profoundly anti-oligarchic and anti-parliamentarian, committed to social and economic reforms through the organization of the industrial and agricultural workers. The Socialist Party obtained its greatest strength in 1941 and in 1971. In 1941 the party polled 18% of the vote, and 1971, 22. 8%. Since 1947, when the Socialists received only 8. 9% of the vote, the party has climbed steadily. In the 1971 municipal elections the PS emerged as the strongest party within the Unidad Popular* coalition, replacing the Communists. A year before, Socialist Allende became the world's first Marxist head of state to win office through a free election.

Partido Socialista Auténtico. The Authentic Socialist Party was a splinter of the Socialist Party (Partido Socialista*) and was founded in 1944 by Marmaduke Grove Vallejo*. The Authentic Socialist Party supported President (1942-46) Juan Antonio Ríos Morales*, a thing which the Socialists refused to do and hence the split. In 1946, the Authentic Socialist Party fused with the Communist Party (Partido Comunista*).

Partido Socialista de Trabajadores. The original Chilean Socialist Party, founded in 1912, was called the Socialist Workers' Party. Soon after its formation, it joined the Comintern and in 1922 changed its name to the Communist Party (Partido Comunista*). It was the party of the workers and of the Marxist Left.

Partido Socialista del Pueblo. The People's Socialist Party was founded in 1964 as a non-Marxist organization which supported the candidacy of Christian Democrat Eduardo Frei Montalva* in the Presidential elections of that year. The party was formed by a group
of Chilean Socialists who refused to support Socialist
Salvador Allende Gossens* for the Presidency. The
party was not entered in the Electoral Register (Registro Electoral*) and hence ceased to exist. Many of its
members joined the Movimiento Nacional de Izquierda*.

Partido Socialista Democrático. The Socialist Democratic Party was founded in 1959. Its principle doctrine was to establish a socialist society without a
class struggle. A year later, the Socialist Democratic
Party was incorporated in the National Democratic Party (Partido Democrático Nacional*).

Partido Socialista Internacional. The International
Socialist Party was founded in 1931 and was a precursor of the Socialist Party (Partido Socialista*), which
was founded two years later. In 1932, the International Socialist Party merged with the Revolutionary Socialist Party (Partido Socialista Revolucionario*) to
form the Unified Socialist Party (Partido Socialista
Unificado*).

Partido Socialista Marxista. The Marxist Socialist
Party was founded in 1931 in opposition to the government (1927-31) of Carlos Ibáñez del Campo*. Two
years later, it became the Socialist Party (Partido Socialista*).

Partido Socialista Popular. The Popular Socialist
Party was a splinter of the Socialist Party (Partido
Socialista*). It was formed in 1948 and represented
the extreme left-wing of the Socialist Party. In 1956,
the Popular Socialist Party joined the Popular Front
(Frente de Acción Popular*), and two years later was
re-incorporated in the Socialist Party of Chile.

Partido Socialista Revolucionario. The Revolutionary
Socialist Party was a precursor of the Socialist Party
(Partido Socialista*) and it was founded in 1931. A
year later, it merged with the International Socialist
Party (Partido Socialista Internacional*) to form the
Unified Socialist Party (Partido Socialista Unificado*).

Partido Socialista Unificado. The Unified Socialist
Party was formed in 1932 to bring together all Marxist
Socialist groups into one party. In 1933, it became
the Socialist Party (Partido Socialista*).

POPULATION. In the first quarter of 1971, the population
of Chile was estimated to be 9.8 million, increasing at
an annual rate of 2.8%. The census figure for 1952
showed some 6 million people living in Chile, whereas
in 1958 the population was 7.3 million, and in 1962
8.1 million. Seven-tenths of the Chileans live in the
Central zone, and three-fifths of the population is urban. Population density varies from 72 to the square
mile in Central Chile, to 20 per square mile in Forest
Chile, and to a mere 1 per square mile in the Archipelago (south of Puerto Montt* to Punta Arenas*). In
1970, the birth rate in Chile was 35.9 per thousand,
with a higher ratio in the cities than in rural Chile.
The death rate of 17 per thousand is one of the highest
in the world. The infant mortality rate of 127.3 per
thousand live births is only surpassed by Japan, Ecuador, and Guatemala, and is highest in rural Chile.
     Approximately one-half of the Chilean population is
suffering of malnutrition. The International Labor Office has disclosed that 11.9% of the people suffer from
simple malnutrition; 27.3% from serious malnutrition;
and 11% from desperate malnutrition. In the past, the
natural increase in population derived mainly from mi-
gration: the Europeans arriving to those areas undergoing development, and the Chilean peasants arriving
from the periphery to the urban centers. While European immigrants have almost ceased to come to Chile,
the country is undergoing, at present, an intense urbanization of the populace. Cities are expanding as a
result of rapid industrial development. Because of
this urbanization, the Chilean Government is facing a
serious housing problem. More than 80,000 Chileans
live in slums (callampas*) in the greater Santiago area
alone. The influx of people migrating to the cities
from the interior is in constant increase, and the Corporación de la Vivienda* (CORVI), a government-sponsored housing agency, is attempting to meet the rising
demand curve in housing units.
     The make-up of the Chilean people can be divided
roughly into three ethnic groups: the Mestizo, the European, and the Indian. Ninety-eight per cent of the
Chileans are classified as either mestizo or European,
and the remaining 2% as Indians. Exact figures vary,
but the most conservative sources estimate the population to be 68% mestizo and 30% European. Eighty-
one per cent of the Chilean people are literate.

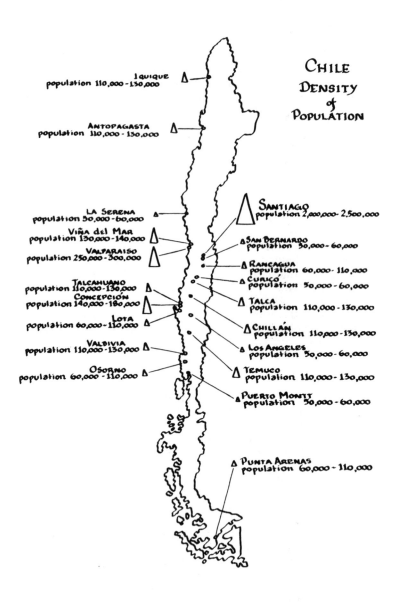

CHILE
DENSITY
of
POPULATION

Iquique
population 110,000-130,000

Antofagasta
population 110,000-130,000

La Serena
population 50,000-60,000

Viña del Mar
population 130,000-140,000

Valparaiso
population 250,000-300,000

Talcahuano
population 110,000-130,000

Concepción
population 140,000-180,000

Lota
population 60,000-110,000

Valdivia
population 110,000-130,000

Osorno
population 60,000-110,000

Santiago
population 2,000,000-2,500,000

San Bernardo
population 50,000-60,000

Rancagua
population 60,000-110,000

Curicó
population 50,000-60,000

Talca
population 110,000-130,000

Chillán
population 110,000-130,000

Los Angeles
population 50,000-60,000

Temuco
population 110,000-130,000

Puerto Montt
population 50,000-60,000

Punta Arenas
population 60,000-110,000

PORTALES PALAZUELOS, DIEGO, 1793-1837. The son of
    a prosperous family, Portales became a very astute
    businessman and a powerful politician. He spoke for
    the landed aristocracy and the wealthy traders, showing
    contempt for those who toiled in the fields and for the
    poor. In 1824, Supreme Director Ramón Freire Ser-
    rano* granted him a monopoly control on tobacco, tea,
    and liquor (see ESTANCO*). The concession stirred up
    a storm of abuse, but Portales insisted that it was
    time for business to play a greater role in politics.
    He then organized a conservative political group known
    as the estanqueros*, who later became members of the
    Pelucone* Party. The rout of the liberals at the Battle
    of Lircay* in 1830 delivered the country into the hands
    of the pelucones, the landed aristocracy. Portales was
    called to serve as Minister of the Interior, Foreign Af-
    fairs, War, and Navy in the conservative regime of
    1830, and for all practical purposes he became the dic-
    tator of Chile until 1837. His mission was to impose
    law and order in government, and he even spoke of the
    "religion of government."
        The Constitution of 1833* embodied Portales' belief
    in the concentration of power and in a highly centralized
    government. In 1836, a three-year war with Peru and
    Bolivia was attributed to Portales' decision to fight the
    Peru-Bolivian Confederation*. The war occurred when
    the Bolivian dictator Andrés Santa Cruz moved to fede-
    rate his nation with Peru. Portales interpreted the
    move as a political and economic threat to Chile and
    single-handedly declared war on the two countries. The
    war was won, the Bolivian dictator was exiled, Chilean
    military prestige was enhanced, and the federation was
    broken up. Portales, however, was an early victim
    in the conflict. He was in Quillota* when a group of
    Chileans, led by José Vidaurre Garretón, organized an
    uprising against him. Portales was arrested and sen-
    tenced to death without a trial. He was brought to Val-
    paraíso and executed on June 6, 1837. After his death,
    a general amnesty was declared, and the Conservatives
    continued to rule for a little more than two decades.

PORTILLO. A ski resort in central Chile, three hours
    south of Santiago*. It was the site of the Winter Olym-
    pics in 1966.

POSITIVISM. A philosophical system based on science as
    the only valid knowledge and facts as the only possible

objects of knowledge. It was originated by the French thinker Auguste Comte in the 1820's, and by the end of the 19th century it had become widespread in Western Europe and in three Latin American countries: Mexico, Brazil, and, to a lesser degree, Chile. Comte believed that knowledge had to go through three different theoretical states: the fictitious state (theology); the abstract state (metaphysics); and the positive state (science). His system was based solely on positive, observable, scientific facts and their relation to each other. All speculation or search for ultimate origin was rejected. Progress through law and order for Comte was a necessary norm of human history, and capitalism was the ultimate stage that man would reach after industrialization.

Comte believed that society would regain its unity and its organization based on a new spiritual power, that of the scientists, and a new temporal power, that of the industrialists. The system would also create a "religion of humanity" and a sociocracy made up of a corporation of positivist philosophers. Education would be in the hands of the elite as would government. It is easy to see how the cult of "law and order" and "government by the elite" turned into dictatorship in Mexico and Brazil. If the same did not happen in Chile, it can be explained by the fact that Chilean Presidents, from the time of independence through the end of the 19th century, had quasi-dictatorial powers. Positivism, never very strong in Chile, found adherents from two groups: the Liberals and the Free Masons. These groups were opposed to the excesses of theology, to ecclesiastical supremacy, and to religious training in the public schools. With the advent of parliamentarism (1891-1925), Positivism lost its appeal in Chile.

POTRERILLOS. The third of Chile's great copper deposits was located at Potrerillos (province of Atacama*) up to 1959. In that year production from the mine was exhausted and Chileans were lucky to find a new mine, located 12.5 air miles from Potrerillos (see EL SALVADOR). The Compañía Minera de Potrerillos was purchased in 1913 by William Braden*, and was later sold to Anaconda*. For over 50 years it yielded only low grade ore until it finally stopped production. From 1927 to 1959, the Potrerillos mine averaged only 55,000 short tons of copper per annum.

PRADO, PEDRO, 1886-1952. Chilean novelist and poet of
distinction, who is considered to be Chile's leading
stylist of modernist prose. From 1915 to 1916, he
presided over "Los Diez" ("The Ten"), an association
of writers, painters, poets, architects, sculptors, and
musicians. His major works are Alsino (1920), an al-
legory based on the myth of Icarus, in which the author
dramatized the condition of the Chilean peasant, and
Un juez rural (1924), a rural novel. He has also
written La casa abandonada (1912), in poetic prose,
and La reina de Rapa Nui (1914), a novel of adventure.
Prado is also known for his essays, parables, and
poems in prose.

PRAT CHACON, ARTURO, 1848-1879. Chilean naval hero
who fought in the War of the Pacific (Guerra del Pacífico*), dying in action. After a few years of schooling
in Santiago, he entered the Naval Academy in Valparaíso*. He participated in the war with Spain in 1865
and became a captain in 1873. Throughout his career
he pursued studies in mathematics, astronomy, and
other sciences associated with naval operations, and
he also managed to obtain a degree in law. During
the War of the Pacific he was commander of the sloop
of war Esmeralda. His martyrdom at Iquique made
him the naval hero of the war. On May 21 Chileans
commemorate the death of Arturo Prat, who rather
than surrender to the superior Peruvian fleet preferred
to die.

PRAT ECHAURREN, JORGE, 1918- . Lawyer by profession and the organizer of a neo-Nazi party in Chile.
In 1941, he was president of the Conservative Youth
of Chile. He worked as a banker in 1952, becoming
president of the State Bank (Banco del Estado) a year
later. In 1954 he became Minister of the Treasury in
the cabinet of President (1952-58) Carlos Ibáñez del
Campo*. He was a candidate in the Presidential election of 1964, organizing an ultra-rightist party, Acción Nacional*, which backed him. But just before
the elections he withdrew. A year later he ran for
the Senate, but was defeated.

PREMIO NACIONAL DE LITERATURA. The Chilean equivalent to the U.S. Pulitzer prize for literature. Given
every year to the most outstanding literary figure in
the country.

PRESA CASANUEVA, RAFAEL DE LA, 1907- . He was a
member of the Agrarian Labor Party (Partido Agrario
Laborista*), and was elected to the Chamber of Deputies in 1954.   In that year he left the party to form a
new political group called the Partido Agrario Laborista
Recuperacionista*.   In 1960, he joined the Partido
Democrático Nacional* (PADENA), a left-of-center party which backed the Presidential candidacy of Salvador
Allende Gossens* in 1964.   Presa Casanueva abandoned
the party in that year to organize a new party called
Nueva Izquierda Democrática*, which backed the Presidential candidacy of Eduardo Frei Montalva*.   In 1965,
President (1964-70) Frei named Presa Casanueva to be
ambassador to Portugal.

PRESS, THE.   Traditionally, Chileans have enjoyed a free
press.   More than 60 dailies and hundreds of weeklies
and bi-weeklies, representing every opinion across the
political spectrum, are published in Chile.   The most
important newspapers and magazines are found in the
large cities, with Santiago having the largest number
of them.   In the past, the Chilean press has been controlled by the nations' economic elite.   For example,
Agustín Edwards, owner of the Banco Edwards, controls three Santiago newspapers, El Mercurio, La Segunda, and Las Ultimas Noticias, as well as two Valparaíso papers, El Mercurio and La Estrella.   In the
capital, La Tercera de la Hora, the organ of the Radical Party, is controlled by the Banco Español-Chile,
and El Diario Ilustrado, linked with the Conservative
Party, represents the interests of the large landowners
and industrialists.
     La Unión of Valparaíso is pro-Catholic, and the
economic elite pretty much control the press in the
south and north of Chile, where most of the papers
lean toward the right-wing National Party (Partido Nacional*).   Outside the control of the economic elite
are other important newspapers and magazines published
mainly in the Santiago-Valparaíso area, and whose orientation is leftist.   They are: El Clarín, a sensationalist morning paper; Las Noticias de la Ultima Hora,
the organ of the Socialist Party; El Siglo, a Communist
daily published in the capital; the weekly satirical magazine Topaze; the weekly tabloids La Voz and La Flecha
Roja, both representing the interests of the Christian
Democratic Party; and Mensaje, a Jesuit journal of
high quality which deals primarily with the role of the

Church in bringing about socio-economic reforms in
Latin America.

Chile's most respected newspaper is El Mercurio of
Santiago, with good coverage of domestic and international affairs. During the government of President
(1964-70) Eduardo Frei Montalva*, El Mercurio sup-
planted La Nación as the mouthpiece of the government.
The magazine Ercilla, also published in Santiago, is a
good source to read to follow political developments in
Chile. Even though politically the Chilean press is
considered as one of the best in the world, both the
right and the left deserve criticism for presenting usually only one side of an issue. Generally the conser-
vative-controlled press does not recognize social problems, and devotes very little space to social unrest.
The left-controlled press, on the other hand, is often
sensationalist. Objectivity thus is lost because of the
political position most magazines and newspapers reflect. The government of President (1970-76) Salvador
Allende Gossens* has promised to keep the freedom of
the press, and to take a stand in opposition to inaccu-
rate reporting. President Allende would like to see
the press itself free of the control of the economic
elite.

PRIETO VIAL, JOAQUIN, 1786-1854. A career army officer who was twice President of Chile (1831-36; 1836-
41). The rout of the Liberals during the Civil War of
1829-30 (Guerra Civil de 1829-30*) had delivered the
country into conservative control. Prieto Vial had
participated in the conflict, leading the rebellious Conservatives to victory. In 1831 he was elected President, and a 30-year conservative rule began. Prieto
Vial sought to impose order upon unruly factions, and
called upon Conservative Diego Portales Palazuelos*
to serve as Minister of the Interior, Foreign Affairs,
War and the Navy. Portales became the virtual dictator of Chile from 1830 until his death in 1837.

Prieto Vial embodied Portales' belief in the concentration of power in a highly centralized government
and promulgated the Constitution of 1833*--a document
which stood until 1925. During his government, Prieto
Vial paid considerable attention to the economic problems of the Republic. Government expenditures were
curtailed, new port facilities were built at Valparaíso*,
and the nation's merchant marine was organized. Rivalries between the ports of Valparaíso and Callao in

Peru resulted in a three-year war (1836-39) with the Peru-Bolivian Confederation*, organized by the Bolivian dictator Andrés Santa Cruz. Santa Cruz's move to federate his nation with Peru had been interpreted by the Chileans as a political and economic threat to their nation. Chile won the war, Santa Cruz was exiled, and the federation was broken up.

During Prieto Vial's second term, the government became more stable. Material and cultural progress was made, and the Chileans began the task of building a nation. The Venezuelan Andrés Bello Edwards* was commissioned by the Chilean government to stimulate intellectual activities in the country and improve education. Militarily, Chile had shown its superiority over both Peru and Bolivia (in a surprise attack on the port of Callao, the Chilean navy had captured the entire Peruvian fleet). So, by the time of the elections of 1841, Chileans were satisfied with their conservative government and chose to continue it with Manuel Bulnes Prieto*.

PROJECT CAMELOT. A social science project which came into being in 1964 with funds provided by the U.S. Department of the Army. Its purpose was to study the likelihood of insurgent movements developing in Chile and the ways that might be used to arrest them. According to the U.S. Army, the project was to be a three- to four-year effort funded at about one and one-half million dollars annually. A large amount of primary data collection in the field was planned as well as the extensive utilization of already available data on social, economic and political functions. The project, with its implicit connotations of counterrevolution and possible U.S. intervention, was highly criticized by the Chilean government, causing an uproar in political as well as academic circles. After one year of adverse publicity, a Congressional hearing, State Department censure, a Presidential veto, and growing leftist agitation in Chile, the project was cancelled.

PROPRIEDAD AUSTRAL, MINISTERIO DE. The Ministry of Austral Property was created by Statute No. 4660 on October 31, 1929. Its functions were primarily to supervise Chilean possessions in the south, including the Antarctic region. This Ministry ceased to exist on April 9, 1931, and its name was changed to the Ministerio de Tierras, Bienes Nacionales, y Colonización*.

PROVINCIAL GOVERNMENT see CHILE: GOVERNMENT.

PROYECTO DE REGLAMIENTO PROVISORIO PARA LAS
    PROVINCIAS. The "Project for the Provisory By-laws
    to Demarcate the Chilean Provinces" was promulgated
    in 1825 by members of the Federalist Party (Partido
    Federalista*). The project recommended that Chile be
    divided into eight provinces: Aconcagua*, Colchagua*,
    Concepción*, Coquimbo*, Chiloé*, Maule*, Santiago*,
    and Valdivia*; and that each province should elect a
    governor.

PUDAHUEL. The international airport serving the city of
    Santiago de Chile.

PUERTO AYSEN. Capital of the southern province of Aysén;
    population: 14, 700 (1971 est.).

PUERTO MONTT. Capital city of the south-central province
    of Llanquihue*; population: 82, 600 (1971 est.).

PUNTA ARENAS. Capital city of the southern province of
    Magallanes*; population: 62, 000 (1971 est.).

PUREN. Site of a battle fought in 1558 in south-central
    Chile between the Spanish Conquistadors, led by García
    Hurtado de Mendoza*, and the Araucanian Indians, led
    by Caupolicán*. The Indians lost and took refuge in
    the mountains. The pursuing Spaniards found them,
    however, and took them as prisoners. Later the In-
    dians were shipped to Cañete where they were all sen-
    tenced to death, including Caupolicán.

                            -Q-

QUECHEREGUAS. Site of a battle fought in 1818 between
    troops loyal to Spain and troops fighting for Chilean
    independence. The army of independence, led by
    Ramón Freire Serrano*, occupied the town after a
    lengthy struggle.

QUILMO. Site of a battle fought during the so-called "War
    to the Death" (Guerra a Muerte*) on September 19,
    1819. The army fighting for independence, under the
    command of the governor of Chillán* Pedro Nolasco
    Victoriano, defeated the royalists, who were led by

Vicente Elizando. Although Chile formally declared
itself independent of Spain in 1818, the Spaniards continued to attempt to regain their colonial hold in Latin
America, sporadically fighting in Chile until the year
1864.

QUILO. Site of a battle fought on March 19, 1814, between
troops loyal to Spain and troops fighting for Chilean
independence. The battle was a victory for Bernardo
O'Higgins* and his army of independence.

QUINTANA, HILARION DE LA, 1774-1843. Argentine patriot
who crossed the Andes with the South American liberator José de San Martín on February 2, 1817, to free
Chile from Spanish rule. At the battle of Chacabuco*
in February, 1817, Bernardo O'Higgins* and San Martín routed the Spanish troops, and three days after the
victory O'Higgins was proclaimed Supreme Director of
Chile. From April 16 to September 7 of the same
year, O'Higgins was summoned south to fight the Spaniards, and he appointed Quintana interim governor of
Chile. The latter remained in Chile for another three
years fighting alongside the Chileans for their independence. In 1820, he was summoned back to his country
to be governor of Buenos Aires, and in 1823 he was
sent to Peru on a commission by the Argentine government to fight for the liberation of that country.

-R-

RANCAGUA. 1) Capital city of the central province of
O'Higgins; population: 75,800 (1971 est.).
2) The site of a very important battle fought some
75 miles south of Santiago between Chilean patriots
under the leadership of Bernardo O'Higgins* and royalist Spanish troops under the leadership of Mariano
Osorio*. The battle--one of many during the Chilean
struggle to obtain independence from Spain--was fought
on October 2, 1814. It was a great setback for the
forces of independence. The Spanish forces routed
the troops of O'Higgins, forced him to seek safety in
Mendoza, Argentina, and marched on to the capital.
The country was once again subject to the colonial
rule of the Spaniards. A wave of repression against
Chilean patriots fighting for independence began, last-
ing throughout the period known as the "Reconquista

Española de Chile*" (1814-17).

REAL PATRONATO. Papal grants and concession to govern
the relationship of Church and State in the Spanish-
American colonies.

REALISTA. One who favored the Spanish Crown during the
Chilean struggle for independence (1810-22).

RECABARREN CIENFUEGOS, MANUEL, 1827-1901. Lawyer
by profession and member of the Liberal Party (Partido Liberal*). He participated in the Civil War of
1851 (Guerra Civil de 1851*), opposing the conservative government of Manuel Montt Torres*. As a result of his rebellious activities, he was exiled, returning to Chile in 1862. It was the beginning of a 30-
year liberal rule (1861-91) and Recabarren decided to
run for Congress. He was elected deputy, then senator, and served in the cabinets of three Presidents,
Domingo Santa María González* (1881-86), José Manuel
Balmaceda Fernández* (1886-91), and Jorge Montt Al-
várez* (1891-96). Recabarren participated in the Civil
War of 1891 (Guerra Civil de 1891*) against President
Balmaceda Fernández.

RECABARREN SERRANO, LUIS EMILIO, 1876-1924. Revolutionary leader of humble origins who worked as a
printer. He was elected a deputy to Congress in 1906
on the Democratic Party ticket (Partido Democrático*),
but was expelled from Congress upon his refusal to
give an oath in the name of God and the Scriptures.
He settled in Iquique* and in 1908 founded the socialist
newspaper El Despertar de los Trabajadores (The
Awakening of the Workers). A year later, he formed
the first labor union in Chile (Federación Obrera de
Chile--FOCH*). He was one of the founders of the
Socialist Workers' Party (Partido Socialista de Trabajadores*) in 1912, and in 1920 left it to found the
Chilean Communist Party (Partido Comunista Chileno*
--PCch). He was elected a deputy in 1921 on the
Communist Party ticket, travelled to Russia in 1922
and returned to Chile in 1923. He committed suicide
on December 19, 1924.

RECONQUISTA ESPAÑOLA. The Spanish reconquest of Chile
during the struggle for independence was attempted between the years 1814 and 1817. The Spanish had de-

feated the Chilean patriots at the battle of Rancagua*
(1814), and had imposed the royalist regime once again,
taking repressive measures against those who were in
favor of overthrowing the Spanish hegemony in Chile.
Many patriots were exiled to the Juan Fernández* Island and to Mendoza, Argentina.   Arbitrary arrests
were made, and free speech and assembly were suppressed.   Some 7000 Chilean exiles began to conspire
with their Argentine neighbors to overthrow the Spanish
rule in Chile.   The Argentine "Army of the Andes, "
(Ejército de los Andes*) led by Liberator José de San
Martín*, was assembled in the western cordillera* for
the final blow against the Spanish.   In February 1817,
after an incredible march over the Andes, San Martín
and Bernardo O'Higgins*, with some 5000 men, defeated the Spanish at Chacabuco*.   This prevented the
restoration of Spanish power in Chile.   Three days after the battle, O'Higgins was named Supreme Director
of Chile, and a year later Chile formally declared its
independence from Spain.

RECOPILACION DE LEYES DE LOS REYNOS DE LAS
INDIAS.   A collection of laws and regulations relating
to the Spanish-American colonies, published in 1563 by
Luis Velasco, viceroy of New Spain (Mexico).   A more
complete collection was published in Spain in 1596,
another in 1628, and in 1681 the Spanish government
brought out the definitive edition comprising nine volumes.   Another version, consisting of three volumes,
was published in 1791, and the last, comprising 12
volumes, was published in 1805 under the title
Novísima Recopilación de las Leyes de Indias.   This
code covered all phases of colonial life in Spanish
America.   It contained numerous humanitarian regulations protecting the Indians.   Many, however, were not
effectively enforced in the New World.

REDUCCIONES.   Indian villages established in the Spanish
colonies in America, supervised by the Church or by
royal authorities.   The Indians were gathered in these
settlements to be converted to Christianity, but more
often than not they provided a much needed labor force.
The most famous reducciones under religious control
were those established by the Jesuits in Paraguay in
the 17th century.

REGIDOR. An alderman or councilman in the cabildo*,
elected by the townsmen to represent them. As early
as the 17th century, the whole municipal system of the
colonies was honeycombed with patronage and graft.
As a result, officials were no longer elected but appointed, and the office of the regidor usually went to
the highest bidder.

REGIONALISTAS DE MAGALLANES. A group of politicians
in the southernmost province of Magallanes* founded
the Regionalistas de Magallanes, a political entity
whose main purpose was to keep a free port in Punta
Arenas* and a decentralized form of government in
this Chilean province. In the Presidential elections of
1952, the Regionalistas presented their own candidate,
Arturo Matte Larraín, who lost to Carlos Ibáñez del
Campo*. The Regionalistas de Magallanes do not constitute a political party and are only influential in the
local government of the province.

REGISTRO ELECTORAL. The Electoral Register where by
law all Chilean political parties must be entered.

REGLAMENTO CONSTITUCIONAL PROVISORIO. In 1812,
the "Provisional Constitutional Rule" was established
in Chile to provide for a junta government with three
presidents and a unicameral chamber of congress--a
senate--to be appointed by the junta. The Spanish
liberal Constitution of 1812 was adopted in Chile to
rule in the name of King Ferdinand VII of Spain. José
Miguel Carrera Verdugo* was one of the sponsors of
the Reglamento Constitucional Provisorio, later becoming president of the junta government.

REGLAMENTO DE LA AUTORIDAD EJECUTIVA DE CHILE.
In 1811, the by-laws to establish the Provisional Executive Rule in Chile were adopted by Chilean patriots
fighting to obtain independence from Spain. The executive power was to be vested in three members of a
junta government, who would appoint a senate for life.
A military coup d'état, however, dissolved such provisions on November 15 of the same year.

REGLAMENTO PARA EL GOBIERNO PROVISORIO. The by-
laws to establish a provisional government in Chile
were promulgated in 1814, replacing the Reglamento
Constitucional Provisorio* of 1812. The new by-laws

provided for a Supreme Director, who was to enjoy full executive powers (quasi-dictatorial), and a seven-member senate, to be appointed by the Supreme Director. The rout of the Chilean patriots fighting for independence at Rancagua* in 1814 brought back Spanish rule in Chile, however, and the Reglamento para el Gobierno Provisorio was abolished.

RELACIONES EXTERIORES, MINISTERIO DE. The Ministry of Foreign Affairs was created in 1925 and lasted until 1930. It was re-established in 1941, and it is made up of the following departments: Immigration; Exports and Imports; Foreign Policy; Protocol; Boundaries; and Foreign Service. The historical antecedents of this ministry date back to 1871, when a constitutional decree separated the Ministry of Foreign Affairs from that of the Interior. From 1887 to 1925, the ministry also included a department of worship (culto), and was called Ministerio de Relaciones Exteriores y Culto* (1887), and Ministerio de Relaciones Exteriores, Culto y Colonización* (1888-1924). In 1891, and for a period of five months (April to September), the Ministry also included the Departments of Justice and Education, being called Ministerio de Relaciones Exteriores, Justicia, Culto e Instrucción Pública*. Following the separation of Church and State provided by the new Chilean Constitution of 1925*, The Department of Religion was abolished within the Ministry of Foreign Affairs.

RELIGIOUS PRACTICES. Ninety-five percent of the Chileans are Roman Catholics, or at least nominally so. The remainder are Protestants, Indians who still practice indigenous religions (less than 1%), and Jews (less than 1%). The Constitution of 1833* established the Roman Catholic Church as the State Church, while prohibiting other religious practices within the country. The Constitution of 1925* separated Church and State, and guaranteed liberty of conscience to people of other faiths. In spite of the separation, however, the association between Church and State has remained very strong, at least until the expiration of the term of President (1964-70) Eduardo Frei Montalva*. Chile is divided into three archdioceses: Santiago, La Serena, and Concepción. There are 16 bishoprics, and numerous churches in every community. Many schools, hospitals, and large territorial holdings are in the care of various religious orders. The mestizo population, concentrated in the Central zone, appears to be the most traditional and orthodox in its adherence to the Church, whereas Chileans of other regions show less attachment to organized religion. Civil marriage is the only marriage recognized by the State. Also see THE CHURCH.

RENGIFO CARDENAS, MANUEL, 1793-1846. Chilean patriot who was exiled to Argentina in 1814 after the Battle of Rancagua*. After the Spanish were routed at the Battle of Chacabuco*, he returned to Chile taking an active part in politics. A Conservative, he held various ministerial posts during the first two decades of conservative rule in Chile (1831-51). In 1831, Joaquín Prieto Vial* became the chief executive, naming Rengifo Cárdenas Minister of the Treasury. The latter paid considerable attention to the financial and commercial problems of the young republic. He was responsible for the adoption of measures curtailing government expenditures, the development of new ports, the adoption of a new tariff law, and the organization of a national merchant marine. Ten years after his first cabinet appointment, he was once again named Minister of the Treasury by President (1841-51) Manuel Bulnes Prieto*, also serving as Minister of Foreign Affairs and the Interior in Bulnes Prieto's cabinet. Rengifo Cárdenas was elected deputy (1828-43) and senator (1843-52) to Congress, dying before finishing his Senate term.

REPARTIMIENTO. Apportionment of Indians to the colonists in a system of forced labor. Theoretically, the Indians were to be considered free men subject to the Crown of Castille. They were to carry out public works supervised by the colonists, were to paid for but liable to tribute. The same system had previously been introduced by Spain in her overseas possession--Majorca, the Canaries, Morocco--but in reality differed slightly from enforced slavery. The Indians usually turned a deaf ear to any inducement of work, and since manual labor was unacceptable to a Spaniard, the natives were forced to work in mines and in public constructions or receive very severe punishment. In Chile, the repartimiento never succeeded because of the resistance of the Araucanians for more than 300 years to being subjugated by the Spaniards.

REPUBLICA DE CHILE. The Republican regime began in
    Chile in 1810. On September 18, Chilean patriots set
    up a junta government to rule in the name of exiled
    Spanish King Ferdinand VII. They dissolved the royal
    audiencia*, decreed free trade, and entered into rela-
    tions with the independent government of Argentina.
    For eight years Chile took up arms to prevent a resto-
    ration of Spanish power, and independence was formally
    declared in February 1818. Chile's history as a Re-
    public can be divided into five main periods. The
    years from 1810 to 1831 saw independence established,
    and were characterized by a conflict between the parti-
    sans of centralized government and those who wanted a
    federal government. From 1831 to 1861 there was a
    highly centralized government, based upon the conser-
    vative Constitution of 1833*. Liberalism, with greater
    local autonomy and individual freedom prevailed during
    the years 1861 to 1891. Parliamentary rule was es-
    tablished in Chile from 1891 to 1924. The period from
    1925 to the present has seen the growth of a relatively
    stable and democratic nation, characterized by growing
    industry, literacy, trade unionism, inflation, and the
    nationalization of natural resources. The entrenched
    oligarchy is losing its traditional prerogatives, and is
    beginning to give in to the growing demands for radical
    social and economic reforms. (See also CHILE:
    GOVERNMENT.)

REPUBLICA SOCIALISTA. On June 4, 1932, a military
    coup d'état overthrew the government (1931-32) of Juan
    Esteban Montero Rodríguez*, and a military junta as-
    sumed the executive power. Colonel Marmaduke Grove
    Vallejo*, chief of the Chilean air force and a pro-
    claimed nationalist, led the revolt which established a
    12-day Socialist Republic. The military uprising of
    June 4 also marked the birth of the present Socialist
    Party (Partido Socialista*). In September 1970, the
    Chileans elected the first Marxist government in the
    Western Hemisphere. Socialist Salvador Allende Gos-
    sens* was sworn into office on November 3, 1970,
    pledging to initiate the socialization of Chile and the
    establishment of a Socialist Republic.

RETTIG GUISSEN, RAUL, 1909- . Lawyer by profession
    and active member of the Radical Party (Partido Radi-
    cal*). He has served in Congress as a deputy and a
    senator, distinguishing himself for his oratorical bril-

liancy. He was twice president of the Radical Party--
in 1950, and from 1960 to 1964. He has also served
as dean of the Law School of the University of Chile.

REVOLUCION DE LA INDEPENDENCIA. Chile's evolution
from a colonial state to independence included four
main periods between 1810 and 1818, known as the
Revolution for Independence. The first period was
characterized by the brief one-year rule of a junta
government proclaimed on September 18, 1810 to rule
in the name of King Ferdinanc VII. The junta government entered into relations with the independent government of Argentina, decreed free trade, and dissolved
the royal audiencia*. The second period, from 1811
to 1814, was marked by intense rivalries among Chilean patriots. A royalist plot to restore colonial rule
was countered by José Manuel Carrera Verdugo* and
Bernardo O'Higgins*. When the two Chileans began to
quarrel between themselves and refused to cooperate,
the Spanish forces, increased with new troops, routed
the armies of both Carrera and O'Higgins and marched
on the capital. The third period saw the restoration
of Spanish rule in Chile, with its repressive methods
to prevent another Chilean uprising. The fourth period
was opened by the triumph of the patriots at that battle of Chacabuco* in February, 1817. O'Higgins was
proclaimed Supreme Director of Chile, and the country
formally declared its independence from Spain in 1818.
In succeeding years, the Chileans tried to institution-
alize their young republic and prevent Spain from re-
conquering its lost colony.

REYES BASOALTO, NEFTALI RICARDO see NERUDA,
PABLO.

REYES PALAZUELOS, VICENTE, 1835-1918. Lawyer by
profession and member of the National Party (Partido
Nacional*). He was active in politics, serving in
Congress as a deputy and a senator from 1870 until
his death. In 1877, he was named Minister of the
Interior in the cabinet of President (1876-81) Aníbal
Pinto Garmendía*. He distinguished himself as an
able political orator, and in the 1880's joined the
Liberal Doctrinary Party (Partido Liberal Doctrinario*),
becoming the party's president in 1885. In 1889, he
was elected President of the Senate. The political
party known as the Alianza Liberal* nominated him to

run for President in 1896, but Reyes Palazuelos was
defeated at the polls by Federico Errázuriz Echaurren*.

REYES VICUÑA, TOMAS, 1914- . Architect by profession
and member of the Christian Democratic Party (Partido Demócrata Cristiano*). In 1951, he became president of the rightist party known as the Falange Nacional*. Several years later he joined the Christian Democrats and backed President (1964-70) Eduardo Frei
Montalva* in the elections of 1964. In 1965, he was
elected senator for an eight-year term. Since then,
he has become one of the executive directors of his
party.

RIESCO ERRAZURIZ, GERMAN, 1854-1916. Lawyer by
profession and active member of the Liberal Party
(Partido Liberal*). In 1900 he was elected a senator
to Congress, and a year later, backed by the Liberal
coalition Alianza Popular*, he was elected President
(1901-06) of Chile. During his administration the
boundary conflict with Argentina was settled (1902),
providing for the arbitration of any future disputes,
and for the neutrality of each nation regarding any
conflicts involving the other. The boundary line bor-
dering Argentine Patagonia was fixed by the arbitration
of the king of England. To celebrate the agreement,
a statue of Christ the Redeemer was erected on the
border between Chile and Argentina, high on the Andes
mountains.
    Chile also signed a peace treaty with Bolivia (1904),
with the northern province of Antofagasta being awarded
to Chile. Serious strikes in the provinces of Valparaíso*, Antofagasta*, and Santiago*, forced the government of Riesco Errázuriz to promote the construction
of low-income housing for the workers. Before the
end of his term, many public works got under way to
erect public buildings, pave streets, construct highways and bridges. These works, however, were completed during the administration of the next Chilean
President (1906-10) Pedro Montt Montt*. After he
stepped down from the Presidency, Riesco Errázuriz
dedicated himself to his law practice, while at the
same time remaining active in politics. He died in
1916 from a cardiac seizure.

RIOS MORALES, JUAN ANTONIO, 1888-1946. Lawyer by
profession, man of business, and active member of the

Radical Party (Partido Radical*).   He served as a
deputy in Congress, and was named Minister of the
Interior (June 1932) and of Justice (September 1932).
In 1942 he ran for the Presidency of Chile, backed by
the Falange Nacional*, the Alianza Democrática de
Chile*, and the Radical Party, winning by some
56, 000 votes.   After his inauguration, Chile declared
a policy of neutrality in World War II, refusing to
break relations with the Axis powers.   Shortly thereafter, however, economic difficulties and popular pressure induced Ríos Morales to sever relations with
Germany, Italy, and Japan.

As a result of this action, Washington included Chile
in its Lend-Lease Program, and the Export-Import
Bank made new loans to Chile's developing industry.
Industrialization was on the priorities list in the administration of Ríos Morales.   A mill for making copper
wires was built; a national hydroelectric plant was
erected; and plans to begin work on a new steel mill
(Huachipato*) were drawn.   Improvements were made
in the Chilean railroads and the expansion of the educational system.   Ríos Morales' last year in office
was troubled by a precarious economic condition due
to a decrease in the price of copper, by a rising inflation, and by labor strikes.   The President was highly
criticized for traveling to the United States in October
1945, and his entire cabinet resigned.   Labor trouble
continued throughout the early months of 1946.   Because of ill-health, the President resigned and was
succeeded by Radical leader Alfredo Duhalde Vásquez*.
Like his predecessor, Ríos Morales failed to live to the
end of his elected term, dying in June 1946.

ROBLE.   Site of a battle fought between troops loyal to
Spain, under the leadership of Juan Antonio Olate, and
troops fighting for the independence of Chile, under the
leadership of José Miguel Carrera Verdugo* and Bernardo O'Higgins*.   The Spanish troops were defeated
on October 17, 1813.

RODRIGUEZ ERDOIZA, MANUEL, 1785-1818.   Lawyer by
profession and Chilean patriot who belonged to the
Moderado* Party and fought in the wars for Chilean
independence with José Miguel Carrera Verdugo*.   In
1811, the junta government named him Secretary of
War, and a year later he joined the army with the
rank of captain.   From 1811 to 1814 he became in-

volved in the internecine quarrels among Chilean patriots, and was accused of conspiring against Carrera
Verdugo. As a result, he was arrested in 1813 but
was later released. In 1814 he participated in the
Battle of Rancagua* and was exiled to Argentina with
many other Chileans. He continued to side with Carrera Verdugo, and, in 1817, after Bernardo O'Higgins
was elected Supreme Director of Chile, Rodríguez was
asked to leave the country; he refused to do so and
was arrested. He escaped from prison but was arrested again for conspiring against O'Higgins. He
spent several months in jail before being freed.

In 1818, he was asked to defend the city of Santiago
while O'Higgins was away. In two days, Rodríguez
was able to organize an army known as the "Hussars
of death" (Húsares de la muerte). He accepted the
executive power of the land but delegated it to O'Higgins when the latter returned. Fearing that Rodríguez
might turn the people against him, an order was issued by O'Higgins to have him arrested. Rodríguez
was taken to Quillota but was assassinated on the way.
Chilean historians are not in agreement as to who is
responsible for giving the order of execution. Miguel
Luis Almunátegui Aldunate* has hypothesized that
O'Higgins was responsible, whereas Justo Abel Rosales
was convinced that Bernardo de Monteagudo gave the
order.

RODRIGUEZ GONZALES, PEDRO JESUS, 1907- . Lawyer
by profession and active member of the Christian
Democratic Party (Partido Demócrata Cristiano*). In
1949, he was president of the Falange Nacional*, and
a trustee of the Catholic University (Universidad Católica). After the election of Christian Democratic
President (1964-70) Eduardo Frei Montalva*, Rodríguez
González was named Minister of Justice (November 3,
1964).

ROJAS, MANUEL, 1896- . Chilean novelist whose ambi-
tion was to create the modern Chilean novel. His
work can be divided into two main periods: the first,
beginning in 1926 and ending in 1936; the second, beginning in 1936 and ending in 1951. The first period
is characterized by regionalism. The novelist describes
primarily the seamy side of Chilean life: city slums,
tenements, centers of vice, prisons, waterfront districts. His early writings include Hombres del sur

(1926), El delincuente (1929), Lanchas en la bahía
(1932), and Travesía (1934). The second period emphasized the alienation and despair of modern man, in
such works as La ciudad de los Césares (1936), and
Hijo de ladrón (1951). In these works the influence of
existentialist writers can be detected, especially that
of Fyodor Dostoyevsky. Rojas portrays life in a re-
alistic manner, and his greatest achievement is his
remarkable study of lower class Chilean society.

ROTO.   "Torn"; a poor Chilean city-dweller.

RUIZ TAGLE PORTALES, FRANCISCO,   -1866. Proprietor of an entailed estate in Los Andes, and member of the conservative Pelucone* Party. He was a
deputy in the Congress of 1811 and participated in the
struggle for Chilean independence. Nevertheless, he
was not proscribed during the Spanish Reconquest (Reconquista Española*), but held municipal offices in
Santiago under the restored regime. As governor ad
interim, he delivered the city of Santiago to the patriots after their victory at Chacabuco*. After the
battle of Maipú*, he again became an avowed patriot,
holding various congressional offices during the
troubled years that followed the abdication of Bernardo
O'Higgins*. In 1829, he ran for the Vice-Presidency
of Chile, losing to Liberal Joaquín Vicuña*. During
the Civil War of 1829-30 (Guerra Civil de 1829-30*),
he was selected by Diego Portales Palazuelos* to be
President ad interim of Chile, holding office for a
little more than a month. Chile was undergoing a
period of constant disturbance and many provinces
within the country refused to recognize Ruiz Tagle
Portales. In light of this, the President was asked
to resign by Portales Palazuelos, doing so on March
31, 1830. Thereafter, Ruiz Tagle Portales retired
from an active political life.

-S-

SAAVEDRA RODRIGUEZ, CORNELIO, 1821-1891. A career
army officer who fought the Araucanian Indians (Araucanos*) and was able to push them as far south as
Villarica. He conducted the last punitive expedition
against the aborigines in the year 1882. For his role
in the extermination of the Indians and his participation

in the war against Spain in 1865, he was promoted to
the rank of brigadier general. He also served in the
Chilean Congress as a deputy and a senator from 1861
until his death.

SALA Y GOMEZ ISLAND. A dependency of Chile. It lies
2, 100 miles west of Chile, at a distance of 250 miles
east-northeast from Easter Island*. The island is
small, measuring only 4, 000 by 500 feet, and is administered by Valparaíso* Province. It is positioned
at 26° 28' south latitude and 105° 28' west longitude.

SALAS CORVALAN, MANUEL DE, 1754-1841. Politician
and lawyer who participated in the struggle for Chilean
independence. In 1811, he was one of the promoters
of the junta government of Santiago set up to achieve
separation between Chile and Spain. A year later, he
was one of the drafters of the Constitution of 1812*.
He was a member of the Exaltado* Party, and filled
municipal and other local offices in the capital. In
1812 he was named Secretary of Foreign Affairs, but
two years later was captured by the Spaniards and
exiled. After the patriots' victory at the Battle of
Chacabuco* (February 12, 1817), he was permitted to
return to Chile. Following the formal declaration of
Chilean Independence in 1818, he devoted himself to
civic matters, working unceasingly to encourage agriculture, mining, industry, and education. In 1823 he
formed part of the junta government that ruled after
the resignation of Bernardo O'Higgins*. In the same
year he was elected deputy to Congress, and was
largely instrumental in the founding of the orphanage
Academia de San Luis, the National Institute, and the
National Library.

SALITRERAS DE IQUIQUE. The Saltpeter refinery of Iquique* was the site of many labor disturbances during
the first quarter of this century. From 1907 to 1925
labor strikes were organized to improve the economic
and social condition of the worker. On December 21,
1907, the workers organized a strike at the Santa
María elementary school. Guards were called in to
break the strike and violence resulted. More than
3000 of the 7000 workers were fired upon and wounded
or killed. In the years that followed, armed conflicts
between the workers and the police continued. Many
labor leaders were imprisoned for years, and the need

for stronger unions was recognized. In 1920, the
workers joined the Federación Obrera de Chile* (FOCH).
Two years later the Chilean Communist Party (Partido
Comunista de Chile*) was founded, and the Iquique saltpeter workers joined it en masse. For these reasons,
many worker representatives in the union were imprisoned. It was not until 1927 that relations between
labor and management improved and that labor demands
were finally met in part.

SALUD PUBLICA, MINISTERIO DE. The Ministry of Public
Health was created by Statute No. 25 on October 14,
1959. The main functions of this ministry are: to
provide health care for all Chileans, even for those
who cannot afford to pay for medical services; to fight
venereal diseases and birth defects; to lower the infant mortality rate; and to conduct research for the
prevention of disease. The historical antecedents of
this ministry date back to 1837, when the first organic
law for the creation of ministries was passed. The
Ministry of the Interior was responsible at the time
for matters dealing with public health. It was not until 1932 that Public Health was assigned its own ministry, known as the Ministry of Public Health (Salubridad
Pública*). Four years later, the Ministry changed its
name to Ministry of Health and Social Assistance (Ministerio de Salubridad, Previsión y Asistencia Social*),
and from 1953 to 1959 it was called Ministry of Health
and Social Prognostication (Ministerio de Salud Pública
y Previsión Social*).

SALVADOR, EL. El Salvador is a relatively new copper
mine discovered in 1959 and located only 12.5 air
miles from Potrerillos* in the province of Atacama*.
Discovered after production had stopped at nearby
Potrerillos in 1959, the new mine was symbolically
called El Salvador (The Saviour). El Salvador, in the
short period of 11 years has raised its production from
42,298 tons in 1959 to about 100,000 short tons of copper in 1970. The rated annual capacity of El Salvador
is estimated at 8,500,000 short tons of ore. Today
El Salvador is producing copper at capacity rate--and
a bit more. (See also ANACONDA).

SAN FELIPE. Capital city of the north-central province of
Aconcagua; population: 30,200 (1971 est.).

SAN FELIX AND SAN AMBROSIO ISLANDS. Dependencies
of Chile discovered in 1574 by Juan Fernández. San
Félix Island, and its small satellite, San Ambrosio
Island, are volcanic and uninhabited; their position is
26° 17' south latitude and 80° 7' west longitude.

SAN FERNANDO. Capital city of the central province of
Colchagua*; population: 42, 800 (1971 est.).

SAN FRANCISCO CHURCH. Located at Alameda Avenue and
Londres Street, this 16th century church, which sur-
vived the earthquake of 1647, is the oldest church in
Chile. The simplicity of the interior is typical of
American colonial art. The walls are broad and plain,
and the confessionaries were wood-carved by Indians.
The church's most valuable relic is a wooden statue
of the Virgin brought by Pedro de Valdivia*.

SAN MARTIN, JOSE DE, 1777-1850. Argentine patriot who,
with Simón Bolívar, is considered one of the liberators
of the South American continent. He studied in Spain
and returned to his native land, where in the brief
span of eight years, he led a highly successful military career. He was a lieutenant colonel at the age
of 31. In Chile, he is remembered for his invaluable
help in overthrowing the Spanish yoke. His legendary
Andes Army (Ejército de los Andes*) was victorious in
two key battles: Chacabuco* (1817) and Maipú* (1818).
San Martín also participated in the Peruvian campaign,
but decided to withdraw from the military and political
scene after meeting with Bolívar in Guayaquil (Equador).
At that historic meeting, which took place on July 26,
1822, the two leaders could not reach an agreement to
insure the independence of Peru. San Martín decided
to let Bolívar finish the arduous task of liberation and
returned home. San Martín lived in Mendoza, Argentina for a few months, and then in France, where he
spent the last years of his life, dying in modest cir-
cumstances.

SANFUENTES ANDONAEGUI, JUAN LUIS, 1858- . Of a
distinguished Santiago family, he was educated at the
University of Chile*, receiving a law degree in 1879.
After a brief service in the navy during the War of the
Pacific (Guerra del Pacífico*), he became involved in
politics as a member of the Liberal Democratic Party
(Partido Liberal Democrático*), and was elected to

Congress as a deputy (1888). During the Civil War of
1891 (Guerra Civil de 1891*), he sided with President
(1886-91) José Manuel Balmaceda Fernández*. When
the latter resigned, Sanfuentes abandoned politics, only
to return to it a few years later. In 1900 he became
a senator and in 1903 he was named by President
(1901-06) Germán Riesco Errázuriz* Minister of the
Treasury.

During the Riesco Errázuriz administration Sanfuentes
was also counselor of the Mortgage Loan Bank (Caja de
Crédito Hipotecario) and the Savings Bank (Banco de
Ahorros). An expert in financial affairs and an astute
politician, in 1915 Sanfuentes won the nomination of the
Liberal Democratic Party to run for President. He
was elected by a narrow margin and immediately embarked upon the task of rebuilding the nation, especially
in the economic field. He succeeded in reducing the
public debt, and in pushing through a program of extended public works. Never popular with his electorate,
he remained neutral in the presidential elections of 1920.

SANTA MARIA GONZALES, DOMINGO, 1825-1889. Lawyer
by profession and active member of the Liberal Party
(Partido Liberal*). He supported the re-election of
General Manuel Bulnes Prieto*, twice President of
Chile (1841-46; 1846-51), and as a reward was appointed intendant of Colchagua*. His liberal politics
got him into trouble during the Manuel Montt Torres*
regime (1851-61), and he was proscribed. Recalled
to Chile during the administration (1861-71) of José
Joaquín Pérez Mascayano*, he became Minister of the
Treasury and later Minister of the Court of Appeals.
In 1865, he was sent to Europe on a diplomatic mission during the war with Spain, and also planned to organize a plan of defense with Peru. During the War
of the Pacific (Guerra del Pacífico*) he held various
important cabinet posts, including that of War.

In 1881 he became President of Chile for a five-
year term. During his administration, he insisted
that Chilean forces occupy Lima until a settlement
with Peru was reached. Although the final agreement
did not come until 1929, the Chilean President recalled
his troops in 1884. As chief magistrate, Santa María
González helped to liquidate the war with the Araucanian Indians (Araucanos*). Treaties were signed with
the Indian chieftains in 1884. The Indians were pushed
further south and were assigned certain lands in per-

petuity. His last two years in office saw him confronted with numerous political and religious controversies. His establishment of civilian cemeteries angered many conservative leaders in Chile, and his administration became the most stormy since that of Montt Torres. After his retirement, Santa María González edited the Code of Civil Procedure (Código de enjusticiamento civil), which was adopted in Chile.

SANTIAGO. 1) The largest city in Chile, having a metropolitan population of about 2.5 million inhabitants. Founded by Pedro de Valdivia* in 1541, Santiago became the capital of Chile after the battle of Maipú in 1818. The city is situated on a wide plain, 1,950 feet above sea level, and is backed by the majestic Cordillera* de los Andes, which reaches heights of more than 20,000 feet, some 60 miles from the city. The metropolitan area extends approximately eight square miles, and is crossed from east to west by the Mapocho river. Santiago is essentially a modern capital, with skyscrapers, big department stores, and traffic problems. More than half of Chile's manufacturing is done here, whereas some 54% of the industrial activities of the country are conducted in the greater Santiago area. The Palacio de la Moneda* located in the downtown area, is the seat of the government. The city boasts two of the leading universities in South America: La Universidad de Chile, and La Universidad Católica. Population: 2,561,000 (1971 est.).
   2) A province of central Chile; population: 3,038,397 (1971 est.); area: 17,685.8 sq. km.; capital city: Santiago*.

SARMIENTO, DOMINGO FAUSTINO, 1811-1888. Argentine writer and statesman who came to Chile after he was exiled by dictator (1835-52) Manuel de Rosas. A self-taught educator, Sarmiento became the director of the Escuela Normal*, and a contributor to the newspaper El Mercurio of Valparaíso*. He took up the defense of a progressive concept of culture, espousing romantic freedom of expression and the vitalizing effects of French writers on Spanish-American literature. He was the first to introduce Romanticism in Chile, but was challenged by the Neo-classicists headed by the Venezuelan scholar Andrés Bello López*. Soon a controversy took place between these two outstanding foreigners who had made Chile their home. Bello defended the aristocratic concept of literary standards, preferring the purity of the Castilian tongue and the values of Spanish culture over the French. Sarmiento defended French linguistic influence, saying that Spanish Americans had to turn to the French language for new expressions. The polemic between the two writers lasted until Sarmiento returned to Argentina, soon after the overthrow of Rosas, to become President (1868-74).

SECRETARIA DEL ESTADO. The Department of State was established in 1814 to create a provisional government to rule independently of Spain. It consisted of three secretariats: Government, Treasury, and War, which in 1817 became ministries. Today the functions of the Chilean Department of State are similar to those of the U.S. State Department.

SECURITIES see THE ECONOMY: Internal: N. Securities.

SEGUNDA, LA see THE PRESS.

SEGURO OBRERO. The Social Security building in Santiago and the site of a clash between right-wing demonstrators and the police, which took place on September 5, 1938, a day after the Presidential elections. The incident occurred when the Nazi-inspired Movimiento Nacional Socialista de Chile* organized a demonstration in Santiago after their Presidential candidate, Carlos Ibáñez del Campo*, had been defeated at the polls. Members of the party were unhappy with the outcome of the elections. Led by Nazi leader Jorge González Von Marées*, they occupied the Seguro Obrero building in the hope that the population would rise in support of their cause. González Von Marées directed the operation with a radio transmitter. When some of the rebellious youth and members of the police were killed as a result, González Von Marées was arrested and the building was abandoned by the demonstrators. The Chilean press deplored the violence used in the demonstration and accused the Right of extremism.

SEMANA ROJA. The "red week" commemorates the organization of a workers' movement which was formed on October 22, 1905. On that day, workers were striking and waving a red flag because there was a meat shortage in Chile. When 200 of them were brutally killed by the police, a nationwide strike was called. Four

years later, railroad workers formed the first union in
Chile known as the Gran Federación Obrera de Chile*
(1909). By 1922, almost all Chilean workers were organized into labor unions.

SEWELL. El Teniente, one of the world's largest underground mines, is located at Sewell, 75 miles southeast
of Santiago*, at an elevation of 8,000 feet, on the
crater wall of an old volcanic peak. The nearest city
to Sewell is Rancagua* (province of O'Higgins*). (See
also: KENNECOTT COPPER CORPORATION).

SIGLO, EL see THE PRESS.

SILVA ALGUE, WALDO, 1820-1892. Lawyer by profession
and active member of the National Party (Partido Nacional*). From 1856 to 1867 he served as Minister
of Public Instruction (Education) and organized the Library of the National Institute (Biblioteca del Instituto
Nacional). He was also instrumental in the establishment of various high schools and public libraries.
From 1860 to 1891 he served in the Chilean Congress
as a deputy and a senator. In 1891, as President of
the Senate, he helped organize the revolt against President (1886-91) José Manuel Balmaceda Fernández*.

SIMIAN GALLET, EDUARDO, 1915- . He studied in Santiago obtaining a degree in mining engineering in 1938.
He has worked for CORFO* and was sent to the south
of Chile, to Magallanes*, to probe the terrain for oil.
In 1945, he was responsible for the first production of
commercial petroleum and by-products in Chile. In
1950 he was Manager of ENAP*. After the inauguration of President (1964-70) Eduardo Frei Montalva* he
was named Minister of Mines (November 3, 1964).

SOCIEDAD DE LA IGUALIDAD. The Society for Equality
was founded on April 14, 1850 by Francisco Bilbao
Barquín* and Eusebio Lillo Robles*. The aims of this
society were to give power to the people and to recognize the equality of all Chileans. It was based on the
French motto "liberty, equality, fraternity," and it
proposed to create free schools for all those who
wanted to attend. The society was anticlerical and
had hostile encounters with the authorities in power.
An attempt on Bilbao's life was made with the purpose
of destroying the Society and its leaders.

SOCIEDAD PORTALES CEA Y CIA. A privately owned firm
    which was given the tobacco, tea and liquors monopoly
    in Chile in 1824 (see ESTANCO). It was founded by
    the Chilean statesman Diego Portales Palazuelos*.

STEEL. A domestic steel industry was established in Chile
    in the early 1950's. The need for the formation of
    this industry was based on the principle that steel pro-
    duction measures the material progress of a nation un-
    dergoing industrial expansion. The drastic curtailment
    of steel imports during the war years also gave support
    to the concept of establishing an integrated iron and
    steel plant. Chile is one of the few South American
    countries that has good grade iron ores, limestone and
    coal, as well as an abundance of hydroelectrical energy.
    Since the construction of the first steel plant, the
    Huachipato* plant, finished in 1950, Chile's steel indus-
    try has developed into an efficient modern enterprise,
    capable of supplying the country's basic steel require-
    ments. As a result of successive improvement, mod-
    ernization and expansion programs, steel ingot produc-
    tion has increased from 178,000 metric tons in 1951 to
    over 600,000 metric tons annually in the period 1965-
    1970. This achievement has been made possible with
    financial and technical assistance from the United States.

SUBLEVACION DE CAMPINO. A military revolt led by
    Colonel Enrique Campino Salamanca* on January 25,
    1827, against the federalist government (1826-27) of
    Agustín Eyzaguirre Arechavala*. Chile's experiment
    with federalism had been a failure as different con-
    gressmen and supreme directors succeeded one another
    leaving the country in a state of anarchy. Frequent
    revolts and coups, such as the one led by Campino,
    made it even more difficult to achieve any political
    organization and stability in the country. Campino's
    revolt precipitated two major events: the dissolution
    of Congress and the resignation of the President. The
    colonel's success, however, was short-lived. A few
    days after the revolt his very companions abandoned
    him and chose as interim President one of his enemies,
    Ramón Freire Serrano*. Campino was arrested but
    later released.

T

TALCA.   1) A province of central Chile located south of
Santiago*; population: 242, 146 (1971 est.); area:
10, 141. 1 sq. km. ; capital city: Talca*.
2) Capital city of the province of the same name;
population: 93, 700 (1971 est.).

TALCAHUANO.   Site of a naval battle which took place on
October 28, 1818, between a Spanish vessel, the María
Isabel, and the Chilean fleet, composed of four vessels,
the San Martín, the Lautaro, the Chacabuco, and the
Arauco.   The episode ended with the capture of the
María Isabel.

TARAPACA.   Province of northern Chile; population:
155, 908 (1971 est.); area: 58, 072. 7 sq. km. ; capital
city: Iquique*.

TARPELLANCA.   Site of a battle fought on September 26,
1820, between Spanish royalist troops and the Chilean
army of independence.   It occurred during the so-
called "War to the Death" (Guerra a Muerte*) and resulted in the massacre of the Chilean patriots by the
royalists.

TARUD SIWADY, RAFAEL, 1918- .   Independent Leftist
candidate in the last two Presidential elections and
Director of the Chamber of Commerce.   He was president of the Federation of Students at the University of
Chile and began his political career at a very young
age.   In 1953, he was named President of the Agrarian
Labor Party (Partido Agrario Laborista*), and two
years later he became Minister of the Economy.   In
1957, he was elected to the Senate for an eight-year
term, and was re-elected in 1965.   He has been president of the Business and Economic Commission of the
Senate and a member of the Foreign Affairs Committee.
In the Presidential elections of 1970, he was the nominee of the Social Democratic Party (Partido Social
Demócrata*).

TAX STRUCTURE see THE ECONOMY: Internal: P. Taxes.

TEMUCO.   Capital of the central province of Cautín; population: 130, 000 (1971 est.).

TENIENTE, EL see SEWELL.

TERCERA DE LA HORA, LA see THE PRESS.

THAYER ARTEAGA, WILLIAM, 1918- . Lawyer by profession and member of the Christian Democratic Party
(Partido Demócrata Cristiano*). In 1941, he was national president of the Catholic Youth Organization
(Juventud Católica). When he received his law degree
in 1945, he became an advocate of the Copper Workers
Federation (Confederación de Trabajadores del Cobre),
and of the syndicate of the State Bank (Banco del Estado). During the 1964 Presidential elections he cam-
paigned for the Christian Democratic candidate Eduardo
Frei Montalva*. Upon being elected, Frei named
Thayer as his Minister of Labor (November 3, 1964).

TIERRA DEL FUEGO. A triangular-shaped archipelago located at the southern extremity of South America and
separated from the mainland by the Strait of Magellan.
It lies between 52° 27' and 55° 59' south latitude, and
63° 43' and 74° 44' west longitude. The total area is
28,434 square miles, two-thirds of which is Chilean
and one-third Argentinian. The Chilean territory,
which was raised to provincial status in 1929, com-
prises the southern tip of the province of Magallanes*.
The terrain is varied but rugged, comprised chiefly
of mountains, volcanic rock and glacial lakes, and the
climate is cool in summer and cold in winter, with
up to 200 inches of rainfall in certain areas.
      Tierra del Fuego was first discovered by Ferdinand
Magellan in 1520. García and Gonzalo de Nodal were
the first to circumnavigate the archipelago in 1619,
but no systematic exploration of Tierra del Fuego occurred until the period 1826-36 when Phillip Parker
King and Robert Fitzroy investigated the islands. For
350 years after Magellan's voyage the region was left
to its indigenous peoples, the Ona and Yahgan Indians,
but, with the introduction of sheep farming and the
discovery of gold, an influx of European immigration
began in 1880. The current population (in 1960 the
population of the Chilean portion was 6100), includes
Yugoslavs, Spanish, British and Italians, as well as
Chileans and Argentines. Few of the Indians have
survived. The economy is based chiefly on sheep
raising and petroleum exploitation.

TIERRAS Y COLONIZACION, MINISTERIO DE. The Ministry of Land and Colonization was created by Statute No.
243 on May 15, 1931. Its main functions are to safeguard all public land within the national territory of
Chile and to give protection to the Indians and their
rights to own all the land assigned to them by the
peace treaty of 1883. The antecedent of this Ministry
dates back to 1837, when it was part of the Ministry
of the Treasury. In 1887, the Ministry of Land and
Colonization was under the jurisdiction of the Ministry
of Industry and in 1924, under the Ministry of Agriculture. Three years later Land and Colonization was
part of the Ministry of Development (Ministerio de Fomento*) until it became a separate ministry in 1931.

TOCORNAL GREZ, MANUEL ANTONIO, 1817-1867. Son of
Joaquín Tocornal Jiménez*, lawyer by profession, and
member of the Conservative Party (Partido Conservador*). In 1846 he became a member of the Chamber
of Deputies and three years later was named Minister
of Justice. He was encouraged by Andrés Bello López*
to write an historic account of the first national government in Chile. His memoirs (1847) did much to clarify
the order of events after 1810. He acquired a reputation both in law and in oratory, and in 1862 was named
Minister of the Interior in the cabinet of President
(1861-71) José Joaquín Pérez Mascayano*. Just before his death he became a member of the Senate and
succeeded Bello as president (rector) of the University
of Chile.

TOCORNAL JIMENEZ, JOAQUIN, 1788-1865. Chilean patriot who fought in the struggle for independence and
served his native city Santiago in numerous municipal
offices, both before and after his exile to Argentina in
1814. He was one of the youngest present at the National Assembly that proclaimed Chile an independent
nation (September 18, 1810), and formed part of the
first junta government. He was a presiding officer of
the Chamber of Deputies when he was named Minister
of Foreign Affairs in 1832. He also presided over the
convention that drafted the Constitution of 1833*. From
1833 to 1837 he held nearly every cabinet post in the
government of (1831-41) Joaquín Prieto Vial*. In 1841
he was a candidate for the Presidency but lost to
Manuel Bulnes Prieto*, and shortly afterwards became
superintendent of the Casa de la Moneda*. He con-

tinued to represent the Conservative party in Congress until his death, as both a deputy and senator.

TOCORNAL TOCORNAL, ISMAEL, 1850-1929. Lawyer by profession and active member of the Liberal Party (Partido Liberal*). He served in Congress as a deputy and a senator, and during the government (1901-06) of Germán Riesco Errázuriz* was named Minister of Industries and Public Works. In 1909, he was Minister of the Interior in the cabinet of President (1906-10) Pedro Montt Montt*, and a year later acted as President of Chile when Montt left for Argentina on an official visit. In the Presidential campaign of 1920, he ran as the Liberal Party candidate but lost to Arturo Alessandri Palma*. In 1925, he became president of the Central Bank of Chile (Banco Central).

TOMIC ROMERO, RODOMIRO, 1914- . Lawyer by profession, active member of the Christian Democratic Party (Partido Demócrata Cristiano*), and Presidential candidate in the elections of September 4, 1970. He was president of the Student Federation of the Catholic University and of the Law Review of the same institution. In 1935 he was one of the founders of the political party known as Falange Nacional*, and was its president from 1946 to 1952. He has served in the Chamber of Deputies and in the Senate from 1941 to the present, and in 1957 was a representative to the International Conference on Christian Democracy in São Paulo, Brazil. After Eduardo Frei Montalva* was elected President of Chile (1964-70), Tomic was sent to the U.S. as the Chilean ambassador. He returned to Chile in 1969 to campaign for the Presidential elections of 1970, and won the party's nomination. He lost the election, however, to Marxist Salvador Allende Gossens*, who received 36% of the vote to Tomic's 28%.

TOPAZE see THE PRESS.

TOPOGRAPHY see CHILE.

TOQUI. (Araucanian) Indian chief.

TORO Y ZAMBRANO Y URETA, MATEO DE, 1727-1811. A man of considerable fortune, he held commercial and political offices of high rank, including those of mayor and corregidor* of Santiago, Governor of La Serena*,

Brigadier General of the Chilean Army, and Governor ad interim when he received the title of Conde de la Conquista on March 6, 1771. In 1809, when the French troops invaded Spain, Toro y Zambrano swore that Chile would not serve Joseph I, brother of Napoleon Bonaparte, as King of Spain. A year later, the brigadier general was given command of Chile and became the first president of the first junta government in Chile. There were two loci of opinion in the first junta government: some patriots wanted to declare the independence of Chile immediately, and others wanted to be governed by the real audiencia*. Toro y Zambrano, as the first president of the junta decided to rule Chile independently of Spain. It took the country eight more years to formally change its status as a Spanish colony and declare complete independence from Spain.

TOURISM   see THE ECONOMY: External: F. Tourism.

TRABAJO, MINISTERIO DE.   The Ministry of Labor was created by statute no. 2 on June 5, 1932. Prior to this date, all that was pertinent to Chilean labor laws was handled by the Ministry of Industries and Public Works (1907), and by the Ministry of Hygiene, Social Security and Labor (1924). The main functions of the Ministry of Labor are to supervise the labor laws of the land providing for workers' insurance, retirement plans, and a minimum wage. In 1959, the Ministry of Labor changed its name to the Ministry of Labor and Social Security (Ministerio del Trabajo y Previsión Social*), adding a social security service for all Chilean workers.

TRABAJO Y PREVISION SOCIAL, MINISTERIO DE   see TRABAJO, MINISTERIO DE.

TRANSPORTATION   see THE ECONOMY: Internal: J. Transportation. . . .

TRATADO DE CUZCUZ.   A peace treaty signed on May 17, 1830 between Conservatives and Liberals to put an end to the civil strife that had begun a year earlier (see GUERRA CIVIL DE 1829-30). The conservative victory at Lircay* delivered the nation into conservative control for the following three decades.

TRATADO DE LIRCAY.   A peace treaty signed on May 3,
    1814 between Chilean patriots and the Viceroy of Peru,
    Fernando Ascabal, which stipulated that Chile was to
    remain a colony of Spain subjected to the will of the
    Spanish King Ferdinand VII. Sporadic fighting continued,
    however, between the army fighting for independence
    and the troops loyal to the Spanish King. When the pa-
    triots suffered their greatest setback at Rancagua* on
    October 2, 1814, the country saw Spanish power re-
    stored for approximately three more years.

TRATADO DE OCHAGAVIA.   A peace treaty signed on De-
    cember 16, 1829 to put an end to the civil war between
    Conservatives and Liberals (see GUERRA CIVIL DE
    1829-30). The treaty provided for a junta government
    to consist of three presidents, Antonio Pinto Díaz,
    Francisco Ruiz Tagle Portales*, and Augustín Eyza-
    guirre Arechevala*, until elections could be set up for
    a new President. The treaty was not observed by
    either side and the civil war continued until May of the
    following year.

TRATADO DE TANTAUCO.   A treaty signed in 1826 to in-
    corporate the island of Chiloé into the national territory
    of independent Chile. Chilean patriots had fought for
    almost four years to liberate the island from Spanish
    control.

TRES ACEQUIAS.   Site of a battle fought on August 26, 1814,
    between troops fighting for Chilean independence and
    royalist troops fighting to retain Spanish control of
    Chile. The troops of independence were led by Ber-
    nardo O'Higgins* and José Miguel Carrera Verdugo*,
    but were defeated by a superior Spanish force.

TRILALEO.   Site of a battle fought during the so-called War
    to the Death (Guerra a Muerte*) on November 1, 1819.
    Spanish royalist troops, under the command of Vicente
    Benavides*, defeated the independents led by Pedro
    Nolasco Victoriano. Benavides won, occupied the city
    of Chillán, and committed many atrocities against cap-
    tured Chilean patriots.

TRIVELLI FRANZOLINI, HUGO, 1913- . Agrarian engineer
    and economist and member of the Christian Democratic
    Party (Partido Demócrata Cristiano*). In 1944, he was
    the drafter of an Agrarian Reform program in the gov-

ernment (1942-46) of Juan Antonio Ríos Morales*.
From 1949 to 1950, he was an agrarian economist on
the National Economic Council (Consejo Nacional de
Economía), also serving as Chilean representative on
the Economic Commission for Latin America (ECLA*).
From 1953 to 1954, he was General Director of Agri-
culture and Director of the Agrarian Development Pro-
gram for ECLA. From that time until 1964, he served
on the Food and Agriculture Organization (FAO) of the
United Nations. He was named by President (1964-70)
Eduardo Frei Montalva* as Minister of Agriculture on
November 3, 1964.

TUCAPEL.   Site of a battle between the Spanish Conquistadors* and the Araucanian* Indians. It occurred in
December 1553 and marked the beginning of a 300-year
struggle between the Spaniards and the Araucanians.
Pedro de Valdivia*, at the command of the Spanish
forces, attacked the Indians at Tucapel. Soon he and
his men were surrounded, however, by a larger Araucanian force, and were taken prisoners. The Araucanians executed all the Spaniards, while the chieftains
Caupolicán* and Lautaro* tried to spare them. Pedro
de Valdivia, one of the last to die, pleaded for his
life, promising to leave Chile for good, but another
Indian toqui*, Leucotón, killed him with a blow on his
neck. It was one of the most disastrous battles for
the Spaniards in their campaign to conquer Chile.

-U-

U.N.   see UNITED NATIONS.

UFUCh.   Another important student organization is the Unión
de Federaciones Universitarias de Chile (also see
FECH).   Founded in 1960, UFUCh has been controlled
during the decade of the 1960's by students of the
Christian Democratic Party (Partido Demócrata Cristiano*).   Socialist and Communist students withdrew
from UFUCh because they refused to share membership with representatives of the Catholic universities.

ULTIMAS NOTICIAS, LAS   see THE PRESS.

UNIDAD POPULAR.   A coalition of six left-of-center parties
formed in 1969 to aid the Presidential candidacy of So-

cialist Salvador Allende Gossens*. The following were
the participating political entities which formed the coalition: the Communist Party (Partido Comunista*); the
Socialist Party (Partido Socialista*); the Radical Party
(Partido Radical*); the Social Democratic Party (Partido Social Democrático*); the Movimiento de Acción
Popular Unida (MAPU*); and the Acción Popular Independiente (API*). The basic program of the Unidad
Popular can be summarized by these six points: 1) to
establish a revolutionary government which would put
an end to imperialism and to the capitalistic structure
prevalent in Chile; 2) to establish a new social order;
3) to give power to "the people" (i.e., the working
class); 4) to begin the structural change of society with
the elimination of a class system; 5) to undertake a
comprehensive agrarian reform program which would
eliminate the latifundio (large landed estates of more
than 1000 acres) and set up a collective system of
farming with the establishment of farm cooperatives;
and 6) to make Chile a power within the Latin American system.

One of the goals of the Unidad Popular is to abolish
the Organization of American States (OAS), since it is
considered by the Latin American Left to be an instru-
ment of imperialism and U.S. domination in Latin
America. A new organization truly representative of
the Latin American countries would then be instituted.
In the March 1971 municipal elections, the Unidad
Popular coalition obtained 50.8% of the vote, an impressive increase over the 36.3% it received in the
1970 Presidential elections. Within the coalition, the
Chilean Communist Party increased its vote from 15.9%
of the total last year to 17.3%, with the biggest increase
going to Allende's own Socialist Party. The Socialists
nearly doubled their representation to 22.8%, replacing
the Communists as the strongest faction within the coalition. The relatively moderate Radical Party obtained 8.1% of the vote, with the remaining 2.6% going
mainly to MAPU.

UNION, LA see THE PRESS.

UNION DE FEDERACIONES UNIVERSITARIAS DE CHILE
    see UFUCh.

UNION LIBERAL. A political combination of various parties
    of the Right, including the Partido Liberal*, the Par-

tido Nacional*, the Partido Liberal Democrático*, and the Partido Democrático*. It was formed in September, 1919, when two other coalitions of the right, the Alianza Liberal* and the Coalición* dissolved. The Radicals (Partido Radical*), who had formed part of the Alianza Liberal, refused to join the Unión Liberal. Prior to the Presidential elections of 1920, the Unión Liberal joined the Conservative Party to form the Unión Nacional*.

UNION NACIONAL. The National Union Party was formed in 1920 through the merger of the Unión Liberal* with the Conservative Party (Partido Conservador*). The aim of this coalition was to present Luis Barros Borgoño* as the Presidential candidate in the elections of 1920, to oppose the Alianza Liberal's* candidate Arturo Alessandri Palma*. Alessandri won, but the congressional elections of the following March gave the Unión Nacional a majority in the Senate. As a result, Alessandri was forced to include two members of the Unión Nacional in his cabinet. The Unión Nacional played an active role in opposition to the Alessandri government, and in 1925 chose Ladislao Errázuriz Lazcano to run for the Presidency. When on January 23, 1925, Alessandri was recalled from his self-imposed exile in Italy to become once again President of Chile, the Unión Nacional lost public support and was dissolved.

UNION NACIONAL LABORISTA. Political party formed in 1958 to back the Presidential candidacy of Independent Antonio Zamorano Herrera*. In the September 4th elections, Zamorano obtained very few votes, and when his party failed to win representation in Congress in March, 1959, the National Labor Union was dissolved.

UNION REPUBLICANA. An independent political party formed in 1932 and dissolved five years later. Most of its members came from professional groups, and created the party after the fall of Carlos Ibáñez del Campo's* government (1927-31). The aims of the party were the preservation of the democratic system and the implementation of universal suffrage in Chile (Chilean women were not allowed to vote until 1952). In 1937 the party fused with another political group known as

the Acción Nacional*, forming the new party, Acción
Republicana*.

UNION REVOLUCIONARIA SOCIALISTA. A political party
organized in Chile in 1932 after the 12-day experiment
with a Socialist government known as the República
Socialista*. A year later, the party formally joined
the Socialist Party of Chile (Partido Socialista*).

UNION SOCIAL REPUBLICANA DE ASALARIADOS DE CHILE
(USRACH). A political party organized in 1925 and
dissolved in 1928. All the members of the new party
were from the Chilean working classes and opposed the
candidacy of Emiliano Figueroa Larraín* for the Presidency of Chile. When Figueroa was elected in 1925,
USRACH protested and demanded his resignation.
Figueroa finally resigned in 1927 and Conservative
army colonel Carlos Ibáñez del Campo*, then Minister
of War, was chosen to succeed him without opposition.
USRACH denounced President (1927-31) Ibáñez del
Campo, but the latter, having arisen to the rank of
general, proved to be above all a man of the sword.
In 1928 he declared USRACH an illegal party, dissolved
it, and persecuted many of its members as Socialist
and Communist sympathizers.

UNION SOCIALISTA. A political party organized in November, 1937, and dissolved a few months later to form
part of the political coalition of various right-wing
parties known as the Alianza Popular Libertadora*.

UNITED NATIONS (U.N.). Chile has been a member of the
United Nations since its inception in 1945. Two Chil-
eans have served as president of the U.N. General
Assembly, José Maza (September 20 to December 20,
1955) and Rudecindo Ortega (November 1 to November
10, 1956). The most important organs of the United
Nations in which Chile participates are: the United
Nations Population Commission; the Economic Commis-
sion for Latin America* (ECLA); the United Nations
Conference on Trade and Development (UNCTAD); the
Industrial Development Board of the United Nations Industrial Development Organization (UNIDO); the Com-
mission on Human Rights; and, the United Nations Development Program (UNDP). The seat of the United
Nations in Latin America is located in Santiago de
Chile.

UNIVERSITY OF CHILE (UNIVERSIDAD DE CHILE). The
University of Chile was founded on September 17, 1843
during the Presidency (1841-51) of Manuel Bulnes
Prieto*. The renowned Venezuelan scholar Andrés
Bello López* was its first president. The University
of Chile, together with the Catholic University (Universidad Católica), has become known as an excellent
center of higher education in Chile, and has made
great strides in the Departments of economics, engineering, mathematics, and in the humanities. It is
one of the few universities in Latin America which
publishes an economic abstract for the Latin American
countries.

URMENETA GARCIA, JOSE TOMAS DE, 1808-1878. A man
of considerable fortune and a philanthropist, he administered many mining enterprises and developed the copper industry in Chile. He was the founder of the first
Firemen Corps (Cuerpo de Bomberos) and served as
its superintendent. A member of the National Party
(Partido Nacional*), he was elected to the Chamber of
Deputies in 1846, and to the Senate in 1855. In 1871
he was the National Party's Presidential candidate but
lost to Federico Errázuriz Zañartu*, who was backed
by the Fusión Liberal Conservadora* coalition.

URRIOLA BALBONTIN, PEDRO ALCANTARA, 1797-1851.
Chilean patriot who fought during the struggle for independence and was taken prisoner by the Spanish royalists after the battle of Rancagua*. Released just before independence was won in 1817, he resumed his
military career, reaching the rank of colonel in 1828.
Ten years later he was commander general in the war
against the Peru-Bolivia Confederation*. In 1839 he
returned to Chile from Peru and ran for Congress,
winning a seat in the Chamber of Deputies. Mixing in
the political disturbances of 1850, he headed the bar-
racks revolt against the government a year later (see
MUTINY OF URRIOLA), and was killed in the streets
of Santiago.

USRACH   see UNION SOCIAL REPUBLICANA ....

-V-

VALDES VERGARA, FRANCISCO, 1854-1916. Chilean
    writer and politician. He was a candidate in the Pres-
    idential elections of 1901, but lost to Liberal Germán
    Riesco Errázuriz*. In 1877 he was secretary general
    of the Chilean delegation in Bolivia, and two years
    later served as Chilean consul general in Panama. In
    1882 he won representation in the Chamber of Deputies
    and served on various economic commissions in the
    Chilean Congress. In 1889 he was administrator of
    Customs in Valparaíso, and two years later he was
    named Minister of the Treasury. Although he lost the
    Presidency to Riesco Errázuriz, Valdés Vergara was
    named by the new President as Director of Customs in
    Chile. From 1913 until his death he served in the
    Senate.

VALDIVIA. 1) A province of central Chile located south of
    Santiago*; population: 298,445 (1971 est.); area:
    18,472.5 sq. km.; capital city: Valdivia*.
        2) Capital city of the central province of the same
    name; population: 97,000 (1971 est.).

VALDIVIA, LUIS DE, 1560-1642. Spanish Jesuit who came
    to Chile in 1593 with the first Jesuits to be sent there.
    He served as rector of the Santiago College, one of the
    first high schools organized in Chile, and prepared a
    grammar of the language spoken in the Spanish colo-
    nies. He also became known as a defender of the In-
    dians, opposing the system of personalized service to
    which they were subjected, and believed that much of
    the difficulties with the Araucanians* arose from the
    ill-treatment they received. He thus acquired wide
    fame for his piety and learning.

VALDIVIA, PEDRO DE, 1500-1553. Conqueror of Chile.
    He was born in Estremadura, Spain. He went to the
    New World in 1535, and two years later joined Fran-
    cisco Pizarro's forces in Peru to fight against Diego
    de Almargo*. He quickly won the favor of Pizarro,
    who in 1539, sent him to conquer Chile. Because of
    Almagro's tragic expedition, Valdivia had great trouble
    recruiting men. By 1540, however, he had managed
    to gather a force of 150 men for the expedition. Val-
    divia's march from Cuzco to central Chile revealed
    his courage and leadership abilities. He was plagued

by mutinies, hardships in crossing the desert, and the hostile Araucanian Indians (Araucanos*), the toughest and most unyielding adversaries the Spaniards were to meet in the Americas. In 1541, Valdivia's men reached the Mapocho Valley, where on February 12 the city of Santiago* was founded. Six months later, the Araucanians attacked and destroyed the city, killing some Spaniards and destroying nearly all of their supplies. The settlers set about the task of rebuilding the city while still surrounded by hostile Indians. After the burning of Santiago*, La Serena* and Valparaíso* were founded. In 1548, Valdivia received aid and reinforcements from Peru, raising the number of Spaniards in Chile to 500. Valdivia's influence continued to spread southward, where in the early 1550's, the cities of Concepción*, Imperial Valdivia, and Villarica were founded. In December 1553, under the command of Lautaro*, a former slave of Valdivia's, the Araucanians defeated the Spaniards in the Battle of Tucapel*, killing Valdivia and most of his men.

VALDIVIESO Y ZAÑARTU, RAFAEL VALENTIN, 1804-1878.
Chilean priest and politician. He studied at the National Institute, receiving his law degree in 1825 and practicing law for 8 years. He ran for the Chamber of Deputies and was elected in 1833. A year later, he was ordained into the priesthood, but continued to act as a deputy in Congress. A few years in the missions in northern and southern Chile established his reputation as a friend of the poor and an accomplished orator. In 1842 he published La Revista Católica and became a member of the Theological Faculty of the newly erected University of Chile*. Although he was an illustrious prelate, this did not prevent his proscription during the Conservative government (1851-61) of Manuel Montt Torres*.

VALPARAISO. 1) A province of north-central Chile; population: 732, 372 (1971 est.); area: 5, 118 sq. km. ; capital city: Valparaíso*. The following Chilean dependencies are governed by the province of Valparaíso: the Juan Fernández Islands*; Easter Island*; the Sala y Gómez Island*; and, the San Félix and San Ambrosio Islands*.
2) The second largest city in Chile, with a port considered to be "the greatest commercial center" on the Pacific coast of South America. The distance between

this city and the capital is 116 miles by rail and 91 by
road (the newly constructed Pan American Highway).
Twenty per cent of the Chilean industry is in the province of Valparaíso. Local products include: sugar,
textiles, varnishers, paints, pharmaceuticals, and bio-
chemical products. Population: 307, 000 (1971 est.).

VANGUARDIA NACIONAL DEL PUEBLO. A political party
of the Left founded in 1958 by the fusion of three
groups of workers: the Labor Party (Partido del Trabajo), the National Workers Alliance (Alianza Nacional
de Trabajadores), and the Anti-imperialist Radical In-
trasingent groups (Intransigencia Radical Anti-imperi-
alista). Many of its members had belonged to the
Socialist Party (Partido Socialista*). In the parliamentary elections of 1961, the Vanguardia Nacional del
Pueblo elected one candidate, Baltasar Castro, to the
Senate. Three years later, the party joined the Frente
de Acción Popular* (FRAP) coalition and backed Senator Salvador Allende Gossens* in the Presidential elections of September 4. Unable to elect any of its candidates to Congress, the Vanguardia Nacional dissolved
in 1966.

VANGUARDIA POPULAR SOCIALISTA. Political party of
the Right founded in 1938 and dissolved three years
later. Its historical antecedent was the Nazi-inspired
Movimiento Nacional Socialista de Chile*, and its doctrine was based on nationalism and anti-imperialism.
Like its predecessor, the party received strong opposition in Chile. Its history was marred with political
incidents and street fights. Increasing disturbances
in 1941 convinced many of its members to dissolve
the party. This was done in May of that year.

VARAS DE LA BARRA, ANTONIO, 1817-1886. A lawyer by
profession, President of the National Institute (Instituto
Nacional), and founder, with Manuel Montt Torres*,
of the National Party (Partido Nacional*). He was
elected to the Chamber of Deputies in 1843, and continued to serve in that body almost uninterruptedly
until his death. He also held various ministerial posts
in the governments of Manuel Montt Torres (1851-61)
and Aníbal Pinto* (1876-81). In 1861, the National
Party chose him as their Presidential candidate, but
he refused to run. In Congress, he was known for
his oratorical skills.

VASSALLO ROJAS, CARLOS, 1908- . A lawyer by profession, he dedicated most of his life to journalism. In 1954, he was named Minister of Public Health in the government (1952-58) of Carlos Ibáñez del Campo*. He was also secretary to the Minister of Foreign Affaris and Chilean delegate to Unesco. He participated in the 10th General Assembly of the United Nations as a member of the Chilean delegation.

VEGAS DE SALDIAS, LAS. Site of a battle fought on October 9, 1821, during the so-called "War to the death" (Guerra a Muerte*). Spanish royalist troops, led by Vicente Benavides*, encountered Chilean troops fighting to maintain their recently-won independence, led by Joaquín Prieto Vial*. The episode ended with the flight of Benavides, who tried to reach Peru but was captured before he was able to cross the border.

VEGAS DE TALCAHUANO, LAS. Site of a battle fought on November 25, 1820 during the so-called "War to the death" (Guerra a Muerte*). Spanish royalist troops, led by Vicente Benavides*, met Chilean troops, led by Ramón Freire Serrano*. The battle ended in victory for the Chilean patriots who were fighting to preserve their recently-won independence.

VERA PINTADO, BERNARDO DE, 1780-1827. Born in Mexico, he grew up in the Platine provinces (mainly Argentina), and came to Chile in 1799, where he received a law degree. During the Chilean struggle for independence (1810-17), he was accused of subversive activities to overthrow the Spanish colonial regime. He also maintained correspondence with Argentine patriots. After the battle of Rancagua* in 1814 and the restoration of Spanish power in Chile, Vera Pintado was exiled to Argentina. In Mendoza he joined the Army of the Andes (Ejército de los Andes*) under the Argentine liberator José de San Martín*. Vera Pintado returned to Chile and took part in the battle of Chacabuco* in 1817. He also wrote the first national anthem of Chile, and did much to stimulate early literary expressions in the country, writing for the newspapers Gaceta del Supremo Gobierno de Chile and the Gaceta de Santiago de Chile.

VERGARA ECHEVERZ, JOSE FRANCISCO, 1833-1889. Engineer by profession and member of the Liberal Party

(Partido Liberal*). He participated in the War of the
Pacific (Guerra del Pacífico*) in 1879, and a year later
was named Minister of War and the Navy. In 1881, he
was Minister of the Interior in the government (1881-
86) of Domingo Santa María González*. In 1886, he
was chosen by the National Party (Partido Nacional*),
the Radical Party (Partido Radical*), and his own Liberal Party to be their Presidential candidate. Unable
to win the support of the Conservatives, he withdrew
from the race, allowing José Manuel Balmaceda Fernández* to run as the Liberal candidate.

VIAL DEL RIO, JUAN DE DIOS, 1799-1850. Lawyer by
profession and supporter of Bernardo O'Higgins* during the Chilean struggle for independence. Vial del
Río was elected to the first National Congress in 1811.
After independence was won, he held various ministerial posts in the governments of O'Higgins (1817-27) and
of Ramón Freire Serrano* (1823-26). From 1834 until
his death, Vial del Río served in the Senate, and was
twice named President of that body (in 1839 and in
1843).

VIAL SANTELICES, AGUSTIN, 1772-1838. Lawyer by profession, member of the Exaltado* Party, and Chilean
patriot. He was a deputy to the first National Congress of 1811. During the next three years he served
in the junta government, but was arrested after the
patriots' defeat at the battle of Rancagua*. Exiled to
Juan Fernández Island, he was able to return to Chile
after the battle of Chacabuco*. During the regime of
Bernardo O'Higgins*, Vial Santelices was exiled once
again, but was recalled to Chile a year later to serve
as Minister of War, and then of the Treasury. Elected
to the Chamber of Deputies, he was the originator of
the Estanco* state monopolies. In 1831, he ran for
the Senate and was elected, serving as President of
the Senate a year later. He died in office.

VICUÑA GUERRERO, CLAUDIO, 1833-1907. He studied at
the National Institute (Instituto Nacional) and devoted
himself to agriculture. He became a deputy in 1873
and a senator in 1879. In the revolt against President
(1886-91) José Manuel Balmaceda Fernández*, he loyally supported the President. He was deprived of office
and went into exile after Balmaceda's defeat. He returned to Chile in 1895 and received a widespread

ovation for his defense of President Balmaceda. He
headed the Liberal Democratic party (Partido Demócrata Liberal*), founded a newspaper, and in 1901 was
the choice of the Liberal Alliance (Alianza Liberal*)
for the Presidency but refused to run and led his followers to support Germán Riesco Errázuriz*.

VICUÑA LARRAIN, FRANCISCO RAMON, 1778-1849. Chilean patriot who suffered at the hands of the Spaniards
and was imprisoned after the battle of Rancagua* (1814)
during the struggle for independence. He had held
various posts in the municipality of Santiago before he
was exiled in 1815. He returned to Chile after the
battle of Chacabuco* (1817), won by the Chileans, and
became regidor* of Santiago. In 1825, he was named
Minister of the Interior and Foreign Affairs by Ramón
Freire Serrano*, and briefly acted as Supreme Director during Freire's absence from Santiago. In 1828,
Vicuña Larraín was Vice-President of Chile and acted
as President a year later when President (1827-29)
Francisco Pinto Díaz* became ill. Pinto Díaz returned
to power later that year but resigned shortly thereafter.
He was succeeded by Vicuña Larraín. Great confusion
ensued in the government. General Joaquín Prieto
Vial* led a revolt and Vicuña Larraín fell from power.
These events led to a civil war in Chile (see GUERRA
CIVIL DE 1829-30).

VICUÑA LARRAIN, MANUEL, 1777-1843. Of a distinguished
Navarrese family, he was intimately connected to other
wealthy Chilean families of the colonial period. His
education was obtained at the University of San Felipe
(later to be called the University of Chile*), and he
was ordained priest in 1803. Thirty years later, he
was elevated to the Bishopric of Santiago and gained a
reputation for administrative ability and eloquence.
With his large inherited fortune he was able to undertake many works of charity, and in 1840 became the
first Archbishop of Chile. He also served as a senator and counselor of state.

VICUÑA MACKENNA, BENJAMIN, 1831-1886. Lawyer by
profession and member of the Sociedad de Igualdad*.
He participated in the Civil War of 1851 (Guerra Civil
de 1851*), was taken prisoner and condemned to death.
He somehow managed to escape, fled to California,
and spent the next few years traveling in the United

States and Mexico. From abroad he wrote many articles relating to the Chilean struggle for independence
and to the history of early Chile. His articles attracted the attention of Andrés Bello Edwards*, and
Vicuña Mackenna gained a reputation as a historian
and publicist. Returning to Chile in 1856, he began
to write for various newspapers, and edited La Asam-
blea Constituyente, in which he attacked Conservative
President (1851-61) Manuel Montt Torres*. In 1863,
he became editor of El Mercurio of Valparaíso* and
was elected a deputy to Congress. Two years later
he served as a special envoy to the United States, and
to Europe in 1870.
    As a diplomat, he collected many historical docu-
ments on his trips, writing more than 100 volumes of
history when he returned to Chile in 1875. He was
the founder of the Liberal Democratic Party (Partido
Democrático Liberal*), and was its Presidential candidate for the elections of 1876. He chose not to run,
however, in spite of his popularity. He loyally supported and recorded the cause of Chile in the War of
the Pacific (Guerra del Pacífico*). His premature
death left the citizenry of Santiago in a state of shock
and grief. Today one of the main streets of Santiago
is named after him, and his most enduring monument
is located in the famous Santa Lucía Park (Santiago).

VIDAURRE GARRETON, JOSE ANTONIO, 1798-1837. He began his military career in 1813, and in the short span
of four years attained the rank of captain. During the
period of political anarchy (1826-30), he took part in
many intrigues. In 1829, he organized a battalion of
infantry known as the Cazadores de Maipú, and his
services at the battle of Lircay* won for him the commission of colonel. He participated in the Mutiny of
Quillota* and was suspected of conspiring against Minister Diego Portales Palazuelos*. Accused of compli-
city in the assassination of Portales, Vidaurre Garre-
tón was executed in the same plaza in which the minister had died.

VIDELA VERGARA, BENJAMIN, 1907- . A career military officer who received the commission of brigadier
general in 1957. In 1953 he was Under Secretary of
War, and two years later was named Minister of Public Works and Communications. He also served as
Minister of Defense and of the Interior in the cabinet

of President (1952-58) Carlos Ibáñez del Campo*. In 1956, he was executive vice-president of CORFO*, and was also the first president of the political party known as the Democracia Agrario Laborista*.

VIEJA GUARDIA. (Literally, the "old guard.") It refers to the followers of President (1886-91) José Manuel Balmaceda Fernández* and his liberal ideals. The group was formed after the President took his own life in 1891.

VILLAGRA, FRANCISCO DE, 1511-1563. One of the Spanish Conquistadors*, he came to America in 1537 and may have taken part in the campaign against Diego de Almagro*. Soon after, Villagra arrived in Chile, where he held minor offices, including that of corregidor* of Santiago*. He hoped to succeed Pedro de Valdivia* after the latter's death in 1553, but Diego Hurtado de Mendoza* received the coveted appointment instead. In 1561 Villagra became governor of Chile, dying two years later in office.

VIVIENDA Y URBANISMO, MINISTERIO DE. The Ministry of Housing and Urban Affairs was created by statute no. 16391 on December 16, 1965. The main functions of this ministry are to provide adequate housing for all Chileans under government-sponsored programs and to supervise the cost of materials of construction in the land. The Ministry consists of various departments, the most important of which is the Department of Urban and Rural Planning. The Corporación de la Vivienda (CORVI*) is under the direct control of the Ministry of Housing and Urban Affairs.

VOZ, LA see THE PRESS.

-W-

WALKER MARTINEZ, CARLOS, 1842-1905. The son of an English industrialist, he studied at the National University receiving a law degree in 1866. He was elected deputy to Congress in 1870 and became well known for his conservatism. He joined the "Society of the Friends of the Country" (Sociedad de Amigos del País), an organization formed to oppose liberalism, and fought for that cause to the end of his life. He traveled to Europe

and the United States, and on his return to Chile held
minor posts in the Ministry of the Interior and the
Ministry of Foreign Affairs. In 1891, he sided with
the conservative Congress against President (1886-91)
José Manuel Balmaceda Fernández*. After the ouster
of Balmaceda, Walker Martínez became known for his
persecution of Balmaceda's followers. In 1894, Walker
Martínez was elected senator, and four years later he
became Minister of the Interior in the government
(1896-1901) of Federico Errázuriz Echaurren*.

WAR OF THE PACIFIC see GUERRA DEL PACIFICO.

WHEELWRIGHT, WILLIAM, 1798-1873. Born in Massachu-
setts, he engaged in South American trade early in his
life. In 1822 he was shipwrecked off the coast of
Buenos Aires and two years later he made his way into Chile. Encouraged by the Chilean statesman Diego
Portales Palazuelos*, Wheelwright established a passen-
ger line to serve the west coast of South America from
Valparaíso*. In addition to his promotion of steam navigation, Wheelwright obtained British capital and was
responsible for the development of Chilean railroads,
coal mines, telegraph lines, and public utilities.

WILLIAMS REBOLLEDO, JUAN, 1826-1910. Son of John
Williams (a companion of Lord Cochrane*), Juan Rebolledo Williams was born in Chile. In 1844 he entered
the naval school and had a distinguished naval career,
carrying out many improvements in the Chilean navy.
He fought against the Spanish fleet in 1865 during the
Spanish intervention on the west coast of South America, and was responsible for the modernization of the
Chilean navy during the War of the Pacific*. He also
explored the southern tip of Chile, venturing as far as
Antarctica.

-Y-

YAÑEZ PONCE DE LEON, ELIODORO, 1860-1933. Lawyer
by profession and member of the Liberal Doctrinary
Party (Partido Liberal Doctrinario*). Upon receiving
his law degree in 1883, he was employed as a relator
in the court of Appeals in Santiago. In 1894 he was
elected a deputy to Congress and a year later became
Vice-President of the Chamber of Deputies. From

1901 to 1917 he served in various ministries, and in
1924 he was elected to the Senate. He supported the
uprisings against President (1927-31) Carlos Ibáñez del
Campo* and as a result was exiled to Paris from 1927
until 1931. On his return to Chile, he remained active
in politics until his death.

YRRARAZAVAL   see IRRARAZAVAL.

-Z-

ZAMORANO HERRERA, ANTONIO RAUL, 1908- . From
his earliest years he followed the religious vocation
and became a priest in 1932. He spent the next 25
years as a professor in the Seminary of Iquique*. After filling minor posts in the bishopric of Monsignor
Lablé Márquez, he abandoned the priesthood and devoted his life to politics to bring about social reforms
in Chile. He was elected a deputy to Congress in
1957 and a year later he organized the political party
known as Unión Nacional Laborista*. He was a candidate in the Presidential elections of 1958 but obtained
very few votes.

ZAÑARTU SANTA MARIA, MIGUEL JOSE DE, 1786-1851.
Chilean patriot who participated in the uprisings of
1810 fighting for his country's independence. He was
enlisted in the army of Bernardo O'Higgins* and was
forced into exile after the battle of Rancagua*. He
returned to Chile in 1817 and was named Secretary of
State by the newly-formed O'Higgins government. He
also participated in the political events that led to independence in 1818. He was a strong supporter of
O'Higgins and received various diplomatic appointments
to Argentina and Peru. With the ouster of O'Higgins
in 1823, Zañartu Santa María went once again into
exile, returning to Chile in 1830. He was elected a
deputy to Congress and resumed his diplomatic career.
In 1831, he was named Chilean plenipotentiary minister
to Peru by President (1830-31) Tomás Ovalle Bezanilla*.

ZAÑARTU ZAÑARTU, ANIBAL, 1847-1902. Lawyer by profession and conservative politician who served in the
Chilean Congress as a deputy and as a senator. He
was named Minister of the Interior by President (1886-
91) José Manuel Balmaceda Fernández*. In the revolt

of Congress against President Balmaceda, he loyally
supported the President.   In 1901, Zañartu was once
again named Minister of the Interior in the administration of President (1896-1901) Federico Errázuriz Echaurren*.   When President Errázuriz Echaurren died in
office, Zañartu, who was next in the line of succession
assumed the Presidency of Chile (May 1, 1901).   After
a little more than four months in office, Zañartu resigned for reasons of health.

ZAÑARTU ZAÑARTU, MANUEL ARISTIDES, 1840-1892.
Lawyer by profession and member of the Liberal Democratic Party (Partido Liberal Democrático*).   He was
a senator when named by President (1886-91) José
Manuel Balmaceda Fernández* to be Minister of the
Treasury.   He had previously served as a deputy to
Congress.   In the revolt of Congress against Balmaceda, he loyally supported the President and went into
voluntary exile after Balmaceda's ouster.   He returned
to Chile and was named president of the Liberal Democratic Party in 1892, just before his death.

ZEGERS HUNEEUS, JORGE, 1835-1889.   Professor of Law
at the University of Chile, writer, conservative politician, he came from a wealthy Santiago family and received a law degree from the national university.   He
was a member of the Chamber of Deputies and of the
Senate.   An enemy of President José Manual Balmaceda Fernández*, he organized the congressional forces
that opposed the President in the Civil War of 1891
(Guerra Civil de 1891*).   An eminent writer of juris-
prudence, he is remembered for his works: Reseña
histórica de la constitución chilena; La constitución
chilena; and, Derecho constitucional comparado.

ZEGERS SAMANIEGO, JULIO, 1833-1918.   Lawyer by profession and Chilean politician who led the Congress of
1891 to oppose President (1886-91) José Manuel Balmaceda Fernández* (see GUERRA CIVIL DE 1891).
Zegers Samaniego was a member of the Chamber of
Deputies and also served in the Senate.   He was in
favor of a parliamentary regime in Chile to be modelled after that of England.

ZENTENO DEL POZO Y SILVA, JOSE IGNACIO, 1784-1847.
A career military officer who fought in the struggle
for Chilean independence.   He was a loyal supporter

of Bernardo O'Higgins* and in 1813 served the patriot government as military secretary. Enlisted in the army of O'Higgins, he was forced into exile after the battle of Rancagua*. Like many other Chilean expatriates, he went to Mendoza, Argentina, and began to plot the overthrow of the Spanish colonial government in America. He became a close associate of general José de San Martín* and participated in the Chilean campaign of 1817 as a member of the army of the Andes (Ejército de los Andes*). After O'Higgins became Supreme Director of Chile, Zenteno was promoted to colonel. In 1821, he was named political governor of the province of Valparaíso*. In this Chilean port he devoted a great deal of attention to the navy. He was primarily responsible for the modernization of the Chilean navy. Because of a disagreement with Supreme Director (1823-26) Ramón Freire Serrano*, Zenteno went into voluntary exile. After his return to Chile, Zenteno resumed his military career, served as a deputy to Congress, and was elected Vice-President of the Chamber of Deputies. Interested in journalism, he founded the newspaper El Mercurio* of Valparaíso and contributed to another paper, El Ferrocarril.

Bibliography

Agricultura e industrias agropecuarias, Año agrícola, 1965-
66--Comercio exterior de 1968--Comercio interior y
comunicaciones de 1966--Finanzas, bancos, y cajas
sociales de 1967--Industrias de 1967--Minería de 1966.
Santiago: Dirección General de Estadística, 1969-70.

Aldunate Phillips, Arturo. Un pueblo en busca de su des-
tino. Santiago: Editorial Nascimento, 1947.

Alegría, Fernando. Literatura chilena del siglo XX. Santiago: Editorial Zig-Zag, 1967.

Almanaque Mundial, 1971. New York: Editora Moderna,
1970. Annually.

Almeyda Arroyo, E. Biografía de Chile. Santiago: Editorial Zamorano y Caperán, 1943.

Altamirano, Carlos. "América Latina necesita su propria
teoría revolucionaria," Punto Final. No. 70, December 17, 1968, Supplement, pp. 1-8.

Amunátegui y Solar, Domingo. Historia de Chile. Santiago:
Nascimento, 1933.

"The Andes: A Nationalist Surge," Time. July 26, 1971,
p. 38.

Anuario de los paises del ALALC. Buenos Aires: Instituto
de Publicaciones y Estadísticas S.A., 1968 (3rd edition)

Armbrister, Trevor. "Will Chile go Communist?" Saturday Evening Post. Philadelphia, September 5, 1964,
pp. 69-73.

Bannon, John Francis and Peter Masten Dunne. Latin
America: An Historical Survey. Milwaukee: Bruce

Pub. Co., 1963.

Barrera, Manuel. Los partidos políticos chilenos: trayectoria y organización. Santiago: Universidad de Chile, 1966.

Barros Arana, Diego. Historia general de Chile. Santiago: R. Jover, 1902.

Barros Borgoño, Luis. La misión del vicario apostólico don Juan Muzi, notas para la historia de Chile. Santiago: Imprenta de "La Epoca," 1883.

Barros Grez, Daniel. Pipiolos i pelucones; tradiciones de ahora cuarenta años. Santiago: Imprenta Franklin, 1876.

"Basic Aspects of the Economic and Financial Policies of the Chilean Government," The New York Times, January 25, 1971, p. 73 C.

Bianchi Gundián, Manuel. Chile and Great Britain. London: Organ, 1944.

Bohan, Mervin L. and Morton Pomeranz. Investment in Chile. Washington, D.C.: Department of Commerce, 1960.

Bowers, Claude G. Chile through Embassy Windows 1936-1953. New York: Simon and Schuster, 1958.

Butland, Gilbert J. Chile: An Outline of its Geography, Economics, and Politics. London: Royal Institute of International Affairs, 1953.

_____. The Human Geography of Southern Chile. London: George Philip, 1957.

Cáceres C., Leonardo. "La elección parlamentaria de marzo," Mensaje, Vol. XVIII, no. 177, March-April, 1969, pp. 68-70.

Carrasco, D. Adolfo. Descubrimiento y conquista de Chile. Madrid: Establecimiento Tipográfico "Sucesores de Rivadeneyra," 1892.

Castedo, Leopoldo and Francisco Encina. Historia de Chile.

Santiago: Editorial Universitaria, 1969.

Chilcote, Ronald H. "The Press in Latin America, Spain, and Portugal," Hispanic American Report, Stanford, Calif.: Stanford University Press, August, 1963.

"Chile abre Comercio con Cuba," El Mercurio (International Edition) Santiago: February 16-22, 1970, p. 1.

"Chile Copper Nationalization Looms as Bill Nears Passage," The Denver Post, May 3, 1971, p. 18.

"Chile: The Last Best Hope," Look. New York, June 2, 1964, pp 80ff.

"Chile: Mandate for Allende," Time. April 19, 1971, pp. 24-25.

Chile and the United Nations. New York: Permanent Mission of Chile to the United Nations, 1967.

"Chile's Foreign Policy," The New York Times. January 25, 1971, p. 73 C.

The Chilean Presidential Election of September 4, 1964. Washington, D.C.: Institute for the Comparative Study of Political Systems, 1965.

Chonchol, Jacques and Julio Silva. El desarrollo de la nueva sociedad en América Latina. Santiago: Editorial Universitaria, S.A., 1969.

Clissold, Stephen. Bernardo O'Higgins and the Independence of Chile. New York: Praeger, 1969.

"El cobre," Polémica. Santiago: No. 5, May, 1969.

"Consecuencias políticas del paro de la CUT," El Mercurio (International Edition). Santiago, July 6-12, 1970, p. 5.

Constitución política de la República de Chile. Santiago: Editorial Nascimento, 1925.

"Constitución política y reglamiento del senato," República de Chile. Santiago: Imprenta Universo, 1954.

Cortes, Lía and Jordi Fuentes. Diccionario político de Chile (1810-1966). Santiago: Editorial Orbe, 1967.

Corvalán, Luis. Cosas nuevas en el campo. Santiago: Imprenta Lautaro, 1960.

Cruchaga Ossa, Alberto. Estudios de historia diplomática chilena. Santiago: Editorial Andrés Bello, 1962.

Daugherty, Charles H. (ed.). Chile: Election Factbook. Washington, D. C.: The Institute for the Comparative Study of Political Systems, 1963.

Davies, Howell (ed.). The South American Handbook. London: Trade and Travel Pub., 1965. Annually.

Debray, Régis. Conversación con Allende. Mexico City: Siglo XXI editores, 1971.

Delano, Luis Enrique and Edmund Palacios (eds.). Antolología de la poesía social de Chile. Santiago: Editora Austral, 1962.

Demografía y asistencia social de 1966. Santiago: Dirección General de Estadística, 1969. Annually.

Dennis, William J. Tacna and Arica. An Account of the Chile-Peru Boundary Dispute. New Haven, Conn.: Yale University Press, 1931.

Diccionario biográfico de Chile. Santiago: Editorial La Salle, 1944 (5th edition).

Doussinague, José M. Pedro de Valdivia. Madrid: Espasa-Calpe, 1963.

The Economist. London, 1969, Weekly.

Education in Chile. Washington, D. C.: United States Office of Education, 1967.

Encina, Francisco Antonio. Historia de Chile desde la prehistoria hasta 1891. Santiago: Nascimento, 1952, Vols. 1-20.

_____. Las relaciones entre Chile y Bolivia (1841-1963). Santiago: Editorial Nascimento, 1963.

_____. Resumen de la historia de Chile. Santiago:

Zig-Zag, 1954.

Endesa. Santiago: Corporación de Fomento de la Producción, 1948.

Escudero, Alfonso M., O. S. A. Apuntes sobre el teatro en Chile. Santiago: La Universidad Católica de Chile, 1967.

Estadística Chilena. Santiago, Dirección General de Estadística, Monthly 1960-70.

Evans, H. C. Chile and its Relations with the United States. Durham, N. C.: Duke University Press, 1927.

"External Payments Considerations to the Fore," Quarterly Economic Review of Chile. London, February 28, 1964, pp. 3-6.

Eyzaguirre, Jaime. Breve historia de las fronteras de Chile. Santiago: Editorial Universitaria, 1968.

_____. Historia de Chile; genesis de la nacionalidad. Santiago: Zig-Zag, 1965.

Figueroa, Pedro Pablo. Diccionario biográfico chileno (1550-1887). Santiago: Imprenta "Victoria," 1887.

"El fraude de la 'nacionalización pactada,'" Punto Final. No. 83, July 15, 1969, pp. 8-9.

Galdames, Luis. A History of Chile. Chapel Hill, N. C.: University of North Carolina Press, 1941.

Gil, Federico Guillermo. The Political System of Chile. Boston: Houghton Mifflin, 1966.

Goldenberg, Mauricio. Después de Frei ¿Quién? Santiago: Editorial Orbe, 1966.

Gómez, R. A. Government and Politics in Latin America. New York: Random House, 1964.

Góngora y Marmolejo, Alonso de. Historia de Chile desde su descubrimiento hasta 1575. Santiago: Editorial Universitaria, S. A., 1969.

Gropp, Arthur E. A Bibliography of Latin American Bibliographies. Metuchen, N. J.: Scarecrow Press, 1968.

301

Guía de Santiago. Santiago: Empresa Editora Zig-Zag, 1961.

Guilesasti Tagle, Sergio. Partidos políticos chilenos. Santiago: Editorial Nascimento, 1964.

Gunder Frank, André. Latin America: Underdevelopment or Revolution. New York: Monthly Review Press, 1969.

_____. "The Underdevelopment Policy of the United Nations in Latin America," NACLA Newsletter, Vol. III, No. 8, December, 1969, pp. 1-10.

Halperin, Ernst. Nationalism and Communism in Chile. Cambridge, Mass.: M.I.T. Press, 1965.

Hanke, Lewis. Modern Latin America: Continent in Ferment. Princeton, N.J.: Van Nostrand, 1959.

Heise González, Julio. 150 años de evolución institucional. Santiago: Editorial Andrés Bello, 1960.

Herrera, Felipe. America Latina integrada. Buenos Aires: Editorial Losada, 1967 (2nd edition).

Herring, Hubert. A History of Latin America from the Beginnings to the Present. New York: Alfred A. Knopf, 1961.

Hilton, Ronald. La América Latina de ayer y de hoy. New York: Holt, Rinehart and Winston, 1970.

_____ (ed.). Handbook of Hispanic Source Materials and Research Organizations in the United States. Stanford, Calif.: Stanford University Press, 1956 (2nd edition).

_____ (ed.). The Movement Toward Latin American Unity. New York: Praeger, 1969.

_____ (ed.). Who's Who in Latin America Part IV: Bolivia, Chile and Peru. Stanford, Calif.: Stanford University Press, 1947.

Hirschman, Albert O. (ed.). Latin American Issues: Essays and Comments. New York: Twentieth Century Fund, 1961.

_____. Journeys Toward Progress. New York: Twentieth Century Fund, 1963.

Hispanic American Report. Stanford, Calif.: Stanford University Press, Vol. XVII, No. 6, August, 1964.

_____. Vol. XVII, No. 7, September, 1964.

_____. Vol. XVII, No. 8, October, 1964.

_____. Vol. XVII, No. 9, November, 1964.

Hormazábal, Manuel. Chile: una patria mutilada. Santiago: Editorial del Pacífico, 1969.

Horowitz, Irving Louis (ed.). The Rise and Fall of Project Camelot: Studies in the Relationship between Social Science and Practical Politics. Cambridge, Mass.: M.I.T. Press, 1967.

Inostrosa, Jorge. Hidalogos del mar. (2nd edition). Santiago: Editorial Zig-Zag, 1959.

"Inscrita la candidatura presidencial de Allende," El Mercurio (International Edition). Santiago, February 9-15, 1970, p. 1.

Inter-American Review of Bibliography. Washington, D.C., Department of Cultural Affairs, Pan American Union, January-March, 1951.

"J. Chonchol propone un pacto revolucionario con partidos y organizaciones laborales," El Mercurio (International Edition). Santiago, September 29-October 5, 1969, p. 5.

James, Herman G. and Percy A. Martin. The Republics of Latin America. New York: Harper Brothers, 1963.

James, Preston E. Latin America. New York: Odyssey Press, 1959.

Johnson, Dale. "Special Report: The Two Forces Battling for the Presidency Contrast their Program," South Pacific Mail. Santiago, September 3, 1964, pp. 10ff.

Johnson, John J. Political Change in Latin America: The

Emergence of the Middle Sectors. Stanford, Calif.:
Stanford University Press, 1958.

Labarca Goddard, Eduardo. Chile invadido. Santiago: Empresa Editora Austral, 1968.

Labor in Chile. U. S. Department of Labor, Bureau of Labor Statistics. Washington, D. C.: Agency for International Development, 1962.

Larraín Bravo, Ricardo. Biografías sucintas de algunos proceres de Chile. Santiago: Editorial Nascimento, 1939.

Lavell, Carr B. Population Growth and the Development of South America. Washington, D. C.: George Washington University Press, 1959.

MacDonald, Austin F. Latin American Politics and Government. New York: Thomas Crowell, 1954.

Magdoff, Harry. The Age of Imperialism. New York: Monthly Review Press, 1969.

Maidenberg, H. G. "Latins Accelerate Tempo of Revolution," The New York Times, January 25, 1971, p. 45 C ff.

Maira Aguirre, Luis. "De la chilenización a la nacionalización pactada." Mensaje. Vol. XVIII, No. 181, August, 1969, pp. 334-344.

Mallory, Walter H. Political Handbook and Atlas of the World, 1964. New York: Harper & Row, 1964.

Mecham, J. L. Church and State in Latin America. Chapel Hill, N. C.: University of North Carolina Press, 1934.

Méndez García de la Huerta, Alejandro. La guerra a muerte. Santiago: Nascimento, 1964.

Meza Villalobos, Néstor. La actividad política del reino de Chile entre 1806 y 1810. Santiago: Universidad de Chile, 1958.

Millar, Walterio. Historia de Chile. Santiago: Editora Zig-Zag, 1959.

"The Mining Sector, " Quarterly Economic Review of Chile. London, February 28, 1964, pp. 9-11.

Mitrani, Barbara and Francisco José Moreno (eds.). Conflict and Violence in Latin American Politics: A Book of Readings. New York: Thomas Y. Crowell, 1971.

Montero Jaramillo, Felipe. Política chilena del cobre y sociedades mineras mixtas. Santiago, Chile, Editorial Universitaria, S. A., 1969.

Montt, Luis. Bibliografía chilena. Santiago: Imprenta Universitaria, 1904-21 (3 vols.).

Moreno, Francisco José. Legitimacy and Stability in Latin America. New York: New York University Press, 1969.

Muños Cautivo, Agustín. "Contemporización, rebeldía, y descontento estudiantil. Una investigación sobre la juventud chilena, " Boletín de la Universidad de Chile. Nos. 89-90, November-December, 1968, pp. 4-8.

McBride, G. M. Chile, Land and Society. Milwaukee: Bruce Pub. Co., 1971 (1936).

Núñez, Carlos. Chile: ¿La última opción electoral? Santiago: Ediciones Prensa Latinoamericana, 1970.

Nutt, Katherine Ferris. San Martín: One Hundred Years of Historiography. Hays, Kansas: Fort Hays State College, 1960.

Olavarría Bravo, Arturo. Chile bajo la democracia cristiana. Santiago: Editorial Nascimento, 1966.

"On the Cross of Politics, " Quarterly Economic Review of Chile. London, February 28, 1964, pp. 1-3.

Osborn, Frederick. Population: An International Dilemma. New York: Population Council, 1958.

"PN reconocerá la primera mayoría, " El Mercurio (International Edition). Santiago, August 24-30, 1970, p. 6.

Panorama Económico. Santiago, No. 242, March 1969.

305

_____. No. 244, May, 1969.

_____. No. 245, June, 1969.

_____. No. 246, July, 1969.

_____. No. 247, August 1969.

_____. No. 248, September, 1969.

"Partidos de izquierda mantienen sus posiciones, " El Mercurio (International Edition). Santiago, December 29, 1969-January 4, 1970, p. 1.

"Partidos de la 'Unidad Popular' dieron a conocer programa básico, " El Mercurio (International Edition). Santiago, December 22-28, 1969, p. 4.

Pendle, George. The Land and People of Chile. New York: Barnes and Noble, 1963.

Petras, James. Politics and Social Forces in Chilean Development. Berkeley: University of California Press, 1969.

Pike, Frederick B. Chile and the United States 1880-1962. Notre Dame, Indiana: University of Notre Dame Press, 1963.

Pinochet de la Barra, O. La Antártica chilena. Santiago: Editorial del Pacífico, 1948.

Pinto, Aníbal. Chile hoy. Mexico City: Siglo Ventiuno Editores, 1970.

Pinto Lagarrigue, Fernando. La masonería: su influencia en Chile. Santiago: Editorial Orbe, 1966.

Política, Economía, Cultura. Santiago, July 4, 1969.

Ramírez Necochea, Hernán. Historia del imperialismo en Chile. Santiago: Empresa Editora Austral, 1960.

_____. Origen y formación del partido comunista de Chile (Ensayo de historia del partido). Santiago: Editora Austral, 1965.

Ranstead, Donald D. "Chile Turns Left, " Commonweal. New York, September 4, 1964, pp. 594-96.

El Rebelde. Santiago, No. 5, July, 1969.

Recabarren Serrano, Luis Emilio. Obras escogidas. Santiago: Editorial Recabarren, 1965.

"The Recovery of Basic Resources Is a Sovereign Decision Reflecting the Feelings of all Chilean People," The New York Times, January 25, 1971, p. 72 C.

República de Chile. "Constitución política y reglamiento del senato." Santiago: Imprenta Universo, 1954.

"Resultados de elección de ejecutivo en la FECh," El Mercurio (International Edition). Santiago: November 24-30, 1969, p. 1.

Ríos Gallardo, Conrado. Chile y Perú: Los pactos de 1929. Santiago: Editorial Nascimento, 1959.

Rodríguez Bravo, Joaquín. Balmaceda y el conflicto entre el congreso y el ejecutivo. Santiago: Imprenta Gutenberg, 1921.

Rojas, Manuel. Historia breve de la literatura chilena. Santiago: Editorial Zig-Zag, 1964.

Sachs, Moshe Y. (ed.). Worldmark Encyclopedia of the Nations. New York: Harper and Row, 1963. (Vol.: Americas.)

Silva Castro, Raúl. El modernismo, y otros ensayos literarios. Santiago: Editorial Nascimento, 1965.

Silvert, K. H. Chile, Yesterday and Today. New York: Holt, Rinehart and Winston, 1965.

_____. The Conflict Society: Reaction and Revolution in Latin America. New Orleans: Hauser Press, 1961.

Smith, T. Lynn (ed.). Agrarian Reform in Latin America. New York: Alfred A. Knopf, 1965.

Solberg, Carl. "Immigration and Urban Social Problems in Argentina and Chile 1890-1914," The Hispanic American Historical Review, May, 1968. Durham, N. C.: Duke University Press, pp. 215-233.

Steinberg, H. S. (ed.). The Statesman Yearbook 1964-65. London: Macmillan and Co., 1964. Annually.

Stevenson, John Reese. The Chilean Popular Front. Philadelphia: University of Pennsylvania Press; London: Oxford University Press, 1942.

Subercaseaux Vicuña, Benjamín. Chile, a Geographic Extravaganza, tr. by Angel Flores. New York: Macmillan, 1943.

_____. Crónicas del centenario; la colonia-la patria vieja. Santiago: Sociedad Imprenta y Litografía Universo, 1910.

_____. Monetary and Banking Policy of Chile. Oxford: Clarendon Press, 1922.

Sunkel, Osvaldo. Reforma universitaria, subdesarrollo y dependencia. Santiago: Editorial Universitaria, 1969.

Tierra y libertad por la reforma agraria. Santiago: Acción Sindical Chilena, 1961.

Torres Ríoseco, Arturo. Ensayo de bibliografía de la literatura chilena. Cambridge, Mass.: Harvard University Press, 1935.

_____. The Epic of Latin-American Literature. Berkeley: University of California Press, 1942.

Turner, Jorge. "La izquierda en las elecciones chilenas," Sucesos para todos. Mexico City, April 18, 1970, pp. 20-23.

Urzúa, Raúl. La demanda campesina. Santiago: Editorial Universitaria, S.A., 1969.

Urzúa Valenzuela, Germán. Los partidos políticos chilenos. Santiago: Editorial Jurídica de Chile, 1968.

Valdés Vergara, Francisco. Historia de Chile. Santiago: Litografía Universo, 1923.

Vega, Miguel Angel. Literatura chilena de la conquista y de la colonia. Santiago: Editorial Nascimento, 1954.

Vicuña Mackenna, Benjamín. La guerra del pacífico. Santiago: Editorial West, 1969.

White, C. Langdon and Ronald H. Chilcote. "Chile's New Iron and Steel Industry," Economic Geography, Vol. 37, No. 3, July, 1961.

Wilgus, A. Curtis (ed.). Argentina, Brazil and Chile since Independence. Washington, D. C.: George Washington University Press, 1935.

_____, and Raul d'Eça. Latin American History. New York: Barnes & Noble, 1969.

Young, Peter. "Allende: A Special Kind of Marxist," Life. New York, July 16, 1971, pp. 38-40.

Zamudio, Gosé. La novela histórica en Chile. Santiago, Chile, Ediciones "Flor Nacional," 1949.